AMERICAN POLITICS

AMERICAN POLITICS
Understanding What Counts

Reo M. Christenson
Miami University

HARPER & ROW, PUBLISHERS, New York
Cambridge, Hagerstown, Philadelphia, San Francisco,
London, Mexico City, São Paulo, Sydney

To the students in my Intro class, who unknowingly have contributed so much to this book

PHOTO CREDITS
Title page: American Airlines; ABC: 23. Davis, James Allen, Jeroboam: Roger Lubin, 14, 105; Kent Reno, 43; Templin, 155; Emilio Mercado, 227; Jerry Blankfort, 263. Monkmeyer: Sybin Shelton, 1; Paul S. Conklin, 111, 188; George Zimbel, 289. Stock, Boston: Arthur Grace, 213. UPI: 11, 37, 57, 104, 133, 144, 153, 171, 181, 193, 217, 228, 238, 243, 259, 274, 298, 303. Wide World: 29, 61, 69, 79, 115, 148, 160, 163, 207, 247, 268.

OTHER ILLUSTRATION CREDITS
Figure on p. 100: *General Social Surveys, 1972-1978, Cumulative Data* (Chicago: National Opinion Research Center, 1978), p. 68; Courtesy of Roper Public Opinion Research Center. Figure on p. 103: U.S. Bureau of the Census, *Statistical Abstract of the United States, 1977* (Washington, D.C.: U.S. Government Printing Office, 1977), p. 508, Table 813. Figures on p. 216 and 237: *U.S. Government Manual 1978-1979* (Washington D.C.: U.S. Government Printing Office). Figure on p. 292: Dayton *Journal-Herald,* January 22, 1979, p. 3.

Sponsoring editor: John Michel
Project editor: Céline Keating
Designer: Gayle Jaeger
Production manager: Marion A. Palen
Photo researcher: Myra Schachne
Compositor: TriStar Graphics
Printer and binder: Book Press
Art studio: J & R Technical Services, Inc.
Cover photograph: Michel Craig

AMERICAN POLITICS: UNDERSTANDING WHAT COUNTS
Copyright © 1980 by Reo M. Christenson

All rights reserved. Printed in the United States of America. No part of this book may be used or reproduced in any manner whatsoever without written permission except in the case of brief quotations embodied in critical articles and reviews. For information address Harper & Row, Publishers, Inc., 10 East 53rd Street, New York, N.Y. 10022.

Library of Congress Cataloging in Publication Data
Christenson, Reo Millard, Date-
  American politics.

  Includes index.
  1. United States—Politics and government.
I. Title.
JK271.C53   320.9′73   79-18492
ISBN 0-06-041259-3

CONTENTS   Preface ix

CHAPTER 1   POLITICAL SCIENCE: WHAT'S IT ALL ABOUT   1
Political science: where has it been? 2
Political science: three research examples 5

CHAPTER 2   IN DEFENSE OF POLITICIANS   11
Politicians: our mirror image 12
Why politicians pussyfoot 15
Why people enter politics 19
Rx for success in politics 22
Getting a foot in the door 26

CHAPTER 3   ON CONSTITUTIONS   29
The constitution: the view from 1787 30
Founding fathers: wise but not all-wise 34
Do constitutions really matter? 35

CHAPTER 4   DEMOCRACY AND ITS CONDITION   43
Democracy and human rights 45
Democracy and equality 46
The gestation of rights 49
Are "natural rights" natural? 52
Government by the people—or by the few? 54
Threats to Democracy 55

CHAPTER 5   FEDERALISM: BATTERED BUT IMMORTAL   61
Federalism: roots and branches 62
The Supreme Court: Jekyll and Hyde 65
Taking revolution in stride 68
Is federalism obsolete? 71
The Washington cornucopia: how many strings? 72

CHAPTER 6   PUBLIC OPINION AND POPULAR GOVERNMENT   79
How much direct popular control? 80
How public opinion is formed: socialization 83
Catholics, Jews, blacks, and other religious and ethnic groups 87
The media and the public 92
Political opinions and personal integrity 94
Liberals and conservatives: the fruitful feud 95
Citizens: apathetic and concerned 102
Polls and their pitfalls 107

CHAPTER 7   POLITICAL PARTIES: FREEDOM'S CHILDREN   111
Parties: the family tree 112
Two parties, many parties 114
Our parties: two peas in a pod? 116
Our parties: splintered they stand 120
Parties in decline: good riddance? 122
Party decay: more serious than people think 126
Reviving our parties 129

CHAPTER 8   **ELECTIONS: THE DEMOCRATIC DRAMA**   133
  The candidate—off and running 134
  Money, money, money 135
  Wooing and winning 138
  Campaigning: from New Hampshire to November 140
  The National Convention: a Hallelujah Chorus 145
  Coming down the home stretch 147
  Does propaganda win elections? 149

CHAPTER 9   **INTEREST GROUPS AND THE PUBLIC INTEREST**   153
  The organized and the unorganized 154
  The ingredients of group power 159
  Common Cause, Ralph Nader, and lobbying 162
  Applying the pressure 164
  The diffusion of power 168

CHAPTER 10   **CONGRESS: OPERATION CHAOS**   171
  The committee system: getting down to work 173
  Congressional leadership—sort of 176
  Shooting the legislative rapids 179
  Members of Congress: a close-up view 183
  A day on Capitol Hill 187
  Congress: a rudderless ship? 190

CHAPTER 11   **THE PRESIDENCY—THE VITAL CENTER**   193
  The swelling of the presidency 194
  The anatomy of presidential power 197
  The president and foreign policy 202
  The president as commander in chief 205
  How powerful—really? 209
  The president's hired hands 211
  Concluding notes 216

CHAPTER 12   **THE BUREAUCRACY AND ITS CRITICS**   219
  Bureaucracy versus efficiency? 220
  Fire them—if you can! 223
  Red tape: a necessary evil 225
  Bureaucrats: drunk with power? 228
  The taming of bureaucrats 233

CHAPTER 13   **THE SUPREME COURT: NINE POLITICIANS AT WORK**   243
  The controversial court 245
  The court as policymaker 248
  The court versus Congress: history's verdict 252
  The court at work 257

CHAPTER 14   **THE BILL OF RIGHTS: SIMPLE RULES AND COMPLEX CASES   263**
The First Amendment in U.S. history 265
John Stuart Mill and free speech tested 269
Communists and free speech 272
The First Amendment and the press 275
That leaky wall of separation 276
Privacy and due process 280

CHAPTER 15   **PUBLIC POLICY: CHANGE AND RESISTANCE TO CHANGE   289**
The impetus to legislate 290
Why change comes hard 293
Incrementalism—thinking small 300
The planners—thinking big 302
The utility and ethics of violence 304
Alternatives to violence 307
Our system and its critics 308

Presidential elections 1789–1976 313

Constitution of the United States 316

Glossary 329

Index 333

PREFACE

Another introductory political science text? With scores of them already on the market? Is this book really necessary?

I think so. I have taught introductory political science for twenty-three consecutive years and enjoyed every minute of it. In the course of constantly experimenting, listening, reevaluating, and reshaping my material, I believe I have learned something about what holds students' interest while simultaneously challenging their thought processes.

This book has a different goal than most—to acquaint introductory students with what they *really* need to know, in a style that they will enjoy, while clearing away the clutter of dreary data that students dutifully cram and promptly forget. Another goal is to offer original observations and interpretations that will prove intellectually stimulating both to students and to those who teach the introductory course. Most textbooks are all plains and no peaks. I have tried to avoid this, since it leaves students with little more than a generalized blur as a legacy from their textbook labors.

Although *American Politics*, then, is in some ways a very personal book, it of course seeks to include, in as concise and literate a manner as possible, much of what the profession has learned in this area that students might remember when their college days are past.

This text has some novel features. A chapter entitled "In Defense of Politicians" correctly suggests that the author sees politicians in a more constructive light than most Americans. It is his conviction that politicians are a much-abused lot whose contributions to democracy deserve more credit than they receive. Their failures are usually those of the American people at large—or a product of excessive expectations.

A greater concern than usual for the ethical dimensions of politics and politicians also marks this volume. I hope to help students see more clearly the uniqueness of the politicians' moral dilemmas, the inevitability of adverse public judgments upon them, and the public misunderstandings that contribute to those judgments.

In brief, the book treats democratic politics in a more appreciative manner than is currently fashionable. But a Panglossian approach it is not.

I am indebted to many of my colleagues. Rick Campbell, Alan Engel, Bob Gump, Steve Hatting, Dan Jacobs, Susan Kay, George Rawson, Mostafa Rejai, Glenn Parker, Herb Waltzer, and Jim Woodworth all made useful criticisms of chapters relating to their respective fields. So, too, did teaching assistants Bill Carroll, Pat Dunham, and—most of all—Brian Murphy. Invaluable critiques were supplied by Professor James C. Dick of Wayne State University, Professor George T. Little of University of Vermont, and Professor Mary R. Mattingly of Texas A&I. (If any author is inclined to be overly pleased with his or her handiwork, I suggest he or she ask Professor Dick to critique it. Humility will surely follow—as well as a better manuscript.) My thanks also go to research assistants Michelle Fistek and Karen Tallman, and to Virginia Helm (my daughter, no less!) who has one of the sharpest editorial eyes in the West and who used her talents fruitfully while reviewing the manuscript.

Errors of fact or judgment are mine, if all defensive maneuvers fail.

Reo M. Christenson

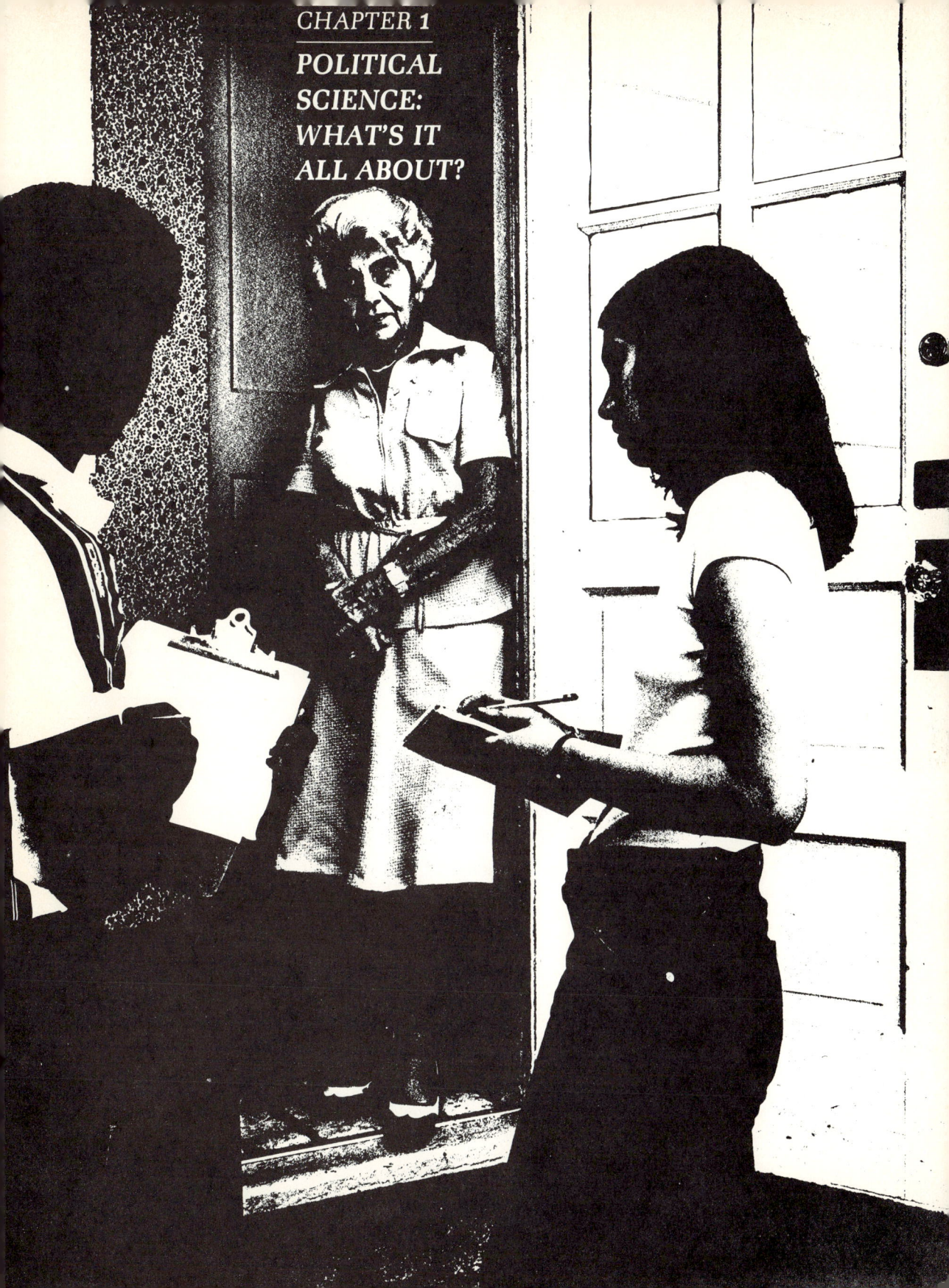

CHAPTER 1
POLITICAL SCIENCE: WHAT'S IT ALL ABOUT?

Political science is the study of politics. Politics has been defined as "the authoritative allocation of values"[1] but a simpler view sees it as the process by which public policy is made and carried out.

Before beginning the analysis of the American political system today, it may be worth examining where political science came from, the road it has traveled, the controversies which have embroiled it, and the current status of the discipline. Although you may yawn as the story begins (forgiveness is hereby granted!), you will soon discover that political science has gone through a rather remarkable transformation, recently involving a battle royal over the domain political scientists ought to occupy and the instruments they should employ. This battle was fought over issues that cut to the bone, and it aroused passions that divided college departments into profoundly hostile camps.

The story is well worth telling and provides an illuminating backdrop against which the succeeding chapters can be developed.

Political Science: Where Has It Been?

Political science has a long history, which can only be described briefly here.[2] From its embryonic beginnings in ancient Greece, political science was considered a branch of "moral philosophy"—a mixture of law, history, economics, ethics, and philosophy. Its emphasis was mainly on "right conduct" and "the principles of the good society." The earliest American colleges and universities devoted a great deal of attention to moral philosophy.

In the late eighteenth and early nineteenth centuries, moral philosophy began spinning off separate academic disciplines—first law, then "political economy" (the forerunner of economics), and then history. In the United States before the Civil War, a great outpouring of literature was produced on the nature of constitutions and the legitimate powers and limits of governments. But this literature did not fit neatly into the categories of either law or history; its unique character led to the establishment of "government" as a separate academic discipline. By the 1880s many colleges offered courses in government, with a few even calling them "political science." Political science journals began to appear, and the American Political Science Association was founded in 1903.

The approach to government taken in the late nineteenth century is today called "traditionalism." Works produced then may be characterized as:

1 Legalistic: that is, devoted to the study of laws and constitutions
2 Historical: treating political science as if it were only a specialized branch of history
3 Institutional: emphasizing the study of institutions, such as Congress, the Supreme Court, the presidency, and the bureaucracy in broad, general terms
4 Philosophical: inquiring into the ethically sound principles of good citizenship and good government

The goal of such works was to prepare students to become good citizens once they graduated.

Around the turn of the century many political scientists became interested in actively promoting political reforms. They tried to facilitate a civil service system (to replace the "spoils" system of government by political cronies), to promote "direct democracy" (the use of initiative, referendum, recall, and direct primaries to give the people more control over public policy and public officers), to improve municipal government by nonpartisan elections and the institution of city manager systems of government.

What all this suggests is that political science was a rather loosely conceived discipline "without a clear intellectual identity," as one critic declared.[3] Others complained that the profession was composed of "political theologians," "political historians" and "political journalists" with only a sprinkling of genuine political "scientists." In other words, there was very little truly scientific study going on.

After World War II a new movement appeared, called "behaviorialism" (which is usually contrasted with "traditionalism.")[4] It came to dominate political science, especially in the graduate schools, just as it already dominated such social sciences as psychology, sociology, and economics. The behavioralists' basic assumption was that political society should (and could) be studied in much the same way they thought that physical and biological phenomena were studied by natural scientists. They wanted to construct hypotheses about political behavior, to test them rigorously with empirical data, and to come up with valid generalizations. In short, they wanted to explain and potentially predict political behavior. As an important part of the objectivity and precision they sought, the behavioralists emphasized measurement and quantification of the variables and statistical analysis of the relationships in their hypotheses.

Finally, behavioralists wished to concentrate on facts, not values—that is, on questions that were subject to scientific analysis rather than on those that dealt with what people *ought* to do (involving value judgments, or so-called normative politics). While the scientific study of politics recognizes the importance of values, they declared, science cannot tell us anything about the relative merits of differing values. Hence, values must be regarded neutrally, as "givens"; the political scientists' job was not to tell us what we *should* do but how to *understand* political beings, their goals, and their behavior as they pursue certain values.

Although behaviorialism gained a clear ascendancy in political science, it did not lack for critics.[5] The latter insisted that political *science* was less scientific than the behavioralists believed. All of us, they maintained, have values that shape our lives, including our professional lives. These subtly influence our perceptions (including what we tend to see as significant) and our interpretations of what we discover. They noted that there are virtually no studies on value-charged questions that are not attacked, as scientifically flawed, by those who dislike the findings. Or by scientists, whatever their values, who are exceptionally advanced in their grasp of mathematical research techniques.

The difficulty of duplicating the laboratory conditions used by some of the natural sciences has not been overlooked by the critics. Society is enormously complex, and people cannot be controlled as readily as rats, mice, and fruit flies. The problem is further complicated if, as many believe, people have free will and can act in unpredictable ways. When people are conscious of being studied, moreover, they may behave somewhat differently than they ordinarily do (a phenomenon known as the Hawthorne effect). Duplicating similar conditions for repeated experiments, holding constant all the variables being tested but one, and suggesting causal significance (as opposed to loose correlations)—all of which are possible in the natural sciences—are often impossible where major social questions are involved, the critics maintained.

Dissatisfaction was expressed as well with much of the specific work done by behavioralists.[6] Behavioralists elected to study only that which can be measured with great precision rather than with that which is important, according to the critics. Mathematically impressive studies usually led to unimpressive findings. Some critics insisted that "what counts cannot be measured,"—that is, the most critically important questions about justice, freedom, morality, community, and human nature are beyond the reach of even the most refined quantitative research techniques.

Some critics feared that behavioralists would distract political science from the most central questions and convert political scientists into amoral, detached, bloodless technicians—mere clinical observers, taking highly scientific X ray pictures of the political process but detached from society's travails, passions and ethical responsibilities. All scientists, the critics maintained, have a responsibility to promote humane values and a humane society. To live under a Hitler or a Stalin and be content to simply examine what is taking place—explaining the course of political developments by elaborate mathematical formulas establishing cause-and-effect relationships, and reporting these in professional journals is to abdicate moral responsibility. Some critics charged that behavioralism rested on a tacit acceptance of the status quo. By studying only "what is" as if that were the sole domain of political science, the profession was distracted from efforts to evaluate and improve our society.

Others contended that the scientific method, applied to politics, necessarily fragments the person (to facilitate the scientific study of human behavior). It therefore can tell us something about the parts but not about the whole. It can deal with patterns of behavior but not with exceptions. Yet these very exceptions in responding to various circumstances, is what makes people human.

Even the development of scientific political theory, which is the goal of political science, ultimately rests on a series of judgments which are not strictly scientific. There is an unbridgeable gap between political theory and the empirical data that supposedly support it. The data are always subject to differing interpretations in a context of arguable definitions.

The events of the 1960s—the black revolution, the student revolution, the so-called equality revolution (concerned with eliminating special privileges and carving out new rights), the renewed concern with poverty and especially with the Vietnam war—brought heavy pressure to bear on the behavioralists.[7] Political science conventions became the scenes of heated disputes about the direction and content of the discipline; personal feelings ran high and some departments were sharply divided between hostile factions of traditionalists and behavioralists.

The latter group insisted that competent political scientists *can* follow the

5
Political Science: Three Research Examples

scientific method, *can* be fair with their evidence, and *can* keep their values from influencing their conclusions unduly at least most of the time. The effort to be as objective as possible lies at the heart of social science and should never be disparaged or minimized. We should not want, the behavioralists warned, a visceral profession whose members passionately follow their personal inclinations and predilections instead of holding to the sober and disciplined requirements of modern science.

Some behavioralists added that they had no objection to research that centers on vital public issues, so long as that research is confined to that which is scientifically knowable. Such research need not be sterile and may provide valuable aid to the policymaker who does hold humane values. Behavioralists reiterated that the scientist is not an authority on values and should never forget this, humbling though it may be. Nevertheless, social scientists can choose research that, even if it fully meets scientific tenets, may be helpful to causes, policies, and goals in which they believe. And more scientifically grounded descriptions and analyses of political relationships can help us do a better job of evaluating the utility of a program or political system in achieving whatever goals we believe to be important.

Even granting the difficulties that restrict the full development of political science as a science, the behavioralists insisted and continue to insist that no one has offered a superior alternative to the behavioral approach. They want to be as scientific as possible, to describe as accurately as possible, to measure as precisely as possible, to theorize as tightly as possible. The alternative is a profession of sloppy observers, theorists, and philosophers.[8]

Currently the profession is highly eclectic, with political scientists pursuing research along many different lines, using many different approaches. Those who apply advanced mathematical techniques to the study of political phenomena still have an edge when submitting their work to most political science journals, but intellectually rigorous research of other kinds also commands respect.

Instead of behavioralism and traditionalism being seen as competitive and mutually hostile, a synthesis that draws on the best of both approaches may be developing. It should be noted, too, that instead of behavioralists and traditionalists constituting two monolithic groups, each consists of numerous subspecies, with their own special interpretations of political science. The assumptions of many of these subspecies overlap at certain points.

Many political scientists would agree with Harold Lasswell that political science "must be at the same time a science of politics, a philosophic examination of the ends and goals of man and a practical profession engaged in advising electorates and men of power."[9]

Political Science: Three Research Examples

A few examples of modern political science research may be helpful to illuminate the state of the discipline today. A glimpse of political scientists at work on quite different problems allows us a better understanding of how they go about acquiring information, thus shedding light on significant and varied aspects of our political world.

Why do Members of Congress (MCs) vote as they do? There are many ways to answer this question. Researchers could speculate on how they would vote if they were in Congress. They could study what competent journalistic observers of Congress have written or read the memoirs of MCs. They could consult a representative sample of MCs and ask *them* why they generally vote as they do.

John W. Kingdon was not satisfied with any of these approaches.[10] Even the latter was unsatisfactory, since MCs have a tendency to generalize in an impressionistic and possibly inaccurate manner when asked this kind of question. Kingdon decided to interview a cross-section of MCs immediately after they had voted on each of a half dozen important and controversial issues. With the vote and the surrounding circumstances, influences and pressures fresh in their minds, they could more accurately analyze why they had cast their vote for or against the bill. From the sum total of these interviews, he could then draw generalizations about the relative influence of personal staffs, congressional colleagues, party leaders, the president (and his legislative liaison agents), and constituents on members' voting.

Kingdon's interviews were fairly brief, since MCs are busy people. He did not record their comments on the spot (since tape recorders sometimes inhibit the free flow of conversation). He also let the MCs explain their decisions in their own words rather than respond to a structured set of questions that might preshape the responses somewhat. After the MCs had expressed themselves, however, he asked supplementary questions. Upon leaving their offices, he would promptly scribble down the results of his interviews, before the passage of time could blur or distort his memory.

To further flesh out his study, Kingdon interviewed:
1 Key congressional staff members
2 Lobbyists actively involved with the issues at state
3 Respected journalists whose beat was Capitol Hill

Their observations about the reasons for the voting behavior of MCs were also fed into Kingdon's calculations.

The study constituted an important addition to our body of knowledge about Congress, based on information assembled and analyzed about as scientifically as a researcher could manage. (What did he discover? Wait until we reach the chapter on Congress, if you can restrain your by now bursting impatience!)

Why do some presidential decisions turn out well while others are disasters? Is there anything about the decision-making process that predisposes a decision to success or failure? Irving Janis decided to find out.[11]

Janis selected six major presidential decisions, four of which met failure and two of which succeeded. The successes were President John F. Kennedy's confrontations with Premier Nikita Khrushchev, which forced the latter to withdraw missiles from Cuba in 1962; and the formulation of the Marshall Plan, which helped rehabilitate post–world War II Europe after the devastations of that war.

The failures were Kennedy's ill-fated attempt at the Bay of Pigs to help Cuban refugees regain control of Cuba in 1961, President Lyndon Johnson's repeated escalations of American military involvement in the Vietnamese civil war; President Franklin Roosevelt's failure, despite repeated intelligence warnings, to prepare for the attack on Pearl Harbor in 1941; and the fateful decision by President Harry Truman in 1950 to permit General Douglas MacArthur to pursue North Korean troops well above the thirty-eighth parallel in an effort to unite Korea into one country, which brought in Chinese troops and led to prolonged fighting.

Janis closely examined the decision making in each case to see if he could identify planning procedures common to the successes or the failures. Although he did not claim to have discovered an infallible formula for successful decision making (doubtless none will ever be found), he did identify a number of procedures that appeared to improve the prospects for making sensible and realistic decisions. These included having the political leader actively encourage dissenting voices, with the leader declining to reveal his preferences at the outset to allow free debate; having several planning groups working independently on the same problem; making sure that expert opinion is solicited from various quarters rather than relying exclusively on highly cohesive top-level political advisers; and holding a final planning session at which misgivings can be freely aired that might have developed but had not yet been brought to light fully. Janis perceived in all of the ill-starred decisions a tendency for "group think" to develop. That occurred when a warm and cohesive "in-group" cherished harmony and unanimity so much that it failed to realistically appraise alternative courses of action and stifled dissenting voices.

What kinds of people become revolutionary political leaders? A colleague, Mostafa Rejai, is undertaking a monumental piece of research to find out. Previous studies have concentrated on a few revolutionary leaders or on comparisons between a small number of them, but they have not covered a sufficiently large sample or involved a sufficiently wide range of potentially significant factors to reach well-founded (if tentative) conclusions.

Rejai's first job was to define a political revolution. He settled on "illegal mass violence aimed at the overthrow of a political regime as a step toward overall social change."[13] Thus a military coup d'état aimed at seizing power but not at changing the political system would not qualify as a political revolution.

He selected 12 revolutionary movements from which to draw his leaders. They were: England in the 1640s, the American Revolution, the French Revolution, the Mexican Revolution of 1910, the Russian Revolution of 1917, the Chinese Revolution of the 1930s and 1940s, the Bolivian Revolution of 1952, the North Vietnamese Revolution of the post–World War II era, the Hungarian Revolution of 1956, the Cuban Revolution of 1959, the Algerian Revolution of 1962, and the abortive French Revolution of 1968.

The next task was to identify the principal leaders of each revolutionary movement (for which adequate data were available). After studying these revolutions, he drew up a tentative list and submitted the names to qualified scholars for comment and possible revision.

In trying to establish common background factors, personal characteristics, and other relevant patterns affecting these leaders, he examined the leaders' experiences in formative years, their relationships with parents and siblings, school experiences, family's socioeconomic status, religion, education, occupation, experiences in foreign countries, involvement in revolutionary organizations and activities, political ideology, attitudes toward people in general and attitudes toward their society and toward the international community as a whole. He also sought to determine their ego strength, inclination toward asceticism and puritanism, self-images, sense of deprivation and status anxiety, esthetic sensibilities, and the specific experiences that overtly seemed to radicalize them. Finally, he analyzed the political milieu in which they found themselves when developing into revolutionary leaders.

A follow-up study of a similar nature will deal with currently active revolutionary leaders (to add a predictive dimension), and a final study will compare revolutionary leaders with nonrevolutionary political leaders in order to identify the nature of what is truly revolutionary.

While the invariable uniqueness of each revolutionary situation and of each revolutionary leader precludes the drawing of rigid generalizations, some of Rejai and Blackwell's findings are revealing. They discovered, for example, that over one-third of the leaders studied had engaged in revolutionary agitation before the age of 20. The majority came from the middle class, a high percentage had renounced an earlier religious orientation, half had experienced relatively untroubled childhoods, and travel abroad had a radicalizing influence on many.

These studies represent only a few among many research techniques used by today's political scientists. They do not, for example, provide an insight into the incredible mathematical rigor which marks many studies appearing in the professional journals (studies that are humbling to those of us with retarded mathematical skills!). But they should provide the reader with a somewhat clearer picture of what political scientists try to do and how they go about doing it. Numerous studies like these have contributed to many of the political descriptions and commentaries found in this book. (First-rate political journalists have contributed a great deal, too, it should be acknowledged.)

Notes

1 David Easton, *A Framework for Political Analysis* (Englewood Cliffs, N.J.: Prentice-Hall, 1965), p. 50.
2 For fuller descriptions, see Francis J. Sorauf, *Political Science: An Informal Overview* (Columbus, Ohio: Merrill, 1965); and Albert Somit and Joseph Tanenhaus, *The Development of Political Science: From Burgess to Behavioralism* (Boston: Allyn Bacon, 1967).
3 Sorauf, *Political Science*, p. 14.
4 For general treatments, see Robert A. Dahl, "The Behavioral Approach in Political Science: Epitaph for a Monument to a Successful Protest," *American Political Science Review* 4 (1961), 763–772; David B. Truman, "Disillusion and Regeneration: The Quest for a Discipline," *American Political Science Review* (December 4, 1965), 865–873; Heinz Eulau, *The Behavioral Persuasion in Politics* (New York; Random House, 1963).

Notes

5. A widely discussed critique was that of James C. Charlesworth, ed., *The Limits of Behavioralism in Political Science* (Philadelphia: The American Academy of Political and Social Science, October 1962). See also Christian Bay, "Politics and Pseudo-Politics: A Critical Evaluation of Some Behavioral Literature," *American Political Science Review* 1 (1965), 39-51.
6. For example, see Bernard Susser, "The Behavioral Ideology: A Review and a Retrospect," *Political Studies* 22 (September 1974), 271-288; and Herbert G. Reid and Ernest J. Yanarella, "Political Science and the Post-Modern Critique of Scientism and Domination," *Review of Politics* 37 (July 1975), 286-316.
7. This was reflected memorably in David Easton, "The New Revolution in Political Science," *American Political Science Review* 63 (December 1969), 1051-1061.
8. Richard Merelman, "On Interventionist Behavioralism: An Essay in the Sociology of Knowledge," *Politics and Society* 6 (1976), 57-78. A useful and balanced overview of political science is George J. Graham, Jr., and George W. Carey, *The Post-Behavioral Era: Perspectives in Political Science* (New York: McKay, 1972).
9. Sorauf, *Political Science*, p. 19. (Sorauf paraphrases Lasswell).
10. John W. Kingdon, *Congressmen's Voting Decisions* (New York: Harper & Row, 1973).
11. Irving L. Janis, *Victims of Groupthink* (Boston: Houghton Mifflin, 1972).
12. Mostafa Rejai, with Kay Phillips, *Leaders of Revolution* (Beverly Hills, Calif.: Sage 1979).

CHAPTER 2
IN DEFENSE OF POLITICIANS

Now that we have examined political science as a discipline, let's take a closer look at its subject matter—the politicans themselves. Politicians are usually regarded with distaste. What are the first words that flash into your minds when somone mentions them? Are they flattering terms—or words and images like corruption, bribery, graft, trickery, big promises, mudslinging, fence straddling, high taxes, logrolling, or insincerity? Many people typically think of politics as a rather devious, double-dealing, manipulative, backscratching, back room dealing, nest-feathering business in which not very scrupulous and not very respectable people engage. It is who you know, not what you know, that counts. According to the stereotype, politics means getting elected by saying what people want to hear, whether you mean it or not. It means smooth words, ambiguous phrases, easy promises, evasive and unethical tactics, flattering voters, smearing opponents, denying all charges, saying one thing and doing another, playing fast and loose with the taxpayer's money. Words like candid, straightforward, honorable, trustworthy seem not to apply.

Politicians: Our Mirror Image

The image of politics and politicians is hardly flattering to democracy. If a democratic form of government and democratic politicians are really this way, democracy must be a very sorry system.

But is this a fair and accurate description of politics and politicians? Probably not. Even members of the general public usually concede that the picture is unfair to politicians they personally know. Members of congress are reelected most of the time, which suggests that the general public is unconvinced that *their* representatives are so corrupt. And, curiously enough, when Americans are asked who they most admire, politicans predominate in the "Ten Most Admired Persons" list.

To a political scientist the art of politics is largely the art of persuading people to do what practitioners of the art want them to do. It is the art of bringing together diverse people with different ideas to follow a common course of action. Politicians must persuade people to entrust them with office and power, and then maintain sufficient public confidence to retain that office and power.

Everyone "plays politics." We all play games with each other in trying to get our way, to advance our interests, and to win friends and influence people. But we do it in less public arenas, free from public scrutiny. Children begin playing politics very early in life. They learn which parent to approach when they want something, what is the best time and occasion to seek a favor, what is the best strategy to use, what parental weakness to exploit, how to play one parent off against another. That is politics, on a lowly scale, but seldom recognized as such.

People play politics when they seek a job. They try to dress in the most acceptable manner, smile winningly, give the answers that will most appeal to prospective employers, emphasize their strongest qualities, and conceal their weakest ones—just like a politician seeking votes.

Most pastors or priests try to be good politicians. They usually present their message without giving undue offense to members of the congregation. If

13

Politicians: Our Mirror Image

there are rival factions in the church, which is often the case, they try to be diplomatic with all factions and avoid taking sides in a way that will arouse hostility. They pay attention to the squeaky wheels. In all sensitive and potentially disruptive matters, they express themselves as discreetly and adroitly as possible, seeking to maintain the broadest possible coalition of support—again just like an officeholder (though the more secure a pastor's position, the less true the above may be).

A final analogy: The behavior of a young man pursuing a young woman (or, for that matter, vice versa) is strikingly similar to that of a vote-seeking politician. He is cheerful, friendly, smiles a lot, always puts his best foot forward. He tries to discover what she likes and to offer it, if possible. He says what he thinks she will be pleased to hear and avoids saying what she will dislike. In sensitive areas, where her opinions are not yet known, he is especially cautious and diplomatic. In general, his conversation focuses on areas of agreement and avoids areas of disagreement. He is not averse to using flattery. He projects his best qualities and conceals his worst. If something discreditable surfaces about him or his past, he is likely to explain it away, minimize it, sugar-coat it, or even doctor the truth a bit. He vows total dedication to her welfare. Sounds like a politician, does it not?

The main differences between politicians and the rest of us are that they deal with public funds and public policy, and they play their game in the open, for all to see, with the press watching their every step and reporting it (not always fairly) in the papers and on TV. Those differences raise an important point. How flawless would you look if shrewd, cynical observers were exploring your past, dissecting and publicly assessing your strategies, noting your weaknesses, your contradictions, your evasions, your concealments? Suppose that your critics were probing for and publicizing every occasion when you were petty, deceitful, cowardly, selfish, sulky, greedy, and calculating? And if they exaggerated a bit, as people are prone to do, would you look like a very admirable person, particularly if the emphasis was on your defects rather than your virtues (because that is what people like to read)? How would you look, moreover, if you had lived 40 or 50 years and had had many more experiences, faced far more temptations, and made far more blunders than you have yet had a chance to make?

The politician faces a public ordeal unlike that of the business person, the doctor, the lawyer, the sales representative, the plumber, the farmer. Few professionals are examined with the fine-toothed combs used on politicians, and those that are rarely see the results—stressing the negative—spread on the front pages for all to see. During campaigns the opposite party or candidate often makes a systematic effort to discredit opponents, exposing—and often exaggerating—every sin or alleged sin in an effort to break down public confidence in them. Who else faces a similar ordeal? If politicians look more unsavory than other people, it may be for these reasons rather than because of their uniquely shabby morals.

Other factors must also be considered. The media give endless attention to the "bad guys." When Arkansas' Wilbur Mills, who chaired the powerful

A candidate meets the voters

House Ways and Means Committee, was caught frolicking with "The Argentine Firecracker" Fannie Fox and Ohio Congressman Wayne Hays was found to have a secretary on his staff who could not type but presumably performed more interesting services, and New York Representative Adam Clayton Powell took Miss Corinne Huff, Ohio's 1960 Beauty Queen, with him on Caribbean vacations (at the taxpayer's expense)—the press had field days and the public greedily drank in the details, convinced anew that this is the way things are in the nation's capital. The other members of the House were assumed to be of equally dubious character because a few failed to keep their noses clean.

Perhaps the rest have not been caught, but with muckraking journalists, zealous prosecutors and political opponents hard at work, misbehavior is far less likely to go unnoticed in politics than in any other occupation. The writer believes that in terms of their general moral principles, politicians are neither much better nor much worse than other people. Because they are watched so closely by reporters and political opponents alike, their official conduct is probably more honorable, on the average, than that of the average professional. What makes people more upright than being watched closely, day and night, by a swarm of reporters with a vested interest in discovering a scandal which will titillate their readers and reflect credit on their investigative skill?

This generalization has special application on the national scene, where the best of the nation's reporters are clustered. It is less true on the state and municipal level, where public attention is less concentrated, and where the quality of journalism is lower. Indeed, a close correlation generally exists between the alertness, competence, and courage of the local press and the degree of integrity manifested by local officials. If newspapers chronically deplore the moral level of local politicians, they are indirectly indicting themselves. Finally, since the public is largely indifferent to county government and the press gives it only scanty coverage, county government *is* often as corrupt as the popular image of government holds government to be. The same can be said for municipal government, sometimes. But in Washington, members of the House, Senate, and the administration find it in their self-interest to keep their records clean. While scandals are bound to break out from time to time, and Congress *is* reluctant to investigate or chastise its own peers,[1] the level of probity is usually high compared to other professions.

In defense of politicians, several other points should be made. Politicians are responsible for imposing taxes, and people hate taxes. Politicians make laws that restrict our freedom (although some laws really enlarge our freedom, when all things are considered). Individuals who exercise authority over us, regulate our behavior, and impose taxes are people we are disposed to resent. We seem to want to believe the worst about them. One primitive tribe, it is said, reserved one day a year in which the tribal members could throw dung at their chieftain. This was probably very therapeutic as well as great sport, because people seem to need to stick our their tongues occasionally at those who govern them.

Why Politicians Pussyfoot

People are often irked by the failure of so many politicians to take clear-cut, unequivocal stands on all the issues, especially controversial questions. Those in office seem to pussyfoot and to want to be all things to all people.

But from another perspective, there is good reason for politicians' reticence. If politicians routinely took strong, straightforward stands on issues that hotly divide people, they would do so at their peril. Many voters would be angry with them for being "wrong" on issues close to their heart and would carry their anger with them to the polls. They would try to punish the politicians for taking such a stupid or unenlightened position. The accumulation of grievances among alienated voters might well cost legislators their jobs.

Perhaps politicians should ignore the probable impact of what they say and do on their future. Maybe they should just do what is "right" and cast all prudence to the winds. But how many other professionals are regularly faced with decisions that could wreck their careers? Doctors, architects, teachers, business managers, and lawyers may err, but the damage is usually minor and transient. They do not find themselves suddenly unemployed, their careers derailed, perhaps never to be on track again. In a way we expect the same thing of politicians as we do of saints—to disregard their career prospects and to consider only what seems "right." Saints, we might add, are not a dime a dozen.

The picture is even more complicated, however. Many times politicians can see both sides of a question, or three or four sides. They are more familiar with the complexity of problems than most voters, and they may see merit in several positions. Right and wrong are not apparent. Are they to be blamed for not taking that blazingly clear-cut position that voters in their infallible wisdom want them to take? Most legislative issues are matters of judgment rather than of principle. They are questions about which experts disagree, on which reasonable people differ, with many facts in doubt and the ultimate effect of a given policy uncertain. Right and wrong are often as unclear to politicians as they are to you and me.

On many issues, a politician may be well advised to reserve judgment until the relevant committee has held hearings, the committee report has been examined, press comment has been weighed, constituent mail studied, and colleagues' judgments assessed. Most citizens want a public official whose mind is reasonably open during deliberations while they are gradually forming and expressing their opinions. But they also want clear-cut positions *now*, too. They can't have it both ways.

Finally, the most a politician can properly do on many pending issues is indicate where his or her general sympathies and preferences lie. Because the final legislation to be voted on will be very specific and detailed and will contain numerous significant clauses that no one could have predicted in advance, it is not illogical for a politician to speak in generalities. Options are thereby left open until the issues have been resolved in a bill, which legislators can then weigh.

Does this mean politicians should always duck the issues and take wobbly or waffling positions on every controversial question? No, since there are times when they must speak out. But in stating their opinions, they can express them diplomatically, showing respect for the position they reject; their statements will give the public useful insights into their general political posture. If they are always evasive, citizens have a right to be displeased. Still, there will always be inflammatory issues on which crystal-clear stands may cost politicians dearly and on which they understandably will try to avoid antagonizing either side. Jimmy Carter was accused, during the 1976 campaign, of being fuzzy on the issues. But a respected *New York Times* reporter wrote that Carter had not ducked the issues but had stated them "so as not to offend those who take the opposite position."[2] There is nothing discreditable in such a stance.

It is instructive to recall Abraham Lincoln's position on the condition and status of blacks. Speaking in Chicago on July 10, 1858, Lincoln said:

> Let us discard all this quibbling about this man and the other man, this race and that race and the other race being inferior, and therefore they must be placed in an inferior position. Let us discard all these things, and unite as one people throughout this land, until we shall once more stand up declaring that all men are created equal.[3]

But addressing an audience in an Illinois town in the southern part of the state on September 19, 1858, Lincoln declared:

17

Why Politicians Pussyfoot

I will say, then, that I am not, nor ever have been, in favor of bringing about in any way the social and political equality of the white and black races: that I am not, nor ever have been, in favor of making voters or jurors of negroes nor of qualifying them to hold office, nor to intermarry with white people.... And inasmuch as they cannot so live, while they do remain together, there must be the position of superior and inferior, and I as much as any other man am in favor of having the superior position assigned to the white race.[4]

When Stephen Douglas, his opponent in a congressional race, twitted him for these inconsistencies, Lincoln responded, "I have not supposed, and do not now suppose, that there is any conflict whatever between them."[5]

Thus Lincoln, one of our most honorable public figures, was unable to bring himself to publicly take a forthright and unequivocal stand on an issue that divided the nation—and his state—so sharply. Rather than risk the loss of his political dreams, he said what he said. Historian Richard Hofstadter observes, "It is not easy to decide whether the true Lincoln is the one who spoke in Chicago or the one who spoke in Charleston [Illinois]. Possibly the man devoutly believed each of the utterances at the time he delivered it."[6]

For a more recent example of a moral dilemma involving politics and race, take the case of former Senator William E. Fulbright of Arkansas. Fulbright, a Rhodes scholar, was a very able, intelligent, and respected senator. As a member (ultimately chairman) of the Senate Foreign Relations Committee, he was the only major figure who advised President John F. Kennedy not to undertake the ill-fated invasion of the Bay of Pigs (our abortive effort to overthrow Premier Fidel Castro of Cuba by assisting Cuban refugees in a CIA-directed military operation). Later he led a long fight against the Vietnam War.

During the struggle to eliminate racial discrimination against blacks and guarantee them full equality, Senator Fulbright consistently voted against civil rights legislation. He did not lead the southern forces, he spoke as little as possible against this legislation, but he did oppose it when the roll was called. Fulbright was a highly educated person whose views on civil rights were actually more advanced than those of his constituents. He may have been uncomfortable with his vote, but he knew a pro-civil rights stand would be deeply resented and would inevitably wreck his political career. Did he sell his soul for political success?

Perhaps he did, but he probably saw the matter differently. If he had voted for civil rights, his opponent might have won and been an even more active antagonist of civil rights than he was. In that case the civil rights cause would have been harmed in the Senate and in the state, since his opponent would, as senator, have had far more access to the media and to the voters. By yielding to voters' wishes on this issue, Fulbright purchased relative freedom in his area of special interest and expertise—foreign policy—freedom he exercised with a skill and wisdom his successor probably could not have matched. Overall, Fulbright might have thought, the public was better served by this accommodation to local prejudices than by a courageous but losing battle against those prejudices.

The senator might also have argued to himself that as a representative of the people, he was obliged to stand for their views. If the majority was strongly opposed to civil rights legislation, that view deserved to be represented in the U.S. Senate, for that is what representative government is all about.

If that was Fulbright's reasoning, he made a strong case. Or, should politicians compromise on almost anything *but* basic human rights? A strong case can be made for this position, too.

But it should be emphasized that very few votes involve constitutional rights. Mostly they involve debatable questions of an economic or administrative nature on which one might err in judgment while committing no moral offense, whatever the vote. The few issues that do require a stand on important questions of value can be agonizing for politicians, however.

Consider, for example, the issue of the B-1 bomber. During his 1976 primary campaign Jimmy Carter attacked the plane as "wasteful and unnecessary." After becoming president he had the opportunity—and the obligation—to study the issue much more fully and with more Pentagon information at his disposal than during the campaign. Suppose this study convinced him that his campaign position was ill founded, that the national security really required our building a large fleet of B-1 bombers. What was the moral thing to do—honor his campaign position (which won him many liberal votes) or follow his best judgment and urge that Congress build the bombers? (As it happened, President Carter was able to salvage his campaign stance by saying his study as chief executive confirmed his earlier judgment.)

Politicians deserve a bit of sympathy on yet another front.

Consider a hypothetical case. Suppose a candidate has a reputation as someone who care about the interests of minority groups. She is seen as a person of strong humanitarian and underdog sympathies, and she welcomes being seen in that light. A bill before Congress would spend billions to attract investment into the decaying inner city. The goal is noble but close study has convinced her that the program will not work. Nonetheless, the bill picks up momentum and looks as if it will pass. Almost all of the members of Congress who normally support minority group legislation line up behind the bill. The pressure is heavy to vote for it; disappointment—even shock—will follow if she doesn't. There is no dobt that her minority group constituents will feel she has let them down if she votes no. Her explanation of why she voted no will probably be ignored by the press and lost sight of in the excitement over the outcome of the measure. Her opponent in the next election will use her vote against her—in minority districts—as proof of her duplicity and hard-heartedness. How would *you* like to be in her boots?

Take another example. The crime rate is high; people lock their doors in the daytime, buy Doberman pinschers, and demand the return of the death penalty. A bill to funnel increased funds to local law enforcement agencies is before Congress. Almost everyone seems to be for it, despite solid research indicating that existing efforts to federally subsidize these agencies have been nonproductive and that increased expenditures are likely to represent money down the old rathole. A vote against the bill will look like callous indifference to the crime wave and lack of support for local crime-fighting groups—and may be costly in the next election. Not many would enjoy making that decision.

It is surprising how often decisions like these arise in which legislators are deeply skeptical about the merits of a bill, but its symbolic significance almost compels them to vote against their best judgment. If they do otherwise, the voters will misinterpret their action. But we voters rarely empathize with the politicians; we just stand ready to condemn if they don't toe our mark. Putting ourselves in the politicians' shoes when bills like these come along helps us recognize what cruel choices politicians often have to make and how easy it is to judge them too harshly.

But if officeholders are often faced with agonizing moral predicaments with which knowledgeable men and women of good will can sympathize, there is a point at which less excusable behavior begins. Undeniably, some politicians are demagogues. The demagogue tells his audience what it wants to hear—especially on an emotionally charged issue—even when he or she knows the statement is a simplistic distortion. It is demogoguery to demand big cuts in federal spending without indicating where those cuts should be made. Or to rail at federal spending while consistently supporting bills that bring more federal dollars to one's state or district. It can be demagoguery to call for major tax cuts without suggesting *where* the necessary revenue is to come from. It is demagoguery to take cheap shots at people on welfare—knowing the applause this automatically brings—without explaining how welfare laws could be improved.

But demagoguery, springs from soil prepared for it. These sentiments are cut from the same cloth that nonpoliticians wear every day of the week. Chances are that you and your father and mother have expressed the same views dozens of times. The only difference is that politicians seek votes by saying these things publicly while Mr. and Mrs. Average Citizen express their disgruntlement to their neighbors. If it is reprehensible when done by politicians, it is not much less reprehensible when done by John and Jane Doe.

Why People Enter Politics

The reasons people enter politics are probably as varied as the candidates themselves. But a few general explanations can be offered

People enter politics because they want recognition. They like to see their names and pictures in the papers, on TV, on billboards, in campaign literature. John Fischer, a former magazine editor, once noted: "Like the theatre, politics is nourisher of egos. It attracts men who are hungry for attention, for assurance that somebody loves them, for the soul-stirring music of their own voices."[7]

Everyone likes attention and recognition (except spies!) but politicians seem to like them a bit more than most people. Entering politics is one of the quickest ways to gratify that need. Of course, that attention may not turn out to be flattering, but politicians hope it will.

Some people enter politics because it will advance their nonpolitical careers. A young, struggling lawyer gains name recognition that should be helpful. People are more likely to consult a lawyer whose name they have heard than one they have not. The same applies to people in the insurance business, in realty, and perhaps in other occupations.

The political arena attracts some because it is in the family tradition. Father, uncles, and grandfather have been active in politics, and children grow up in a family atmosphere full of political talk. They acquire an interest in politics, just as the family transmits interests in many other topics—with active involvement following almost as a matter of course.

If they are from celebrated political families, following the tradition is even more likely. Young men (and perhaps now women, too) from the Taft family might almost naturally consider a political career, given the family's history: President William Howard Taft was followed by Senator Robert A. Taft Sr. and Charles Taft (his brother, long active in Cincinnati politics) and by former Senator Robert A. Taft, Jr. The same is true of the Stevenson family: Adlai Stevenson I, who became vice-president in 1892, was followed by his son, Adlai Stevenson II, twice nominated for president by the Democrats; in turn, his son, Adlai Stevenson III, became a U.S. Senator. The Massachusetts Kennedys, the Louisiana Longs, the Georgia Talmadges, the New York Roosevelts are other examples. In their cases, not just family tradition but instant and favorable name recognition gives young candidates a big advantage over less fortunate opponents.

Politics, especially on the national level, appeals to those with an appetite for power. As journalist Stewart Alsop correctly observed, "Power, not money, is ambition's ultimate reward. An important politician disposes of more real power than the most exalted chairman, so Washington acts as a magnet to able and ambitious men."[8] When John F. Kennedy was asked why he wanted to be president, he replied, "That's where the power is." Abraham Lincoln was similarly fascinated with power and was motivated as well by a burning desire to be "somebody."

One prominent political scientist, incidentally, has argued that politicians seek power to compensate for their low self-esteem.[9] They need power to reassure themselves that they are really competent people. But another political scientist believes politicians are better adjusted than most people or they would never survive the rigorous "screening" that politicians must undergo to attain and retain political office. The higher the office, the more likely that they are emotionally healthy people.[10]

Some people believe the desire to exercise power is discreditable. But strong personalities almost inevitably seek power, however well-disguised the search. The important question is: Do people seek power for its own sake, or are they at least partly moved by a desire to do something worthwhile? Probably few, if any, want power purely for noble reasons, but many politicians genuinely hope—and try—to use it for good ends. The best of them will not sacrifice all their principles to achieve or exercise power. Power is exceedingly important to them but not all-important. If we can obtain reliable clues to a candidate's attitude toward "power at any price," that is invaluable information for the discerning voter. But it is never a reproach to a politician to say that he or she seeks and enjoys power. Only when that ambition is obsessive and unrestrained by ethical concerns is it a cause for alarm. Then it is indeed a grave menace, both in the political *and* nonpolitical world.

A sense of duty is not irrelevant to political entry. To quote Fischer again:

> Most [politicians] are as much moved by a sense of duty as by their thirst for status. If politics is balm for tender egos, it is equally soothing to the inflamed superego. Perhaps more than most people, politicians are prodded by conscience. Certainly the best of them sincerely feel an obligation to perform a public service.[11]

George Washington, though not a typical politician, is a good example. He accepted the presidency with regret, out of a sense of duty. A sense of duty played a significant part in Dwight D. Eisenhower's decision to run for president. Political scientist David Barber, in *The Presidential Character*, categorizes a number of presidents as "passive-negative" men who were primarily in politics because of a sense of duty.[12] Besides people who run for high office, some people run for the school board or city council because they feel they should. Most of the time, duty is not as important as the itch for recognition or power, but it is a mistake to overlook it. Most of us are a confusing mixture of self-concern and concern for what is right—and politicians are no exception.

In this connection, a number of people seem to enter politics because they are pushed. They have no real intention to enter, although the idea may have flickered in their minds from time to time. But friends or political scouts recognize their valuable political qualities—or their vote-getting capacity—and urge them to seek office. Those who do the urging may stress the shortage of good candidates, the total inadequacy of the leading candidate, the party's need to field a respected ticket, the opportunities to achieve something worthwhile. The potential candidate may be reluctant to give up a secure, comfortable, and well-established way of life. He or she may wince at the demands (and indignities) of a campaign, advance a host of objections, but finally yield to heavy pressures.

Some people enjoy "The great game of politics." Fischer again (what would I do without him?).

> Nearly every skillful politician I have ever met enjoyed the subtleties and excitements of his craft just as a tennis player enjoys a well-played match. Perhaps a better analogy is chess—a kind of chess played with thousands of pieces, each different and everyone likely to start charging around the board on his own at any moment; demanding luck as well as art; and offering to the winners the highest of stakes, and to a loser, oblivion.[13]

A politician planning a political campaign is like a general planning a military campaign. There are a thousand things to consider, hundreds of things can go wrong, and it is exhilarating to see how astutely one can plan strategy. One needs to size up the "enemy" accurately, assess his or her strengths and weaknesses, decide how to blunt the opponent's attack and put him or her on the defensive; what issues to emphasize, what propaganda will be most effective, which media in what proportions, what timing, how to raise the money to finance the campaign, how to build a supporting coalition, how to recruit and energize one's foot soldiers—these are all important decisions. A candidate enjoys the excitement of political rallies, the speculation about how this or that is contributing to or impeding success, the climactic "high" of election day. Day-to-day corporation activities, for many people, pale in comparison to this environment. The same excitement applies to legislative struggles pitting one side against another in a battle of wits that demand all the skill at dealing with complex problems and forces that anyone can muster. Whatever else politics can be, it is rarely dull. And that is what attracts many people into the field.

Some people enter politics because they believe things need changing, or believe they can "do a better job than those clowns now in office." College students who indicate an interest in going into politics usually claim *this* as their motive. It may well be the reason, though probably those who claim it may not be as pure in motive as they think. The preceding six factors are usually stronger incentives, if one probes beneath the surface. But the sincere desire of some people to want to run things better cannot be ruled out altogether. Human beings are a powerfully self-interested lot, but self-interest does not explain all that we do. We have some larger instincts, too.

Rx for Success in Politics

What kind of people make good politicians? Is there any formula for political success?

No one has ever come up with a sure-fire formula that will assure political success. Indeed, many different kinds of people have reached the political heights.

We think of successful politicians as friendly, personable people—and they usually are. But Bob Taft, Sr. became "Mr. Republican" and minority leader in the Senate despite being a rather austere, ascetic, "egghead" type who disliked backslapping and glad-handing. The late Senator Everett Dirksen of Illinois was also a highly successful politician whose face bore no resemblance to Robert Redford. Similarly, Mike Mansfield, former majority leader of the Senate and a phenomenal success in Montana, went far despite a bleak and wintry countenance and a penchant for abrupt expression. Wayne Hays was arrogant, dictatorial and sharp-tongued—but became one of the most powerful men in the House of Representatives before his fall.

In terms of the usual qualities associated with political success, a few generalizations can be offered, however. In our TV age, being reasonably good-looking helps. It is not imperative but it is a plus. Being able to speak fluently is an important asset. Having the capacity to meet people with ease, to make small talk comfortably, and—of great significance—to be a good listener are other major assets. Good listeners are always in such short supply that they promptly endear themselves to others—in politics and out. Anyone who is good at remembering names and faces also has an edge in politics.

Being tall helps. Given an opportunity to choose between a tall person and a short person, the public usually prefers the former. (Executives in big corporations ordinarily are taller than the average American, one study revealed.) Why? Maybe it goes back to the days when physical power was important in defending the tribe against wild beasts and enemy tribesmen. The Bible notes that Saul, the first king of Israel, "from his shoulders and upward, he was higher than the people." 1 Sam. 9:2. For whatever reason, people seem to associate leadership qualities with height, absurd though this may be.

A successful politician needs to be able to accept criticism with some degree of equanimity. If a hostile newspaper editorial would cost you three nights sleep, or a campaign attack leave you quivering with rage—politics probably is not for you. It is a rough and tumble profession, and experienced politicians accept its darts and barbs as part of the game. Politics is not for thin-skinned people, although politicians are normal enough to resent what they regard as unfair criticism. However, they do not let their resentment emotionally incapacitate them.

Successful politicians must be able to choose their words with care, avoiding expressions or phrases that will later come back to haunt them. One ill-chosen phrase that seems derogatory to a church, a race, a nationality group,

Jerry Ford at interview

or an interest group may wreck a political career. An impetuous statement, an extravagant generalization, or even a jocular expression that looks bad in print can cost a politician dearly since opponents are always ready to capitalize on such remarks. Thus, politicians who can say precisely what they mean to say and say it in words that are not readily misinterpreted have an invaluable political skill. National politicians on "Meet the Press" and "Face the Nation" choose their words as if they were picking their way through a minefield. Otherwise, a careless expression may be exploited by the press in a manner disastrous to their career. Politicians are always "persons on guard."

One quality is shared by all successful politicians—a high energy level. This is, in fact, a quality common to highly successful people in almost every walk of life. Politics is a very physically demanding profession. Not only are the hours long but there is a heavy emotional drain associated with constant human contact and with the frictions inevitably associated with campaigns and legislative conflicts. People are forever clamoring for attention, for favors, for help in every imaginable way. Vigilance against verbal misstep must be constant. Because politics is so demanding, a high energy level is called for.

Being lucky is also helpful. Almost all successful politicians received some fortunate breaks in their climb. Although it is true, as someone has said, that the harder you work the luckier you get, a certain amount of sheer good fortune often accompanies success in any field.

There are really two kinds of politicians—those who are regularly reelected but never accomplish much and are not highly esteemed by their colleagues, and those who achieve through hard work and political skill. The former may have gotten elected more or less by accident and continue to be reelected because they have name recognition, help constituents work out problems with the bureaucray, and stay out of trouble. Or they may be public relations wizards, expert at having names appear in the paper even though they achieve very little. (In fact, adeptness at obtaining press and TV attention for activities should be included as one of the qualities most helpful for political success.)

In contrast, real political craftsmen do their jobs conscientiously and win the respect of their colleagues (although not necessarily the attention of the press).[16] These persons are masters of the fine art of politics, which is one of the most valuable of human arts.

Successful practical politicians are people who can be trusted. When they give their word, they can be counted on. Politicians who tell one colleague one thing and another something else, or renege on promises to do this or that, are soon shunned. Most descriptions of effective officeholders stress their reputation as trustworthy. Being as good as one's word wins respect from others.

Politicians who are legislators trying to get a bill passed must first do their homework. They study the bill and its probable impact so thoroughly that others are impressed with their firm grasp of the subject. (Knowledge is power, just as Bacon said!)

They consult with people who are likely to play a key role in the fate of the bill and with influentials whose feelings might be wounded if they are not consulted. Successful legislators are good listeners. When those consulted make cogent recommendations, an attempt is made to incorporate their suggestions into the bill. Where they are less cogent but of great importance to potential supporters or to groups affected by the bill, concessions may be made, where possible. In formulating and revising the bill, words and phrases are selected that will be least offensive to those who are dubious about the bill but might be persuaded either to support it or at least not to actively oppose it. Sometimes the phrases are vague enough to be subject to diverse interpretations, so that groups with different goals can hope that the administrators or the courts will interpret the bill *their* way.

When serious differences between persons and groups with different interests and perspectives persist, the constructive politician searches for a compromise that gives both sides something even if neither is entirely content. Skill at identifying those compromises that can placate opposing factions without simultaneously alienating other groups with a stake in the outcome is an essential part of the political art.

Difficult, complex, and controversial measures are usually passed by assembling a majority coalition of groups and legislators representing many different interests. It is often a delicate and fragile coalition, likely to come unstuck unless the architect of that coalition is highly sensitive not only to divisive substantive considerations but to all of the ego needs involved. The world is full of people whose egos need stroking if their cooperation is to be won. The capacity to soothe those egos and find a compromise that enables all the disparate groups to decide they can "live with" the final product is a remarkably useful one. The ability to reconcile seemingly irreconcilable views and to come up with a solution that reduces tension, defuses harsh feelings, and provides a workable solution is one of the most valuable skills in the human repertory. No one should ever disparage the politician who, in a world of warring interests, of unavoidably contrasting views, of ideologues, demagogues, headline hunters, uncompromising crusaders and of tender, throbbing egos, is able to keep people from each other's throats and enable them, however grumpily, to work together and live together in relative peace. This talent is surprisingly rare and its presence does far more for social harmony than most people realize.

The skillful politician contrasts with the "principled" crusaders who know they are absolutely right in their crusades and who will not give an inch lest their eternal souls be scarred. We need people like this too, to force us to consider the moral dimensions of certain issues. But if politics was composed only of crusaders, it would become a species of civil war. It would create an intolerable society—one in which peace, order, and stability would give way to political carnage. Let us be grateful for the canny politicians who keep us from destroying one another.

These politicians have the same talent, as we have noted, as is possessed by the skillful pastor faced with congregational strife, by the able union leader trying to keep peace between the hotheads and those who are more reasonable, by the competent school principal who can appease angry parents demanding contradictory policies, and by the wise parent who effectively mediates between his or her warring children. Many people are able critics or defenders of a given policy, but few are able to effectively conciliate, compromise, and blend diverse views into a constructive outcome. Politicians who can do this deserve much more press attention than they receive.

Such politicians also make democracy possible, because citizens will not support *any* political system unless it gets necessary jobs done tolerably well. Even though people may incline toward democracy, they will not retain allegiance to it if those who operate the political machinery are too corrupt or ineffectual. Dictators often arrive when legislatures are so inefficient and impotent that the public becomes disgusted with their performance. Thus, politicians who keep the system functioning with a reasonable degree of efficiency enable it to maintain enough public support to keep democracy healthy. Not many people play a more significant social role than that.

Getting a Foot in the Door

Many people are curious about how to get started in politics. It is surprising how many politicians began in campus politics. They run for office, serve on committees, polish their speaking abilities. Serving on a student legislative body is always an educational experience, even if that body has little impact on university or college policy. The political world is one in which establishing good personal relations is all-important; that talent can be developed on a college campus as well as anywhere. In shaping campus policies and programs, many of the same pitfalls exist, and the same skills are required as in the noncollegiate political world. Students who find college politics distasteful and unrewarding are likely to view politics on a larger plane in the same way. So if you have a yen for politics but aren't sure how deep it runs, a plunge into campus politics may help you decide.

It has long been regarded as wise for the budding young politician to earn a law degree. Probably that is still a prudent thing to do. A legal education is not absolutely necessary to being a successful lawmaker (though it does teach care in precise communication as well as in the uses of vagueness), but it has certain practical advantages. Lawyers can schedule their work and office hours to accommodate the needs of political campaigning, since they do not work a 9 to 5 shift. Young lawyers who become assistant prosecutors may handle newsworthy cases as well as being cast in the role of battling for righteous causes.

Prior to running for office, prospective candidates should probably devote a campaign or two to helping another candidate make his or her run. This can give you experience, enable you to get the "feel" of campaign politics, and give you acquaintance with members of the community who are active in politics. Also, it erases or reduces the hostility some people feel toward a young unknown who is too eager to go too far too fast, without going through an appropriate apprenticeship. On the other hand, if a young person's name has come before the public in sufficiently favorable circumstances, the apprenticeship period can often be by-passed.

Becoming a joiner also helps by enabling the fledgling politician to meet more people, make more friends, and understand community sentiment a little better. It provides more opportunities to make speeches; if a candidate's campaign literature indicates membership in a given organization, that might induce other members of that organization to take a more friendly view of the candidacy. The process of becoming a joiner also offers the chance of remembering names and faces and becoming a good listener.

The aspiring young politician is well advised to find some community problem and become an expert on it—to learn all that can be learned about it from every conceivable source and then to seek opportunities to speak on the subject. People will listen to someone who has done his or her homework well, who has absorbed the facts and can comment intelligently on them. There is no substitute for knowledge, no matter what the endeavor. Most people don't want to undergo the time-consuming, onerous job of becoming truly well informed, but they still want to be heard and heeded. Generally, in this matter, people get the respect and attention they deserve.

The farsighted young politician guards well his or her reputation as a person of character. Avoiding not only the illegal and unethical but also activities that might *appear* to be dubious, even if in fact they are not, seems wise. Sooner or later opponents will try to make political gain out of any moral indiscretions they perceive. The judicious person keeps as clean a record as possible out of sheer self-interest. (The genuinely moral person will do the same because it is right; when morality and self-interest merge, it is certainly foolish not to respect the course of action it ordains!) This will also relieve you of the nagging fear that somebody will find you out, thus producing a peace of mind that promoteth sound sleep.

Finally, it has usually been helpful to marry and have a couple of children. Just what the capacity to reproduce has to do with political talent is hard to say, but people seem to trust a mother or a "family man" a little more than a single person.

Finally, prospective candidates should keep in mind the maxim about persevering "if at first you don't succeed." The mere act of running for office gradually gives public exposure, sharpens political wits, and steadily improves a person's chances of going all the way. Of course, a person can stumble badly enough or often enough to convince the public he or she is a political dud. In which case, politics isn't the only career in the world. It's just one of the most exciting.

This chapter has discussed politics and politicians in a typical American milieu—what might be called "mainstream" politics in a pluralist society. It does not describe the politics associated with a major assault on a given political system or upon major political institutions. That requires a somewhat different political style and different political skills. It also requires an analysis we can't make in a book as short as this one. Maybe your professor or teaching fellow will want to talk about revolutionary politics and politicians.

Notes

1. Gerald Parshall and Robert Barr, "Shenanigans in Congress: Why There's No Crackdown," *U.S. News and World Report*, May 24, 1976, pp. 60–64.
2. Martin Schram, *Running For President* (New York, Stein & Day, 1977) p. 308.
3. Quoted in Richard Hofstadter, *The American Political Tradition* (New York: Random House Vintage Books, 1955), p. 116.
4. Quoted in ibid.
5. Quoted in ibid, p. 117.
6. Ibid, p. 116.
7. John Fischer, "Please Don't Bite the Politicians," *Harper's Magazine*, November 1960, p. 16. Courtesy of Harper's Magazine and Elizabeth W. Fischer.
8. Stewart Alsop, *The Center* (New York: Harper & Row, 1968), p. 127.
9. Harold D. Laswell, *Power and Personality* (New York: Norton, 1948), p. 39.
10. Robert D. Putnam, *The Comparative Study of Political Elites* (Englewood Cliffs, N.J., Prentice-Hall, 1976) p. 74.
11. Fischer, "Please Don't Bite the Politicians," p. 16.
12. James D. Barber, *The Presidential Character: Predicting Performance in the White House* (Englewood Cliffs, N.J.: Prentice-Hall, 1977), p. 13.
13. Fischer, "Please Don't Bite the Politicians," p. 16.
16. See Donald R. Matthews, *U.S. Senators and Their World* (New York: Vintage, 1960), pp. 94–95.

CHAPTER 3
ON CONSTITUTIONS

Having considered the actors on the political scene, let us turn to one of the major political institutions—the Constitution. Americans are often displeased with their president, with Congress, the Supreme Court, the bureaucracy, the press, big corporations, big unions, the schools, the climate, and just about everything else about our country. But one aspect of our country seems never to displease them—the Constitution. This we believe in with all the fervor and devotion of converts to a new religious faith. Americans may be desperately unhappy with the way the courts "misinterpret" the Constitution, but that document has become more sacrosanct than even the flag. After all, no one tried to burn the Constitution during the anti-Vietnam War demonstrations. The American attitude is close to that of President Andrew Johnson, who asked to be buried with a copy of the Constitution tucked into his casket. We believe in the Constitution the way true Marxists believe in *Das Kapital* and the way the Chinese used to believe in Mao Tse-tung's Little Red Book.

A document so revered is worth examining. How did we get it and why? Is it really *that* great? Why has it survived so long? How important is it today?

The Constitution: The View from 1787

First, what is a constitution? A constitution can be defined as the fundamental rules and principles that declare the powers and duties of a government and guarantee certain rights to the people. The key words are "fundamental rules and principles," "powers and duties of a government" and "rights." These words and phrases distinguish a constitution from the general body of laws that governs a country. Although the distinction is not always clear, since "fundamental" is not a term with exact meaning, a constitution creates the basic framework of government, establishes its powers and limits, while laws (statutes) deal with lesser structural matters and spell out governmental policies promulgated under authority granted by the constitution.

Americans have a "written" constitution whereas the British have an "unwritten" one. The latter never have convened a constitutional convention such as the one held in this country in 1787. At no time were a group of delegates selected by the British people or the British Parliament and instructed to draw up a constitution to be voted on by the people. Yet the British have a constitution, which consists of:

1. Great historic documents (like the Magna Charta, the Bill of Rights of 1689, and the Westminster Agreements of 1911, all of which set forth the terms that settled great political crises)
2. British common law (consisting of centuries-old court decisions that established certain property and other personal rights and that have endured so long they are virtually unquestioned)
3. Major legislative enactments (such as those enlarging the suffrage and determining the size of Parliament)
4. Important political customs (such as the gradually evolved custom that the king or queen's powers should be exercised by the cabinet).

The constitution so described fulfills the above definition and is revered by the British just as much, perhaps, as we admire ours. It gradually changes, just as ours has evolved since 1787, but it has never been ratified by a formal vote of the British people. Nor is there a formal amending process. Something

31

The Constitution: The View from 1787

becomes part of the British constitution when it is "fundamental" and it has been accepted by the people over a considerable period of time.[1]

The United States Constitution, curiously enough, was formulated almost by accident, by a process of dubious legality and under a cloak of secrecy that would horrify us today. After the Declaration of Independence in 1776, the American states were joined together in a loose cooperative league by the Articles of Confederation. Under the Articles the legislative branch was supreme; there was neither a chief executive nor a supreme court. National defense and foreign policy were managed by the legislature. The government could ask the states for money but lacked power to force the states to comply. It also lacked the authority to regulate interstate commerce. The states were individually sovereign—that is, they could not be coerced to do what they did not wish to do. They cooperated when they wanted to and went their separate ways on other occasions.

The system worked better than one might expect, but problems arose that deeply disturbed many political leaders. The necessary tax revenues were hard to raise, individual states imposed burdensome tariffs on one another's commerce, and the government commanded little respect abroad. When Shays' Rebellion (a popular uprising that accompanied a demand for cheaper money and debtor relief) demonstrated state weakness in maintaining law and order, the critics decided enough was enough. The Confederation Congress yielded to pressure and called upon the states to hold a convention, not to form a new constitution but to revise the Articles. Thus, when the delegates decided to disregard their instructions and devise a wholly new constitution, they were acting illegally. But since the states were later asked to ratify the new document, the delegates' lawlessness was of a singularly responsible nature.

That the proceedings took place in secrecy, with the press excluded and with few if any "leaks," is a sobering and thought-provoking phenomenon. True, the states would have a chance to approve or reject their handiwork, so the public would still have its day. But if anything like that happened in our time, the public would be outraged. Yet the Founding Fathers constructed, in secrecy, a Constitution that has lasted longer than any other ever devised. Conceivably, then, are there times when the public's "right to know" what public officials are currently doing is less important than providing an atmosphere conducive to deliberation, debate, and compromise, by people who aren't worrying about the morning headlines and the evening news broadcasts? Who aren't grandstanding, not trying to be instant heroes, not seeking personal glory as much as trying to do the job?

What philosophical premises did the delegates bring with them into Constitution Hall? Many of them were well educated, steeped in the classics and in history. They were disciples of John Locke, the British theorist who taught that government was a contract between the government and the governed, with the government largely limited to the role of protecting the rights of the people. These included the right to life, liberty, and preeminently, property—property that was the result of one's personal labor. Locke also believed in a system of "natural law," which implicitly contained and vindicated certain rights.[2]

The delegates were also students of Montesquieu, the French theorist who contributed the idea that political power was dangerous if concentrated. It should, instead, be divided among various political branches.[3] Thus "separation of powers" was a natural outgrowth of respect for Montesquieu's central theme, a respect that reflected the delegates' historical experience with what they regarded as "royal tyranny."

Like their mentors, the Founding Fathers at the convention mistrusted human nature, believing that people were prone to abuse their power if given the chance. That mistrust had been accentuated by their experience with King George III, who seemed to epitomize the abuse of power in the absence of an adequate and balanced separation of powers. The behavior of some of the royal governors in colonial days also underlined the point. As the founders saw it, the way to control power was to divide it up, pit power against power, and give each political institution a selfish interest in preventing a "power grab" by another group that would threaten its own political turf. Presumably this would prevent the concentration of power in the hands of a single person or group and hinder the development of tyranny. "If men were angels," to use James Madison's phrase, we would not need this precaution; but since they are not, prudence is necessary to safeguard human liberty.

Article II of the Constitution, which outlines the role and powers of the chief executive, beautifully illustrates the foregoing. The president is the commander in chief of the armed forces, but Congress declares war and raises money for those forces. The president negotiates treaties, but the Senate must ratify them. The president makes major appointments, but the Senate must confirm them. Congress passes laws, but the president can veto them (although Congress can then override the veto).

The founders applied this principle in other areas, too. The central government was delegated important powers, but the states retained a healthy share. The Supreme Court could invalidate federal laws (although this was not too clear in 1787), but the Court could be overridden by constitutional amendments. The state legislatures originally selected the states' representatives in the U.S. Senate, but the people selected the members of the House. The people selected the electors for the electoral college, but the electors were then free to use their best judgment. And Congress could propose constitutional amendments (by a two-thirds vote of both houses), but those amendments must then be approved by the legislatures of, or constitutional conventions in, three-fourths of the states. Dividing up power, balancing power, checking power—the founders applied these principles with great consistency throughout the document. The ancient Greek motto, "Nothing too much," seemed to have guided their every move.

Most of the major constitutional decisions were the product of compromises between groups holding strongly opposing positions. One faction wanted to greatly strengthen the national government; another feared the central government as a potential source of tyranny. One group wanted a strong executive; the other worried lest such an executive develop into a monarchy. One wanted the president selected by Congress; the other feared this would weaken the presidency and make it subservient to Congress. One wanted the states to have equal representation in the legislature; the other wanted representation according to population or wealth. Southern state delegates wanted slaves counted as persons for purposes of representation, while northerners resisted. Southern delegates wished to prevent treaties that, approved by a mere majority, would discriminate against southern trade; northerners saw it in a different light, but finally agreed to treaty ratification by a two-thirds majority of the Senate.

No faction prevailed at any major point unless concessions were granted to the other side. Compromises of this kind are not always the essence of wisdom and statesmanship, but they are the ingredients of successful political negotiations. And while the Founding Fathers were well-educated and public-spirited men, they were also good politicians. This is something worth remembering. (Maybe we should call them the "Founding Politicians.") [4]

Were the founders out to feather their own nests, by creating a political system favorable to their property interests?[5] It is true that most of the delegates were wealthy landowners, or merchants or professional men having ties with the families of wealthy landowners and merchants. (The rest were mostly lawyers, who usually identify with the propertied classes.) And, many of the provisions protected their monetary interests. For example, they denied the state legislatures—which were becoming more responsive to debtor groups—the power to print currency and prevented them from "impairing the obligation of contract." Debts incurred under the Articles of Confederation were reaffirmed as valid under the Constitution. Escaped slaves were to be returned to their owners. No one was to be deprived of life, liberty, or *property* without due process of law. Private property could not be seized for public purposes without just compensation.

But most of these provisions were sensible ones to which many of the poorer people would not take exception. Indeed, concern for the protection of property rights was an attitude shared by most of the colonists. They owned property, too, or expected to do so in the near future. The rather aristocratic founders thus did not carry their class interest bias—which *did* appear in the Constitution—to politically dangerous excess;[5] they were genuinely interested in devising a sound and enduring political system that the general electorate would find acceptable. Keeping one eye cocked on ratification prospects provided one more balancing element in the constitutional architecture. (Luckily, too, because ratification was barely achieved despite the Constitution's defense by one of the most brilliant propaganda documents in history—The *Federalist* papers.)

A final compromise should be mentioned. The phraseology of the Constitution was not so broad and general as to be meaningless; yet it was broad and general enough in critical areas to provide the flexibility needed to accommodate unpredictable future developments. If the Founding Fathers had drawn up a highly detailed Constitution, the document would have lacked the capac-

How the Constitution is amended

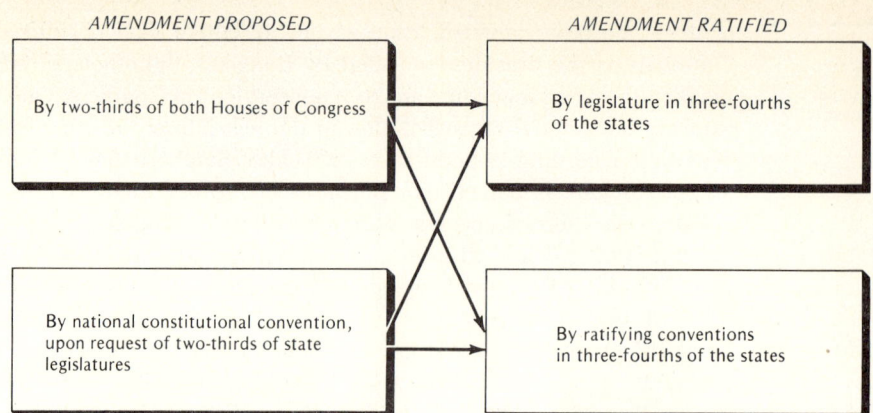

ity to breathe, grow and develop in accordance with the requirements of an uncertain future. It would have been a strait jacket that a lusty nation would soon have cast aside with consequences unknown.

In addition to the fact that the founders were educated, experienced, practical, judicious men, whose handiwork reflected these qualities, the Constitution endured for other reasons. Governments and constitutions tend to be more stable if a country is prosperous, if the people are optimistic about their economic future, if they are militarily secure, and if the people share many common values and social customs. Even then, our constitutional system came close to breaking up in the 1860s, when internal disputes reached such fevered proportions that only 600,000 deaths and four years of national agony kept the Union together and the Constitution intact. Lest we be too self-congratulatory, then, it is important to remember that the Constitution barely did survive, and then only because a numerically and economically superior North forced the South to yield, in violation—some would say—of the principle of government by free consent of the governed. In 1865, then, the Constitution prevailed not through sweet reason but through brute force.

Founding Fathers: Wise but Not All-Wise

The Founding Fathers nonetheless did an extraordinary job of formulating a Constitution that would endure for centuries, but they were not without their blind spots and misconceptions. Their attitude toward slavery vividly illustrates the point. A black was treated as three-fifths of a person for purposes of representation and direct taxation, but not as a person so far as citizen rights and privileges were concerned. Nor did there seem to be any great uneasiness about this. The founders lived at a time when people had not confronted the issue of slavery squarely or perceived the staggering disparity between their rhetoric about natural rights and the status of black slaves. We can judge them too harshly for this. All of us are the product of our time, afflicted with moral blindness and political myopia in ways that will mystify our grandchildren. Our overall history of democratic development (as we shall see later) demonstrates this repeatedly.

The founders were unwilling to let the people directly choose their president, believing they were to ill informed and deficient in general political wisdom to perform such a crucial task. Today we recognize that the public may err from time to time, but no one can think of a better way to select our chief executive than to let the public register its opinion. ("Voters are not fools," as distinguished political scientist V. O. Key once wrote.)

The founders declined to let the people directly select their senators, preferring that this be done by state legislatures. Considering the embryonic state of democratic thought at the time, this was not surprising, but it again reveals the delegates to the convention to be men whose vision was limited by the intellectual climate of the age.

Political parties were anathema to the founders. They called them "factions," believed they were incapable of public-spiritedness, and convinced themselves that one of the "factions" was bound to consist of have-nots, bent on plundering men of property. They tended to see the majority of the people as potential political mobs, intent on leveling incomes and creating a crudely egalitarian state. Today we believe that democracy is unworkable without parties and that they are, in any case, inevitable. How, in a free society, can one prevent like-minded people from joining together, selecting leaders, and seeking to win power in the political realm? The Fathers ignored parties altogether in the Constitution; it was a notable and rather singular oversight.

As another example of fallibility, many delegates in 1787 fretted endlessly lest the big states domineer over the small. Yet rarely if ever have senators and representatives been arrayed against each other along big state–small state lines. Divisions, instead, have reflected economic factors, regional factors, or sociological factors—none of which have anything to do with state size. Finally, the founders failed to foresee the possibility of secession and failed to clarify the question of whether states could or could not secede. Perhaps no effort would have prevented the Civil War anyway. But some believe their inattention to this issue was a serious oversight; others, however, believe that the founders, as good politicians, knew they could not resolve every sticky question or anticipate every future difficulty, and so settled instead the more pressing issues and let the others wait the decisions of time.

The Founding Fathers were fallible men, but they were the wisest of their time. In general, farsighted beyond all we could expect.

Do Constitutions Really Matter?

We need to be reminded that a constitution is not a magic document that, by itself, can drastically alter political reality. A constitution means no more than we want it to mean.

The Spartan lawgiver, Lycurgus, recognized this several thousand years ago. He opposed writing down the fundamental laws of his nation because, as one writer put it, "If you must write the law in order to remember it, the spirit of the law has been already forgotten.... The only proper tablet of the law is the cultivated human soul. For law is secured among men not by tablets of stone but by habits of loyalty."[7]

The truth of this statement can be seen by examining the Soviet Union's constitution under Stalin. It contained some inspiring passages guaranteeing human rights, such as the following:

1. Article 123: Equality of rights of citizens of the USSR, irrespective of their nationality or race, in all spheres of economic, government, cultural, political and other public activity, is an indefeasible law.
2. Article 124: ... Freedom of religious worship and freedom of anti-religious propaganda is recognized for all citizens.
3. Article 125: ... The citizens of the USSR are guaranteed by law: (a) freedom of speech, (b) freedom of the press, (c) freedom of assembly, including the holding of mass-meetings, (d) freedom of street processions and demonstrations.[8]

These provisions were flouted on every hand by one of the worst despots in history.

South American constitutions patterned after ours have remained in force while dictators trampled their human rights' guarantees. Constitutions may be no more than showpieces, designed to conceal the harsh realities that lie behind their façades. Even the American experience bears this truth out.

The Fourteenth Amendment contains the following wording:

When the right to vote at any election for the choice of electors for President and Vice President of the United States, Representatives in Congress, the Executive and Judicial officers of State, or the members of the Legislature thereof, is denied to any of the male inhabitants of such state, being 21 years of age and citizens of the United States, except for participation in rebellion or other crime, the basis of representation therein shall be reduced in the proportion which the number of male citizens shall bear to the whole number of male citizens 21 years of age in such state.

In brief, the amendment says that any state denying blacks the right to vote will have its representation in the House of Representatives reduced in proportion to the scale of the denial.

But from 1870 to the mid-twentieth century, blacks *were* denied the right to vote on a wholesale basis, by literacy laws discriminatorily applied, by "white primaries" (which denied blacks the right to help Democratic candidates in the South, where Democratic candidates always won the November elections), by devious devices to prevent black registration, by terror (the Ku Klux Klan), and by economic punishment of those who still dared to vote. At no time was there a serious move in Congress to deprive southern states of their representation in the House. Any member of the House who proposed such a thing would have been thought a mischievous person of shocking bad manners. He would have been ostracized not only by the southerners but by northerners as well (who had largely lost interest in the plight of the blacks after Reconstruction ended.) No one had to tell potential "troublemakers" not to raise the issue. They could sense in their political bones this was just not done, whatever the Constitution might prescribe.

Similarly, the Fourteenth Amendment required that no state should deprive any person of equal protection of the laws. Blacks presumably were persons. But this did not prevent the South from imposing a host of restrictions that prevented their enjoyment of equal protection of the laws. Meanwhile, the North remained mute, discriminating against blacks almost as egregiously as did the South. Blacks had become "invisible" persons, and their problems were equally invisible.

Other examples of violations of the Constitution besides those involving blacks can be cited. During the Civil War Abraham Lincoln violated many provisions of the Constitution because they hampered his efforts to save the Union. He suspended the writ of habeas corpus, borrowed money, spent unappropriated funds, enlarged the army, censored the mails, closed down dissident newspapers, and denied Congress its rightful share of critical national decisions by refusing to call them into session for almost three months after the firing on Fort Sumter. A leading constituional lawyer called him a "dictator even exceeding those of the Roman model."[9] But he got away with it because a large number of people thought what he did was necessary and more important than respecting inconvenient parts of the Constitution. We live up to Constitutions when we want to, in other words.

Japanese Americans (Nisei) were presumably "persons," too, to whom "equal protection of the laws" applied. But during World War II President Franklin D. Roosevelt, apprehensive lest the Nisei become traitors and sabo-

Japanese American prisoners of war in World War II

teurs, rounded up several hundred thousand of them and herded them into concentration camps. There was no solid evidence of disloyalty; there was only suspicion.[10] The American people approved, demonstrating anew that the Constitution has meaning and effect only to the degree it currently commands support for its specific provisions.

A more recent example is the attempt by several modern presidents to usurp the war-making powers that the Constitution had entrusted to Congress. This, too, was done because the people believed the presidents were making necessary and wise decisions that Congress was ill equipped to handle.

What matters most in a democracy, then, is what the people most want—or are willing to accept if a strong leader comes along who does or proposes to do what the people believe should be done. If such a leader, *especially during periods of national emergency*, takes strong and effective steps to protect the national security, the people are inclined to applaud, whether his acts are constitutional or not. A frightened public wants action and results more than it wants adherence to constitutional requirements. If the latter seem to stand in the way of what seems to need doing, let the leader do the job the most expeditious way possible. That is not only the American way but probably the way people behave in every country when fear comes to the fore. (There will always be learned men, too, who will write learned books and articles justifying what is done.)

Are constitutions, then, virtually meaningless? In dictatorships their value is minimal. In democracies they matter much more.

Constitutions prepared by or used by dictators primarily for public relation purposes, or which win public support by lofty phrases and principles that do not reflect deep-rooted popular feelings, have little significance for obvious reasons. But if a constitution does reflect the values, aspirations, and living traditions of either the general public or the politically active minority of that public, it is a document of major importance. By reflecting widely held values within a society, a constitution becomes an instrument that those who govern normally dare not ignore.

Such a document also has educational value. Typically, an educational system inculcates respect for the principles of a constitution, thus deepening and broadening both the intellectual and the emotional commitment to it. The emotional aspect is not unimportant because if those who really understand the constitutional principles and are deeply committed to them are able to enlist the emotional support of others who "believe in" that constitution in a general, abstract, idealized sense, they can sometimes rally the kind of support that, in constitutional crises, can be crucial.

Various polls have shown that while almost everyone "believes in" the Bill of Rights, a majority or a large minority simultaneously believes that communists or atheists or other unpopular groups are not fully entitled to free speech and a free press.[11] There is a persistent tendency on the part of large numbers of people to limit the full application of the Bill of Rights to "respectable" people or groups. But, of course, dissenters and heretics are those who need its protection most, if freedom is to be truly meaningful.

Many writers believe that a constitution's guarantees of personal freedom are likely to be maintained only if a sizeable number of well-educated, historically minded, and vocal people exists—a core that understands the real meaning of democracy, the necessity of ensuring freedom and fair play for unpopular groups, and that is prepared to raise a ruckus if rights are impaired. Under ordinary circumstances these people can prevail, since the normal apathy of the general public gives this core an opportunity to dominate the public discussion and maximize the impact of its philosophy. The dedicated minority's zealous defense of the democratic idea, and of its necessary application in the dispute at hand, can often mobilize support from a significant number of less committed citizens who become apprehensive about a "threat" to a symbol that they understand only dimly but to which they are emotionally attached.

But if the public is sufficiently frightened by what it regards as a major threat to its military or economic security and believes that threat is caused by or is accentuated by the presence and activities of some domestic group, its hostility toward that group may become so intense that the desire to punish or prevent the group from doing harm overrides any objections that intellectuals[12] may raise to the violation of their rights. Of course in a democracy the majority does have a right to punish violations of law. But the threat to the Constitution comes when people are punished either on grounds of suspicion rather than because of illegal behavior, or for breaking laws that are themselves unconstitutional.

For most people economic and military security always has higher priority than respect for the rights of people who seem to jeopardize that security. Thus when the general public is aroused by a real or imaginary threat, public officials respond to that public and do what it wants done. And if the majority strongly feels that a minority seriously jeopardizes its military or economic security, no constitution and no core of intellectuals can protect that minority from the fear, anger, and suspicions of the aroused majority. The "Copperheads" during the Civil War, the abolitionists prior to the Civil War, persons of Germanic ancestry in World War I, radicals during the "Red Scare" after World War I, the Nisei in World War II, and the communists in the 1950s illustrate the point. All were denied constitutional protection because an intolerant majority apparently wanted it so. The courts can help, and sometimes do, but courts adjust to the national mood, too. There is *no* defense against a people bent on punishing or restraining those they fear. Who will be next?

The democratic wisdom of intellectuals can be exaggerated, however. While the intellectual core of which we have spoken has a more acute understanding of what the democratic idea requires than the average American, this may have greater relevance for some democratic concepts than for others. Intellectuals, moreover, often disagree with each other. For example, some of them sanctioned the imposition of penalties on most of the unpopular groups cited in the preceding paragraph. Other disagreements can be found in our own day. The dominant intellectual view opposing the censorship of pornography has been challenged by other intellectuals who believe the public's less tolerant view may be, in the long run, more defensible. The prevailing intellectual view interpreting the "rights" of criminal defendants more generously than in other countries is not shared by other intellectuals who suspect that the public has a more commonsense appreciation of the needs of society, vis-á-vis that of the defendant. Western world intellectuals are usually indignant at the suppression of literary, artistic, and political dissent in the USSR but are curiously indifferent to the widespread persecution of evangelical-Protestant believers in that country.

One need not read much intellectual history to become aware that ideological fads and fashions sweep over the intellectual community from time to time, warping its views in ways that its successors will repudiate. It is not being suggested, then, that in every debate in which democratic philosophy is invoked, the dominant intellectual view is necessarily the proper one. But on the ultimate questions of the right to political and social dissent and the basic right of due-process protection for hated groups and individuals, the intellectuals are likely to better understand the necessity of living up to what we say we believe. Without their urgent voices sounding alarms, dictators and quasi dictators could more readily convert public prejudices and apprehensions into support for systematic repression. Since intellectuals often see themselves as somewhat heretical, they are more sensitive to the rights of heretics in general. That sensitivity lies at the heart of the democratic creed. Intellectuals, in general, are the keepers and carriers of that creed.

But our Constitution is more than the Bill of Rights. Its general provisions continue to serve us well; if the president and Congress cannot give us policies equal to the demands of the age, the Constitution can hardly be blamed. No constitution can ensure that a country will have the leadership it needs or that the people and their legislators will accept farsighted policies when they are offered. The latter could be our Achilles heel as much as the former. In any case, the Constitution's basic provisions seem as adequate today as they have been since 1787. And that is remarkable, considering the astonishing changes that have occurred in our society—changes that have also made ours a much more democratic society than the Founding Fathers envisioned.

Notes

1. Sydney D. Bailey, *British Parliamentary Democracy* (Boston: Houghton Mifflin, 1966), pp. 1-10.
2. C. B. Macpherson, "The Social Bearings of Locke's Political Theory," *The Western Political Quarterly* 8 (1954), 6-19; and C. B. Macpherson, *The Political Theory of Possessive Individualism: Hobbes to Locke* (New York: Oxford University Press, 1962), pp. 199-203.
3. Baron de Montesquieu, *The Spirit of the Laws* (New York: Macmillan [Hafner Press], 1949), pp. 150-151.
4. The importance of political considerations at the Constitutional Convention is highlighted in John P. Roche, "The Founding Fathers: A Reform Caucus in Action," *American Political Science Review* (December 1961), vol. LV, pp. 799-816.
5. This theory was advanced by Charles A. Beard, *An Economic Interpretation of the Constitution of the United States* (New York: Macmillan, 1921), pp. 17, 18, 35-37, 148-151.

6 See Robert E. Brown, *Charles Beard and the Constitution, A Critical Analysis of 'An Economic Interpretation of the Constitution'* (Princeton University Press, 1956), pp. 73–91; Forrest McDonald, *We the People: The Economic Origins of the Constitution* (U. of Chicago Press, 1958); and David G. Smith, *The Convention and the Constitution* (New York: St. Martin's Press, 1965).

7 John F. A. Taylor, *The Masks of Society* (Englewood Cliffs, N.J.: Prentice-Hall, 1966), p. 4.

8 John N. Hazard, *The Soviet System of Government* (Chicago: The University of Chicago Press, 1964) 3rd ed., p. 241.

9 Edward S. Corwin, *The President: Office and Powers,* 4th ed. (New York University Press, 1957), p. 309.

10 E. V. Rostow, "Our Worst Wartime Mistake, Treatment of Japanese and Japanese-Americans on the West Coast," *Harper's Magazine,* September 1945, pp. 193–201. See also Michi Weglyn, *Years of Infamy: The Untold Story of America's Concentration Camps* (New York: Morrow, 1976).

11 Samuel Krislov, *The Supreme Court and Political Freedom* (New York: Free Press, 1968), pp. 39ff., and CBS Poll, "60 Minutes," April 14, 1970.

12 By intellectuals, I mean educated persons who have a persistent and sophisticated concern for general ideas and principles having relevance to the development and well-being of society. This is a home-grown definition; if the reader has a better one, please forward same!

CHAPTER 4

DEMOCRACY AND ITS CONDITION

In our discussion of the Constitution, we wrote about democracy and some of the threats to it. But we have not defined it or discussed its evolution in the United States, its current condition, or where we may be going. It is time to do so.

There are many species of democracy. The Greek concept of democracy involved direct participation of the citizens in both legislative and judicial matters. Greek democracy, then, was a matter of *direct democracy* rather than representative government. (In reality, Greek democracy was imperfect. Women could not participate in the government and a large population of slaves were also excluded.[1] The closest parallel in this country was the New England town meeting, at which all interested citizens gathered to set public policy. And today many of our states combine representative government with a limited form of direct democracy because they allow the general public to raise issues for the legislature to consider (the *initiative*) or for the voters to decide (the *referendum*). However, only a small percentage of legislative issues are raised or settled in this manner.

The communists think their governments are the only truly democratic ones. They believe Western democracies are really run by the capitalists for their own self-interest, whereas their governments promote the well-being of the great masses of people. If government serves the people and not the rich, it is by that very fact democratic, they argue. Thus Fidel Castro's political order became "true democracy" and Mao Tse-tung's totalitarian despotism was transmuted into the "new democracy." Soviet spokesmen also refer to their system as a "people's democracy."

Non-communist dictatorships often employ a similar line of reasoning. They may violate human rights on all sides, maintain a one-party state, and hold rigged elections, but if the dictator says he or she governs for the good of the people, that assertion magically makes the regime democratic. Benito Mussolini labeled his fascist state "organized, centralized, authoritarian democracy." Former dictator Achmed Sukarno of Indonesia dubbed his regime "guided democracy"; Egyptian dictator Gamel Abdul Nasser termed his political system "partyless democracy."

The ultra-right-wing John Birch Society insists that the American system is a "republic" instead of a democracy. True, we are a republic, since that term describes a nonmonarchial political system in which the people choose representatives to govern them rather than directly decide public issues. But modern usage has blurred the difference between "republic" and "democracy"; we can properly be called either, since most democracies rely on representative legislative procedures rather than direct popular policymaking.

Some political scientists believe a nation is a democracy if it holds free, competitive elections that give the executive and legislature a popular mandate to govern. But, if a majority freely establishes a government that, even with popular support, proceeds to deny virtually all of the rights of a dissident minority except the right to make a futile appeal at the polls, that is not really a democracy. Hitler, Mussolini, and Mao Tse-tung might very well have won a series of free elections, but that would hardly have made their regimes democratic.

In this book the term "democracy" will be used synonymously with the term "liberal democracy"—the brand of government that prevails in the United States, Great Britain, Canada, Mexico, Australia, New Zealand, and Western Europe (plus a few other countries). *Liberal democracy* requires free, competitive elections at reasonably frequent intervals, but it is also necessary that the freely elected government respect the fundamental rights of the individual. In brief, liberal democracy means majority rule *and* minority rights; that is the way most educated Americans understand the term "democracy."

Democracy and Human Rights

What rights do we mean? They are the rights that the countries cited above generally respect and uniformly regard as the proper rights of a free people. These include rights that, if denied, would be "shocking to the conscience of civilized men," or which are "implicit in the concept of ordered liberty," in the words of a famous Supreme Court decision.[2] Among those rights are the ones included in the First Amendment—freedom of speech, press, religion, and assembly. (*Freedom of assembly* is construed to mean the right to freely organize into groups having similar goals, and to seek those goals in an organized manner.) Also included is the right to a fair trial, although not necessarily a trial by jury; Western European democracies typically prefer trial by judges, who ensure the defendant a fair chance to demonstrate his or her innocence.

The right to travel freely within one's country and to travel abroad (unless there are reasonable grounds for believing one is an espionage agent for a foreign power) has come to be regarded as one of the rights of a free person as well. So is freedom from unreasonable searches and seizures—although "unreasonable" is a word that leads to endless litigation. In addition, there is the right to enjoy privacy within one's home, free from police intrusion unless a search warrant has been obtained from a magistrate. Similarly, all liberal democracies respect the principle that the state may not seize one's property, even for legitimate reasons (such as the need to build a highway through your acreage and home) without paying "just compensation." Equality before the law is also a person's democratic right; both the benefits and the penalties of law must apply equally to all, whatever one's nationality, race, or religion. "Reasonable" classifications may be made, however; for example, criminal offenders under 16 may be treated differently from those over 16, and a military draft necessarily has age limits.

Finally, all adults (with a few exceptions, such as persons with felony convictions or those in mental institutions) are entitled to vote and otherwise participate in the political process, including running for public office. The right to vote also means the right to do so in a competitive election in which all candidates can freely seek public support.

All of these rights are normally granted to citizens in liberal democracies. They may be unfairly abridged in some instances because perfection is not attainable either in individual or political life, but liberal democracies believe in and attempt to live by these principles. If they are violated, and the press learns about it, one can generally count on vociferous protests from the press and from better educated citizens who are usually on guard against the erosion of democratic rights.

Democratic rights are not tantamount to all of those contained in our Bill of Rights, the first ten amendments to our Constitution. While many provisions of those first ten amendments fall into the category of "basic" rights, not all do. Countries that lack an Anglo-Saxon heritage do not grant persons accused of crime the right to be free from "compulsory self-incrimination" (a privilege extended to us by the Fifth Amendment). Many Western European democracies see no injustice in requiring defendants to answer relevant questions, so long as no third-degree methods (physical or psychological) are employed to obtain a confession. Nor, as we have said, do they believe a jury is essential to a fair trial. And an indictment by a grand jury (which is required in federal, but not all state, prosecutions) is not considered indispensable to a fair trial in those same countries. But the key provisions and spirit of the Bill of Rights do embody rights seen as fundamental to free persons everywhere.

Democracy and Equality

The democratic idea rests on one supremely important premise—namely, that all persons should be basically equal in terms of rights and legal privileges.[3] Thus, if any person deserves a fair trial, everyone should have a fair trial. If any normal adult has the right to vote, all normal adults have the right to vote. If anyone has a right to worship as he or she pleases, all should have this right. And if anyone deserves the right to speak and write freely, all should have this right.

We are all equally human. We all have lives to live of equal importance to each of us; we all experience pain and pleasure, love and hate, hunger and thirst. All are equal in the sight of God (many would say), and hence all should be equal before the law. Everybody should count, and no one should be regarded as a second-class citizen. This concept of human equality is one of the noblest that has ever been discovered. While living up to its implications is a perpetual struggle that we never fully win, the struggle is what democracy is all about. Every dictatorship rejects the idea, believing that only certain privileged groups—those that hold political power and those who uncritically support the government—deserve human rights.

The "equality of man" once meant only political equality—the right to vote, participate in public affairs, and to be equal in the sight of the law. But it has come to mean more than this. Equality does not mean economic equality; it does not imply equality of income or wealth. Increasingly, however, it has meant greater equality of opportunity.

The state cannot ensure genetic equality, of course, or prevent children from being raised in homes whose atmosphere either aids or handicaps their journey through life. But democratic theory has increasingly recognized a public obligation to modify economic or educational factors that reduce equality of opportunity for less privileged youngsters. Thus governments seek to encourage equal opportunities for self-development and employment by eliminating racial and religious barriers to these goals. Governments also strive to give poorer children better educational and economic opportunities through the distribution of financial aid to poorer school districts, by special vocational training for those who need it, and by free health services for those unable to pay.

These policies rest on the belief that freedom has both its negative and its positive aspects. Implicit in the concept is freedom *from* arbitrary and unreasonable governmental interference in our lives, but it also includes freedom *to* develop one's potentialities to the fullest. Children may be free from dictatorial repression and terror, but this is scant comfort if they lack the health or the educational opportunities to fully develop their talents, or if they face ultimate barriers to self-expression and vocational progress because of religious, racial, ethnic, or political prejudice. Thus, creating conditions that promote "positive freedom"—the freedom to become all that one might be—has emerged as a significant democratic goal. Communist dictatorships partly share this goal but often are unwilling to grant equality of opportunity to those who take religion seriously or who hold the wrong political attitudes.

Democracy, then, is an evolving concept. New meaning has been added to the democratic idea over the centuries, and the development of that idea is not yet complete. From time to time democracy generates new conceptions of human rights that people accept only as history unfolds and as human experience lengthens. This needs to be illustrated more concretely by American experience.

In the eighteenth century even enlightened minds thought it appropriate for voting to be restricted to white male property holders. These persons alone were thought to have a sufficient stake in society to participate in its political decisions and to be sufficiently stable and meritorious to deserve this privilege. Little by little we came to see the inadequacies and unfairness of this vision. First, we extended the vote to nonproperty-owning persons (about mid-nineteenth century); then, we theoretically extended it to black males by the Fifteenth Amendment, and later made theory reality by eliminating a variety of barriers to black voting. We did this through Supreme Court decisions, which invalidated the discriminatory "white primary" and "grandfather clause" in some southern states;[4] by a constitutional amendment eliminating the poll tax; and by federal legislation, which swept away unfair literacy tests and other discriminatory practices that had previously prevented black voting.

We extended the democratic principle further by outlawing slavery (Thirteenth Amendment), giving blacks citizenship (Fourteenth Amendment), by guaranteeing minorities equal access to hotels, motels, restaurants, and other public accommodations (by the Civil Rights Act of 1964), by forbidding racial discrimination in hiring and promotions, and by protecting minorities against the more blatant forms of housing discrimination and against discrimination in the selection of juries and grand juries. While subtle forms of discrimination still exist, some "reverse discrimination" has also taken place, with blacks and other minorities sometimes given preferential treatment as corporations, universities, and government agencies seek to protect themselves from charges of racial bias and from the possible withdrawal of federal funds. Thus, although this country's record of denying human rights—for blacks—was one of the worst in history, our record of progress in correcting injustice has, since World War II, been among the best in history.[5]

We were long equally blind, for what now seems equally incomprehensible reasons, to the rights of women. That women should be granted the same rights as men is an idea so simple, so obvious, so irrefutable that it almost surpasses belief that humane and enlightened men (and women) so long failed to grasp the point. But if we had lived in the nineteenth century, conditioned by the social attitudes of that day, we might have been blind, too. Change has come gradually. The Nineteenth Amendment gave women the right to vote in 1920, and today's feminist movement has destroyed most of the other *legal* barriers to full equality for women.

The democratic idea has prevailed in many other areas, too. The secret (Australian) ballot, introduced in the late nineteenth century, made genuinely free elections possible. Its presence dispelled fears of offending local sentiment or displeasing powerful people who could retaliate in one way or another if one voted "wrong."

The electoral college initially was an elitist notion. It assumed that the voters would select electors—believed to be superior persons to the rank-and-file voters—who would exercise their best judgment in selecting a president. If their judgment differed from that of the people, so be it. But when political parties emerged about 1800 (the Federalists and the Republicans), electors were pledged to support a specific party. Popular voting for electors became, in effect, a direct contest between specific parties and their candidates. Electors can still vote their conscience in theory, but in practice they rarely do.

As indicated earlier, the founders ordained that state legislatures should select United States senators, doubting that the general public could safely be entrusted with choosing members of both House and Senate. The latter was expected to be a somewhat aristocratic body, composed of the "better class" of citizens. But in 1913 the people ratified the Seventeenth Amendment calling for direct election of senators. Democracy was on the move again.

Long before, however, a major democratic advance had taken place. In the early nineteenth century candidates for president were nominated by a congressional caucus, thereby depriving the voter of a direct voice in that critical decision. But in 1832 the supporters of Andrew Jackson nominated him at a national convention attended by popularly selected delegates. The Whigs (and other parties) soon followed suit, thus enlarging the popular role in a manner we now take for granted.

When the Supreme Court, through several decisions in the 1960s,[6] declared that each vote should carry about the same weight in elections, it also forwarded the democratic notion of equality. Prior to these "one man, one vote" court pronouncements, voting districts were so constituted that one person's vote might count much more heavily than another's. For example, the town of Victory, Vermont, with a population of 55, had one representative in the Vermont General Assembly, while Burlington, with a population of 60,000, also had but one representative. In California the state constitution entitled each county to have one representative in the upper house. Some counties of 25,000 to 50,000 persons thus had as much representation in one house as the county of Los Angeles.[7] Under these circumstances persons in sparsely populated areas had much greater proportionate voting impact than those from more densely populated areas. (Just why people's votes should count more if extensive pasture land, fields, and woodlots separated them from their neighbors was never fully explained.) The Supreme Court promptly extended "one man, one vote" not only to both houses of all state legislatures but also to the national House of Representatives—to the distress of previously overprivileged rural and small-town residents. (I've extended the concept still further—semantically—to "one person, one vote!")

One could argue that national polls (such as those taken by Gallup, Roper, and others) have brought us closer to the democratic ideal. Legislators, of course, do not necessarily have to reflect the outcome of the opinion polls in making their voting decisions, but popular sentiment surely should be taken into account. Prior to the polls, legislators were also sensitive to public opinion, but in determining what that opinion was they had to rely on less precise data. Letters, newspaper editorials, random encounters with voters, and discussions with local political leaders could provide a crude measure; but today's polls provide a more accurate picture of the public mind.

The Gestation of Rights

We have surely come a long ways since 1787 toward a more democratic nation, both in terms of realized human rights and in terms of popular control of government. But we are not at the end of the road. Other potential rights are struggling to be born, and our lengthening experience and broadening perception of human needs may ultimately vindicate their claims. Not all of the alleged rights being claimed today will be recognized, of course, since it is one thing to assert a "right" and another for that claim to seem so compelling that the nation will eventually accept it. But some of the proposed reforms to broaden the spectrum of rights will probably win their way.

Should we wipe out the electoral college and have fully direct election of presidents?[8] Critics of the electoral college correctly charge that on three occasions (1824, 1876, and 1888) men became president who received fewer popular votes than their opponent but more electoral votes. This is possible because of the winner-take-all system whereby the candidate who receives the most popular votes in a state thereby wins *all* of the state's electoral votes. Thus, a tiny victory margin in a handful of large states could enable the winner to overcome lopsided losses in most of the other states—and become president despite being a loser in terms of total votes cast. Is it democratic for a person to become president who has received fewer votes than his opponent? Also, if no candidate gets a majority of electoral votes, the election is thrown into the House of Representatives, where each state casts one vote. Is this consistent with the democratic premise that citizen votes should bear substantially equal weight? (This does not mean that there are not formidable arguments for the electoral college, but the possible outcome of a minority victory is hard to reconcile with majority rule.)

Another possible inequality arises from the fact that each state now has two senators. Is it democratic for the relatively few citizens of Nevada to have the same influence in the Senate as the more numerous citizens of California? Unfortunately nothing will change this situation except a constitutional amendment to which each small state consents—that will happen when shrimp learn to whistle!

A whole set of issues about the rights of the poor must also be resolved in the future. Currently, for example, one's fate in the court depends heavily on the quality of legal counsel available to the defendant. The poor must usually depend on inexperienced young "public defenders" appointed by the court, while well-to-do persons can hire expensive attorneys who can do a much more skillful job of protecting them. Should justice be dependent on one's bank account? We have a long way to go before we can accurately boast of "equal justice under law."

In this connection, the poor and uneducated are more likely to be arrested than the affluent and to be treated with less courtesy during and after arrest. They are likely to receive less lenient treatment from the sentencing judge, also. (This seems to be a universal phenomenon, not an evil confined to this country.) Although the situation is patently undemocratic, no one has devised an effective and practicable way to remedy the evil. Some injustices seem beyond the capacity of law to correct.

The poor also suffer educational disadvantages. Do they have a democratic "right" to equality of educational opportunity at the college level? We now have such equality (at least in theory) on the elementary and secondary levels of education. Some people claim that the children of poor parents have as much "right" to a college education as those of prosperous parents. Has the democratic state an obligation to convert this claim into a right? Or is a college education a privilege rather than a right?

Besides the poor, other segments of society are beginning to claim rights. The area of sexual rights has been opened to debate. Should homosexuals be free from all discrimination in employment and other areas, or has the community the right to uphold certain traditional moral standards? In a related issue, should publishers and consumers of pornographic materials be free from any censorship of these materials? Or has the state a right to intervene to protect the young, a healthy image of women and "the quality of life" from the free circulation of these materials?

Other issues affect the work place. Does everyone have a "right" to a job, a "right" that the state is obligated to fulfill? Or is this strictly a matter of economic policy, with the government mediating between the twin evils of unemployment and inflation? And what about older workers? Do compulsory retirement laws interfere with a person's "right to work" if that individual remains capable of doing a job well despite his or her age? Or do other factors make such retirement laws a "necessary evil"?

Perhaps an even more basic concern of older Americans—and of all of us, eventually—is the issue of the rights of the dying. Is there a *right* to die? Does a person, confronted with a painful terminal illness, have the right to demand the cessation of treatment that prolongs dying? Or even the right to take a lethal substance if that is his or her wish? Should someone facing life imprisonment have the "right" to take his or her own life? Is this the ultimate freedom? Or does this push freedom's claims to excessive lengths?

At the other end of the age spectrum, an issue of particular concern to the young is the military draft. Is there a right *not* to fight in a war that one regards as unjust? We are not referring to the right of conscientious objection to *all* wars, a right now recognized by all or almost all liberal democracies. Rather, the issue is whether young men (and women) can decline to fight in a war they regard as "immoral and unjust" (as many Americans regarded the Vietnam War and as many French regarded the war against Algerian independence). Suppose they believe that their supreme right is the right to decide whether they are being asked to kill for a sufficiently good cause? Does the state have too much power if it can force them to participate in killing people they believe do not deserve to die? Or is "selective conscientious objection" an appealing idea but an unrealistic or impractical one that no democracy will ever concede?

Which of these, and other alleged rights that have not yet even come to mind, may some day be accepted as unquestioned democratic rights is anyone's guess. All asserted rights face an uphill struggle when first advocated, and many wither for lack of either rational or widely felt emotional support. Some make headway fairly rapidly (as has the right of women to receive equal pay for equal work), while some rights struggle for centuries before receiving legal vindication.

Interestingly, those who drafted the Bill of Rights made allowance for rights that the people might claim but that were not included in the first ten amendments. The Ninth Amendment states that "The enumeration in the Constitution, of certain rights, shall not be construed to deny or disparage others retained by the people."

But while the founders understood that rights might expand, they couldn't have foreseen the rash of alleged rights that have been asserted in recent years. So many have been claimed, in fact, that a "revulsion of common sense" is said to be brewing. For example, Jerry Rubin wrote a book explaining in detail how to steal, insisting that this was his right under the First Amendment.[9] Policemen and firemen claim the right to go on strike, whatever the impact on the community. It is claimed that alcoholics are handicapped persons and that no employer can legally discriminate against them in hiring and firing. Transvestites assert the right to try on women's clothing in women's clothing stores.[10] Are we becoming so confused by desires masquerading as rights that concern for individual liberty is overriding the "right" of society to protect itself from irresponsible behavior that threatens society's health?

It is a truth well known to sensible philosophers that every principle, however sound, eventually meets an equally sound counterprinciple that limits the former's scope and application. Thus, individual freedom is a very great good, but carried too far it can lead to the excesses that anger people and provoke demands for a "strong man" to restore "order and discipline." If individual freedom were our sole concern, we would abolish government altogether since government exists largely to restrain people from acting on their antisocial impulses. But anarchy provides not only total individual freedom but an environment in which the most powerful, ruthless, predatory, or cunning people prevail over the weak, the scrupulous, and those less endowed with a militant spirit of "me first." Thus, we prefer government, with all of its shortcomings, to a state of anarchy that differs little from the conditions of the jungle. We will have more to say about this at the conclusion of the chapter.

Are "Natural Rights" Natural?

Are there genuinely "natural rights," as the Founding Fathers believed, or are all democratic "rights" no more than the cultural prejudices of a given society at a given point in its experience? Does a system of human rights represent nothing more than the prevailing sentiment of a culture whose members are conditioned to believe certain things because of their unique traditions and experiences? If so, the implications are sobering indeed since any critic who challenges our treasured values and "rights" can argue that we cherish them only because a singular set of circumstances has conditioned us to do so. Thus, if one culture practices infanticide and another abhors it, there is no objective standard for deciding which is right. If one society practices slavery and another regards it as an abomination, defenders of the latter can only say, "We disagree with slavery but only because we've been conditioned by our environment to oppose it. If we were raised in your culture we would find slavery quite acceptable." They would be expressing the doctrine of *cultural and moral relativism*. Hitler would be exonerated by this outlook, and President Carter's stress on human rights would reflect no more than his own narrow cultural prejudice.

The author takes exception to the view that we have no firm basis for judging any social value as superior or inferior to its opposite.[11] Granted that most moral concepts and most laws are purely "conventional," the product of a particular culture rather than of "natural laws" that reflect universal reason. But it is also true that there appears to be another order of laws emerging that embodies timeless, universal, and transcendent principles. These include injunctions that forbid:

 Punishing persons for crimes they have not committed
 Inflicting wanton injury upon other persons
 Slavery
 Genocide
 Punishing children for the crimes of their parents
 Convicting someone of a criminal offense without a fair trial
 Achieving confessions by torture
 Treating equal judicial cases unequally
 Compelling people to affirm what they do not believe
 Denying equal rights to women
 Imposing legal penalties purely because of race, color, or religion
 Arbitrarily denying normal adults a voice in the political decisions of that society

Laws that condemn such practices are, in effect, political-moral absolutes that have always been valid (even when unrecognized) and will never become obsolete, whatever state of development a society may attain.

Laws claiming universality and inherent moral validity must not rest on a society's *current* sense of justice—which admittedly differs widely from society to society. They must rest, instead, on a society's *matured and settled* sense of justice. This requires that an issue (involving an alleged right) shall be raised, argued about, struggled over, and eventually settled in such a way that tensions involving it are gradually reduced and acceptance of the right grows until it hardens into one of the almost unconscious norms of that society. Only then can society's sense of justice be said to have matured on that issue.

This process has occurred in many areas involving our sense of right and wrong. Slavery, confessions by torture, the burning of witches, the denial of rights based on race or religion—these and many other moral issues have been raised, fought over, and eventually settled in many societies. They involve issues that *can only be settled in one way if the issue finally is to be put to rest*. If an issue is temporarily "settled" by a majority at the expense of a dissenting minority, the settlement will not endure. The issue will be raised again and again until it is finally resolved the *right* way, once and for all. The issues of equal rights for women and for blacks, for example, could never be definitively settled except by granting equal status to both groups.

Why do people finally settle certain issues (such as those listed) in ways we regard as "enlightened" and "right"? Reason and empathy combined with experience enter into the settlement. Reason, in a context of full and free discussion, sustains the settlement; our capacity to empathize with victims of injustice provides emotional support; experience demonstrates that only by resolving the issue in the "right" way can lasting peace on that issue be brought. (Is an innate "moral sense" somehow involved?)

Of course there is no proof that societies can find enduring peace on certain political–moral questions *only* if they settle them in the ways we assume. But it seems more reasonable to believe this than to believe the contrary.

If this reasoning is correct, it places some values on a more solid basis than if they rested on purely personal hunches or on the cultural prejudices of a given culture. They rest, instead, on universal human tendencies, once certain issues have been raised and deliberated upon, to find peaceful consensus only by arriving at similar conclusions.

If this is correct, Hitler was wrong not just because contemporary Americans are repelled by his savagery, but because he was violating an immutable principle of justice—a principle already on its way to being confirmed by the common consent of the human race.

Waiting for *all* societies to arrive at a common agreement on certain rights in order to establish their moral compatibility with human beings' matured sense of justice is a long, drawn-out matter. In the meantime, the best assurance we have that a democratic right is truly a right is to subject it to full and unsparing examination in the marketplace of ideas. If it can survive all assaults upon it, and steadily gain ground even among those not directly benefited by it, we have good reason (though not proof) to believe it merits the label of "right."

Government by the People— Or by the Few?

Like the principle of "natural rights", that of "majority rule" deserves some clarification. We do not, in the strict sense, have government "of the people, by the people, and for the people." In our country the majority does not make and enforce the laws. Most American citizens are onlookers who take only a casual interest in what the government is doing. More accurately, we have *government by the consent of the governed* rather than government by the governed. The majority consents by elections to let this party and this group of legislators and executives govern them for a number of years rather than a competing party and group. For most Americans, that is the extent of their direct participation in self-government.

Those who govern, however, have attempted, during and preceding the campaign, to ascertain what kinds of policies the majority of those who are likely to vote will find most acceptable. Their campaign speeches and pledges reflect their findings. Since public officials, more than most people realize, then try to carry out their pledges, the majority (of voters) has a continuing impact on government though it is inactive in attempting to guide the government between elections.

Communist countries often practice *democratic centralism*—a device that gives top political leaders an opportunity to freely discuss a proposal or issue until a decision is made. Once made, debate ceases until the leadership decides to open the question for reconsideration by that same group.

This is not the case in a democracy. A liberal democracy gives all its citizens a continuing opportunity to influence policy between elections, to apply pressure individually and through organized effort on behalf of what they want and against what they do not want. Thus, democracy means far more than giving the public a chance to vote for competitive slates of candidates. It means an ongoing process of government by the active consent of the majority of those who care about the issue at hand. And it means respect for minority and individual rights.

One school of thought holds that the concept of majority rule in the United States is more fiction than fact.[12] This school believes that a "power elite"—consisting of the top military, corporate and political figures—really makes the most significant political decisions while letting less important leaders—judges, interest group leaders, members of Congress, and media executives—make decisions of lesser import. This power elite, rooted in an economic system dominated by giant banks and massive business corporations, is careful to maintain a democratic façade, however. Through its control of the mass media, it influences the apathetic "masses" more than the latter influence it. In the process it encourages the average citizen to believe that ours is a system of popular government, but the harsh reality is that the people have little influence over major foreign policy decisions or over the economic structure and basic economic policies of the country. That structure vests heavily disproportionate wealth in the hands of a small percentage of the people; inevitably, political power reflects this economic power. With both political parties substantially supporting the status quo, elections do not give the people a genuine opportunity to effect major change.

Members of the power elite, it is said, share common goals and attitudes. All are committed to limited government, to the maintenance of the capitalist system, to a large military budget, and to a willingness to accept minor reforms in order to placate the public and perpetuate their own power. Overwhelmingly male, white, affluent, Anglo-Saxon, and Protestant, members often hobnob together, moving freely back and forth from top corporation posts to top government posts, or from high-ranking military to governmental to corporation berths; they constitute what some call the "Establishment." Not many people move into this elite; those that do reach this eminence because they share the goals and attitudes of the Establishment. Democracy, therefore, is little more than a pretty illusion, an illusion that keeps the public passive while a small minority governs in essentially its own self-interest.

We will not attempt to evaluate this interpretation of democracy at this point. The author disagrees with it and his reasons for doing so are scattered throughout the book. For now it seems sufficient to say that the author finds little evidence that the will of the majority *of those who care* about specific political issues—large or small—is flouted by the top decision makers in this country. The communications media are not united in hostility to the voices of dissent. Dissent and controversy, on the contrary, are diligently fostered by most of the "prestige press" and by the television and book publishing industries. Finally, instead of political power resting in the hands of a small elite, it is very widely dispersed within our system. That power, when exercised, must respect the basic traditions, values, and prejudices of the American people.

Threats to Democracy

In Chapter 3 on the Constitution we spoke of dangers to the freedom of minority or heretical elements that may come if, in some hour of real or imagined national emergency, people focus exaggerated or misplaced fears on these groups and proceed to strip them of their rights in the name of national security. What other dangers to democracy can we foresee?

Democratic governments, to remain in good health, need to have *the power to govern*. In an age when one crisis seems to follow another, citizens need to feel that their government has the will and the capacity to act when action is needed. The action need not be wise or even very successful, but nothing threatens the continuation of any system so much as the widespread feeling that the government cannot pull itself together and do something significant to meet a serious problem. People will forgive governments for unsuccessful experiments; they will not, in times of stress, tolerate indecision for long.

Italy's fledging democracy gave way to Benito Mussolini in 1921 because that government was too weak, too indecisive, to irresolute to deal firmly with the strikes, the violence, and the growing tendency of private groups to take the law into their own hands. When the government hesitated to act in the face of Mussolini's military arm, the Black Shirts, support for democratic government was shaken. The incapacity of the post–World War I Weimar Republic to respond vigorously to economic disaster and local disorders led Germans to yearn for a government that *could* act and act decisively. Hitler followed. Franz Neumann notes that "modern revolutions such as the French of 1789, the two Russian ones of 1917 and the German of 1918 had their immediate cause in the lack of power of the central governments and not in the excessive use or abuse of power."[13] Again, the notorious paralysis of the French government in the post-World War II period led to increasing French disillusionment and cynicism about the government. When the French had had enough of weak government, they were fortunate to have a strong leader available who was committed to democratic principles. But democracies cannot depend on Charles de Gaulles to rescue them from governmental inertia; some de Gaulles turn out to be Napoleons.

In our system and in our time, the necessity for a reasonably effective working relationship between president and Congress is thus imperative. Whether we can count on that remains to be seen.

A second apparent danger to democracy is the tendency of citizens to consult only their short-range interests. People usually accept painful measures if an emergency is clearly apparent, but they rarely tolerate such measures under other circumstances. The resistance of Americans to make the modest sacrifices needed to reduce our ominously high level of oil imports is a case in point. Most of the American people are accustomed to living so comfortably that they balk at making almost any sacrifices for the long-range interests of their country—to say nothing of the interests of other countries. Lacking an emergency, Americans tend to consider short-range comforts vastly more important than the needs of tomorrow. If the people maintain this attitude, we can count on Congress to reflect a similar view.

While there is a reasonable possibility, from time to time, that the chief executive will take the long view of the national interest before a crisis is full-blown, there is almost no prospect that Congress will do so. Thus, the greatest peril in the decades ahead will come not from executive abuse of power so much as from a people and a Comgress that will insist on easy solutions, those which make the fewest demands, whatever the cost for the future. The disasters that follow may invite governmental controls so sweeping that democracy may falter.

A third peril to survival of democracy comes from the quite real likelihood that terrorists will obtain control of atomic weapons and threaten to use those weapons against our major cities unless their outrageous demands are met. If this should happen, the subsequent efforts to protect ourselves from such disaster could lead to governmental controls so intrusive and so sweeping that democracy, as we know it, would give way to a more repressive system.

Perhaps an equally important, although less readily recognized danger to democracy lies in the gradual erosion of those personal qualities that sustain a

One alternative to democracy

self-governing society. Thomas Jefferson beloved that the endurance of a free people depended on the virtue of the people, a virtue he felt was best maintained in a rural, small-town environment.[14] French philosopher Alexis de Tocqueville tended to agree.[15]

Whether or not Jefferson and de Tocqueville were correct in mistrusting the impact of urban life and affluence upon the people, the following statements seem true: the less self-discipline that citizens display, the less freedom a democratic society can afford; conversely, the more self-discipline that citizens manifest, the less coercion is required from the democratic state.

Philosopher Edmund Burke put it this way: "Men are qualified for civil liberty in exact proportion to their disposition to put moral chains upon their own appetites. Society cannot exist unless a controlling power upon will and appetite be placed somewhere, and the less of it there is within, the more there is without."[16]

Self-discipline is not a quality that homes, schools and the entertainment industry have cultivated in recent decades. (By entertainment industry I refer to radio and television, the rock and record industry, motion pictures, the pornography trade, and trash magazines in general.) The emphasis has been on self-expression and self-gratification, not on self-control. The results are not inspiring. Witness the national crime rate, the rapidly rising illegitimacy statistics, the growth in one-parent families, increase in pregnancies of 13 to 15 year olds, the rising rates of abortion and venereal disease, the alarming phenomenon of high school age drunkenness, the common-place use of marijuana by 10 to 13 year olds, the four billion dollar pornography industry, movies which exploit super-violence and illicit sex to ever further extremes, records and rock groups whose indecencies know no bounds, a fading concern with the national interest as "gimme" interest groups proliferate, a Congress increasingly concerned with reelection rather than with the public interest, a general chaos of values as moral "authorities" lose their authority.[17]

If these do not suggest a serious moral decline with grave political implications, what would?

The consequences can be sobering. A society in which a healthy value system and its attendant behavior are being eroded is a society in which freedom's worth will be questioned. A society in which ultra-individualism leads to destructive social consequences can become a society in which the alarmed reaction to signs of social decay may have profoundly antidemocratic manifestations. Society requires a balance between the spirit of unbridled individualism in pursuit of hedonism and the ant-hill collectivist mentality of many communist states. That this balance has been upset in recent decades seems clear to me. What do you think?

Notes

1. For a brief description of Greek democracy, see Dorothy Pickles, *Democracy* (London: Batsford, 1970), pp. 29–41.
2. Palko v. Connecticut, 302 U.S. 319 (1937). The court has recently altered this latter phrase to mean fundamental to an Anglo-American system of ordered justice.
3. This point is eloquently made in E. E. Schattschneider, *Two Hundred Million Americans in Search of a Government* (New York: Holt, Rinehard and Winston, 1960), pp. 46–47.
4. See Alfred H. Kelly and Winfred A. Harbison, *The American Constitution: Its Origins and Development*, 5th ed. (New York: Norton, 1976) p. 465. The "white primary" restricted voting in the Democratic party to whites only; whoever won that primary always went on to win the general election, since the GOP was so weak in many southern states. "Grandfather clauses" limited the suffrage to persons whose ancestors were entitled to vote in 1866, thus effectively disenfranchising blacks.

5 For a good overview, see John Hope Franklin, *From Slavery to Freedom: A History of Negro-Americans*, 5th ed. (New York: Knopf, 1978), and Mary Ellison, *The Black Experience: American Blacks Since 1865* (London: Batsford, 1974).
6 Baker v. Carr, 369 U.S. 186 (1962); Wesberry v. Sanders, 376 U.S. 1 (1964); and Reynolds v. Sims, 377 U.S. 533 (1964).
7 Richard L. Strout, "The Next Election Is Already Rigged," *Harper's Magazine*, November 1959, pp. 35–40.
8 Contrasting views are presented in Neal R. Peirce, *The People's President* (New York: Simon and Schuster, 1968); and Wallace S. Sayre and Judith H. Parris, *Voting For President* (Washington, D.C.: Brookings Institute, 1970).
9 Jerry Rubin, *Steal This Book,* (New York, Grove Press, 1971).
10 "The Sensible Limits of Non-Discrimination," *Time*, July 27, 1977, p. 53.
11 For fuller treatment of this view, see Reo M. Christenson, "The Moral Imperative in Politics," *Polity*, Winter, 1968, Vol. 1, pp. 178–190.
12 Proponents include C. Wright Mills, *The Power Elite* (New York: Oxford University Press, 1946); Michael Parenti, *Power and the Powerless* (New York: St. Martin's Press, 1978); and Thomas R. Dye and L. Harmon Zeigler, *The Irony of Democracy* (Belmont, Calif.: Wadsworth, 1970); for opposing views, see Robert A. Dahl, *Pluralist Democracy in the United States* (Skokie, Ill.: Rand McNally, 1967); and Arnold Rose, *The Power Structure* (New York, Oxford, University Press, 1967).
13 Franz Neumann, "Federalism: Its Nature and Role," in *Federalism Mature and Emergent*, Arthur W. MacMahon, ed. (Garden City, N.Y.: Doubleday, 1955), p. 49.
14 See Thomas Jefferson, *Notes on Virginia*, in *Writings*, Vol. III, H. A. Washington, ed. (Washington: Taylor and Maury, 1853).
15 Alexis de Tocqueville, *Democracy In America*, Vol. I (New York, Knopf, 1945), pp. 60–62, 66–68.
16 Quoted by Norman Graebner, "Government Without Consensus," *Virginia Quarterly Review*, 1978, p. 650.
17 See Thomas Griffith, "Doing As We Damned Please," *The Atlantic*, March, 1979.

CHAPTER 5
FEDERALISM: BATTERED BUT IMMORTAL

Politics is not a dull subject, but of all the chapters in a political science text, federalism is ordinarily the dreariest. It is usually a guaranteed soporific (although, happily, neither addictive nor carcinogenic). But it need not be that way; the story of federalism's development in the United States is actually one of the more fascinating sagas of our political history. Understanding its implications tells us much that we need to know about our political system. Let's see if we can make good on these assertions.

Federalism: Roots and Branches

Federalism is a system of government in which certain powers are granted to the central government and other powers to local governments (states or provinces, usually), with neither level of government able to add to its own powers or subtract from the powers of the other level. The Constitution laid the groundwork for this distribution of power in our country today. Only the people can formally alter the distribution of powers—by constitutional amendments (proposed by two-thirds of the members of Congress or by the legislatures of two-thirds of the states) which are ratified by constitutional conventions or by the legislatures of three-fourths of the states.

The Constitution gives the national government certain delegated (or enumerated) powers, reserving all other powers not prohibited by the Constitution to the states or to the people (as provided by the Tenth Amendment). In Canada (which also has a federal system), this order is reversed: Certain powers are specifically granted to the provinces, with the remaining powers reserved to the national government.

Federalism contrasts with a *unitary system* of government, under which a constitution grants all powers to the central government, which, in turn, parcels out such powers to local governments as it sees fit. The central government can enlarge or diminish local powers as it believes necessary.

A third arrangement is a *confederation*, which is a league of sovereign states joined together for limited purposes; the central government seeks the cooperation of each of the states but cannot coerce any of them. From 1778 to 1789 the United States operated under the Articles of Confederation.

Federalism was the principal political innovation of the American Constitution. As such, it has been a source of great pride to many Americans. Yet it was the product of an expedient compromise rather than of a profound philosophical concept of what the ideal American polity should be. The founders stumbled onto federalism rather than formulating it after a mighty debate over human nature and the necessities of freedom in a diverse land.

No one has better summarized the conflicting forces that made federalism a logical development than political scientist Richard Leach, in *American Federalism*. Leach observes that when the Great Compromise was devised, giving equal state representation in the Senate but representation according to population in the House

> the stage was set for a lengthy and revealing debate on federalism [which] did not materialize.... In the end, the Constitution emerged with no real clues as to what was in the framers' minds as they voted on the several resolutions before them or how they expected the federal

Federalism:
Roots and Branches

system they had brought into being to work in practice. The reasons the framers avoided what now seems to be such a vital question are not hard to imagine. The very necessity for compromise in getting the Constitution drawn up and promulgated virtually ruled out an exhaustive excursion into theory. The framers were agreed on the need for a limited government; they saw the possibilities of federalism in this connection. But they also saw the dangers of going beyond that point of general agreement into the thicket of theoretical niceties which lay just on the other side. So they avoided theoretical considerations and advanced in their place the more utilitarian matter of preserving the union.[1]

Not only was federalism, then, a makeshift compromise in 1787, but its broader implications and practical contours were hardly touched upon. It was a formula for a stronger union that might lead a skeptical public to ratify the Constitution—and that was enough.

The practical wisdom of the framers may well have been correct. (Sometimes practical compromises bear better fruit than the most elegantly devised, rationally consistent, and theoretically refined models.) For their day, the founders built wisely. The system did win public support; it did prove workable; it did endure. And it became a feasible structural model for other societies seeking to build a nation from heterogeneous and clashing minorities.

Americans, then, have looked upon their handiwork and pronounced it good. The longer they looked, the more virtues they ascribed to federalism. By avoiding centralization of power, the Constitution allowed state governments to adapt their policies to the diverse tastes and needs of a diverse people; the states could become experimental laboratories, launching innovations that, if successful, could be imitated by other states (or Washington itself). If unsuccessful, they would adversely affect only a small part of the Union while warning the remainder. Federalism would develop a sturdy citizenry actively participating in their local governance; it would recruit, train, and winnow political leadership for responsibilities at the highest level; it made the governing of a large geographical area feasible; and it confined the evils of local despots and bulwarked the entire framework of liberty by its division of powers.

Generations of Americans have been taught the beauties of federalism using these lines of reasoning. Even today, when disenchantment with government is widespread, federalism goes largely unchallenged. Textbook after textbook recites the standard litany in relatively uncritical fashion. While tribute is regularly paid to American ingenuity in circumventing the obstacles federalism poses to effective government the system itself is usually extolled. Books that mount formidable attacks on the system are usually ignored or minimized.[2]

But federalism today bears little relation to that which existed in 1787. It will be instructive here to review the role of the Supreme Court in dealing with constitutional aspects of federalism and then to discuss the social forces that brought us to where we are today.

Chief Justice John Marshall stressed what has been called *nation-centered federalism*. In *McCulloch* v. Maryland, (1819), Marshall declared that

Maryland could not tax the deposits of a national branch bank, despite the taxing power that states unquestionably possess. Stressing the *supremacy clause* ("This Constitution, and the Laws of the United States which shall be made in Pursuance thereof ... shall be the supreme Law of the Land, "Article VI), Marshall said that when state powers and legitimate national powers collide, the latter must prevail.

Marshall also greatly expanded the potential power of the federal government by ruling, in the same case, that the national government could exercise not only its delegated powers but powers that could be reasonably implied from those powers. This interpretation of the *elastic clause* ("Congress shall have the power ... to make all Laws which shall be necessary and proper for carrying into Execution the foregoing Powers," Article I, Section 9) made possible most of the expansion of national power that came in the last 50 years.

Marshall's "nation-centered" interpretations, coming at a time when state loyalties were intense, made him our most unpopular Chief Justice. They also led to a counterinterpretation of the Constitution—*state-centered federalism*. This perspective, favored and developed by southerners seeking to protect their regional interests, stressed the role of the states (rather than of the people collectively) in the creation, ratification, and proper interpretation of the Constitution. To support their position, they cited the arguments of James Madison in *The Federalist*, No. 45):

> The powers delegated by the proposed Constitution to the federal government are few and defined. Those which are to remain in the State governments are numerous and indefinite. The former will be exercised principally on external objects. . . . The powers reserved to the several states will extend to all the objects which, in the ordinary course of affairs, concern the lives, liberties and properties of the people, and the internal order, improvement and prosperity of the states.

Madison's remarks contrast sharply with the emphasis of Marshall; they fitted perfectly with the mood of the pre-Civil War South, with that of the corporations and their lawyers after that war, and, finally, with that of opponents of the New Deal.

A third vision of federalism that appeared prior to the Civil War achieved full fruition in the twentieth century. In *Dual federalism*, first developed by Chief Justice Roger Taney, and described by Leach:

> The National and state governments form two separate centers of power, from each of which the other is barred and between which is something like a jurisdictional no-man's land, into which both are barred from entering. Each government in its own sphere is sovereign and there is an essential equality between them.[3]

The dual federalists laid great store by the Tenth Amendment, which declares, "The powers not delegated to the United States by the Constitution, nor prohibited by it to the States, are reserved to the States respectively, or to the people." They regarded the reserved powers of the states as invulnerable to penetration by the delegated powers of the national government. These reserved powers, then, severely limited the delegated powers assigned to Washington.

The American Federal system division of powers

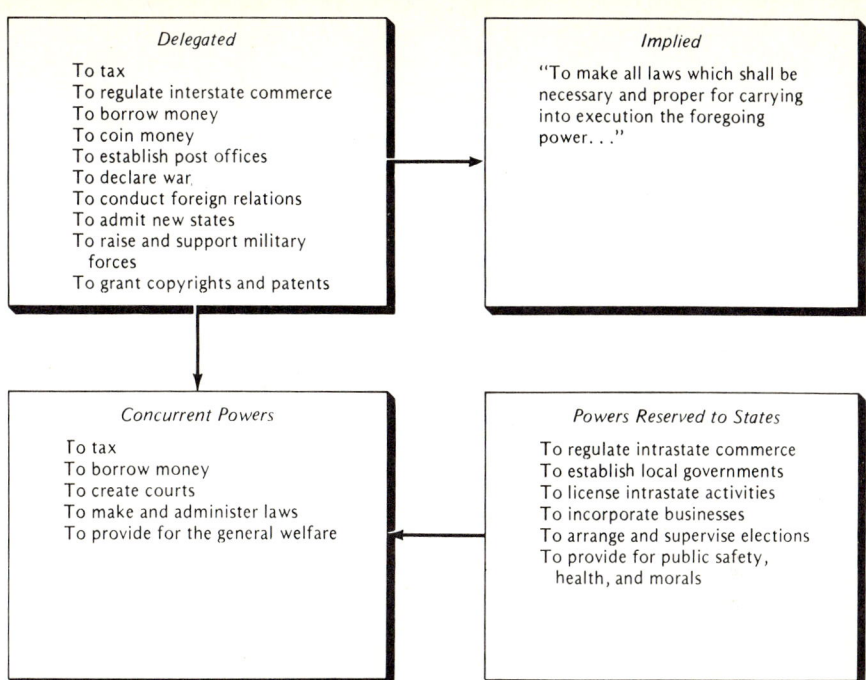

The Supreme Court: Jekyll and Hyde

Because the story is both pertinent and fascinating, the work of the Supreme Court, in grappling with dual federalism and with the reserved powers of the states, should be described. In doing so, I will draw heavily upon Alfred H. Kelly and Winifred A. Harbison's unrivalled work, *The American Constitution*.[4]

The Supreme Court once interpreted the Sherman Antitrust Act (1890), which forbade "every contract, combination... or conspiracy in restraint of trade or commerce among the several states", in a very narrow fashion. The court limited its application to monopolies in transportation (like railroads) and excluded manufacturing monopolies, which Congress was primarily interested in preventing. Control over manufacturing was not a power that the constitution delegated to Washington, said the Court, and Washington could not employ the commerce clause to reach out and penetrate the reserved rights of the states. In other decisions the Court ruled that Washington could not regulate labor relations by banning yellow-dog contracts. (These contracts, forbidding an employee to join a union while working for a given employer, had led to numerous strikes, walkouts, and boycotts that Congress believed were interfering with the flow of interstate commerce.) Such regulation, declared the Court, deprived a worker of "freedom of contract," a freedom believed to be implicitly guaranteed by the Fifth Amendment clause that states that no person shall be "deprived of life, liberty or property without due process of law." A person's "liberty" included the right to agree not to join a union as a precondition of employment.

The Court made other conservative rulings in the period from about 1890 to the mid-1930s. Congress could not pass minimum-wage laws, since a worker's "liberty" enabled that person to work for whatever wage he or she was willing to accept. It could not outlaw the "white slave" traffic, since the regulation of public health, morals, safety, welfare, and order were among the reserved powers of the states. Nor could it forbid the movement in interstate commerce of goods made by child labor—either directly, under the alleged authority of the commerce clause, or indirectly, through placing a heavy federal tax on such goods. Neither the commerce clause nor the federal taxing power could be misused to invade the areas reserved to the states by the Tenth Amendment.

Moreover, proclaimed the Court, the commerce clause could be used to regulate, but not to prohibit commerce. And while activities having a "direct" impact on interstate commerce could be controlled, those having only an "indirect" effect could not. The Court repeatedly looked behind the ostensible constitutional justification for a congressional action to Congress' ulterior motives, ruling out regulations that seemed innocent on their face but that, in the Court's opinion, had the effect of violating the Tenth Amendment.

Finally, quoth the Court, Congress could not regulate agricultural production by paying cooperating farmers to reduce their acreage so that surpluses would not drive prices down to calamitous levels. Even if voluntarism was involved, the result was to control an activity—farming—for which no delegated power could properly be cited.

From these cases, the court appears inflexible in its resolve to interpret the Tenth Amendment strictly and to limit Washington to the exercise of powers clearly delegated to it in the Constitution. In fact, however, cases discussed up to this point were chosen selectively, creating a misleading impression of consistency. Actually, the Court's decisions were hopelessly contradictory in the time period under discussion.

For example, while the Court would not permit a federal tax on goods made with child labor in 1922, it had upheld a federal tax on colored oleomargarine in 1904. Clearly the law attempted to regulate manufacturing, and it *was* a federal tax; but the Court decided that Congress had the power to levy taxes, and it did not inquire into Congress' ulterior motives in this case. The Court also approved a tax on the sale of narcotics, designed to facilitate federal control of narcotics traffic by provisions attached to the tax, which plainly sought to regulate public health and morals. And while the Court would not permit the outlawing of yellow-dog contracts, it did uphold a Utah statute limiting miners to an eight-hour day, an Oregon statute restricting certain types of female labor to ten hours a day, and an Oregon statute that limited employment of both men and women in certain industries to a 10-hour day. Just why these did not violate "freedom of contract" was unclear.

The Court also upheld, in 1903, a federal statute forbidding the sale of lottery tickets in interstate commerce—although the statute did *prohibit* a form of commerce and was an obvious attempt to protect the public morals. Congress was allowed to pass an impure food and drug act, even though this regulation was surely designed to protect the public's health. And despite its earlier "white slave" decision, it later upheld a federal law, only technically different from its predecessor, which forbade the transportation of prostitutes in interstate or foreign commerce; in this case the Court contended that the commerce clause could be used to "promote the general welfare, material and moral."[5] Less than ten years after its initial decision gutting the Sherman Act, the Court backed away from its narrowly construed interpretation of the commerce clause by a new interpretation that later enabled it to sustain antitrust suits against the Standard Oil Company, the American Tobacco Company, the U.S. Steel Corporation, and other manufacturing trusts.

Thus we find the Court zigging and zagging in its attempt to assign powers in our federal system, making desperate efforts to explain its inconsistencies with tortured hair-splitting. Critics contended that the Court, from case to case, was either rationalizing its conservative economic and social preferences or responding to social pressures it could not withstand. After the Court struck down half a dozen New Deal measures in its effort to restrain national power and protect its crazy-quilt pattern of federal-state powers, Franklin D. Roosevelt launched his famous attack on the Court in 1937. Although the President's effort to "pack" the Court with additional Justices sharing his views failed, the Court took a reading of public opinion and decided to reverse course. Aided by new Roosevelt appointees replacing retiring conservative justices, the Supreme Court set about systematically repudiating virtually the entire body of restrictive principles that had been inconsistently used to protect the reserved rights of the states.

Can Washington regulate labor relations? Yes, said the Court, because strikes *do* affect the flow of commerce. Can Congress outlaw child labor? Yes, because the commerce clause need not be interpreted narrowly, and Congress *can* prohibit the movement in interstate commerce of undesirable commodities or goods produced by undesirable methods. Furthermore, the Court would no longer question Congress' motives if a statute, on its face, was reasonably related to a congressional power. This applied to regulatory taxes as well as laws drawing on the commerce clause. And the Court wiped out the distinction between direct and indirect effects on commerce.

Asserting that the commerce clause "is an affirmative power commensurate with the national needs," the Court adopted a permissive view that Congress could regulate any economic practice, however local it might seem, if it could be shown to have a practical economic effect upon commerce.[6] The already heavily breached walls of Jericho, erected in deference to the Tenth Amendment, were now leveled almost to the ground.

The revolution in federal-state relations was fueled by other interpretations of the Court. The highest tribunal sanctioned an exceedingly liberal interpretation of "spending for the general welfare," spending that indirectly brought further large chunks of "reserved powers" under federal control. A benign judicial view was taken of federal appropriations for local airports, hospitals, employment services, slum control and urban renewal programs, sewage disposal facilities, and a host of other programs (so-called "grants-in-aid"), even though these contained, as a prerequisite to their distribution, certain regulatory provisions designed to ensure that they were spent efficiently for the purposes intended. These controls, unconstitutional if imposed directly, became constitutional so long as the states were free to either accept or reject the accompanying funds. In reality, the states felt obligated to request their full share of funds drawn from general federal tax revenues (to which their citizens had contributed) and being accepted by surrounding states.

In addition to major federal breakthroughs achieved through the commerce clause, the taxing clause, and the spending clause, Washington was empowered to almost raze federal-state barriers during wartime. The power to wage war, said the Court, was "a power to wage war successfully."[7] During wartime, then, Washington could regulate prices, wages, and rents; impose rationing; allocate workers and scarce resources; and do virtually anything else that might promote the war effort.

In brief, the Court had seemingly resolved to give Congress and the president a virtually free hand in making social and economic policy. From 1937 onward the Court would focus primarily on civil liberties and civil rights, relinquishing responsibility for overseeing federal policymaking in the areas that had preoccupied it previously.

Federalism, as the Founding Fathers perceived it, was in a shambles by 1940. In most of the significant areas of national policy the only restraint upon Washington was its own sense of propriety. Federalism, seen as separate spheres of federal and state power, each protected from encroachment by the other, had suffered such a drastic transformation as to be scarcely recognizable from earlier textbook descriptions. It was still federalism—but so twisted and wrenched out of shape as to be little more than a caricature of its earlier condition. Not that the states were doing less than before; on the contrary, the scope and range of their powers had also expanded. But only a few pockets of state and local activity could still claim immunity from federal control if Washington chose to exercise that control.

Taking Revolution in Stride

Why has the public taken this development in stride? Why has there not been a great popular outcry against the manhandling of the Constitution and the mutilation of the sacred philosophy of the Founding Fathers? Americans are alleged to be a conservative people, so far as their fundamental institutions are concerned, and one of their most fundamental institutions—federalism—had been desecrated in wholesale fashion.

A number of reasons account for this change in attitude. Foremost among them, the United States had become a nation rather than a collection of states. American citizens began thinking of themselves as Americans first and state citizens hardly at all—in sharp contrast with the early days, when the inhabitants conceived of themselves first of all as citizens of Virginia, or Georgia, or New York and only secondarily as Americans. A century and a half of common experience and commingling has changed us, with mass communications greatly accelerating our sense of oneness. With the entire nation consuming the same products, watching the same TV, reading the *Reader's Digest*, singing the same songs, laughing at the same jokes, scanning the same reports from the Associated Press and United Press International, being educated in substantially the same way, a common culture developed. The homogenization process has been greatly enhanced by the automobile, which enables us to travel the length and breadth of the land and helps reduce regional singularities. We have also fought several major wars, wars of sufficient magnitude and peril to help forge a sense of common purpose and common destiny.

Added to this is the growing recognition that our domestic problems are essentially national rather than regional, and must be dealt with nationally. The great internal issues that have concerned Americans since Franklin Roosevelt's presidency have been unemployment, inflation, subversion, energy, race relations, labor relations, agricultural surpluses, poverty, crime, and pollution. These are not local problems; they are national in origin and in scope. If they are to be dealt with effectively, national programs, not those of the separate states, must be developed. This lesson was imprinted harshly upon us during the Great Depression of the 1930s, when state incapacity to cope with pressing economic problems became painfully apparent. Since the depression the imperatives of national innovation, direction, and financing in dealing with economic and social problems have become equally evident. The prag-

Washington finances local public works during Depression

matic public, more concerned with pressing realities than theoretical purity, has adjusted its expectations and its premises accordingly.

The adjustment has been facilitated by several factors. First, average citizens have only the dimmest notion of what federalism is all about. Asked to define it, they respond with stuttered gibberish. They believe devoutly in federalism, but as a symbol without known substance. The vast alteration of the federal-state landscape has taken place, then, without much awareness that something of great constitutional import was happening. If Americans had been asked to ratify a constitutional amendment empowering Washington to do what it was doing, they would probably have reacted negatively, fearful lest the foundations of this republic be undermined by the visible concentration of power in Washington. But since the New Deal revolution has taken place step by step, under a confident and reassuring chief executive, it has seemed less ominous and even rather natural.

Americans have been soothed, too, by all the rhetoric that filled the air, and fills it to this day, about how terribly important the states are, how much we treasure vigorous local self-government, and how determined we are to keep government "close to the people." Comforting theories have been devised to describe modern-day American federalism. It has been called "cooperative federalism"—emphasizing that since federal and state governments have always worked together to achieve our public ends, the latest developments only build on our past. In the recent past former Governor Nelson Rockefeller of New York called for "creative federalism," a concept stressing cooperative relations among the Federal government, municipal governments, private organizations, and the states. "All are regarded as a working team, dedicated to positive action in solving the problems facing the nation, with perhaps a different combination of forces at work in each different problem area and with the national government not always the senior partner."[8] The Nixon Administration added its bit by proclaiming a "New Federalism":

> The New Federalism calls upon us to act as one nation in setting the standards of fairness, and then to act as congeries of communities in carrying out those standards. We are nationalizing equity as we localize control, while retaining a continued federal stewardship to insure that national standards are attained.[9]

These versions of federalism are not necessarily inaccurate, but they do mask the magnitude of the shift toward federal power and federal initiative on the major issues and obscure the shrinkage of the reserved powers that remain in theory constitutionally protected from federal incursion. And great though federal powers now are, their scope under Supreme Court interpretations has not yet been fully explored. Washington annually embarks upon new policies further extending national power and further reducing the states to a handmaiden role. The people, only faintly sensing the erosion of state prerogatives and pragmatic about the direction of national policy, remain undisturbed. If apprehensions do arise about the concentration of power in Washington, there are sure to be mollifying speeches about the administration's profound commitment to grassroots government.

Is Federalism Obsolete?

We have gone far, very far, toward the creation of a unitary rather than a federal system of government. There is, some would say, much to be said for a fully unitary system at this state in American history.[10] If we had such a system, we could eliminate the shocking range of penalties now possible in various states for similar criminal offenses. Why should a second-offense criminal get one year's imprisonment in one state, three in another, five in another, and ten in still another—as now occurs under our federal system—for having committed the same crime? This is justice? This is equality before the law? This is fair?

Why should not property laws be uniform? Is there any real advantage in having a host of different state laws governing the ownership and transmission of property? Would uniformity in this area destroy any diversity of real value? On the contrary, some would say, it would promote our common economic interests by removing differences that serve no valid purpose.

In addition, our state tax systems are an astonishing hodgepodge, adding up to highly regressive results. Why should Washington not have the power to establish a single, rationally conceived, nationwide tax system, returning revenues to the states in accordance with a fixed formula and confining additional state taxes (where individual states wanted them) to limited categories that make economic sense and are also compatible with our sense of moral justice? The costs of tax administration would be cut sharply, new enterprise would settle in areas offering natural economic advantages instead of seeking out states offering special tax incentives, and the tax system as a whole would be rationalized. A great deal of smuggling could also be avoided, such as that which now occurs because of varying state taxes on cigarettes.

A unitary system might also empower Washington to pass legislation enabling cities that overspill state boundaries to deal with their problems in a coherent, unified fashion. Washington could facilitate the establishment of *metropolitan government* across state lines wherever that is needed rather than endure the hamstringing of metropolitanwide action by local governments bent on protecting their special privileges.

Every value now ascribed to federalism could be retained under the unitary system. The states could continue to tailor most of their policies to the special tastes, needs, and traditions of their people. Members of Congress, who have no appetite for homogenization for homogenization's sake, would impose national authority only when the national public, after the prolonged debate that accompanies major legislation, agreed that an overriding national interest did indeed exist. This was the basis for previous expansions of national power. So long as the states were handling problems adequately, Washington manifested no impulse to thrust their efforts aside and impose its more uniform system. Only when state and local governments demonstrated their impotence, or when overarching national considerations were at stake, did the federal government choose to act. If Washington up until now has shown reasonably good judgment in supplanting local prerogatives, there is little reason to believe it would show bad judgment if its potential scope were broadened.

Under a unitary system Washington would probably behave no differently from the way Britain does. The British Parliament has unlimited power to abolish, modify, enlarge, or limit the powers of local boroughs and shires in Great Britain. But does Parliament, drunk with power, impose stifling, deadening, constricting authority over local governments? Does it take advantage of every flimsy excuse for demonstrating its political muscle by reducing the powers of local governments? There is excellent reason for Parliament's restraint. British voters believe it makes eminently good sense to leave many governmental functions in local hands, and the Members of Parliament (MPs), desiring reelection, respect their wishes. Indeed, MPs, being normal Britons with a normal quota of good judgment, share their constituents' views on the desirability of vigorous local government. Only when local inability to do a job is evident, or when a principle superior to that of local autonomy is involved—one supported by a majority of British citizens—does the central government enlarge its powers at the expense of local government. Given the sociological similarities between our country and Great Britain, Congress would do the same. The sociological differences between the United Kingdom and the United States are not of a nature that would invalidate this parallel.

The assumption that if Washington *could* kick the props out from under local government it *would* promptly do so is manifestly without foundation. Members of Congress do not have less sense than the readers of this book; their careers depend on pleasing their constituents. They would be as unlikely to withdraw local powers cherished by the local citizens as they would be to deride the average citizen during campaign speeches.

But while all of this may be true, it is also fanciful. There is no more prospect of the United States formally abandoning federalism than of our adopting Zen Buddhism as a national religion. The nation's sentimental attachment to federalism runs so deeply as to be wholly immune to rational attacks upon it. And even if this country did adopt a unitary system, Congress might be quite unwilling or unable to agree upon the kind of reforms believed desirable under that system. In fact, if Washington were constitutionally empowered to "legislate for the general welfare" (an expansion of its present power to *spend* for the general welfare)—thus giving us, in effect, a unitary system—probably very little would change. The states would be permitted to remain intact; their powers would be continued, and Washington would only assume fresh power when a strong public demand for that development took place. The formal change from a federal to a unitary system would seem monumental, but the results would be minor. The more things change, the more they remain the same!

The Washington Cornucopia: How Many Strings?

Given the fact that a unitary system is unlikely to be adopted, we should concentrate, then, on the current operation of the present system. The size and nature of Washington's involvement with the states needs greater elaboration.

People seem to believe that Washington has become a colossus while state and local governments retain modest governmental dimensions. It is true that Washington's budget has grown enormously—from $3 billion in 1929 to $30 billion in 1947 to well over $500 billion today. But while the number of federal employees has increased only 37% since World War II, the states have more than tripled their employees.[11] Since 1955 state and local spending has risen about 700%, compared to a Washington increase of 400%. Thus, state and local employment and proportionate spending have increased much more rapidly during recent decades than has Washington's personnel and budget.

Most of the increase has come about through greatly enlarged spending for education and welfare, both of which are administered by state and local governments. To help them meet these costs, Washington has returned vast amounts of tax money to them. Federal aid for such local responsibilities as education, health, housing, and welfare has leaped 600% since 1964. Today, about one-fourth of all the money spent by the states and localities comes from Washington, compared to only 12% in 1962.

Most of Washington's help has come through the grants-in-aid system earlier described. Grants-in-aid have been established for a host of "good causes;" currently over 20 federal departments and agencies administer about 600 separate programs that cover welfare, unemployment compensation, public health care, public housing, school lunches, hospitals, airports, urban renewal, library services, vocational education, aid for handicapped persons, law enforcement, and highways. Most of the grants are conditional; to qualify for federal funds, the states must be prepared to match those funds on a percentage basis that ranges from 10 to 33%. Usually the statutes also require that the states adhere to certain standards in spending the money. For example, some common requirements are that the monies be spent by persons recruited and operating under a civil service system; that proper accounting procedures be established for handling the funds; that the aid shall be administered without racial, religious, or sexual discrimination; and that local units give their citizens an adequate opportunity to express their sentiments on the proper use of these funds. Washington thus sets minimum standards; the states and localities are free to raise those standards as much as they please.

Grants-in-aid have been used to accomplish many purposes not immediately visible to someone perusing the federal budget. In addition to pressuring states and localities into giving women and minorities more opportunities, grant-in-aid programs have tried to ensure minimum incomes for needy groups, to upgrade the quality of local administration, to stimulate local experiments in dealing with problems, to help solve problems without creating new federal bureaucracies, and to help poorer states meet certain public needs by distributing funds more generously to them (proportionate to their per capita income) than to wealthier states. States with a relatively low income per resident, for example, may get larger proportional educational grants than the more prosperous states—in order to equalize educational services throughout the nation.

As administered, grants-in-aid give certain regions an advantage over others, leading to considerable discord among representatives in Congress. New England and the Midwest complain that they get back from 71 to 83 cents of every tax dollar they contribute to support these grants, while the South and West receive from $1.14 to $1.20.[12] If these complaints were heeded, of course, the very basis for many grants-in-aid would be destroyed. The poorer states are intended to receive more funds.

While most federal grants are given for quite specific purposes (in *cate-*

gorical or *program grants*), about one-third of the dollar total has been given in so-called *block grants*, which funnel dollars into broad areas. For example, a block grant may be given for health services, instead of specifying money for smaller categories such as public-school nursing services, hospitals, immunization programs, rat-control measures, prenatal instruction for low-income mothers, and so forth. The states say such block grants give them more flexibility in meeting their problems. Some states may need more money for rat control than others and less for prenatal care. Block grants, it is argued, give them a better opportunity to use federal money wisely rather than being "straitjacketed" by Washington perceptions of state and local needs. Thus, there has been heavy pressure from the states and localities for more block grants—pressure welcomed by conservatives in Congress who usually favor taking power from Washington and giving it to the states. Conservatives believe that local people can make more judicious judgments on these matters than "Washington bureaucrats," who are not exposed to grass-roots opinion.

While Washington has yielded somewhat to these pressures, it has also resisted rather stoutly. Members of Congress (MCs) realize that constituent gratitude for Washington appropriations will accrue more directly to them if grants are specific and detailed than if Washington hands the states a lump of money and the latter distribute that money as they see fit to specific groups. The states will *appear* to be the major benefactor if they apportion the funds, whereas MCs will *appear* in that role if they do the job. Since Washington raises the taxes that finance the benefits, Washington politicians would like to receive as much credit as possible.

Resistance springs from another consideration, too. Many MCs (especially liberals) do not trust the states to do a good job of dividing up the melon and administering it properly with "no strings attached."

The states have a much poorer system of bookkeeping and management than does the national government. They are often delinquent in their accountability for the use of public funds. More important, perhaps, is the subservience of state and local governments to powerful interest groups.[13] Business is *a* powerful interest in Washington, but it is often *the* dominant interest in states and localities. The state educational lobbies also have vast power, as do state medical societies, bar associations, and many other groups.

For all its vulnerability to special interests, Washington does represent a better balance of interests than do any of the states or cities. Almost all interests are represented in the national government, but certain interests are clearly overrepresented at local levels. For example, the Du Pont (synthetic materials) interests have enormous political power in Delaware, as does coal in West Virginia, the auto interests in Michigan, oil in Texas and Louisiana, and cattle interests in some western states. In some cities major industrial enterprises supply much of the employment and have preponderant local political power.

Liberals believe that the interests that suffer most at the state and local levels are the poor and minority groups. While the latter have powerful champions and, sometimes, articulate organized lobbies in Washington, they are less articulate and organized at local levels.

It was at the local level, too, where segregation was most fiercely defended, requiring the Supreme Court and the national government to break down tenacious resistance to desegregated schools and desegregated public life in general. Those who have read American history recall that it was Nebraska that, in World War I, forbade the teaching of foreign languages in elementary schools, Oregon that indirectly forbade parochial schools, California that discriminated against citizens of Oriental ancestry, and Louisiana that gave birth to a colorful gubernatorial despot—the Kingfish, Huey Long[14]—to say nothing of a host of petty tyrannies in smaller localities.

Corruption is more of a problem at the local level as well. Where has it been more shameful than in New Jersey and Maryland, which used to spawn a scandal a day? Look at the periodic police scandals in New York City and the never-ending cases of nepotism, misfeasance, malfeasance, and conflicts of interest in Chicago. Or the "court house gangs" in county governments! Largely because the press does a poorer job of covering local government (since the public is less interested in local news than in the bigger, more dramatic national stories covered by national television), more people get away with more abuses at the local level. Or so, at least, many close observers conclude. It is one thing to idealize "grass-roots government" which is "close to the people," and quite another to look squarely at political realities at the local level.

Administrative efficiency is also very low locally. The worst administered public programs seem to be Medicaid and unemployment compensation, both locally run. Welfare programs in general are not much better managed—and they too are local responsibilities. As for the caliber of state legislators, no knowledgeable person believes that they are as a whole as intelligent, well educated, and generally capable as are their counterparts in Washington.

One textbook spoke for most political scientists when its authors wrote: "The federal government . . . has proved to be far more innovative, progressive and responsive in its policy making and in its use of new techniques and new technologies than have the state and local governments."[15] While it is true that California did pioneer in air pollution control, New York in water pollution laws, Oregon in the initiative and referendum, Wisconsin in various social welfare policies, state and local governments have, on the whole, been remarkably timid and unimaginative in dealing with local problems. Whether or not this is because our best minds find problem solving in Washington more attractive than coping with local dilemmas, these observations seem broadly accurate.

Whenever a generalization is made about 50 states and thousands of local governments, many notable exceptions are bound to be present. Wherever an exceptionally able governor or mayor is elected, state and local government is likely to be of higher quality. But the general indictment of grass-roots government contains so much truth that Washington is not eager to give local governments carte blanche to deal with local problems by unrestricted use of large amounts of federal money.

Despite this reluctance, pressures have been potent enough to bring about more block grants and what has been called *revenue sharing*. This program sets aside a specific portion of federal tax revenues for automatic annual return to the states on a largely "strings-free" basis. Revenue sharing achieved attention in Washington at a time when tax money was flowing more rapidly into federal coffers than was needed while states and cities—burdened with heavy educational, welfare, and inner-city problems—were sorely in need of fiscal help. Under President Nixon, as part of his "New Federalism," Washington authorized a "revenue-sharing" program that now gives the states over 10% of all the monies they receive from Washington.

Shortly after revenue sharing went into effect, the fiscal fortunes of states and cities began to improve, while Washington was beset with federal deficits on a huge scale. It is highly doubtful that Washington would have introduced the program if it had been able to see the comparative fiscal positions of national and local governments today, but apparently revenue sharing is here to stay. Fewer schoolchildren and more pensioners are compounding the problem.

Whatever the objective circumstances may be today, the national mood has increasingly been one of skepticism about and disillusionment with Washington. Accompanying this has been a powerful desire to return government "to the people"—meaning to state and local governments. While it makes eminently good sense to recognize that Washington has overextended itself and certainly cannot effectively administer its multitudinous programs from Washington except in terms of general criteria and broad directives, the national impulse to turn to local government for salvation finds little to recommend it from American history. More disillusionment lies ahead, in the opinion of this writer (and I respect his opinion!).

Notes

1. Richard Leach, *American Federalism* (New York: Norton, 1970), pp. 7–8.
2. Such as William H. Riker, *Federalism: Origin, Operation, Significance* (Boston: Little, Brown, 1964); and Franz L. Neumann, "Federalism and Freedom: A Critique," in *Federalism Mature and Emergent*, Arthur W. Macmahon, ed., (Garden City, N.Y., Doubleday, 1955).
3. Leach, *American Federalism*, p. 13.
4. Alfred H. Kelly and Winfred A. Harbison, *The American Constitution: Its Origins and Development*, 5th ed. (New York: Norton, 1976).
5. *Hoke v. U.S.* (1913).
6. *Wickard v. Filburn* (1942).
7. *Home Building and Loan Association v. Blaisdell* (1934)
8. Leach, *American Federalism*, quoting Gov. Rockefeller.
9. Rowland Evans, Jr., and Robert D. Novak, *Nixon in the White House* (New York: Random House, 1971), p. 243.
10. This section borrows shamelessly from Reo M. Christenson, *Heresies Right and Left* (New York: Harper & Row, 1973), Chap. 5.
11. Many state employees, however, work under programs subsidized by Washington, which thus distorts somewhat the picture of a seemingly stable level of Federal bureaucrats. Samuel C. Patterson, Roger H. Davidson and Randall Ripley, *A More Perfect Union* (Homewood, Ill., Dorsey, 1979), p. 573.
12. Robert Sherrill, with James David Barber, Benjamin I. Page, and Virginia W. Joyner, *Governing America* (New York: Harcourt Brace

Jovanovich, 1978), p. 459. For a dissenting view, see Ann R. Markusen and Jerry Fastrup, "The Regional War for Federal Aid," *The Public Interest,* Fall, 1978, 87–99.

13 See Grant McConnell, *Private Power and American Democracy* (New York: Random House [Vintage Books], 1970), pp. 104–105, 109. See also Sherrill, et al, *Governing America,* p. 469.

14 See Robert Penn Warren, *All the King's Men* (New York: Random House [Modern Library], 1953).

15 Sherrill et al., *Governing America,* p. 466.

CHAPTER 6
PUBLIC OPINION AND POPULAR GOVERNMENT

Ours is supposed to be a government "of, by and for the people." How much of this is myth and how much reality? Is our government really run "by the people" and "for the people?" Many people seriously question this. They suspect the politicians in Washington and the state capitals actually run the show with average Americans having little to say about it. Or powerful special intersts control the politicians, thereby sabotaging government "by the people." Is democracy at bottom a fraud and a farce, purporting to be government by the people when actually it is government by shrewd, calculating, selfish men (and not many women) who use the government to advance their economic interests—while maintaining a democratic façade to deceive the people into thinking that the government is really theirs? A disturbingly large minority of people seem to believe this.[1]

How Much Direct Popular Control?

Let's look at this issue. There is no way that the people, collectively, can directly run the government. They are busy with their jobs, their family, their garden, their bowling and TV. They have little time for running the government, even if this were technically possible. Most people also have little interest in government. They are primarily involved in their day-to-day activities; government is a remote abstraction that they grumble about but aren't interested in doing something about. Except, perhaps, to vote. And many do that out of a sense of duty, or habit, or because of subtle social pressure, rather than from an authentic desire to participate in self-government.

We could have a system of national referenda, whereby every adult in the United States could vote (if he or she wished) on all of the political issues facing the nation, or even on the most important issues, which someone would frame for the electorate. But not many thoughtful people think this makes sense. Most problems are so complex that bills dealing with them run to scores of pages of highly legalistic and technical language that the public would never wade through. Only greatly simplified measures could be offered the electorate, measures that would fail to do justice to the complexities of the problems with which they dealt. And while the voters would be confined to a yes or no vote on a given bill, legislators could deliberate on alternative bills as well as upon numerous amendments to these bills that might have merit.

If the public voted on just the major bills, it would still make judgments based on little more than hunch and prejudice; those judgments would be largely shaped, moreover, by massive propaganda campaigns, by shrewd sloganeering and emotional appeals, as self-seeking groups sought support from a bewildered electorate. Although elected legislators are not always that well informed and that coolly rational, at least they (or the legislative leadership of a particular bill) have heard all sides and given some thought to the public interest.

The general public also holds many contradictory views without realizing it. It believes, for example, that Washington is too big, too powerful, and too costly. At the same time polls show it favors wage and price controls (when inflation is high), national health insurance, federal action to ensure a job for everyone who wants one, more spending to control pollution, and more feder-

How Much Direct Popular Control?

al aid for big cities, for education, and to help black people. It also wants fewer government services.[2]

This rather absurd stew of simultaneously held opinions makes the voter look like a dunce—but only if we ask the voter to assume intellectual burdens he or she should not be expected to bear. Ours *is* a chaotic, confused, and bewildering world. To expect the average voter to have studied numerous, complex political and economic issues in some detail and to have formed coherent and consistent views that take account of the probable consequences of *this* action as against *that* action is to expect far too much. Skilled, full-time legislators fall short as well—but they at least can be expected to make more informed, rational judgments than Jane and John Doe, preoccupied as they are with the problems and strains of their personal lives.

Experience has shown, moreover, that there is a low voter turnout on referendum elections, a turnout that draws disproportionately from the more well-to-do citizens. The growing tendency of voters to indiscriminately reject school bond issues or school tax levies is not reassuring evidence of mass responsibility. Nor do referendum elections take into account the intensity of opinion, a crucial factor that representative government clearly does consider—and clearly should. Referenda do not make room for those political compromises that characteristically emerge from legislative chambers when hotly disputed matters are at stake—compromises that reduce public passions and promote political stability. As for direct popular decisions on delicate and complex foreign affairs issues, no foreign policy expert on this planet believes mass opinion is adequate to this task.

Thoughtful people, then, have deep misgivings about the growing tendency within the states to use the referendum as a means of letting the mass public make major policy decisions. The public may welcome the opportunity, but the overall implications of this process are exceedingly grave. If offhand opinions are better than those that come from a closer study of issues, the assumptions underlying education will have to be abandoned. Mass decision making is one more example of a good idea—popular government—carried so far that it degenerates into folly. There is no realistic substitute, in modern societies, for representative government.

How important is public opinion in our democracy? Abraham Lincoln once said, "With public opinion on your side, anything is possible; without it, nothing."

One facet of public opinion that is of enormous importance is often underestimated. Whatever power any elite groups, or the "invisible government," may have, it is sharply limited by the basic value system and public expectations of the great mass of Americans. The policymakers of this country, whether visible or invisible, cannot defy this system and maintain their power. To illustrate, the people are deeply committed to a system of representative government and free elections. In general, they want free speech, a free press, and freedom of religion. They are opposed to public ownership of the nation's productive facilities (mines, farms, factories). They want a national military establishment that is a second to none. They want to maintain a system of social security, unemployment compensation, workmen's compensation, and other policies that protect the people from economic disaster. They want government to act when inflation or unemployment becomes serious. A score of other popular values and expectations could be cited that policymakers must respect—or find their power evaporating.

Public opinion, then, sets the outer limits within which policymakers exercise discretion. The latter may be powerful, but only when they respect these public attitudes. This towering fact gives substance to what we call "popular government." Even though this aspect of public opinion is not conspicuously evident at any given time, its silent presence is fully recognized by policymakers. They know that *latent* public opinion can promptly become an *active* and all-powerful opinion if cherished values are flouted. Any president, for example, who recommended nationalizing the nation's farms would become politically dead overnight. The same could be said for a president who proposed to abolish our system of social security without an adequate substitute, or who called for repeal of the Nineteenth Amendment (granting suffrage to women).

Less extreme examples make the point, too. Although President Franklin D. Roosevelt had just been reelected in 1936 by the biggest margin in history (until then) and was at the pinnacle of his career in terms of public approval, he lost much of that approval when he proposed "packing" the Supreme Court with additional members so it would not block his programs. Most citizens favored his New Deal measures, but many of them became so disturbed by a proposal that violated their sense of propriety and smacked of impatient power hunger that they withdrew a significant part of their support. Roosevelt had to struggle throughout his second term for congressional support and often failed to get it primarily because he misread the public mind on this issue.

Similarly, Richard Nixon was in a powerful political position after his smashing victory over George McGovern in 1972. But when the public became convinced that Nixon had repeatedly lied, cheated on his income taxes, and obstructed justice by collaborating in a cover-up of illegal activities, his power as chief executive dissolved.

Thus, we begin our study of public opinion by recognizing that policymakers command power only if they are sensitive to what the people will not stand for. Jane and John Doe often are indifferent to what goes on in the political world, but when politicians violate their basic premises and expectations, that indifference can quickly give way to an indignation that destroys political careers.

(It is interesting to speculate on how many times presidents have dared do things they expected would arouse public disfavor. George Washington's promulgation of the Jay Treaty with Britain in 1795, continuance of Thomas Jefferson's embargo of warring European nations from 1807 to 1809 when the public regarded it as a failure, Harry Truman's firing of the popular General Douglas MacArthur for insubordination in 1951, Gerald Ford's pardon of Richard Nixon in 1975—these and a few others can be cited. But such instances are remarkably rare throughout our 200-year history. Presidents may miscalculate what the public will approve, but very, very seldom do they take important steps that, at the point of decision, they anticipate will meet with strong public disapproval. As for Congress, it almost never takes such a stand.)

So, public opinion in a general sense sets the boundaries within which public officials can safely operate. Within these boundaries public opinion also exercises a powerful influence, since virtually no decisions are made without attention to the opinions of those who care and make themselves heard.

If those who care disagree in about even numbers, policymakers may safely exercise their own judgment. If, however, a clear and persistent majority for or against a proposal is apparent, that majority will almost certainly be heeded—and for very good reasons. Politicians like to get reelected, and the best way to do that is to please the majority of those who are interested in the outcome of an issue.

Even this generalization needs to be refined. If a majority of interested persons mildly favors a given proposal, but a minority is intensely opposed, the minority will probably prevail. Why? Because they are likely to vote for or against a legislator because of his or her vote on *this* issue, while the majority will probably forget about that vote (if they ever knew what it was). Thus, when we say that policy in a democracy is ultimately determined by the majority of those who care, the degree of caring is usually of crucial importance.

Note the word "usually." Powerful interest groups give some organized elements of the population greater power than their numbers and degree of caring warrant. Courts are somewhat less concerned about public opinion than are legislative bodies, as attested by various pro-busing decisions to cope with racial discrimination in the public schools. The Federal Reserve Board, which has been granted policymaking independence in its effort to control the nation's money supply, is less responsive to public opinion than other government agencies. Legislation that slips past during the last hectic hours of a legislative session faces a less severe public opinion test. Powerful congressional committee chairs (like Senator Russell Long of Louisiana, chair of the Senate Finance Committee), who hold unrepresentative views can exact prices from other Members of Congress in return for clearing a given bill under their control. MCs worry less about public opinion on foreign policy matters (unless the public happens to be deeply concerned) than when domestic policy is involved. Even in these cases, however, if decisions are made that clearly affront the majority of those who care, subsequent political decisions in these areas will almost certainly reflect that displeasure.

Qualified, then, by quasi exceptions such as these, public opinion largely determines both what is done and what is not done in a democracy. The more important the issue, the more surely this rule prevails.

How Public Opinion Is Formed: Socialization

Many factors enter into the shaping of a person's opinions, including family, school, church, social groups, race, region, and nation. In addition the media—TV, radio, newspapers, and the publishing industries—play a role. And in our time the entertainment industry seems to have quite a lot of influence in shaping youthful attitudes and values. Let us look at each of these.

Not much needs to be said about the family, since its influence on political (and other) opinions is so well known.³ A close correlation normally exists between parental views on politics and those of their children. This is less true if adolescents do not get along with their parents, and their rebellion happens to take a political form. (A fairly rare occurrence). Such a development is likely only if politics is of great importance to the parent or parents so that repudiation of their political views is an appropriate form of revenge.

Partisan preferences are primarily determined by parental influence, although the number of young persons calling themselves "independents" (whatever their level of education) has grown substantially in recent years. The influence of higher education and of peer groups sometimes competes effectively with the family in shaping or reshaping other political attitudes but since children are intimately and continuously exposed to their parents during their most impressionable years, it is natural that the family would normally have the greatest impact.

How do families develop the party loyalties which tend to be so enduring? A hop, skip and jump through history may illuminate this phenomenon.

The Civil War was an event of such traumatic magnitude, involving issues so vital, that it set the broad pattern of party allegiance for nearly 70 years. Since the Republican party (the GOP) was the party of Lincoln and the party that won the war, millions of families in the North developed an abiding attachment to it. Similarly, since the Democratic party had been the party of secession, southern whites developed an equally tenacious loyalty to it. Although the Civil War was over and party attitudes toward that war were largely irrelevant to the campaigns and issues that followed, most Americans continued to vote a straight party line because the GOP "saved the Union" and because the Democratic party supported secession. It was really quite silly, and shows how irrational voting behavior can be. If voters were asked, in the 1920s, why they were voting Democrat or Republican, they would have given every answer except the real one—family tradition. Not that the voters' rather vague, fuzzy reply would be intended to deceive; they were usually not conscious of the roots of their loyalty. (Of course, the Republic and Democratic parties took continuing positions on controversial issues that were close enough to their supporters' views, to make allegiance possible. But the emotional attachment, harking back to an earlier period, gave stability to partisan ties.)

Although the Civil War was far and away the major determinant of voting patterns for 70 years, the election of 1896 had such emotional impact that it realigned voting patterns to some degree and was of enduring symbolic significance for both major parties. William Jennings Bryan, the Democratic presidential aspirant, aroused both fervent devotion and fervent hostility in 1896 and during his subsequent campaigns as Democratic standard bearer. Bryan (and the Democratic party) became identified with the interests of the debtor, the poor, the economically oppressed, and the working person. His eloquent attacks upon the bankers and the rich in connection with his campaign for free silver (which would have put more money in circulation and hence brought an inflation helpful to debtors) stamped him as the champion of the "common man." Meanwhile, the GOP, which denounced Bryan, the "Great Commoner," as an unsound, impractical, visionary fanatic, was seen as the party of "sound money," of prudent, successful people, of persons with conservative leanings. Although this image did not prevail, in most instances, against the more powerful images created by the Civil War, it altered the loyalties of many voters for decades to come.

The election of 1928, because it centered around the alleged danger of electing a Roman Catholic (Al Smith) to the White House, was another major historical event that shaped enduring loyalties for or against the Democratic party both by Catholics and anti-Catholics. So did the prohibition issue, which was of great importance to millions of voters. The Democrats, who favored the end of Prohibition and the GOP, which wanted it continued, attracted the warm allegiance of many voters from 1928 to 1932—an allegiance that persisted for "wets" and especially for "drys" long after 1933, when the Eighteenth Amendment was repealed. The issue had such great emotional content for millions that it had a powerful partisan carry-over effect for decades.

Next to the Civil War, however, no historic event affected family voting loyalties as much as the Great Depression and the New Deal. The depression involved not only a massive and scary stock market crash but the closure of thousands of banks, unemployment of one-fourth of the workers, and the bankruptcy of thousands of businesses. Vast numbers of farmers and home owners were unable to pay the interest on their mortgages and lost their homes. The depression hit so hard and lasted so long (in 1940, the unemployment rate was still over 15%) that it was bound to have a lasting impact on the politics of the era. People developed intensely favorable or hostile attitudes toward Franklin D. Roosevelt and his New Deal, that fundamentally realigned party loyalties. The Democrats not only won the 1932 election but became the party commanding enduring majority support. The public has deviated from Democratic party presidential loyalty from time to time, if especially attractive Republicans like Dwight Eisenhower headed that party's ticket or particularly unappealing figures like George McGovern led the Democrats, but voter loyalty to a Democratic Congress has remained consistent since 1932. (The only exceptions were in 1946 and 1952.)

Franklin Roosevelt was generally perceived as a vigorous, confident, determined reformer who disciplined big business, helped the labor unions, and brought about a measure of economic recovery. The legislative achievements of his first six years were probably the most impressive of any president in American history. Since the term "New Deal" often means little to students today, a brief recital of its major features is in order. Included in the New Deal legislative package were the following:

1. The Federal Deposit Insurance Corporation, which insured bank deposits against bank failure
2. An agricultural law, which protected farmers from disastrously low prices
3. The Civilian Conservation Corps, which provided jobs for unemployed youth
4. The Works Progress Administration (WPA), which gave millions of

jobless a chance to build roads, bridges, and schools instead of receiving a dole
5. The Home Owners' Loan Corporation, which protected property owners from losing their homes
6. The Federal Housing Administration (FHA), which helped potential home owners borrow money at low interest rates
7. The Wagner Act guaranteeing workers the right to organize or join unions without suffering discrimination.
8. The Tennessee Valley Authority (TVA), to generate electricity (and jobs) as well as reduce floods
9. A minimum-wage law
10. The Social Security Act, protecting the aged, and the jobless[4]

The impact of these measures, plus Roosevelt's buoyant, reassuring personality, created Democratic loyalties that, like those created by the Civil War, persisted long after new issues had arisen making these legislative achievements largely irrelevant. People vote for party images, kept alive by skillful party propagandists who play upon the past, to a much greater degree than many people realize. Often we vote the past more than the present.

It looked for awhile as if the Democratic party was going to be labeled the "war party" and the Republicans as the "peace party." It was a silly notion, spawned by a partisan spirit run amok, but the perception was potentially very damaging to the Democrats. A Democratic president led us into World War I, Roosevelt was president when Pearl Harbor was attacked, Truman brought us into war against North Korea, and Lyndon Johnson was largely responsible for our massive involvement in the Vietnam War. On the other hand, President Eisenhower, a Republican, had promptly extricated us from the Korean War in 1953.

President Nixon had a splendid opportunity to persuade the public that the GOP was the "peace party" when he became president in 1968. The Vietnam War had come to be regarded, by many, as Johnson's war, and Johnson was a Democrat. But instead of opting for a quick end to what had become an unpopular war, President Nixon dragged out the withdrawal of American troops for four years, allowing Democratic liberals to take the lead in urging a more rapid end to American involvement. By not following in Eisenhower's footsteps, Nixon blew the party's chances of gaining a major and perhaps long-lived advantage over the Democrats.

Family tradition, then, shaped by history, has a large influence in shaping political opinions, but schools also have a role. Schools help transmit accepted American values and attitudes to their students. Schools have long been skittish about introducing controversial (to say nothing of heretical) ideas to students, since parents are likely to come storming in to the principal and demand, "What's going on here, anyway?" But standard American attitudes about the Constitution, free elections, free enterprise, free speech, fair trial, fair play, competition, and other such concepts were directly and indirectly taught and reinforced in the schools. Occasionally a teacher with an unusually forceful personality or persuasive qualities advanced controversial opinions that made a lasting imprint on their students, but this was infrequent. The typical school atmosphere was one of caution—some would say timidity—because teachers are solicitous of their personal security. Offended parents make life difficult for principals, who in turn make life difficult for "troublemakers" on their staff. (In some high schools, however, heterodoxy has become fashionable in recent years!)

Do churches, too, help shape political opinion? It is doubtful that there is much difference between the political attitudes of those who attend the major churches and those who do not. True, many (and perhaps all) of the major churches have liberal wings that have taken activist positions on many political issues. It is unclear, however, whether this liberalism springs from their church as much as from other liberal influences to which its members were exposed, or from members' personal interpretation of certain passages of Scripture. In general, the major churches appear to have a minor influence on the political attitudes of their members.

Some of the smaller churches, however, clearly do shape some of the political views of their members. Christian Scientists are predisposed to take a dim view of governmental initiatives in the field of health. Mormons are more likely to oppose welfare programs than most people are. Jehovah's Witnesses are indoctrinated with the belief that governments are largely under the control of the devil. Members of conservative religious groups are strongly inclined to oppose abortions (as do many Catholics), the unfettered distribution of pornography, and the advertising of cigarettes and liquor. Their conservative religious views are normally accompanied by conservative political views, including a belief that politics is a sordid business. Unitarians, on the other hand, are liberal on virtually everything. And Quakers oppose a large military budget and policies that seem militaristic.

Catholics, Jews, Blacks, and Other Religious and Ethnic Groups

In the past Catholics have tended to be more pro–labor union than Protestants, more liberal on welfare issues, and more conservative on many moral issues. In recent years these differences have declined. Catholics remain more inclined to vote Democratic than non-Catholics. It may be useful to inquire into the reasons for this since we are interested in knowing not only what political influences various groups have on their members but also why they take the positions they do.

In the nineteenth and early twentieth centuries most of the Catholic immigrants (often Irish or Italian) settled in the large cities at a time when many of these cities were dominated by Democratic political organizations (called "machines" by those who disliked them). The political "bosses" who ran the "machines" often had ward and precinct organizations whose leaders made themselves useful to the potential voters in their prescribed area. They helped them find jobs, brought food when things were desperate, intervened with the local magistrate if the voters' children got in trouble, and generally acted in a benevolent way. In return, they counted on and usually won support at the polls in a reciprocally useful relationship.

From the time of William Jennings Bryan onward, the Democrats were often regarded as the party of the "common man," especially of the skilled, semiskilled, and unskilled workers. The Catholic immigrants largely fell into these categories. As such, they were prime candidates for the labor unions, which increasingly were headed by Catholics loyal to the Democratic ticket.

The Democratic party, eager to consolidate and strengthen its standing with Catholic voters, developed a habit of giving the chairmanship of the party's national committee to a Catholic. By the time the Democrats ran New York's Al Smith as the first Catholic for president in 1928, people who were prejudiced against Catholics usually found themselves more comfortable in the Republican party. Many of them feared a Catholic president would take orders from the pope. Dark stories circulated about the horrors that secretly took place in convents and monasteries, stories reminiscent of the 1830s and 1840s, when religious bigotry was at its height in this country. The more lurid the tales and the more open the hostility against a Catholic candidate, the more strongly the Catholics leaned toward the Democrats. The propensity to vote the Democratic ticket remained during the Roosevelt and Truman years, dropped somewhat when Adlai Stevenson ran against the almost universally admired Dwight D. Eisenhower in 1952 and 1956, but strongly recovered when the Democrats nominated Catholic John F. Kennedy in 1960. Today, Catholics ordinarily support Democrats more than they do Republicans, but the margin has been reduced as the "Catholic issue" has faded.

Jewish voters, whose Democratic party attachment is much stronger than that of the Catholics, offer another instructive example of group impact on personal voting patterns. This preference draws on many streams of influence.[5] Jewish immigrants from Europe came from a continent that experienced far more clerical and anticlerical divisions than the United States has known. Christian (usually Catholic), political parties long competed with parties having a democratic socialist flavor. It was only natural that European Jews would have identified with non-Christian parties, which were also the more leftist parties and which had the least identification with the frequently anti-Semitic status quo. In this country the Republicans were the less liberal party and the most attached to a status quo also perceived as somewhat anti-Semitic.

Jewish tendencies to vote Democratic were strengthened by the ancient Hebrew prophets' calls for social justice—a justice that elevated the cause of the poor and the downtrodden to a position of prominence. The Democratic party was seen as the one with the greatest interest in the poor, while the Republicans were seen as the party of the rich, the comfortable, and the "better set" that excluded Jews from their clubs.

The Jewish tendency to vote for Democrats was given a major boost by Franklin D. Roosevelt, who appointed many Jewish intellectuals to his "brain trust," an advisory group, and later led the war against Adolph Hitler—who had slaughtered nearly 6 million Jews in the most barbaric act of genocide in history. When Democrat Harry S. Truman strongly championed the establishment of the state of Israel in 1947, Jewish tendencies to vote for Democrats were strengthened. Eisenhower's secretary of state, John Foster Dulles, followed a more "even-handed" policy toward Israel and the Arab states, further cementing the Jewish-Democratic relationship. Since World War II, then, Jews have ordinarily voted Democratic by margins of three or four to one.

The black vote also demonstrates the role of historical experience in shaping a group's voting bent. Blacks decisively favored the GOP from 1865 to 1933 since Republican Abraham Lincoln was the "Great Emancipator" and southern whites, who kept the blacks "in their place," were solidly Democratic. To black voters these perceptions clearly outweighed whatever substantive policy differences might exist between the parties or the relative merits of particular nominees.

But all this changed with Roosevelt's New Deal. Blacks were especially hard hit by the Great Depression, and New Deal policies designed to rescue the impoverished were of special importance to them. The image of the Democratic party as the party of action, of concern for the "little guy," and of economic reform—combined with Roosevelt's personal popularity—was so clearly etched on black minds that the 70-year-old identification with the GOP was washed away. Eleanor Roosevelt's open championing of black rights (including black opera star Marian Anderson's right to sing in Constitution Hall against the protests of the Daughters of the American Revolution) further accelerated the movement to the Democrats. So did Roosevelt's wartime order establishing the Fair Employment Practices Commission, President Truman's surprisingly advanced civil rights program (which included desegregating the armed forces), Dwight Eisenhower's lack of enthusiasm for the Supreme Court decision outlawing segregation in public schools in 1954, and the role of liberal Democrats in strongly backing fair housing and equal employment legislation in the 1960s. When the GOP nominated Barry Goldwater, a conspicuous opponent of civil rights legislation, in 1964, the party lost its chances of winning much black support.

(The political loyalty of another social group seems somewhat anomalous. Business people, contrary to their apparent economic self-interest, consistently support the GOP. Studies show that business failures are higher under Republican than Democratic administrations, while the profit rate is higher under Democratic administrations.[6] But, no mattter, business people feel a spiritual kinship with Republican politicians that overrides the economic record. Republican oratory is their kind of talk, and Republicans are their kind of people; these count for more than the statistical record. Let Marxists chew on that awhile!)

Concepts of class and class interest play a considerable part in determining voting loyalties but the picture is more confusing than might be expected. A majority of blue-collar workers tend to see the Democratic party as the party most sympathetic to their interests, yet a large minority of them vote Republican. White collar workers logically belong to the "working class," but these workers have often identified more with management than with labor and have been more friendly to the GOP than have blue collar workers.

How people perceive themselves is more politically significant than the objective facts concerning income, education, and job prestige that theoretically determine one's class. Almost one-third of the American people do not think of themselves as members of any class, while those who are more class-conscious tend to branch off, rather evenly, between self-identified members of the working class and of the middle class. About one-third of those who think of themselves as middle class hold blue collar jobs, and vice versa.

The reluctance of those who would empirically be classified as working class to think of themselves as working class, with economic and political interests that would lead to political unity, is the despair of many socialists. But matters of religion, snobbery, ethnicity, moral value systems, parental attitudes, the appeal of particular political personalities, and historic political relationships often override embryonic concepts of class consciousness or class interest. Party loyalties often have very complex and obscure roots, nourished by many complex and obscure forces; they remain among the most significant and enduring political facts in American history.

The impact of one's social group has other applications. A person whose fellow workers hold certain political views in common is likely to move toward those views in order to gain greater social acceptance, unless contrary views are strongly held; then, the person—unless especially combative—may simply decline to express his or her opinions. But if your views are lightly held, the adjustment may not be difficult to make. The same holds true if one is a member of a country club, and winning the approval of its members is important. This principle applies to any social group whose favor is coveted. People may not consciously tailor their views to others' tastes, but gradually they may find themselves seeing things in the others' way.[7]

Probably adult political opinions are shaped as much by whom one marries as by any single influence. The strongest personality in the home, if interested in elections and political issues, is likely to impose many of his or her political views on the more passive mate. That depends, of course, on the degree of amity that exists between them. If there is discord and ill will, political conversion is unlikely; indeed, a contrary effect may take place. But since opinion adjustments are one way to promote greater domestic tranquility, and since most marital partners prefer peace and harmony, adjustments are frequently made, consciously or unconsciously.

Residence in a given region has often influenced the formation of political views. For whites, only extraordinary strong personalities living in the South from 1820 to 1865 did not accept the dominant views on slavery. This was no less true on racial attitudes after the Civil War up to the 1960s. To have favored full equality for blacks, including the elimination of arbitrary voting barriers and the full desegregation of southern social and political life, would have led to the ostracism of the individual holding such views. Southern whites absorbed the dominant white views on race as naturally and unconsciously as they absorbed the belief that family, church, and school were desirable institutions, or that the United States was the greatest country on earth. No formal indoctrination was needed; people acquired the proper attitudes in a thousand subtle ways, simply by living in an environment that took white supremacy for granted.

Similarly, people automatically acquire many views because they are born into a given country. American children learn to believe in democracy, to dislike communism, to believe in the virtues of competition, and to trust that a massive nuclear arsenal will prevent atomic wars directly involving the United States. They come to believe that industrialization promotes human well-being, that politicians are often crooked, and that, whenever possible, political problems should be left to state and local governments. They learn these things mostly from school and home, but the total national environment also tends to impose or reinforce those beliefs. It is difficult to be an American and not believe them.

We are also influenced by the spirit of the times, a spirit frequently conditioned by major historical events that jolt us into different perspectives: Americans tended to be isolationist in world affairs (Latin America excepted) until the two World Wars and Soviet domination of Eastern Europe transformed our mood into one of interventionism. We then intervened to prevent the spread of communism all over the world through the creation of the North Atlantic Treaty Organization (NATO) to block any Russian designs on Western Europe; the Southeast Asia Treaty Organization (SEATO) to restrain the communists in Indochina; through the Korean War, the Berlin airlift, the Greek-Turkish aid plan and other treaties binding us to help nations protect themselves from communist aggression. American opinion overwhelmingly supported these preventive and interventionist acts. (Children raised in the Soviet Union learned to see these acts as American imperialism, intended both to protect and promote capitalist investments and trade abroad and to repress the efforts of oppressed people to throw off the yoke of colonialism.)

But when the disastrous Vietnam War ended—with nothing to show for our efforts but increased inflation, debt, and thousands of dead or crippled veterans—American attitudes shifted again. Further involvement in foreign disputes, at least, in a direct military sense, was now frowned upon.

Similarly, Americans long tended to believe that government should not meddle with the nation's economy, allowing "natural" economic forces to correct whatever economic problems or abuses arose. Nor should the government spend much money on programs to relieve personal economic insecurity. But when the Great Depression hit with devastating force in 1929, Americans began to see things differently. From that point on they would demand that the government in Washington accept responsibility for keeping workers employed and the economy prosperous. And they warmly supported social security, unemployment compensation, disability insurance, farm price supports, and other programs designed to provide an economic safety net for individuals who might otherwise be impoverished through no fault of their own. Thus a continuing preference for "local responsibility" was balanced with a new-found awareness of what local governments could not do that the people wanted done.

Major national experiences do more to politically educate a nation than all the books that professors, journalists, and others write. The average person draws certain broad conclusions from national or international events that directly affect his or her life, and these are passed on to children. Books reach a minority of the people, are usually challenged by other books, and generally have a small impact on the broad currents of public opinion. (A few exceptions, through the sweep of history, might be the Bible, the Koran, Charles Darwin's *Origin of Species*, Karl Marx's *Das Kapital*, and Sigmund Freud's works. These have been challenged, too, but they have left their mark on people's opinions, including the hidden value framework within which political opinions arise.)

The Media and the Public

How important are TV and the press in shaping public opinion? Here we must speculate since it is exceptionally difficult to isolate the impact of TV and the press from the impact of other forces that affect public opinion. We can make some educated guesses, however.

More people get their news from TV than from newspapers, surveys show, and people find television news more believable,[8] although this does not tell us how much influence television has. Conceivably, newspaper editors and columnists who interpret the news have more impact than TV editorials, which are usually pretty bland. In deciding what is newsworthy (from a chaotic jumble of news stories) and how much emphasis to place on stories or how to treat them, TV and the press subtly affect our own notions of what news is important and how we should perceive it.

For the most part, those who determine what we see on TV news programs and in newspapers make their decisions according to their estimate of what their readers will think is important or interesting. But to an undetermined but significant degree, their personal value system and interests intrude from time to time. This is particularly true where moral questions are involved, such as abortion, pornography, the death penalty, the feminist movement, racial equality, and the like. On most of these issues the people who report, process, and comment on the news tend to be more liberal than the American people. (See Seymour Lipset, "The New Class and the Professoriate," *Society*, Jan–Feb., 1979.) This may be less true in small towns and some cities, but it is certainly true of those who work for the national TV networks and most big-city newspapers. (Publishers, on the other hand, are less liberal than their employees.) Newspapers and communications personnel, in general, tend to be somewhat more cynical than the average person, to be more tolerant of deviant behavior and ideas, and to be impatient with moral conservatism.

Because television's overriding interest is in maximizing its audience, TV talk shows tend to be receptive to people who attack cherished American values and institutions. These people have a shock value that raises the Nielsen rating (so important to attracting advertising dollars), so they are heard more frequently than their proportionate support in the population might lead one to expect. Given this national platform so frequently, these dissenters doubtless appear to be more numerous than they really are and thus have more credibility than if TV did not exist.

Television has influenced public opinion in other ways. During the 1950s the televised congressional hearings of Senator Joseph McCarthy's reckless and irresponsible charges of communist infiltration into the army had much to do with the decline of support for the senator. The first Kennedy-Nixon debate in 1960 helped convince the American people that Kennedy was indeed a worthy candidate for the presidency. Television's overemphasis upon Carter's 1976 victory in the New Hampshire primary, along with its downgrading of Senator Henry Jackson's victories in Massachusetts and New York, may have contributed significantly to Carter's nomination that year.[9] "Sixty Minutes" undoubtedly makes a considerable impression upon the views of millions of Americans.

The network TV news programs tend to represent about as objective reporting as one can expect in a world in which total objectivity is not possible. The same seems true of the Associated Press and United Press International news services. Since they provide stories for newspapers of every political slant, their news accounts are usually quite unbiased.

Some newspapers influence public opinion much more than others, of course. Most students of the media believe that the *New York Times*, the *Washington Post*, and the *Wall Street Journal* are publications that have extraordinary impact. They have it for many reasons. First, they are superior papers, judged by professional standards. They are responsible and sometimes courageous, qualities that attract top journalistic talent. Second, they are read by the politicians in Washington who play the largest part in making and administering public policy. Third, national TV news and editorial departments get much of their news from these papers, which means their news orientation is appreciably affected by them. Finally, opinion leaders throughout the nation are educated by these papers and take their cues from them. They are "national" newspapers, not just city dailies.

These newspapers share prominence as political opinion moulders with magazines like *Time* and *Newsweek*—and, to a lesser degree, *U.S. News and World Report*. *Time* and *Newsweek* devote themselves to the interpretation of the news; their readers' opinions are unquestionably affected by the slant that these prestigious weeklies give to the news. When people have strong opinions or predispositions, they are not easily influenced by even their favorite magazines or commentators; but when strong feelings are not present, the influence is considerable. Other magazines that may be unusually important in the opinion formation of leaders are the *New Republic, Commentary, Foreign Affairs, The Washington Monthly, Harper's, Fortune,* and *Business Week*.

One should not overlook the influence of a few columnists who have unusual prestige and a large following. Persons like David Broder, George Will, Joseph Kraft, Milton Friedman, Paul Samuelson, and Jack Anderson are read closely by many people who are themselves opinion moulders on a lesser scale.

Political reporters also may play a very important role in screening prospective presidential candidates. They come to know leading political figures rather well from first-hand observation, and their published analyses can sometimes make or break a struggling candidate. (See James David Barber, *Race for the Presidency* (Englewood Cliffs, N.J.: Prentice-Hall, 1978, p. 77.)

Finally, the mass entertainment industry probably has a great deal to do with the shaping of the political values and attitudes of the young.[10] Insofar as "pure" entertainment is concerned, this has little direct political significance (although attitudes toward violence and the police may be affected). But at a time when moral beliefs increasingly impinge on public affairs (such as public policy on abortion, pornography, homosexuality, drugs, the integrity of the family, etc.), the influence of the mass entertainment industry takes on special significance. Its offerings are often intimately related to attitudes bearing upon sexual behavior, life styles, and public policy related to these areas. That the mass entertainment industry promotes "liberal" attitudes goes without saying. In fact, the members of that industry are probably more "permissive" and more hostile to traditional American values on sex, the family, religion, and authority than any cultural group in the nation. Since they speak to young people at a time when many of them are in a rebellious mood and are questioning traditional values, it would not be surprising if the industry had an important impact. How much influence, however, is something no one knows.

Political Opinions and Personal Integrity

Once the various family and other environmental influences have created our political opinions and inclinations, we protect and reinforce them in certain ways. We expose ourselves to TV commentators, newspapers, columnists, news magazines, and political candidates who tend to share our views; we shy away from those who don't. We tend to remember facts or statements that buttress our opinions and to forget those that attack them. We minimize facts we dislike and exaggerate those that reinforce our views. We tend to believe our favorite candidates hold views more similar to ours than they really do. We interpret their comments generously and uncritically, while putting unflattering interpretations on similar statements by politicians we dislike. The nearer we come to an election, the more virtuous our favorite candidates become and the more menacing their opponents appear.

How rationally, then, do we really form our opinions? Are we the helpless victims of our happenstance environments, with our intelligence limited to providing convenient rationalizations for what our environments have predisposed us to believe?

To an uncomfortable degree this seems to be the case. Our opinions *are* largely shaped by the accidents of environment, even if this does tend to challenge our dignity and self-respect. Almost no one formulates an opinion based on a thorough study of the available facts, a systematic exposure to contrary views, and a dispassionate weighing of the evidence. Even if one tried, the final judgment would take place in a context of established personal values that have largely subjective roots.

Fortunately, our opinions need not be wholly the product of chance. Those who come to understand and appreciate what intellectual integrity means are able, to some extent, to establish a degree of personal autonomy in forming opinions that partially rescues them from the tyranny of chance.

We probably cannot, by the application of our intellects, change our value system very much. That system is relatively fixed by the time we reach adolescence. But relatively objective rational considerations may alter our beliefs concerning the most effective ways to pursue our value-directed goals. Thus, one's value system might require that health care should be available equally to all, regardless of income. But whether this is best achieved by one form of national health insurance rather than another, or by some combination of public and private insurance, or whether national health insurance might introduce such a cumbersome bureaucracy that the nation (including the poor) would be ill served by it—these are choices that can be made after a careful examination of the alternatives and of the experience of other nations.

Or one can believe that welfare recipients should have a reasonably generous minimum living standard but discover that a certain payment level would give those on welfare more income than persons working full time at the minimum wage. That would involve another personal value—a belief that public policy should encourage people to work. Study and reflection, then, can show that various values may give conflicting signals, and that our value priorities, once clearly perceived in a context of relevant facts and alternatives, lead to different policy stands than those we had originally held. Thus, we may quite rationally change our policy opinions without altering our value system.

Intellectual integrity, once adopted as a value, requires us to give due weight to facts we dislike and to cogent opinions we find distasteful. Instead of ignoring them or minimizing them, this integrity demands that we give them due respect and adjust, not our values, but our strategy for maximizing public policy reflecting those values. In adhering to intellectual integrity, we become more rational human beings, and we win more independent control over our opinions and our lives than if we do not respect it.

None of us practices intellectual integrity fully and at all times. The more deeply we are emotionally committed to an opinion, the more difficult it is to adhere to such integrity. But the consistency of its presence is one of the surest marks of the truly honest person.

Liberals and Conservatives: The Fruitful Feud

No appraisal of public opinion should overlook the liberal-conservative conflict that is such a permanent feature of the policy-shaping terrain. Most Americans are not highly ideological. That is, they have no coherent, integrated general philosophy about the proper role of government, a philosophy which consistently guides their thinking on specific issues. (Only about half of the voters know what liberal and conservative mean and far fewer than that think consistently in these terms.) But the more ideologically concerned voters tend to be the most politically active elements in the nation. And if we can accurately identify a citizen, politician, columnist, editor, magazine, or newspaper as liberal or conservative, that label tells more about them, by far, than any adjective we can apply. If liberals dominate a group, we can predict with considerable accuracy what stand that group will take on a wide range of issues. If a legislator is a bona fide conservative, his or her vote can be prophesied correctly over an equally wide range.

We turn first to the political liberal. The meaning of that term has changed quite dramatically since the early nineteenth century, when modern liberalism first developed, and it has been subject to constant revision as new issues have arisen and as our national experience has shed new light on the validity of current dogmas.

In the early nineteenth century a liberal was someone who wanted to prevent the government from meddling with the economy, especially in matters of trade. Tariffs, subsidies, export quotas, import controls, governmental privileges to favored businesses—these were seen as well-meant but essentially pernicious interferences with free trade and a free market. Let businessmen compete freely, and the free market would direct their economic activities far better than any governmental edict, the liberals believed. Drawing on the teachings of Adam Smith's *The Wealth of Nations*, liberals held that the search for profit would direct entrepreneurs into production and trade channels that would best serve buyers and thus the nation. Those who defended this economic order are now called "classical liberals," and they sound very much like the business conservatives of today. But in the twentieth century, liberalism came to mean something quite different. Experience demonstrated that unregulated profit seeking produced monopolies, exploitation, ruthless and unfair forms of competition, customer gouging, economic booms and busts, and a degree of economic insecurity for individuals that seemed intolerable.

First, what a modern liberal is not. The liberal is not just "Someone who favors change;" it depends on what *kind* of change. If fascism or communism were to come to the United States, either would represent change but the liberal would be appalled by them. Nor would he or she favor repeal of the progressive income tax, elimination of the Food and Drug Administration, aid for parochial schools, or a million other changes that might be made. It all depends on what *kind* of change is being proposed.

Modern liberals typically hold a series of attitudes toward public policy that constitute their political ideology. (An ideology is a reasonably coherent body of ideas concerning social good and social change.)

First, they favor the use of governmental power, at all levels of government, to improve the well-being of economic underdogs. The economic lower class is the constant object of their solicitude. Governmental programs that help those on the lower end of the income scale win their enthusiastic approval. Thus, liberals usually want to raise the minimum wage, provide more generous benefits for the unemployed, supply more adequate assistance for those on welfare, help migratory workers, install national health insurance, and so forth. For this reason liberals normally worry more about unemployment than about inflation. The unemployed are often the poorest of the poor so that getting jobs for them has higher priority than preventing inflation—if a policy choice must be made. (Of course if inflation reaches a sufficiently severe level, its control becomes the highest priority for liberals, too.)

One of the best criteria for identifying liberals is their attitude toward taxation. Liberals yearn to place higher taxes on upper-income groups while reducing them for lower-income groups. Closing "tax loopholes" that benefit the rich enlists their warm support as well. And, they favor using the tax system to "redistribute wealth" from the more affluent to the less affluent elements of our society.

Liberals were ardent supporters of the civil rights movement of the 1960s. They favored open housing laws and gave busing to achieve integration strong support, at least during the early phases of the controversy over the latter issue.

Liberals have a reverent attitude toward the Bill of Rights, which they interpret in interesting ways. The oppose almost all aid for parochial schools, believing such aid violates the "establishment of religion" clause in the First Amendment (even though such aid would help poorer parents send their children to the school of their choice). During the raging disputes over the rights of domestic communists in the 1950s, they insisted the communists should have full constitutional rights, including the right to advocate violent overthrow of the government, the right to propagandize freely, to seek support at the polls, and to be free from political harassment by the House Un-American Activities Committee. Liberals are very zealous about guaranteeing criminal defendants full notification of their rights and full protection from police coercion or unreasonable searches and seizure. (What is "unreasonable" to them may seem "reasonable" to nonliberals.) Where the conservative would stress "national security" and "law and order," the liberal stresses individual freedom and the need to guard against abuses of law enforcement powers.

Liberals tend to take permissive stands on various moral issues. They would not interfere with the distribution of pornographic materials to adults. They were among the first to advocate lifting severe criminal penalties for the use of marijuana. They are willing for public funds to be used to finance abortions for those on welfare or those receiving Medicaid. And they supported the Supreme Court's decision forbidding prayers and Bible reading as official school exercises. Liberals do not like big business very much. They are not socialists (with a few exceptions), but they cast a wary, vigilant, and suspicious eye on big corporations, which they suspect are usually up to no good. Liberals used to adore labor unions, but these days their ardor has cooled. Their reflex sympathies still tend to be pro-union, but union abuses of power (plus the fact that union members often are not economic underdogs any longer) have diminished their devotion to unions and union causes. Still, in a showdown battle between unions and big corporations, liberals tend to side with unions more often than not.

Stiff enforcement of consumer and environment laws automatically elicits liberal support. If big auto companies and big corporations in general stoutly resist these laws, that is taken as evidence that the laws are beneficent.

In recent years liberals have opposed a large military budget, preferring to spend some of this money for domestic programs to help underdogs. They have been the strongest critics of the CIA, at least in part because the CIA has backed right-wing governments of which liberals disapprove. In general, liberals are internationally minded, feeling that the United States has an obligation to help economic underdogs abroad as well as at home. They were the strongest supporters of foreign economic aid until it became apparent that much of that aid was not helping the poor as much as it was helping sustain right-wing governments or was ending up in the pockets of landlords, bureaucrats, and clever entrepreneurs.

It should be emphasized that conservatives (at least the more moderate ones) usually differ from liberals only in degree. Where policy disputes arise on which reasonable people can differ, liberals and conservatives disagree *within a broader area of agreement.* For example, conservatives in Congress usually support the minimum wage, but when liberals would raise that wage 30 cents an hour, conservatives prefer a 20-cent raise. (Many conservatives, however, would like to repeal minimum-wage laws altogether.)

Conservatives usually support a progressive income tax, which hits the wealthy harder than the poor, but they prefer a lower maximum tax than liberals. Conservatives believe in the Bill of Rights, too, but in borderline cases, where good arguments can be made on both sides of a given interpretation of those rights, they gave higher priority to the interests of potential victims of crime higher than to certain arguable "rights" of the defendant. (Who is the underdog in these cases?) As an example, liberals tend to believe that incriminating evidence improperly seized by police should not be admissible in court. Conservatives, on the other hand, would permit its admission while calling for appropriate punishment of police who have violated the law.

Conservatives would not abolish unions or leave business unregulated. But they would usually not let strikers have food stamps or other welfare-type benefits, and they would give the auto companies a longer period in which to meet standards of exhaust emission controls or gasoline mileage. They would not vote to eliminate a foreign economic aid program costing $3 billion; instead, they would trim it by $1 billion dollars.

Still, conservatives often do oppose many programs, when they are first proposed, and then grudgingly accept them after they have been in effect awhile. But their general sympathies remain consistently probusiness, pro–law enforcement, anti–government spending (except for the military), antibureaucracy, anti–high taxes, pro–traditional moral values, antiwelfare, and pronationalism.

In recent years a new group labeled the Neoconservatives has received a good deal of public attention. Disillusioned liberals, they have moved to a point between the liberals and the conservatives. Most of their prolific writing has been critical of liberal goals and "illusions," criticism largely growing out of disappointment with the results of Lyndon Johnson's sweeping array of liberal-oriented "Great Society" programs.

Neoconservatives want to preserve most of the gains from the New Deal and post-New Deal period, and accept the need for welfare state programs to help the poor and eliminate unnecessary economic insecurity for the average American. They are more internationalist than nationalist in foreign affairs. But they deplore unnecessary bureaucracy, oppose "soak the rich" tax proposals, dislike the egalitarian tendencies they think liberals have, are dubious about affirmative action programs, are keenly aware of the limitations of government in bettering the human lot, are skeptical of proposals to give the public more direct control over public policy, and look upon the "free market" with more respect than do most liberals. In general, they are moral conservatives.

Intellectuals (Irving Kristol, Daniel Bell, Norman Podhoretz, Daniel Moynihan, and Nathan Glazer are regarded as leaders of the group), the Neoconservatives have had a notable impact on opinion leaders but have made a relatively small imprint on the average American. They are part of a national drift toward the Right; they are learned men who have made a thoughtful and essentially moderate appraisal of what America has experienced since 1965. They are perhaps closer, in outlook and temperament, to the Founding Fathers than any other intellectual group in the nation.

At present liberals are pining for the Big Cause that will bring fresh excitement and meaning into their lives. In earlier years they fought hard battles against the big trusts and Wall Street, made common cause with beleaguered labor unions, battled for the New Deal against its foes, sounded the alarm about Adolf Hitler, thundered against Senator Joseph McCarthy, gave their hearts to the civil rights crusade of the 1950s and 1960s, demonstrated fervently against the Vietnam War, and reveled in the Watergate revelations and Nixon's impeachment.

With these soul-stirring causes only a memory, liberals continue to concern themselves with the Equal Rights Amendment, the rights of homosexuals, equal access to abortion by poor women, consumer protection, environmental protection, anti-nuclear power, and a rearguard battle against governmental economies at the expense of the poor. But while these issues are extremely important to segments of the liberal camp, they do not provide the deep emotional satisfaction for all liberals which the earlier causes had brought. When will the next Big Cause appear? We don't know but life will be less sweet for liberals until it comes along.

Some people argue that the terms "liberal" and "conservative" are becoming out of date, in view of Democratic politicians' tendency, in an age of growing conservatism, to adopt conservative positions on policy issues. However, although the differences between liberals and conservatives occasionally blur when strong opinion tides are flowing, the underlying divisions continue to manifest themselves on concrete issues. They may be more conspicuous at one time than another, but they are an omnipresent and inevitable feature of political life. They will not go away—in this country or in any other—but they do require redefining from time to time.

What produces a full-fledged liberal or conservative? Conservative or liberal parents, you may say. But where do the original conservative or liberal impulses come from that are then transmitted to children? Both liberals and conservatives will give flattering explanations of why, at bottom, they are what they are (humanitarians versus hard-headed realists, for example); but no definitive answer can ever be given to the time origin of these political stances. Certainly there are many liberals who love the poor and unfortunate

How Americans saw themselves on a Liberal–Conservative scale (1977)

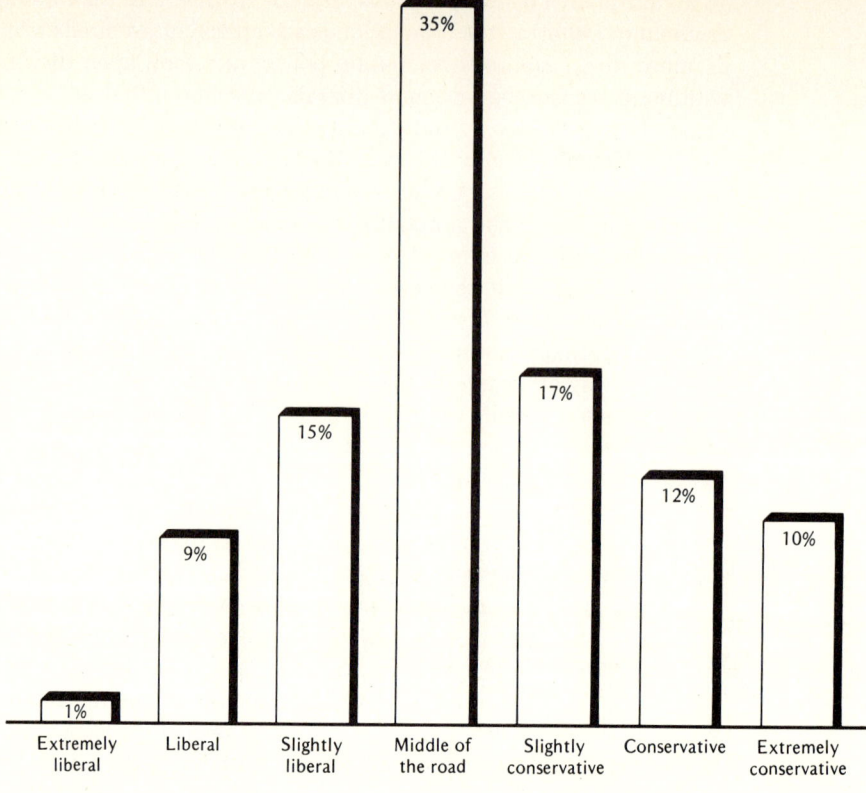

in the abstract but not the poor next door. And many conservatives are not so much philosophically conservative as anxious to preserve their wealth, maintain their status in society, and convince themselves that they are superior to less successful people. But not all liberals and conservatives are so motivated. And, many people are, of course, partly liberal and partly conservative.

In both camps one can find "knee-jerk" representatives. If something has a nice humanitarian ring to it, knee-jerk liberals will promptly endorse it, without bothering to ask many questions about visible costs, invisible costs, feasibility, and cumulative effects in conjunction with other programs. One can always find arguments, after taking a stand the heart approves, which makes one's position sound reasonable. Knee-jerk conservatives make their decisions in the same fashion, arriving at a conclusion first and looking for plausible arguments afterwards.

Liberals or conservatives who, while unavoidably retaining their general predisposition, withhold judgment on a proposal until they have had a chance to carefully evaluate it should be cherished. They are rare birds, indeed. If they sometimes acknowledge that their ideological opposites are right and their soul mates are wrong, they have the kind of integrity and open-mindedness that marks them as valuable national assets. Once this characteristic becomes known, they can work with both liberals and conservatives in a highly constructive relationship. Our head tends to follow our heart so consistently that those who can resist the knee-jerk tendency (in the political world) can become either leaders or mediators.

In most legislative bodies neither liberals nor conservatives are in a clear majority. Each side needs to win over a number of middle-of-the-roaders in order to prevail. This usually means they must moderate their positions and concede something to the other side. Relatively open-minded liberals or conservatives can be of great value in bringing these adjustments about.

A nation needs both liberals and conservatives. It needs intelligent liberals to criticize the status quo, recommend reforms, and breathe fresh vitality into our political institutions. But it needs intelligent conservatives who will ask sharp and searching questions to ensure that the liberals have thought things through, considered all the costs, and given enough attention to the practical problems that a proposal will involve and the long-range effects, as nearly as these can be determined. The American Essayist Ralph Waldo Emerson once wrote of liberals and conservatives, "Each is a great half but an impossible whole. Each exposes the abuses of the other but in a true society, in a true man, both must combine."[11]

Liberalism and conservatism are related to another important political question. Those without strong partisan attachments usually feel they vote for the "best person" rather than a mere party candidate. Many people take pride in voting this way and hold in some disdain those who are "party regulars." How defensible is this attitude?

For anyone who is exceptionally well informed about candidates' experience, policy views, and personal integrity, voting "the man and not the party" makes a good deal of sense. But those who are not very well informed may be voting for "the man, not the party" only because they recognize the name, shook the candidate's hand, liked his or her engaging manner, or had other trivial reasons. It is interesting, moreover, how often the "independents" somehow find the members of one party rather consistently more attractive than members of the other party—though they may be unaware that this pattern exists.[12] (Only about one voter in six is a true independent, although one in three thinks he or she is. About two-thirds are regulars and another one-sixth vote for one party most of the time.)

If a person knows that he or she is mostly a conservative or mostly a liberal—and does not know much about the candidates—it is rational to vote along Republican or Democratic party lines for state and national candidates. Not all Republicans are conservatives and not all Democrats are liberals, but this is generally the case. And since those labels predict voting behavior more accurately than any other labels, they enable the not-too-well-informed voters to support candidates who generally agree with them. In fact, the most politically alert, interested, and knowledgeable voters (who are usually the most ideological voters) tend to be party regulars much more often than do apathetic voters. So, voting "the man, not the party" often may be less laudable than it seems.

Citizens: Apathetic and Concerned

Why one votes as one does is an interesting question; whether citizens should feel guilty if they do not vote is a controversial one. Some political scientists do not concur in the popular view that voting is a "civic obligation" and that people ought to vote if they want to be good citizens. Citizens with little knowledge or interest in politics should not be nagged or shamed into voting and should not vote because it is the "thing to do." They should stay on their job or pull weeds in the garden or watch soap-operas instead. The better informed should decide elections; there is no merit in doing what one does badly. Of course, if voting appeases your conscience, despite your woeful ignorance about what you're doing, this is not the unpardonable sin.

But suppose people *want* to be well informed and just do not know how. Indeed, it is no easy task to know the positions of each and every candidate, and we have all had occasion to refrain from voting when our knowledge of the candidates did not permit an informed choice. And there are times, too, when we do vote but regret not knowing as much about the candidate as we should. To minimize those occurrences, however, conscientious voters can follow a few suggestions.

Several organizations and publications—including the Americans for Democratic Action, the American Conservative Union, the *New Republic* and *Congressional Quarterly*—print key congressional votes. These can help voters evaluate Members of Congress—but not their challengers. *Time* and *Newsweek* campaign stories often shed useful light on the more prominent national candidates. Public TV sometimes carries programs featuring savvy political observers who have educational value. Newspaper editorials in respected papers (if they are not strongly partisan) can be helpful. If one or two political issues are of overriding importance, organizations that are concerned about those issues can provide some information on candidate stands (if they have taken any). But for most state and national races, the best course probably is for the voter to know where he or she stands on the conservative-liberal scale, find out which candidates are regarded as relatively more liberal or conservative, and vote accordingly.

Although some textbooks devote a good deal of space to discussing this country's comparatively low voting turnout,[13] the problem seems overblown. If middle-class nonvoters went to the polls, there is no evidence that they would vote much differently from middle-class voters. It is true that if the poor and the various minority groups that now have a low voting turnout were class-conscious and voted as blocs for candidates espousing feasible programs specially tailored to their needs, a larger turnout *would* have an important political impact on our system. But their situation might not change drastically even then. No one really knows how to help these groups, in politically feasible ways, except by strengthening the economy in general. And no group has a magic answer to that problem. Indeed, though many might disagree, there seems to be no practicable national program that minority group leaders or champions of the poor currently espouse that would be enacted if these minorities voted in larger numbers. The principal difference might be a greater federal effort, when fighting inflation, to simultaneously appropriate more

Citizens: Apathetic and Concerned

money for public service jobs. This is not unimportant but neither would it make the dramatic difference that critics of nonvoting sometimes imply. (The author hopes classes using this book will debate the author's admittedly debatable view.)

Those concerned with low voter turnout sometimes suggest that the fault may lie in our system of voter registration. If we had automatic voter registration, as some countries have, our turnout would probably rise slightly. But there is no good reason to believe this would increase the wisdom of the nation's choices, or even alter those choices very much.

Of course if people do not vote because, although interested in politics, they feel the political system is unresponsive to the voters, that would be a serious development. Some evidence suggests the percentage believing this is rising, but this rise may reflect the collective disillusionment of our people over Vietnam, the impeachment of Richard Nixon, highly publicized cases of congressional corruption, and the growing inability of government to successfully cope with our major problems. It may also reflect people's increasing awareness that, in a highly populated and complex nation, only rarely can a single individual make a difference in the outcome of elections or on policy choices. It cannot be otherwise. Thus, the flurry of talk about the "political alienation" of ever larger numbers of voters may be less serious than many political scientists believe. Given a charismatic presidential candidate or an overriding national issue, it is probable that voting percentages will return to normal.

Voting turnout in presidential elections

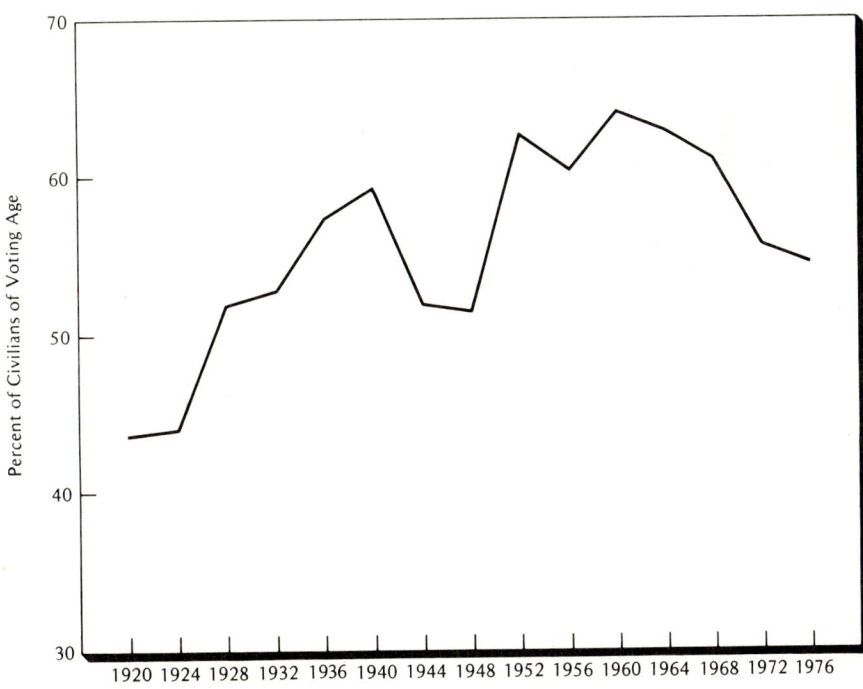

One-issue groups are gaining importance

Although elections rarely hinge on individual votes, sometimes the lone individual *can* make an impact on our political system. Phyllis Schlafly almost single-handedly fought off the Equal Rights Amendment. She read widely on the subject and then combined her personality, forensic talent, and formidable energies (along with outside financial support) to speaking before as many local and national audiences as possible. She is widely credited with (or discredited for) having blocked ERA ratification in a number of crucial states.

Other examples could be mentioned. Rachel Carson's memorable book, *Silent Spring*, helped arouse national interest in ecology.[14] Her carefully researched descriptions of what insecticides were doing to birds, insects, and fish were too ominous to ignore. And, of course, Ralph Nader's exposé of the auto industry, *Unsafe at Any Speed*, not only led to better engineered cars but helped launch the consumerist movement.[15] Howard Jarvis was largely responsible for getting "Proposition 13" on the California ballot, leading to major reductions in California property taxes.

Few of us can be Schlaflys or Carsons or Naders, but each of us can be more influential than the average, if we become better informed and politically active, and join others with similar beliefs to achieve our goals. Each indi-

Citizens: Apathetic and Concerned

vidual also has the right to run for political office; success in this undertaking can substantially increase one's influence. Furthermore, the majority of those who care about a given issue and make their voices heard nearly always get their way. All in all, the average American probably has as much power as he or she individually deserves to have.

Are the American people sufficiently well-informed to be equal to their responsibilities? Some writers stress how ill informed the average American is and how little he or she really knows about complex governmental issues. Half of the people cannot even name their state representative or both of their national senators. Less than half know which party controls Congress. Their accurate knowledge about issues such as atomic energy, economic policy, the Middle East, and so forth could be exhausted in less than two minutes each. As political philosopher James Bryce once wrote:

> [The common man's ideas] when examined, mostly resolve themselves into two or three prejudices and aversions, two or three prepossessions for a particular leader or party or section of a party, two or three phrases or catch-words suggesting or embodying arguments which the man who repeats them has not analyzed.[16]

How, then, can such poorly informed people really exercise intelligent control over a country that faces hundreds of difficult questions, on many of which the average American knows next to nothing? Well, just as it does not matter too much if many people do not vote, it matters less than one might think if most people know little about politics and political issues. The crucial point is that "an attentive public" (about 10%) follows public affairs closely and makes its voice heard—at the polls, in letters to Members of Congress and editors, and through joining with others in organized political activities.[17] The policymakers know they are being watched and evaluated by this minority. The voices of this well-informed minority, along with those of editors, columnists, authors, lobbyists, organization leaders, people like Ralph Nader, and others, contribute to the overall discussion of a given issue. Issues are thereby thoroughly thrashed out, and people with every conceivable view contribute. By the time a policy decision is reached, about all the relevant information this nation can offer has entered into the picture. If this information had been duplicated three times over, the decision would have been no better. Thus, so long as all opinions are heard and no issue evades a thorough scrutiny before a decision is made, and so long as the general goals of the larger electorate are roughly known, we need not worry unduly because so many millions of people know so little about issues. In a democracy, of course, the majority has a right to prevail even if its judgment is wrong (constitutional rights excepted), but since the majority of those who really care almost always get their way, this factor also is accounted for.

It could be added that whereas one-fourth of the American people are almost totally illiterate on political matters,[18] most middle-class Americans are somewhat better informed (even if their information level is not high). They read a newspaper, hear Walter Cronkite, John Chancellor, or Frank Reynolds, peruse the *Reader's Digest*, and (often) read *Time, Newsweek*, or *U.S. News*. They have a fairly accurate picture of what is going on, even if they are not very politically active or sophisticated.

For those who worry because complicated matters are really beyond even the average American's capacity to knowledgeably judge, several observations are in order. First, "experts" are often—and, in fact, usually—divided on most issues. Second, even the most brilliant minds are often wrong. Their capacity to predict the long-range repercussions of given policy choices are almost as limited as are those of the average citizen. The "brightest and the best" minds in Washington took us into the disastrous Vietnam War.[19] The same minds almost unanimously favored massive federal aid to education, a policy that we now discover has not improved the quality of education one whit. They strongly backed a major program of foreign economic aid in the 1950s and early 1960s, which also turned out to be a major disappointment. They wholly failed to anticipate the need for a national energy policy until the energy crisis burst upon them. The misjudgments of the experts, if one reviews the past, are endless.

In sum, their expertise does not put them far ahead of the average American; they can make just as flagrant blunders. If this nation's wisdom does not prove equal to the demands of our times, it will not be because of the unique deficiencies of ordinary citizens as much as the lack of adequate wisdom by the top minds of our country. The latter know far more facts than the former but not much more about the meaning of those facts, about which of those facts are the truly significant ones, or which of our options will make the most sense over the long run.

Finally, the average American is probably as capable of judging the character and competence of presidential candidates as "experts" are. Experts notoriously disagree on the virtues and qualifications of candidates, too. All of us develop some ability to "size up" people we meet, and the average American's job is less to decide complex issues than to decide whether a particular person and party are better qualified at this time to lead the country than another. They can be wrong here, too, but probably they can be trusted as much as any body of "experts." If you find politics confusing and nearly incomprehensible, with everybody disagreeing with everyone else, everyone sure he or she is right and very few really knowing what they're talking about, and if this tends to turn you away from politics entirely, don't worry excessively. If you are a good husband or wife, parent, friend, neighbor, and worker, you are a valuable national asset, whether you are involved in politics or not. But you're missing a lot of fun!

Polls and Their Pitfalls

We have referred to polls as a means of measuring public opinion. How reliable are the polls and how do they reach their results?

Some polls are reliable and some are not. Just as there are competent and incompetent doctors, lawyers, professors, mechanics, and raspberry pickers, there are competent and incompetent pollsters. The best of them, however (like George Gallup and Louis Harris), are highly professional and very reliable when it comes to picking winners in presidential elections and in predicting the percentage of votes they will get. Over the last seven elections, Gallup has come within two percentage points of the victor's winning margin—very impressive. (Pollsters only claim to come within a 3% margin of error at best. However, that means that if the polls show a candidate winning 40% of the vote, he might get anywhere from 37% to 43%.) But even the best pollsters do less well on primary elections, where people's opinions are less well established and where voting turnouts are less predictable.

Gallup usually polls only about 1500 people, but these people are drawn at random from precincts randomly selected throughout the country.[20] This process gives him an accurate cross section of Americans, containing proper proportions of farmers, city dwellers, blacks, Chicanos, rich, poor, southerners, factory workers, Jews, Poles, and people with no hair. The number polled seems small but if the sample is truly random, experience has shown that the results are substantially the same as if the pollster used 3,000 or 10,000 or 200,000. Innumerable experiments have verified these results, so political scientists trust the best pollsters on their presidential election reports.

Pollsters must write their questions in a professional manner, since slight differences in wording can produce dramatically different results (where public opinion on issues is concerned). For example, one responsible polling organization discovered that 50% of the public have a great deal of confidence in "established religion" but only 35% have confidence in "organized religion." About 63% had great confidence in the "Army, Navy and Air Force" but the figure dropped to 48% for the "Military" and to only 21% for "Military leaders." And while 21% had great confidence in "Organized Labor" only 7% felt this way about "Big Labor" [21]

On matters of public policy, pollsters sometimes came up with widely varying results. For example, in November 1974 the Louis Harris poll reported that 66% of the voters favored giving Israel whatever it needs in military equipment, while a Yankelovich poll one month earlier, worded slightly different, announced that only 31% wanted American arms sent to Israel.[22] Morality issues also yield surprisingly different results in polls, depending on wording. Thus in February 1976 a New York Times–CBS News poll found 67% agreeing that "the right of a woman to have an abortion should be left entirely up to the woman and her doctor." But in April 1975 Gallup found that only 33% of respondents answered in the affirmative when asked, "Are you in favor of a law which permits a woman to have an abortion even if her husband is against it?" And in March 1975 a National Opinion Research Center poll revealed that only 46% approved of legal abortion if the woman simply did not want more children.[23]

Devising questions that are as objective as possible is a very specialized skill. The best pollsters usually pretest questions on sample groups of people to reduce the dangers of questions being biased or misinterpreted.

Similarly, responsible polling organizations train their interviewers carefully so that they will not ask questions in such a way as to bias the results by the inflection of their voices or their demeanor in general. Finally, the data must be processed with care and the results placed in an illuminating rather than a misleading context, with attention given to recent events that might affect the poll. Polling has become a highly professional enterprise, and one must be on guard against the findings of amateurish or scheming pollsters.

Poll results usually do not determine what decisions policymakers will make but they are watched attentively. They are a valuable instrument for testing the claims of private interest groups that the public wants this or that. They may make policy-makers more cautious and more interested in reaching a compromise decision that all sides can "live with." And the more crucial the issue, the more important the polls become. Used properly, they can be an asset to democracy.

To repeat a point made earlier, virtually all political scientists believe poll results should be respected by political leaders but not venerated. The job of leaders is to lead, not simply to reflect last Tuesday's poll. As Brian Murphy puts it, public opinion is a barometer, not a compass.[24] Whatever the limitations of the educated mind, political leaders sometimes see farther and more clearly than John Q. Public. The democratic statesman is not someone who is contemptuous of public opinion but someone who can appeal to the best that is in us. That is what leadership at its finest will attempt to do. The best that a people are capable of is not always visible from Gallup poll results.

Notes

1. See Joan Huber and William Form, *Income and Ideology* (New York: Free Press, 1973), p. 135. One of the best brief treatments of political elitism is Kenneth Smorsten, *A Preface to Action* (Pacific Palisades, Calif.: Goodyear, 1976), ch. 2.
2. Everett Carl Ladd, Jr., "What the Voters Really Want," *Fortune*, December 18, 1978, pp. 40-44.
3. For systematic studies of the family's impact on children, see Bernard Berelson and Gary A. Steiner, *Human Behavior* (New York: Harcourt Brace Jovanovich, 1967), p. 105; Fred Greenstein, *Children and Politics* (New Haven, Conn.: Yale University Press, 1965); and David Easton and Jack Dennis, *Children in the Political System* (New York: McGraw-Hill, 1969).
4. Two useful overviews of the New Deal are Basil Rauch, *The History of the New Deal 1933-1938* (New York: Creative Age Press, 1944); and Morton Keller, ed., *The New Deal: What Was It?* (New York: Holt, Rinehart and Winston, 1963).
5. Lucy S. Dawidowicz and Leon J. Goldstein, *Politics in a Pluralist Democracy* (New York: Institute of Human Relations Press, 1963), pp. 76-81, 84-90.
6. See R. D. Corwin and Lois Gray, "The GOP's Strange Appeal to Business," *Fortune*, July 1971, p. 127-128. Also see John K. Galbraith, "The Trouble With Economists," *New Republic*, Jan. 14, 1978, p. 21.
7. See P. F. Lazarsfeld, B. R. Berelson, and Hazel Gaudet, *The People's Choice* (New York: Columbia University Press, 1948), pp. 16-27.
8. NBC Poll reported in the *Washington Post*, January 9, 1976.
9. See Paul A. Weaver, "Captives of Melodrama," *New York Times Magazine*, August 29, 1976, pp. 6-7.
10. By entertainment industry, I mean radio and television, motion pictures, pornographic and trash magazines, and the rock concert and record business.
11. Clinton Rossiter, *Conservatism in America* (New York, Knopf, 1962), p. 56.
12. Cobbe and Elder, *Participation in American Politics*.
13. Voter turnout has dropped from 63.1% in 1960 to 53% in 1976, the lowest since 1948. For a concerned viewpoint, see Arthur Hadley, *The Empty Polling Booth* (Englewood Cliffs, N.J.; Prentice Hall, 1978).
14. Rachel Carson, *Silent Spring* (Boston: Houghton Mifflin, 1962).
15. Ralph Nader, *Unsafe at Any Speed* (New York: Grossman, 1972).
16. James Bryce, *The American Commonwealth*, vol. II (New York: Macmillan, 1912), p. 254.
17. Roger W. Cobbe and Charles D. Elder, *Participation In American Politics* (Boston, Allyn and Bacon, 1972), p. 107.
18. Charles E. Lindblom, *The Policy-Making Process* (Englewood Cliffs, N.J.: Prentice-Hall, 1968), p. 44.
19. David Halberstam, *The Best and the Brightest* (New York: Random House, 1972).
20. George Gallup, *The Sophisticated Poll Watcher's Guide* (Princeton, N.J.: Princeton Opinion Press, 1972), section 2.
21. Seymour M. Lipset, "The Wavering Polls," *The Public Interest*, Spring 1976, p. 83.
22. Ibid., p. 70.
23. Peter Skerry, "The Class Conflict over Abortion," *The Public Interest*, Summer 1978, pp. 72-73.
24. Who is Brian Murphy? One of Miami University's brightest graduate students, that's who he is.

CHAPTER 7

POLITICAL PARTIES: FREEDOM'S CHILDREN

Although many Americans know almost nothing about politics, they do know that we have two major parties called Republicans and Democrats. And in most cases they have at least a faintly flickering loyalty to one of them.

If average citizens cannot define what a "party" is, well-informed Americans would also stumble over that. Even political scientists have trouble arriving at an agreed upon definition. But it is roughly accurate to say that a *major political party* is a loose coalition of persons seeking to control the government by winning elections. This definition, of course, will not suffice for minor parties—the America First party, the Vegetarian party, and the Prohibition party are historical examples—which are organized not to control the government but because some people want publicity for an organization leader or for certain strongly held minority opinions.

Theoretically, parties serve many vital democratic purposes. Defenders of parties insist that parties are useful for the following functions

1. Nominating candidates
2. Providing the electorate with competitive choices
3. Harmonizing discordant elements in society by making the compromises necessary to form a majority coalition
4. Enabling the voters to hold elected officials accountable for their conduct of public office
5. Coordinating the activities of an otherwise splintered government
6. Making the necessary policy and personnel decisions that government requires
7. Providing links between the various levels of government

Whether or not parties are really essential for these functions—or whether we are just conditioned to believe that they are—is a matter to be discussed later. Certainly many Americans would sleep soundly if informed that political parties had mysteriously evaporated from the face of the earth. They might even drink a toast to that event.

Parties: The Family Tree

As indicated in an earlier chapter, the Founding Fathers held "factions" (their term for the rudimentary parties of their day) in low esteem, regarding them as selfish aggregations of persons hostile to the public interest. Far from saluting them, they wanted to minimize their baneful effects. If parties had never been born, the founders would have rejoiced. But early in George Washington's Administration repeated arguments broke out between Alexander Hamilton and Thomas Jefferson, which culminated in 1796 with the birth of our first political parties.

Jefferson stressed the equality of all men, the virtues of farmers and farm life, and the wisdom of limited government; he spoke for the sentiments and interests of the small farmers, laborers, debtors—and slave owners—groups that were predominant in the South and West. Hamilton spoke for the commercial interests—bankers, shippers, speculators, manufacturers, and the large landowners. Since both sets of interest groups were affected by government policy, it was a wholly natural development for them to form loose political alliances in order to protect and advance those interests. These alliances were called *parties*.[1]

Hamilton's party was called the Federalists, Jefferson's the Democrat Republicans. Jefferson's party soon dropped the Democratic prefix, but later evolved into the Democratic party, which now has the distinction of being the longest-lived political party in the world. The Federalists gradually faded away after Jefferson's election in 1800; for several decades Americans carried on under an essentially one-party system, not because opposition parties were suppressed but because the Federalists had lost support and a more viable party had not yet arisen. Andrew Jackson, however, so frightened and infuriated his enemies (they called him "King Andrew I" and were sure he was hell-bent on destroying constitutional government) that his opponents formed a Whig party. (The Whigs were the antimonarchist party in Great Britain.) The Whigs agreed on little except their hatred of Jackson. Indeed, they dared not call a party convention, knowing they could never agree on a statement of party principles. But parties can arise, and persist for awhile, on no more common ground than a deep-seated antagonism to a prominent political personality or an equally deep-seated attachment to a popular political figure. Lacking internal political unity, as well as broad popular support, the Whigs were able to win elections only when they nominated military heroes like William Henry Harrison and Zachary Taylor. (The badly divided Rspublican party in the post–World War II period could also win the presidency only by nominating another military hero—Dwight D. Eisenhower.)

The indigestible issue of slavery splintered the major parties and led to the birth of the modern Republican party in 1854. The Democratic party became the proslavery party, a development that plagued it for decades to come. (In the 1950s and early 1960s the *southern* Democrats were still the major anti–civil rights faction in the nation, although northern Democrats dominated the national party and the national conventions.)

The Republicans—also called the Grand Old Party (GOP)—largely controlled national politics for over 65 years after the Civil War. The assassination of their first president, Abraham Lincoln, had transformed a much maligned political leader into a revered national saint. The party that had "saved the Union" won the enduring loyalty of northern pro-Union voters, the Homestead Act of 1862 (granting 160 acres of free land to homesteaders) won vast amounts of good will, and the party's friendly policies toward manufacturing and commerce consolidated a coalition of diverse elements that was one of the strongest and most enduring in political history. Only unique political circumstances enabled the Democrats' Grover Cleveland and Woodrow Wilson to temporarily wrest the presidency out of their hands.

The depression and Franklin D. Roosevelt shattered that coalition. The latter's New Deal policies and leadership in World War II created a new coalition that has consistently controlled Congress (except for a few years) since 1932. Since that date Republicans have won the presidency only with Eisenhower at the helm or when the Democrats were badly divided. But though only 20% to 25% of the voters characterize themselves as Republicans these days, the Republicans still manage to put up formidable candidates in presidential election years. The voters' attitude seems to be that they favor the

Democratic party over the Republicans but are not bothered if the Democrats run Congress and the Republicans run the White House. This may not promote efficient, active, and productive government, but from time to time it has pitted a moderately liberal legislative institution against a moderately conservative executive branch.

Two Parties, Many Parties

American political system has long been an essentially two-party system. While third parties appear from time to time, they are ordinarily side shows. In most European democracies, on the other hand, many parties compete for power. Why, then, should the United States have a predominantly two-party system?

In Europe deep-seated divisions existed in the nineteenth century that were not present in this country. In many European states there was a monarchist and an antimonarchist faction. We were spared that. There was also a clerical and an anticlerical faction—which grew out of the religious wars that our nation was also spared. Somewhat later, powerful socialist sentiment appeared in Europe, while only a marginal interest in socialism arose in the United States. Sometimes internal nationality loyalties ran so deeply in culturally pluralistic European countries that they gave rise to separate political parties, again not so in our magnificently heterogeneous land.

With the nation speaking a common language, educated in common values, basically agreed on representative, secular government and on a capitalist economy, the social environment was favorable to a two-party system. Once it became established, and seemed to work well, we tailored our laws to reinforce its presence. And the longer we had it, the more natural and beneficent it seemed to be. The third parties that occasionally surfaced were viewed as temporary aberrations that would sink beneath the political waters in a few years.

One of the political arrangements that undergirded and solidified the two-party system was our *single member district system*. That refers to the practice of carving out an electoral district for each representative to which a state is entitled and then letting the prize go to the candidate who wins the most votes. That may seem the only way of doing things, yet many European countries use a different system. They create electoral districts large enough to include, say, five representatives and then divide up the winners in proportion to the party votes cast. If one party receives about 40% of the total vote, it is allowed 40% of the five representatives—or two. If three other parties each receive from 16% to 24% of the total vote, each is allowed one representative. But if the large district had been divided into five smaller districts, the party winning 40% (a plurality) would probably have won all five seats if its strength was quite evenly distributed throughout that district. Thus the *proportional representation system* tends to give relatively small parties representation in the legislature.[2]

The electoral college system also discourages minor parties. Although not required to do so by the Constitution, each of our states has chosen to give all of its presidential electors to the party receiving the most votes. If these electors were divided according to the proportion of votes cast for the various parties, even small parties (in the larger states) could win some electors and hence have visibility as well as bargaining power.

Thus, tradition combined with the single member district system and with our winner-take-all electoral college system strongly predispose us toward a two-party system.

A two-party system has important consequences. Where two major parties compete for a majority of the votes, both are likely to be rather moderate, centrist parties since the great American middle tends to be neither strongly liberal nor strongly conservative. Thus, no matter which party wins, the losers do not feel devastated. Party differences being rather modest, policy changes following a change of party administration are usually minor. In consequence, the two-party system promotes a more harmonious society, one in which political passions are less intense and hence less potentially disruptive.

On the other hand, a multiparty political system is one in which voters find party choices that more closely correspond to their particular views since more shadings of political beliefs are represented. In this country, many people vote Democratic or Republican who are not very pleased with either party or its candidates—because there is no real alternative. To vote for small and impotent parties would seem to be throwing their vote away. So, people are less enthusiastic party supporters than in multiparty countries, but also less disconsolate losers.

In two-party systems both parties are coalitions of many disparate groups—coalitions that hang together during an election campaign because they have more mutually compatible views and interests than if they joined together in any other conceivably victorious manner. The alliance is usually loose, informal, and restless, but it is the best arrangement that the current political situation permits. Such coalitions can produce majorities, and majorities have more governing "legitimacy" (that is, the public recognizes their "right to govern") than any alternative. They thus tend to produce more stable government.

In multiparty systems important social or economic groups often form their own parties, which represent their beliefs and interests in undiluted fashion, rather than forming coalitions with other groups (and parties) before elections in an effort to seek a majority. After the election, then, no party usually has won a majority. In order to form a government commanding majority support, a coalition must be shaped that can win the support of a majority of the legislature *after* the election. The various party leaders bargain among themselves to see what coalition arrangement will give each of them the greatest influence and the best possible cabinet (or executive) positions. Eventually a majority coalition takes shape and exercises control of the government. The job then becomes one of holding the coalition together; if one element of that coalition secedes, the government may come tumbling down and a new coalition must be stitched together—or new elections must be held.[3]

Thus, the principal difference is whether a potential majority coalition is formed *before* the election (as in two-party systems) or *after* the election (in multiparty systems). In either case compromises must be made between various groups with divergent ideas—compromises that are not entirely satisfactory to anyone but that seem preferable to any feasible alternative. Most American political scientists believe the two-party preelection coalition is the better since the resulting government is more united and less precarious than the multiparty model. Some multiparty coalitions are so fragile they dare not take strong and decisive action lest the delicately balanced structure fall apart. Near-paralysis may be the result.

Multiparty systems usually are associated with cabinet-type governments rather than presidential governments. These cabinets, which usually give several parties representation in the ministries, are led by a prime minister or premier, and hold power only so long as they are backed by a majority of the legislature. On the other hand, presidents hold office for a fixed number of years, whether they retain majority legislative support or not.

Our Parties: Two Peas in a Pod?

Many Americans see this country's two parties as so similar in programs and goals that it makes little difference who wins. Some (though not many) even decline to vote for this reason. They view the major candidates and their more active supporters as groups seeking the spoils of office but without real commitment to significant and differing policy goals.

It is true that both parties, seeking a majority of the votes, tend to cling rather closely to the center of public opinion since that is where most of the votes usually are. To embrace positions that most voters might reject is to invite defeat. But this does not mean election choices are meaningless. No well-informed person can study presidential elections since 1945 and conclude that the public was regularly presented with two peas in a pod. Harry S Truman's bill of fare in 1948, including an advanced civil rights program, a major new farm program, national health insurance, and an attack on the Taft-Hartley labor bill, was decidedly different from that of his opponent, Thomas E. Dewey. Adlai Stevenson offered the nation ideas and programs that differed appreciably from those of Dwight D. Eisenhower in 1956. John F. Kennedy supported Medicare, federal aid to education, and a strong civil rights position in 1960; Richard Nixon did not. The differences between Lyndon B. Johnson and Barry Goldwater—over Social Security, Vietnam, labor unions, the extent of government, and so forth—in 1964 were such that only a political ignoramus could fail to see them. Hubert Humphrey called for a more active federal government in domestic affairs in 1968 than did Nixon; more important, everything about their political backgrounds suggested that their administrations would have different goals and a different tone. In 1972 George McGovern offered many programs of first-rank importance that Nixon rejected. And in 1976 it was clear to the reasonably discerning voter that Jimmy Carter would be in the activist Democratic tradition while Gerald Ford would move away only slightly from the status quo.

In sum, those who believe our two parties give the voter no real choice have not read their history or followed recent political affairs very closely. Of course, socialists, communists, and members of the Far Right are unhappy

Harry Truman gives 'em hell

with the choices offered by the two major parties, but noncentrists have always had that complaint.

Still, the more ideologically minded members of both parties (who are usually the most active members) are generally dissatisfied with the comparatively moderate nature of the party leader's positions. Intense Republican conservatives tend to believe their presidential candidate has compromised his principles in his hunger for votes. Intense Democratic liberals feel the same about their candidate; he too has struck a shameless bargain with the devil by flirting with middle-of-the-road voters. Since truth, virtue, and righteousness reside only on incontestably conservative or liberal territory, they gnash their teeth over the wayward tendencies of candidates so eager to win that they stray from the true faith.

Sometimes these party "purists," as they are sometimes called, manage to win control of the party machinery and nominate their man. This happened when Barry Goldwater and George McGovern were nominated. But in both cases, significantly, the candidates went down to inglorious defeat; the public instinctively recoils from candidates perceived as too liberal or too conservative. So the party ideologues, who would often rather stand "on principle" and lose rather than compromise and win, were given a chance to do just that in 1964 and 1972. It was a great trip while it lasted, but the journey ended on the rocks.[4]

Still, it is possible to be too disdainful of those who "stand on principle" rather than compromise to win. To be willing to make numerous compromises, especially on economic issues, in order to win is one thing. But to be willing to make *any* compromise to win is something else. If, for example, the national majority is in a vengeful mood and is out to punish some unpopular minority by depriving it of its constitutional rights, a party that refused to pander to the public is a party that might lose an election but ultimately win respect for refusing to yield to a transient and destructive popular passion. A party that always makes winning its highest and only aspiration is no more admirable than a football coach who believes that winning is everything—whether by fair means or foul. No magic formula identifies the point at which a stand for democratic principles is called for, win or lose. That decision, properly taken, requires judgment and an educated conscience. But that point can surely come.

Discontent with the policies of the party toward which individuals and groups normally lean has led to several alternative forms of protest. It frequently leads the disaffected minority to try to seize control of the party and convert it into a more leftist or rightist party. Ordinarily, this effort fails; the minority's candidate fails to net a majority of convention delegates. The most the dissatisfied minority can then hope for is either a party platform that incorporates some of its cherished positions or a vice-president who is sympathetic with many of its views. Sometimes, on the other hand, its diligence in the primaries and in gaining control of local party machinery enables it to nominate the candidate—as happened with Goldwater and McGovern and almost happened with Ronald Reagan in 1976. At other times the disgruntled minority may, either before or after the convention, refuse to accept frustration and form a third party.[5]

This happened shortly after the Civil War when some voters found both the Democratic and the Republican parties insufficiently sympathetic to the plight of the farmers. The latter were believed to be victimized by the railroads, bankers, and middlemen, by high freight rates, high interest rates, and high prices. The indignant voters formed local Populist parties, elected local candidates, and eventually won so much support that a candidate very much to their liking captured the Democratic presidential nomination—William Jennings Bryan. (Bryan ran three times but never won.)

In 1912 persons loyal to former President Theodore Roosevelt refused to accept the Republican convention choice of William Howard Taft, and Roosevelt ran on a Progressive party ticket. The decision split the GOP, leading to victory for Democratic nominee Woodrow Wilson.

A more issue-oriented and less personality-oriented Progressive party found the Democratic ticket in 1924 (headed by conservative corporation lawyer John W. Davis) too much to swallow and united behind Wisconsin's able Senator Robert M. La Follette. La Follette's following consisted largely of labor union elements, grumbling midwestern farmers, reform-minded liberals, and socialists. La Follette captured only 13 electoral votes, while lacklustre but "safe" Calvin Coolidge won a landslide victory.

Again, in 1948, Democrats who were unhappy with Harry Truman split into two groups. Southern Democrats who could not stomach Truman's strong civil rights stand formed a "Dixiecrat" party with Senator Strom Thurmond as standard bearer. The more liberal Democrats, unable to nominate William O. Douglas as the party nominee and distressed with Truman's "hard line" against the Soviet Union, formed a new Progressive party headed by former Vice President Henry A. Wallace. The double split seemingly doomed Truman's chances, but a plucky, folksy, hard-hitting campaign, combined with the cool national reception given to Republican Governor Thomas E. Dewey, led to one of the biggest upsets in American election history.

Third parties sometimes play a very significant part in our political system. They force one or both major parties to pay more attention to problems they are ignoring or underestimating, and they give disgruntled, highly ideological activists an outlet for their energies and their unhappiness. In an effort to avert the emergence of third parties, the major parties usually make concessions to minority views. But often they dare not concede too much, or they will alienate other groups in their party who are strongly opposed to the minority view. Calculating how far to go in placating one rebellious faction without losing the support of other factions requires a delicate balancing act by party leaders.

Frequently third parties remain unborn only because the unhappy faction knows that the formation of a new party would only ensure victory for the least acceptable major party. Much as they may deplore the failure of their party to take the strong liberal or conservative positions they favor, they dislike even more the prospect of taking action that will divide the party and allow the other major party to govern. After all, it is even less liberal or less conservative than their own party.

While persons who call themselves Democrats far outnumber persons who call themselves Republicans, neither party has enough hard-core supporters to ensure victory at the polls. Indeed, persons labeling themselves "independents" have outnumbered Republicans in recent years. Most of these "independents" should be more properly termed "independents leaning Republican" or "independents leaning Democratic" since they generally end up rather consistently voting for one party. But about one "independent" out of six really deserves the label.

Studies used to show that most of those who took pride in being "independents" and who "voted for the man, not the party" were among the least well informed citizens. Many, indeed, were apathetic and rarely bothered to vote. In recent years, however, an increasing number of young people, college educated or not, have moved into independent or semi-independent ranks. About half of the young and one-third of all adults now consider themselves independent. *Ticket-splitting* (voting for some Republicans and some Democrats in the same election) is becoming a more common practice,[6] to the consternation of those who believe that party deterioration is an ominous development.

Independents are usually the last to make up their minds, and since the undecided vote is normally decisive in a close election, that vote is assiduously courted. A presidential nominee's first responsibility is to consolidate the support of party regulars, but the closer the election comes, the more the candidates appeal to independents. Since the latter's policy or symbolic tastes cannot be intuitively perceived, candidates dispatch pollsters to ascertain what is on their minds. The results tend to shape candidates' strategy, with each attempting to say what will be most persuasive to the independents without taking obviously incompatible stand with previous remarks. These appeals, it should be added, often take the form of generalities and imagery with a low policy content. With both candidates focusing on some of the same emotional themes, the independents must decide which candidate is the most "sincere" or which candidate's personality is the most pleasing (or the least displeasing). For voters who know the least and care the least about politics, these considerations are usually decisive.

Earlier, we discussed the factors that contribute to party loyalties and that are passed along from generation to generation (the Civil War, the Bryan campaign of 1896, the issues of Catholicism and booze and the New Deal). In recent decades partisan loyalties have been waning. Labor union members and Catholics are less reliably Democratic than they used to be, for example. But the Democrats continue to draw important support from the wobbly remnants of Franklin Roosevelt's coalition. Catholics, union members, blacks, Jews, Chicanos, liberals, lower-income workers—these remain the groups that identify more readily with a Democratic candidate than with a Republican. For the GOP, business people, small-town residents, farmers (unless prices are down and a Republican is president), and the more conservative voters in general are that party's natural constituency. Fortunately for the GOP, more people think of themselves as conservatives than regard themselves as liberals.[7] But fortunately for the Democrats, an appreciable minority of self-styled conservatives continue to vote Democratic while very few self-styled liberals vote Republican.

In general, the voters in recent years found themselves more comfortable with liberal Democratic party attitudes toward economic policy but more compatible with conservative Republican attitudes toward the cultural-moral issues (abortion, pornography, soft drugs, homosexuality, etc.). President Carter came closer to satisfying both of these public attitudes in his 1976 quest for the presidency than did any of his opponents. Where the inflation-fed popular drift toward greater economic conservatism will leave the Democrats is a major unanswered question.

Our Parties: Splintered They Stand

Although our major parties bring together many different factions, they are remarkably decentralized, compared to parties in most other countries. Each national party is little more than a loose alliance of state parties, which in turn are a loose alliance of local parties. The national party committees can give assistance to national congressional candidates, but they cannot dictate who those candidates shall be, what policies they shall espouse, or what strategies they shall employ. It is quite common, for example, for congressional candidates to take positions that sharply diverge from the national party platform or from policies advocated by the party's presidential candidate. Not only is this done with some frequency, but efforts by the national party or its presidential candidate to force the local candidates into line is usually resented by the voters. Such action may strengthen the heretical local candidate by demonstrating his or her "independence" of the "party bosses," as Franklin D. Roosevelt learned when he unsuccessfully sought to "purge" anti–New Deal Democrats in 1938. Other presidential candidates also have learned that their campaign efforts to discourage support for those "disloyal" to the national ticket are nearly always rebuffed by the voters.

Thus the heterogeneity of American society leads to a decentralized politics, which, in turn, makes it extraordinarily difficult (more accurately, impossible) for a political party to present a united front on matters of policy—either between or during elections. Parties, to repeat, are coalitions, and the price for maximum unity is a willingness to allow diversity of opinion within the party.

This situation differs from that in Great Britain, where the national party headquarters has more power.[8] If a party candidate chosen by local voters is unsatisfactory, the national organization can veto him or her. It can deny the candidate the privilege of running on the party label, obliging him or her to file as an independent. (The local party organizations have been becoming more rebellious in recent years, however.) British party members have accepted this because they are accustomed to and believe in the value of relatively unified, disciplined parties operating under generally centralized control. They accept this because, for the British, it is more important for a party to deliver on its pledges (which requires party unity) than for local members of Parliament to represent local opinion more faithfully. The British voter typically is thus more party oriented and less candidate oriented than the American voter. The personality, character, and constituent services of the parliamentary candidate matter less than the fact that the candidate does or does not support a party that currently is in or out of favor with the voters. (All of this, of course, reflects the fact that Britain is a more homogeneous country than the United States.

But, to avoid misunderstanding, British parties are not indifferent to the personal merits of a candidate. They want candidates with intelligence, wit, judgment, and other attractive qualities because such nominees help win a few more votes and because able Members of Parliament (MPs) not only improve the general party image but also provide a better pool of competent people from which the prime minister can select his or her cabinet. But party loyalty is a prerequisite to winning national party approval.

How are the American parties organized to do their work, and how important are these organizations? The national committees, with representatives from each state, perform party services of limited significance. They select the site of the national party convention and make arrangements for that gathering. The national committee chair is chosen by the convention's nominee and serves at his pleasure—if that nominee wins the presidency. During the presidential campaign the party chair helps direct the campaign, using his or her

How the major parties are organized

```
Congressional Campaign Committee;  ←  National conventions
Congressional Campaign Committee       National Committee
                                       50 state committees and conventions
                                       State legislative and Congressional
                                          committees
                                       County committees
                                       City, town, and village committees
                                       Ward or district committees
                                       Precinct committees
```

committee to raise money and to prepare and distribute campaign literature. If the party's nominee loses, the chair may be replaced by another person chosen by the strongest of the competing factions within the party. The defeated nominee loses control of the committee, which in any case has only minor functions to perform between presidential campaigns. During this interim the chair's principal role is to be a gadfly to the party in power—and to give "Meet the Press," "Face the Nation," and "Issues and Answers" a top party official to interview. Ordinarily, the chair carefully refrains from making statements that might indicate any preference for the party's potential presidential candidates who are readying for a run at the top slot during the next campaign. Neutrality is the watchword. (Some national committee chairs, it should be added, are active in helping to recruit, train, and finance congressional candidates.)

Beneath the national party committee are arrayed the state congressional district, county, city, and ward committees. The state committees are blissfully independent of the national committees and primarily concern themselves with state politics. Their chair is sometimes chosen (in fact, though not in form) by a dominant state political figure—generally a governor or senator. The state and local committees play roughly the same role as the national committees but in a more limited arena. They arrange meetings, raise money, distribute literature—and usually do not take sides in state primary election contests. American political campaigns are directed by, and revolve around, individual candidates rather than standing, official party organizations. The latter are usually little more than paper organizations; powerful city organizations like those of former Mayor Richard Daley of Chicago are rare indeed. Thus the parties' basic building blocks are wasting away.

Parties in Decline: Good Riddance?

Political scientists have long warned that political parties are in decline, but the American people seem unconcerned. Put on their scale of worries, the steady deterioration in influence and activity of organized political parties rates about 267th, if indeed it rates at all. But the evidence that parties are losing their power and place in American politics is very strong. Let us take a look at some of that evidence.

Popular commitment to parties has been dwindling. As previously stated, fewer people than ever before identify themselves as Republicans or Democrats when polled. A growing number call themselves independents, who have little or no party allegiance. (Presidents like Eisenhower, Nixon, Lyndon Johnson, and Carter, who have downplayed their partisan affiliation and attempted to govern on a relatively nonpartisan basis, probably contributed to this phenomenon.) Less than two-thirds of the voters call themselves Democrats or Republicans and only one-fourth of the voters are strongly partisan.

Ticket splitting is become more frequent. More people are voting for a person rather than a party and doing so with an air of moral superiority. This phenomenon is strengthened by the growing number of *single issue voters*, persons who vote for or against candidates because of their stand on abortion, ERA, gun control, gay rights, nuclear energy, or some other issue of intense concern to them. Rather than evaluating candidates' overall ideology or record or following a partisan predilection, these citizens cast their votes solely on the basis of the candidates' position on a single issue.

The direct primary system has enfeebled the parties. Instead of candidates being chosen by party conventions or party caucuses, as was done in the past, the winning candidates are persons who win the most primary election votes. They usually owe nothing to the regular local party organization and may even have won their nomination by advertising their independence of the "party bosses." When local party leaders lost the power to select party nominees, this dealt a near-mortal blow to the local organizations. Their principal power had been shorn away, much to the pleasure of the early twentieth-century reformers, who were enthralled with the notion of taking politics "away from the bosses" and "giving it back to the people." They got their way but also gave us a more atomized and chaotic politics. (The United States is the only country that uses the direct primary on a widespread scale to choose party candidates.)

Precinct organization has become almost extinct in many cities. Whereas the old-time precinct leader knew most of the members of his precinct, did various favors for them, and rounded them up on election day, precinct leaders today are either nonexistent or largely inactive. The earlier precinct captains gave the party a human face and an image of helpfulness and accessibility that has now departed.

Running for office is now a do-it-yourself operation. Local candidates form and direct their personal organizations, during the primary campaigns, and the primary winner continues this pattern through the general election campaign. His or her personal organization collects campaign funds, prepares literature, distributes that literature, and attempts to prod supporters to the polls. The permanent party organization is largely an onlooker. Its limited services are sought by the candidate only after the primary victory.[9]

The presence of television and the development of computerized, direct-mail fund-raising operations—drawing on massive mailing lists compiled by liberal or conservative groups—have accelerated the personalization of American politics. Individual candidates can reach the voters directly through television ads and raise the money to finance those ads without having to rely on the established party apparatus for help.

This personalization, it might be added, reflects this country's heightened emphasis on individualism—an emphasis that celebrates the primacy of the individual's tastes, inclinations, and goals while depreciating the obligations and values of community and collective responsibility. The spirit of individualism has left its mark on almost every aspect of our society—at a cost more serious than is usually realized.

The national party organization has even lost its power to select the president. There was a time when a number of presidential aspirants came to the convention, hoping the party leaders would tap them for the grand prize. Since no candidate commanded the backing of a majority of delegates, a handful of top party leaders from the large states and cities would select the party nominee. Now the winning candidate almost always comes to the convention with a majority of delegates committed to him; the convention only formalizes a decision already made in the presidential primaries (and in party caucuses, to a lesser degree). Again, the party organization has lost a vital and invigorating function.

Television tends to stress personalities, thus downplaying parties. As a communications medium TV can more readily dramatize its news with a focus on the individual candidate and his or her personal qualities.[10] That the candidate is the *party's* nominee is almost lost sight of, as is his or her general attachment to the general policies of the party. Candidates also have a tendency to minimize or ignore their partisan role, hoping to woo independents and dissident members of the opposition party by obscuring their party affiliation. (As members of a clearly minority party, Republican candidates are especially prone to adopt this stance.)

Civil service has weakened parties. Merit system reforms restricting jobs to the winners of competitive exams has deprived party leaders of job rewards they once doled out to those who served the party. The withering of the "spoils system" *may* have ensured more qualified public jobholders, but it also guaranteed that party leaders would get less cooperation from party members since there were fewer loaves and fishes to distribute in return for active party cooperation.

Dwindling party cohesion has hurt parties, too. The failure of party members to act rather cohesively in Congress, especially in the Senate, has added to the diminution of party significance. If party members pulled together and took common stands on major issues, parties would be more meaningful than they have become. But, in addition to the centrifugal political forces already at work in our heterogeneous, decentralized nation, party leaders often exercise little party leadership on major policy issues. When the president is a member of the same party that controls Congress, some party teamwork takes place, but congressional leaders like John McCormack, Carl Albert, and Mike Mansfield applied minimal partisan pressure on behalf of party measures. (Tip O'Neill and Robert A. Taft, Sr., constitute exceptions to this rule.)

Congressional leaders often are given little opportunity to jointly formulate a *party* program with the president. They are consulted a little, but mainly they receive an executive-drafted program that is more the president's program than a party program. Not having helped formulate it, they have less interest in pushing that program. The ensuing free-for-all usually blurs party responsibility for the legislative outcome.

Tensions between the executive and legislative branches affect parties negatively. The United States has always had a system of divided government, with Congress and the president having separate (though overlapping) responsibilities and viewing each other as potential competitors for power. Even if the president and the majority of Congress are members of the same party, their differing bases of support and their institutional rivalry tend to erode the normal spirit of partisan cooperation. But since World War II an additional complication has arisen. The opposition party has controlled Congress almost as often as has the president's party, presenting a disorderly picture to the public and preventing the public from pinning responsibility on either party for what is or is not done. The opposition party blames the president, and the president reciprocates. The public is confused but some citizens feel that with each party sharing power and keeping a vigilant eye on the other's transgressions, good should somehow emerge from this turmoil. One thing that does not emerge is public respect for parties that take stands, unite to put them into law, and accept responsibility for the outcome. The public does not know who to blame or who to praise. The parties are barely discerned amidst the smoke of battle.

Federal law gives presidential candidates, rather than their political parties, millions of dollars with which to finance their campaigns. Many political scientists would like to have seen the money go to the parties, in recognition of their stewardship role. Turning the money over to the candidates only accentuates the independence of those candidates from their parties.

Finally, party squabbling, enmities, and intrigues have hurt the party system. The public feels, not without justification, that many party members support or oppose measures not because of their merits, but because the president is or is not a member of their party. For example, Richard Nixon, before becoming president, had always opposed wage and price controls, had always taken a hard line toward the communist countries, and had always opposed deficit financing. All of these were in line with conservative Republican opinion. But as president he instituted wage and price controls, cultivated friendly relations (détente) with the Soviet Union and China, and defended deficit financing. This switch was not all that remarkable; many presidents adopt different policies in office than those they espouse as candidates. But when the Republican party not only accepted these policies but praised him for his statesmanship, many people marveled that partisan feelings could bring such an about face. There was no doubt that adoption of the same policies by a Democratic president would have been denounced vociferously by the same party that praised Nixon for his performance.

Nor is a phenomenon like this unique to the GOP. Democrats, too, go along with policies undertaken by their party leader that would bring spasms of indignation if a Republican were president. The question that such conduct raises is, If the partisan spirit is that supple and unprincipled, is partisanship useful? It would seem instead to lead merely to endless and unnecessary bickering, squabbling, sniping, posturing, jockeying for advantage, a ceaseless effort by one party to defend its champion, and a persistent and mean-spirited attempt by the other party to discredit him and erode his standing with the public.

Could it be that the Founding Fathers were right in their distaste for, and mistrust of, parties—that nonpartisan government is really better after all? Why not a government in which public officials are praised or blamed because of their true accomplishments and actual defects rather than because of their party affiliation? Why maintain a purely artificial element—the spirit of partisanship—which adulterates the process by constantly injecting a phoney and disruptive element into it? If there were no parties, each of us could evaluate a candidate on the basis of his or her true strengths and weaknesses, rather than have our judgment subtly corrupted by our tendency to be hypercritical of the candidate from the other party and hyperdefensive of our candidate. That spirit is not much credit to us, but partisanship inevitably brings it about.

As for the criticism every government needs, a nonpartisan system could supply this as well as a partisan one, it would seem. Responsibility would fall to persons in and out of Congress who genuinely oppose policies carried forward by the government. There would never be a shortage of critics since almost every policy produces ideological opposition or resistance from those disadvantaged by it. So long as we had a free press, we could be sure an administration would be carefully scrutinized, evaluated, and held accountable for its shortcomings. There would be plenty of praise and blame, and it would reflect people's true feelings and interests, uncontaminated by a spurious spirit of partisanship. Parties? Out—and good riddance!!

But although the abolition of the party system sounds plausible, a closer look will show some flaws in the argument.

Party Decay: More Serious Than People Think

The other side of the argument, that parties are not only useful in many ways but may be indispensable to democracy, must now be examined: What do parties do, and what would we be lacking without them?

Without parties elections would become personality contests to a much greater degree. Although people do not have a very sophisticated knowledge of parties, they usually do know that the Democrats and Republicans have certain persistent leanings. Republicans are more probusiness, anti-labor union, and anti-public spending for social welfare programs, and they give inflation control higher priority than unemployment reduction; in brief, Republicans are more conservative than the Democrats. Knowing this about the major parties provides invaluable cues to intelligent voting. It enables people to vote for party representatives who roughly reflect their own views. Without parties, voters would have to discover the policy leanings of many candidates. This the average voter could not do, partly because the self-advertising, the image gimmickry, the charges and countercharges of a campaign would leave most voters thoroughly confused.

Most Americans are not serious students of public affairs. They are casual students, who take a limited amount of interest in politics and politicians. They would never take the trouble to closely study the campaign literature, read widely about the candidates, sort out truth from fiction, and come up with reasonably accurate analyses of the various candidates—especially when the absence of parties would lead to a profusion of candidates, far more than we have now. Even those most able and willing to ferret out the necessary information about the throng of candidates would have a near-impossible job on their hands. *No political system should make excessive demands on the public knowledge of its people.* A nonparty system would do precisely that.

Without parties would we often not have adequate surveillance of those in power. On the national scene newspapers are preponderantly conservative in their *political* stance. Newspapers have given strong editorial support to almost every Republican presidential candidate since World War I—Harding, Coolidge, Hoover, Landon, Wilkie, Dewey, Eisenhower, Nixon, Ford. Only Goldwater failed to win majority newspaper support.[11] Thus, conservative politicians could count on a friendly press while liberal politicians would get rough treatment. This happens now, true, but it is at least partially counterbalanced by Democratic party criticisms of conservative Republican officials.

In the absence of parties how confident could dissenting legislators be that their criticisms would be adequately reported by the press? Most newspapers now feel some obligation to give both parties a reasonably fair shake, at least in the news columns. Arguably, they would not feel as obliged to report criticism they disagreed with, if no parties were around.

Partial party responsibility some of the time is better than none at all. Even if we have had frequent periods of divided government in Washington, such divisions may prove transient aberrations rather than permanent trends.

Party responsibility means that a given political party takes control of the government, formulates a program, and accepts responsibility for that program. Its members are willing to be judged by the electorate for their collective performance in office.

We do not have real party responsibility in Washington since individual members of Congress usually seek reelection based on their own voting records, their constituent services, and their public relations skills. But party members tend to vote together on many issues partly because of sharing a common ideological inclination and partly because of a sense of party fraternity that develops within Congress. If the president is a member of a given MC's party and the president rates high with the public, his "coattails" improve the reelection prospects of that MC. This is true especially if he or she was marginally elected in the previous election; long-term incumbents rarely need to worry about the state of executive popularity. There is a desire, therefore, to support the president when he is a party member—a desire reinforced by subtle ties of partisan feelings that increase from time to time. While this desire is not strong enough or consistent enough to give us a sufficient degree of party responsibility, it at least moves in that direction. It gives the public some basis for deciding that the party in power should or should not be kept in office.

Being able to "kick the rascals out" is a prime feature of democratic government. But how is that accomplished if no party controls the government? Do voters simply vote out the incumbent in the legislature—even though he or she may have dissented from the course of action taken by the majority? That, of course is unfair. But few voters take the time to find out who voted for what and make a selective judgment of who merits support. To expect voters to do so makes unrealistic demands on the public knowledge of the average voter. The most we can realistically hope is that the better informed voters will decide that they do or do not like what the party in power is doing and then make a party judgment. In view of the diversity that now exists within parties, that is a crude and highly imperfect way of evaluating the quality of those who govern, but it is the best we can currently do. And it is clearly superior to the almost blind judgment that would otherwise be made.

Parties can exercise a restraining influence on executives. Often the latter's arrogance, impetuousity, or bad judgment lead them into dangerous policies. Party leaders who see their president taking action that imperils the party's national reputation are inclined, through self-interest, to warn him. Sometimes, it is true, party leaders become so protective of their president that they are more interested in defending his excesses and misjudgments than in steering him onto safer ground; the spirit of partisanship can blind them to their true self-interest. (Watergate is a case in point.) But despite this not infrequent tendency, it is better to have party leaders on hand with a permanent concern for the reputation of their party, and hence a lasting concern for responsible presidential conduct, than not to have them. A president's friends in the executive office may be reluctant to speak candidly to him since they owe their jobs to him. But congressional leaders from his party do not sup at the presidential table; their jobs survive whatever anger a president may feel about their criticisms. Every president needs advice from those with an interest in his success but who can also feel independent enough to speak their mind. Only a party system can ensure such advisors.

Parties help MCs make intelligent decisions. Legislators do not have time to study all of the multitudinous measures that come before them. They must rely, to a large extent, on persons they trust who generally share their outlook on public affairs. Party leaders who are in close touch with committee chairs from the same party supply this help. The presence of parties enables those with a moderately liberal or moderately conservative orientation to cooperate more effectively in support of roughly common objectives and common principles. In the absence of parties such cooperation would be much harder to organize.

In the absence of parties, wealthy, skillfully led, organized special interests would have even more power than they do today. Walter Burnham has made this argument for political parties. Parties, he says, "are the only devices thus far invented by the wit of man that can, with some effectiveness, generate countervailing power on behalf of the many individually powerless against the relatively few who are individually or organizationally powerful."[12]

In a wholly atomized, free-for-all, anarchic Congress (which one without parties would be) the poorer, less political savvy, less organized or unorganized groups would receive short shrift. It would become a Congress of the jungle, with the most cunning, ruthless, and aggressive groups dominating the scene.

Political parties may check the rise of demagogues. Jeanne Kirkpatrick has wisely observed that "party loyalty is our best protection against surge movements: men on horseback and various kinds of demagogic, sudden-flash parties."[13] People with no party commitments can more readily support charismatic candidates whose basic values and goals are not well known. When party leaders play an important part in selecting a party's nominee, greater safety exists. These leaders know, from close observation and contact, something about an experienced politican's judgment, trustworthiness, and steadiness under fire. For this and other reasons, Kirkpatrick deplores the fact that we are becoming preoccupied with "media skills; organizational skills; direct-mail, computerized fund-raising appeals; 'turn out the vote' techniques, and public relations.... It may take only technical skills to be nominated and elected, but it surely takes political skills to govern."[14]

Reviving Our Parties

All of the arguments for the value of political parties have special validity when parties are comparatively strong and cohesive. The arguments lose validity in proportion to the degree that parties are feeble. While American parties are not exactly feeble, they are much less united and powerful than they once were and than they now are in many other democracies. Political scientists for years have been advocating reforms, therefore, that would make our parties stronger and more active in formulating policy and more accountable for their behavior.[15] Stronger parties would weaken the cherished independence of individual representatives and senators, but that independence is usually a matter of being free from party control but under the sway of powerful organized interests from their district or state. That is hardly an independence to be prized.

How could stronger parties be brought about? Reformers have suggested the following:

1. Congress should pass election laws that give professional party leaders a larger voice in selecting party candidates at party conventions
2. Parties should hold "preprimary" conventions before the primary elections are held that choose congressional nominees, with these conventions identifying which of the various potential nominees is favored by party leaders in the relevant congressional district or state
3. National party conventions should select their vice-presidential candidate from a list of three to five persons recommended by the presidential nominee (instead of rubber stamping his preference)
4. Party conventions should be held every two years to give local delegates a voice in making party policy in between presidential election years
5. Congressional committee chairs should be denied to senators and

members of Congress who frequently oppose the party's program
6. States should repeal primary laws that permit *crossovers*, the practice of allowing Democrats to vote for Republican primary candidates and vice versa
7. Parties should create grass-roots, dues-paying organizations that encourage greater local participation in party policy and party affairs
8. The opposition party should develop a "leadership council" that can speak for that party on policy matters
9. Any public financing adopted shall make those funds available through the parties rather than directly to the candidates

Although these and other proposals have often been made, little is done about them. The gradual decay of the parties continues.

One proposal for strengthening the parties not mentioned in the above list seems particularly noteworthy. That is the suggestion that the president regularly consult his party leaders in Congress on both substantive policy and on strategy. If the president and his party's legislative leaders jointly formulated a *party* program, instead of the president drawing up an *administration* program and urging his party leaders to support it, we would make enormous strides toward party government and party responsibility. The legislative leaders would be much more eager to push through a program they had helped devise—which in turn would strengthen the chances of a legislative program passing. Rank-and-file legislators would find it harder to balk at a party program, partly constructed by their own leaders, than one that the president alone had formulated. They could still vote against it, if they wished, but the pressure to back the party program would be substantial. The public would know this was the party program and could hold the party responsible for it. The public would be faced with the kind of choice it can best make—deciding if a general program and the people who devised it deserved a vote of confidence or deserved repudiation. Perhaps most important, if presidents consulted party leaders on all significant domestic and foreign policy initiatives, we would be protected from the kind of presidential abuse of power that gave us Vietnam and the long list of Nixon abuses of power. A president would be making decisions with powerful, experienced political leaders, who could divert him from a reckless, vengeful, or ill-advised course of action. Decisions collectively made by the president and party leaders could still be wrong, but the risks of near-autocratic decisions (as in foreign policy) would be greatly reduced. Nothing would do more than this reform to ensure the prudent government we so need in the nuclear age.

The alternative is a more *personalized* government, one which depends unduly upon the personal wisdom and discretion of the president. This can give us more decisive and, sometimes, more progressive government, but it can also give us more dangerous government. If we can institutionalize *collective* policymaking by the top elected officials of the nations, we would go far toward protecting ourselves from the abuses of power that can most seriously threaten both democratic government and planetary peace.

Although the case for strengthening our parties is compelling, the outlook for action is bleak. The most crucial reform—the weakening or elimination of direct primaries and presidential primaries—can be blasted by opponents as "taking government away from the people and giving it to the bosses." Simplistic, superficial, misleading, and demagogic though this is, it is a powerful and probably insuperable barrier to reform. It seems *so* democratic, and that is enough to win. But some day we may be sorry.

The major hope, then, is that presidents will formulate *party* programs in consultation with top party congressional leaders. Presidents have shied away from this for most of our history, but—just maybe, someday.

History shows, all too clearly, that political parties are the first casualty when dictators come along. Opposition parties are a nuisance, an irritation, and an obstacle to the achievement of total power and to the maintenance of that power, so they are abolished and their leaders jailed. People who are contemptuous of political parties should reflect on that once in awhile.

Notes

1. For general studies of political parties, see Frank Sorauf, *Party Politics in America*, 3rd ed. (Boston: Little, Brown, 1976); William N. Chambers and Walter Dean Burnham, *The American Party System* (New York: Oxford University Press, 1975); Thomas W. Madron and Carl P. Chelf, *Political Parties in the United States* (Boston: Holbrook, 1974); Everett Carl Ladd, *American Political Parties; Social Change and Political Response* (New York: Norton, 1970); and Everett Carl Ladd, *Where Have All the Voters Gone?* (New York: Norton, 1978).
2. Information on proportional representation can be found in Enid Lakeman, *How Democracies Vote: A Study of Electoral Systems* (London: Faber, 1974).
3. Descriptions of coalition politics appear in Lawrence C. Dodd, *Coalitions in Parliamentary Government* (Princeton University Press, 1976).
4. An unflattering description of the "purist" phenomenon is present in Nelson W. Polsby and Aaron Wildavsky, *Presidential Elections*, 4th ed. (New York: Scribner, 1976), p. 22-26.
5. A good account of the role of third parties is Daniel A. Mazmanian, *Third Parties in Presidential Elections* (Washington, D.C.: Brookings Institute, 1974).
6. See Walter De Vries and V. Lance Tarrance, *The Ticket-Splitter: A New Force in American Politics* (Grand Rapids, Mich.: Eerdmans, 1974).
7. Amitai Etzioni, "Public Affairs," *Human Behavior*, August 1978, p. 16.
8. Austin Ranney, *The Governing of Men*, 4th ed. (New York: Dryden Press, 1975), p. 205.
9. See Polsby and Wildovsky, *Presidential Elections*, pp. 166-168. See also Everett Carl Ladd, Jr., " 'Reform' Is Wrecking the U. S. Party System," *Fortune*, November 1977, p. 188.
10. See Thomas E. Patterson and Robert D. McClure, *The Unseeing Eye: The Myth of Television Power in National Politics* (New York: Putnam, 1976), Chapter I.
11. Milton C. Cummings, Jr., and David Wise, *Democracy Under Pressure*, 3rd ed. (New York: Harcourt Brace Jovanovich, 1977), p. 280.
12. Walter Burnham "The End of American Party Politics," *Trans-Action*, December 1969, p. 22.
13. Jeanne Kirkpatrick, Interview on *U.S. News & World Report*, September 18, 1978, p. 55.
14. Ibid.

CHAPTER 8

ELECTIONS: THE DEMOCRATIC DRAMA

Free elections are the climactic events in a democratic society. The politicians may rule for a time, but the people ultimately control their careers. A cartoonist once portrayed a politician watching the vote flood being counted on election night—and shaking his head, saying: "Gad, all that power! It just doesn't seem right!"

The United States is an election-happy country. We have elections for president every four years, preceded by a host of primary elections to narrow the candidate field. We have elections for members of the House of Representatives every two years and for one-third of the Senate, too. We elect state governors, lieutenant governors, treasurers, secretaries of state, attorney generals, and auditors either at the same election or in odd-numbered years. We elect state and municipal judges (something few other countries do) and local prosecuting attorneys. We elect mayors and members of city councils. The list could be extended to county commissioners, county clerks, sheriffs, coroners, school board members, and even officers of farm acreage control committees. Every time we turn around, it seems, another election is being held—to say nothing of all the private elections to choose officers for farm bureaus, churches, lodges, fraternities, student councils, and for every private organization in the land.

Do we elect too many public officials? Most political scientists would vigorously agree since we vote for such a flock of people about which we know almost nothing that elections often become almost farcical.

If we voted for fewer officers (who really knows whether the auditor, coroner, sheriff, secretary of state, and state treasurer are doing a good job?) and concentrated our attention on learning more about the performance or potentialities of these fewer persons, we would be less democratic in a superficial sense but more democratic in terms of accountability. Unfortunately, any effort to convert an elective office into an appointive one produces loud and often demagogic cries (from those who fear losing power) that we are wresting control from the people and handing it over to the politicians and bosses. In almost every case that battle cry is enough to kill the proposal. And so we go to the polls, face a bewildering list of candidates whose very names are unknown to us—to say nothing of their records—and blithely cast our votes. The whole procedure seems to illustrate the ancient truth that there is no principle, however valid in general, that cannot be deformed if carried to extremes.

The Candidate—Off and Running

It is easy to become a candidate for most elective positions. Now that party conventions nominate few candidates, individuals can usually get on the ballot simply by registering with the secretary of state and/or by getting a modest number of bona fide signatures of local or state residents on a petition. The real job, for the more important offices, is raising the money to run an active campaign and assembling a campaign organization that will help do the work. Since official party organizations per se seldom get involved in primary campaigns and have few resources to contribute to the general election campaign, candidates must recruit their own campaign staffs.

Why do people become actively involved in these campaigns? Well, if the candidates are running for governor, U.S. senator, or U.S. representative, they will have a few good jobs ("patronage") to pass out to their supporters if they win. But campaign workers are rarely interested in these positions. They volunteer their services because of personal or partisan loyalty, shared views on public issues, or because they like politics and want to become "involved." For the most part these activists are white, better educated, and more prosperous than average, and they are usually middle-aged. They also tend to be either more liberal or more conservative than the average voter.

Lester Milbrath divides the public into three categories—gladiators, spectators, and apathetics.[1] The first group is composed of activists; the spectators follow politics with some interest but do not participate beyond voting; the apathetics (about 25% of the population) ignore politics altogether. Only about 13% of the adult population have ever bothered to write to an elected officer, less than 5% have volunteered to help in a campaign, and about 10% have given money to a campaign.[2]

Money, Money, Money

Running a campaign, especially for national office, requires a great deal of money. In a presidential election year all candidates spend over half a billion dollars on campaigns. Running for the Senate in a large state usually requires several million dollars, and running a competitive race for the House, several hundred thousand dollars. A campaign for state office is much less expensive but still involves sizeable sums. So, recruiting influential and skillful fund raisers is one of a national candidate's most important tasks.

People contribute cash for a wide variety of reasons. Many do so because they generally agree with the candidate's ideology or his or her stand on some issue of particular importance to them. Contractors or insurance executives may give to local or state candidates in hopes of receiving lucrative contracts in return for their help. (There are lots of roads to be built or repaired and thousands of public buildings to be insured. Frequently contracts for these services go to campaign contributors.) Interest groups give to legislative candidates who are sympathetic to—or at least cooperative with—their goals. Many persons give because they are solicited by a friend or colleague, and they hate to say no. A few give in hopes of being placed on a public official's personal staff. Highly partisan people give because, in the heat of a sharply contested campaign, their favored candidate looks more and more like Sir Lancelot while his or her opponent takes on an increasingly villainous appearance as election day nears.

These days, national candidates often employ direct-mail solicitations. They purchase mailing lists from magazines, charities, public interest groups, book clubs, and other private organizations, making special efforts to obtain mailing lists from organizations that tend to have generally liberal or generally conservative citizen ties. The names of previous contributors to liberal or conservative causes or candidates are especially welcome. No Democratic liberal, for example, is interested in William Buckley's *National Review* mailing list, and no Republican conservative wants *The Nation's* circulation list. By computerizing the names and addresses of thousands or even millions of persons who are in the target area of potential contributors and then preparing painstakingly drafted letters appealing for financial help, campaign committees and professional fund-raising organizations have raised vast amounts of money for candidates like George McGovern, Barry Goldwater, George Wallace, Morris Udall, and Ronald Reagan. Tax laws that enable political contributors to qualify for a tax credit (for half of their campaign contributions up to $100 for a couple and $50 for a single person) have presumably encouraged private contributions.

Although both labor unions, and corporations are forbidden by law to contribute directly to national candidates or campaigns, each has found ways to evade the law. The AFL-CIO, for example, has a Committee on Political Education (COPE), to which union members are encouraged to voluntarily contribute. Members can authorize the union to deduct a small percentage of their wages for political purposes, or they may be solicited individually by union officers. Unions raise millions of dollars annually in this manner and turn over the money to favorite candidates. Unions also help their political favorites by cooperating with specially targeted registration campaigns, by endorsing candidates in union literature, and by helping their normally Democratic members get to the polls. These activities have no specific dollar value, but they are definite assets to the Democratic party and its candidates.

Many business corporations used to help favored parties and candidates by asking their senior or junior executives to contribute toward a fund for them. Although the solicitation was ostensibly voluntary, a refusal would not be regarded as helpful to one's career prospects. In 1972 Richard Nixon's fund raisers collected millions of dollars illegally from corporations by dubious tactics, an activity that later led to numerous corporate convictions.

In 1974 Congress passed a law forbidding individual contributions to a candidate to exceed $1000 but permitting corporations to ask their employees for anonymous donations. Since then, corporations have become far more active on the campaign front. By 1978, nearly 2000 corporate political action committees (PACs) were registered with Washington; each of these can legally give candidates up to $5000 apiece per election. In 1976 these PACs gave about $8 million to congressional candidates—and the figure is expected to continue to rise. As the vice-president of Common Cause (a public interest lobbying organization) commented, "... We're headed to a time when PAC giving becomes the dominant force in our political system."[3] The implications are worth pondering.

More than unions and corporations get into the act, however. If Congress considers a major bill seen as hostile to the interests of doctors, the AMA often contributes handsomely to candidates opposing that bill. Farm organizations similarly give substantial support to their friends in Congress as do a host of other organizations whose interests are promoted or injured by federal or state legislative action. With federal legislation vitally affecting the economic fortunes of almost all the important economic interests in the country, it is easy to see why half a billion dollars can be raised every four years.

To what extent do large campaign contributions taint the political process and make legislators indebted to the "fat cats" or special interests groups? Research has been unable to answer this question definitively. It is one thing to demonstrate that persons receiving large sums of money from groups or individuals subsequently support their donors' interests and another to prove that they did this *because* of the contributions. Perhaps their ideology would have led them in this direction, whether money had been given or not. Members of Congress naturally take a benevolent attitude toward economic interests located in their state or congressional district—campaign contributions or no. However, the legislators will *not* vote for an economic interest if they believe that vote will seriously jeopardize their prospects for reelection. Members of Congress do put their *own* self-interest ahead of the interests of any group among their constituents.

On the other hand, if the pressures for or against a proposed bill are fairly evenly balanced, or if the bill is arousing little public attention, it would be natural for representatives and senators to come down on the side of those who have helped their cause. And political scientists generally agree that money buys *access*. Those who contribute can count on a hearing and a careful consideration of their views. Finally, money rescues a person from anonymity. Anyone who gives a large sum will be known by the candidate. People sometimes will pay to achieve that status.

That money alone cannot win campaigns is usually conceded by students of money and politics. In the presidential elections from 1932 through 1976 the candidate who spent the most money won five times and lost seven times.[4] (Republican presidential candidates routinely outspend Democratic candidates.) Incumbents usually outspend their challengers, but they normally win in any case. In primary campaigns, however, money can make a real difference, especially if none of the contenders is very well known. Advertising gives name recognition, and it can create a favorable image if the money is spent shrewdly.

In an effort to reduce the possibly adverse effects of large contributions in presidential campaigns, Congress enacted a law in 1974 that limits presidential candidates to spending not over $10 million in primary campaigns and $20 million in the general election campaign. In the presidential primaries Washington matches each privately contributed dollar with a public dollar—up to about $5 million.[5] Public money constitutes all of the $20 million that each nominee can spend in the fall campaign. Thus far, efforts to publicly finance congressional and senatorial campaigns have failed, despite a strong effort by Common Cause, Ralph Nader, and others. Some members of Congress oppose such legislation because they believe the voters prefer to finance congressional elections by private, voluntary contributions instead of their tax dollars. Others fear it will give challengers the money needed to more effectively campaign against incumbents. And still others believe it further reduces public involvement in political parties, which they are reluctant to see happen.

Ever since 1925 laws have tried to limit the total amounts of money candidates can spend and contributors can give to campaigns. There have always been so many loopholes in these "Corrupt Practices" laws, however, that they have been largely ineffective.⁶ Nor has a serious effort been made to compel compliance with them or to publicize total expenditures for the voter's benefit.

The Supreme Court has ruled that candidates can give as much of their *own* money as they wish to their own campaigns. To rule otherwise would violate the free speech provision of the First Amendment, the Court declared in an arguable decision.⁷ This gives wealthy candidates a distinct edge over poorer ones, an edge that has shown up. Millionaires who spend accordingly have been winning a disturbingly large number of Senate races recently. Private money is important in another respect. Private individuals can spend as much as they wish on behalf of a party or candidate if their money is not given *to* that party or candidate. That is, they can finance as many ads as they wish, so long as the party or candidate is not involved in supervising the expenditure.

Some students of government believe that full disclosure of how much money is spent and from whence the money comes will adequately serve the public interest. If the public knows the facts, it can judge accordingly. Excessive spending, it is believed, can boomerang on a candidate, with the financially undernourished candidate able to assume the underdog role and accuse his or her opponent of trying to "buy the elections." Others are less optimistic on this score.

Under the latest law each congressional candidate must authorize a single committee through which all contributions and expenditures must be reported. Congress has created the Federal Election Committee to enforce the legal ceilings on candidate expenditures⁸ and ensure that the public is informed of campaign spending involved in time to influence the election. Whether this and subsequent efforts to achieve "clean elections" by reducing the impact of private money will succeed remains to be seen.

Wooing and Winning

A candidate's first job is to win the primary election, thereby enabling him or her to represent a party in the general election campaign. If the candidate is already well and favorably known, the job is greatly simplified. If he or she is not, every available method must be used to win the public recognition. That may mean television, radio, and billboard ads (so far as funds permit); speaking before as many groups as extend invitation; meeting people at factory entrances, supermarkets, shopping malls, or wherever people congregate; mailing out as much campaign literature as money allows; meeting leaders of as many ethnic and economic interest groups as possible; mobilizing people who will help address the envelopes, fold and insert the literature, and lick the envelopes; persuading supporters to allow posters to be placed on their property; and saying *something* that the press will regard as newsworthy.

Candidates for national office may have polls conducted for them not only to learn about public sentiment on current issues but also to illuminate their strengths and weaknesses as the public perceives them. Some commentators are contemptuous of candidates' reliance on polls, believing it signifies an overeager desire to cater to the public's whims and "gimme" tastes. Of course, it can be just that. But any politician worth his or her salt wants an accurate reading of public opinions and attitudes. To desire a more accurate picture of the public mind rather than relying on hunches or on judgments based on inadequate samples is not sinful. The real question is, how does the candidate use this knowledge—to echo the opinions of the moment or to address himself or herself more intelligently to the problems that concern the voters? Statesmanship is always a rare commodity, but even a statesman needs to know what the public does and does not want.

Candidates for national office may or may not identify with the president or presidential candidate of their party, depending on the current standing of that figure. If he is unpopular, they will ignore him (as Democrats usually did with Harry Truman and George McGovern and as Republican candidates did with Barry Goldwater). If his standing is high, as Dwight Eisenhower's was in every election year except 1958 and as Lyndon Johnson's was in 1964, they will try to "ride his coattails." But ordinarily the voters make an independent judgment of the local candidate; Eisenhower, for example, could not persuade voters to back GOP congressional candidates despite his personal popularity and his earnest pleas for a Republican Congress. On the other hand, a genuinely unpopular figure like Goldwater can cost the ticket many congressional seats.[9] Since most votes are cast on a partisan basis, whatever impairs the general image of the party rubs off on national congressional candidates and sometimes even on candidates for state office. The only casualties, however, are usually those who have previously won by a narrow margin or who would otherwise have run a close race.

Incumbent members of Congress have an enormous advantage at the polls. They often do not have a challenger in the primaries, thus avoiding a bruising and often divisive struggle that leaves unhealed scars for the November election. If they face competition at this stage, incumbents win about 90% of the time—even if the public's general estimate of Congress in general is disdainful. Those who lose are often doddering old wrecks or are the victims of political manipulation of election districts (see below).

Although half of the voters may not know who their congressional representative is, half of them *do*, and that is a decided asset for an incumbent. Members of Congress have also been able to do numerous favors for their constituents, creating or consolidating personal support.[10] Their franking privilege has enabled them to mail, at no cost, newsletters to constituents detailing activities on their behalf. Or they can send out questionnaires on public policy, designed as much to remind the voter of the good job they are doing and the consideration given the public's views as it is to elicit that opinion as a voting guide. (In fact, many questionnaires are "loaded" to induce the desired answers, and since the small percentage of voters who answer polls does not constitute an accurate cross section of the voters, questionnaire results are of dubious value in ascertaining public sentiment.) Members of Congress are usually permitted to announce the awarding of federal grants and contracts for job-creating public projects in their state or district, thus receiving useful publicity in connection with a matter of vital local concern. They have access to subsidized television facilities on Capitol Hill, usable to create flattering film clips for distribution to local TV stations. Favorable publicity is for politicians what profits are for corporations.

If they are members of the majority party, representatives in the House sometimes have a further advantage. Every ten years state legislatures "redistrict" since shifts in national population cause some states to lose seats in the U.S. House of Representatives and others to gain. When redrawing the congressional district lines, the majority party members in the state legislature obligingly strengthen their party candidates' chances in congressional elections by excluding areas that contain strong pockets of opposition party strength and including nearby areas that contain pockets of in-party strength. This process, called *gerrymandering*, produces districts of bizarre shapes, but it is a longstanding method—much deplored by the opposition party, which would do the same if given the chance—of tinkering with election districts to perpetuate or strengthen the party in power.

So, incumbent members of Congress win reelection over 90% of the time, whether they are outstandingly good, mediocre, or putrid. In fact, it is a reasonably common occurrence for members of Congress (and other incumbents) to win renomination and reelection even if they are under indictment for serious crimes.[11] Voters' loyalty to long-tenured members of Congress of demonstrably shabby character is better explained by psychiatrists than by mere political scientists.

Campaigning: From New Hampshire to November

Presidential candidates have a rougher road to hoe than congressional candidates. Over 30 states have presidential primaries, and the others have conventions or caucuses that require attention. This compels candidates to face a fearsome obstacle course, unlike that required of any other man or beast on this planet. Candidates often begin planning their campaigns a full year before the presidential election year. Since the New Hampshire elections takes place in March and the Iowa caucus even earlier, high-gear campaigning begins in January of the election year. Meeting the formal technical requirements to become a candidate in the various states, building and managing a personal campaign staff, creating statewide campaign organizations, the endless travel, the painful decisions on how to make best use of limited funds, the stream of meetings with local politicians—all with different advice that *must* be followed—and with newspaper editors and interest group leaders, the speech after weary speech, developing satisfactory answers to the myriad prickly questions the candidate is asked, the hurried meals, the frequent confusion and lack of coordination that normally plague a campaign, the constant questioning by the press, trying to find a little time to read, the efforts to repair goofs which will surely occur when one talks about politics and public policy for month after month, the frantic fund-raising efforts, hour after hour of smiling brightly while shaking a million hands when your own feels like ground hamburger—well, it takes an incredible amount of desire, determination, and raw energy.

In bygone decades candidates could and often did win the nomination without being the popular favorite in the primaries. Winning the favor of a handful of party "king makers" (who controlled most of the delegates in the bigger states) was more important than winning the primaries. But that day is over. The 30 or so states with presidential primaries must be canvassed for convention delegates. And the psychological advantage of coming out ahead in the primaries has gained paramount importance. To have submitted oneself to the electorate in these states and have become a front runner in them, is to put nonprimary opponents in the unenviable position of trying to oppose "the people's choice."

If the candidate is an incumbent president, his job used to be vastly simplified. Everyone knew his name and his record was so well established that primary campaigning demands were minimal. Usually the best stance for an incumbent, both in primaries and in the general election, was to stay on the job, act "presidential," appear to rise "above politics" by disdaining the usual campaigning rites, and let the vice-president respond to attacks upon the president.[12] In brief, the appearance of "no politics" was the best politics. Sometimes it still is but incumbent presidents can't count on it. Jerry Ford faced a stiff primary challenge in 1976; so did Jimmy Carter in 1980. That an incumbent president deserves no opposition from within his party if he seeks reelection is a proposition that no longer holds.

But for nonincumbents a far more strenuous course is required. If he wants to maximize his chances, the candidate must start building campaign organizations on a nationwide scale but with special stress on states with early primary dates. Some of these states select delegates by party caucus, and the candidate must see that his supporters attend in full force so they can outnumber the supporters of any other candidate. (Anyone can attend these county meetings and help select the delegate(s) from that county for the national party convention.) Diligent work by loyal supporters of Goldwater, McGovern, and Carter in these caucus states had a lot to do with their winning the party nomination.

But the major early effort is in New Hampshire. Since it has the first state primary, a vast amount of press and TV publicity is associated with the candidates' experiences and ultimate fate there. Since the results of that primary have almost invariably pointed toward the ultimate nominee, it is not surprising for the communications media to focus heavily on that state—so heavily that they have been subjected to a good bit of criticism for exaggerating its importance. But New Hampshire's predictive record justifies most of the attention it receives, along with the fact that candidates' efforts are so intense in a state small enough to enable candidates to personally meet most of the voters that this gives candidates a unique opportunity to present their personalities and campaign wares in a major in-depth test. New Hampshire is not a microcosm—it has too few members of minority groups, for example—but its citizens are representative enough to reveal the basic political appeal of the candidates. In any case, the winner (plus anyone who makes an unexpectedly strong showing) receives a flood of publicity and valuable momentum. He may have had national name recognition problems before New Hampshire, but that problem is vastly reduced by a victory there.

New Hampshire's importance is helpful to "dark horse" candidates—those not given much chance to win—in another sense. The state is small enough so that a candidate can make an all-out effort there even if his financial resources are limited. But if he wins in New Hampshire (or comes out of nowhere to make a convincing showing), he will attract money for subsequent campaigns. Money gravitates to potential winners, and New Hampshire thus gives the little-known and financially strapped candidate a fair chance against more well-heeled opponents. (See chapter opening photo.)

Still, many observers would like to have Congress establish three or four dates on which, and only on which, states could hold presidential primaries. Or, they would like Congress to ordain some sequential dating system for primaries that would reduce both the number of primary elections and the duration of the primary season.

Few thoughtful persons prefer a single nationwide primary, for a number of reasons. First, it would handicap the little known contender who needs time to pick up speed. Second, the plurality winner (the one with the most, though not the majority of, votes) might well be the favorite only of the most liberal or the most conservative factions in the parties. Finally, the current system is believed to be a sturdy test of a candidate's ability to deal, over a period of time, with the political demands of a large, diverse, heterogeneous country. It is thought to be the kind of pressure test that ultimately reveals much we need to know about a possible president. Prospects for early reform of the system are thus not bright.

An invariable phenomenon accompanies the race for the presindency. Since the people who attend caucus meetings (especially) and vote in primaries tend to be the most interested voters, and since the most interested voters tend to be the most ideologically inclined, the candidates find themselves forced to appeal to Democrats who are more liberal than the party rank-and-file and to Republicans who are more conservative than that party's typical member. This gives an advantage to candidates who are believed to be, or campaign as, strongly liberal or strongly conservative. But while such candidates may attract fervent support in the primaries and caucuses (enough to nominate Goldwater in 1964 and McGovern in 1972), their strong ideological coloration makes it difficult for them to attract independent and middle-of-the-road voters in the general election.[13] Because they are perceived as radicals or near-radicals, the very quality that helped them win the primaries may doom them in November.

The way to avoid this hazard is for candidates to stress the most liberal (or conservative) part of their policy stance during the primaries and emphasize their more moderate positions during the general election. Since almost any candidate's total spectrum of positions probably runs from left to center or from right to center, this posture can be assumed without taking contradictory stands during the primary and the general campaign or without retreating from specifics to generalities. One development always happens: Both Republican and Democratic candidates move from right or left toward the center when the general election campaign begins. The center is where most of the votes are to be found, especially among the independents and undecideds who are the last to make up their minds.

Candidates can follow various other strategies in the primaries as well. One such strategy is to get on the evening newscasts by saying or doing something that will interest John Chancellor, Walter Cronkite, or ABC's team.

In all likelihood the more issue-oriented candidates will be exasperated by television's daily coverage of the campaign. Television is naturally concerned with events that lend themselves to visual treatment (hence, the mind-numbing camera coverage of candidates' shaking hands and riding in motorcades). Commentators often discuss the candidates' strategy in ways that make the candidates wince, and they give minimal attention to the candidates' substantive policy statements. They pounce eagerly on minor misstatements (or, in the case of Gerald Ford, his missteps), often diverting public attention from what really counts. They treat the campaign as a spectator sports event, not as a serious democratic drama.[14] It rarely occurs to TV news people to attempt to assess objectively candidates' past political records in some depth or to interview people who know them well and have a reputation for candor and fairness.

No hour is set aside, for example, for the best-respected and best-informed national political journalists to discuss with each other on TV their impressions of the strengths and weaknesses of the two candidates. Instead they prefer to balance every partisan pro with a partisan con, leaving the public more confused than illuminated. Thus the two most important aspects of a candidate—previous political record and character—are given scant attention by television. Yet they reveal more about a candidate and his presidential capacity than all the froth, fuss, and flutter which television finds visually entertaining to its audience. But since television's one and only god is Nielsen ratings, maybe that is all we should expect. If television fails in its democratic responsibilities, what does that matter so long as the audience ratings hold up and the stations make money?

During primaries in addition to courting TV newscasters, candidates experiment with various campaign themes and styles to see which works best. Any public speaker quickly learns what lines are well received and which fall flat. They recognize which of their policy positions are sources of strength and which are not. As a result of constant trial and error, in this shake—down cruise, the candidates finally come up with "The Speech" which, with minor variations, they may use for the rest of their campaign. It will be low in substantive content but high in the kind of emotion-laden generalities and phrases that appeal to people with limited political interest and a short political attention span. (One journalist referred to these as BOMFOG speeches——the Brotherhood of Man, the Fatherhood of God—and little else!)

But candidates usually cannot avoid the issues entirely. At press conferences, on "Meet the Press," "Issues and Answers," and "Face the Nation," and when interviewed by editors, journalists, magazine writers, and interest group leaders, they may be obliged to answer more specific questions than they would wish. The more explosive the issue, the more certainly they will

Jimmy Carter and Jerry Ford debate

be interrogated on it. The trick is to be able to give an answer that is not *too* evasive but that still will not alienate too many people. Candidates become extraordinarily skillful at sparring with their questioners and at walking the fine line between a vagueness that leads to charges of fence straddling and a specificity that can cumulatively build a rising tide of negative sentiment. The public claims to like the candid, direct, forthright speaker—so long as the candidate is forthright on the right side! Few candidates want to risk taking a forthright stand on abortion, homosexuality, capital punishment, and national health insurance, fearing they might anger a multitude of voters. Thus, the winner in such confrontations is usually the candidate who *seems* more candid and forthright than he really is.

The smartest candidates probably are those who indicate the general thrust of their policy preferences but deliberately become rather vague when asked about the precise nature of the legislation they support. To say that these need to be studied in great detail and talked over with advisors and congressional leaders before settling on their precise outlines is both politically acceptable—and honest. That, after all, is what the ultimate winner would need to do. At the same time, the candidate is giving the electorate enough general information about goals to enable it to make a reasonably informed judgment.

One of the candidate's major concerns is to avoid verbal indiscretions, which the media and opponents can seize upon as evidence of flawed moral or political capacity. George Romney, running for the GOP nomination in 1968, complained of being "brainwashed" on Vietnam by the military; this self-inflicted wound hastened his political demise. Goldwater had spoken of selling the TVA power-generating facilities to private interests, a comment that impaired his chances of winning half a dozen states then warmly loyal to that federal project. Ford, in a nationwide TV debate, said Poland was not under Russian control, a horrendous misstatement that hurt him grievously. Carter spoke respectfully of neighborhoods wishing to preserve "ethnic purity" and spent weeks trying to explain this to troubled black voters. He also said in a *Playboy* interview that he "lusted after" women in his heart—a remark that was innocent enough in reality, but one that brought tears of purest joy into the eyes of Jerry Ford's supporters. How anyone can hope to talk on and on for a year or more about sensitive policy issues without committing some gaffe or other is a mystery.

Other campaign strategies usually involve securing endorsements from as many prominent and respected political and nonpolitical leaders in each state as possible. Newspaper editorial endorsements are also eagerly sought, despite the absence of cogent evidence that this helps very much. And treating newspapermen and women with courtesy and respect is obligatory; although they report the news more objectively than most people believe, their feelings about a candidate subtly influence their reporting nonetheless. John Kennedy's friendly relations with the press, contrasted with Richard Nixon's quite obvious suspicion of and distaste for the press, was a factor of undetermined significance in the 1960 campaign.[15]

Drawing up the campaign schedule involves serious decisions. While New Hampshire (and Iowa!) win priority attention, candidates cannot wholly ignore the other states until after those primaries are over. Anyone who wins or does well in New Hampshire (and Iowa) must keep the momentum going by winning or doing well in the primaries that most immediately follow. Looking like a winner, or at least a solid contender, starts the flow of both publicity and money. The biggest states, with the largest bloc of delegates, must receive special attention, but it is also imperative to win—not just do well—in the last primaries. The Oregon, Ohio, and California primaries, coming just before the convention, are of crucial consequence. Whoever goes into the convention with the most recent victories is likely to become the top banana. Almost always, that person also tops the last preconvention Gallup poll. The importance of late polls are hard to exaggerate if undecided delegates still hold the decisive voice.

The National Convention: A Hallelujah Chorus

Conventions used to really select presidential candidates, not just go through the motions of doing so. The GOP convention in 1976 was almost faced with choosing between Ford and Reagan, but Ford actually had a majority of delegates in his corner before the convention met. Most political aficionados believe it will be exceedingly rare, hereafter, for a convention to meet without knowing in advance who will be the party nominee. With more states opting for primaries, and the states' caucus-convention delegates assiduously courted long before the convention's opening gavel, the convention's task is usually seen as drawing up a platform (dictated or heavily influenced by the potential winner), ratifying the preconvention results and giving television attention to certain party notables.

The national conventions' central task, in reality, is to kick off the nominee's general election campaign. Since so much TV time is allocated to the convention, its managers want to exploit this free publicity. When the job is well done, everything is organized so as to keep party disunity and viewer boredom to a minimum. The latter is not easy when the nominee's identity is already known. And the network TV analysts do their best to ferret out and play up any possible friction or disharmony. The party managers are largely helpless to prevent this media obsession, but they do try to extract as much drama as possible from the nominee's unannounced selection of a running mate. Even if the nominee knows who it will be, every effort is usually made to pretend that the choice is still pending.

To an increasing degree convention time is given over to the presentation of films that portray the candidate as both populist and statesman. The films feature cheerful childhood scenes, various milestones on the road to fame, down-to-earth encounters with hometown folks, and glowing tributes to the candidate's superlative political exploits. While the film falls short of full canonization, it is designed to make the TV audience proud of a country that could produce such a sterling figure.

The candidate's acceptance speech is the climactic event of the conclave—a speech that, since it reaches a nationwide audience, is worked over and polished as if it were the Kohinoor diamond. If it is not a work of art, it is only because the best speechwriters in the country could not bring it off. One of the classic political blunders of modern times was the mismanagement of the 1972 Democratic convention, giving nominee George McGovern a chance to deliver his acceptance speech at 2:30 AM. Even burglars were in bed by then.

Candidates, incidentally, make a ritualistic endorsement of the platform but are free later to emphasize those portions they most agree with and to ignore those they reject. We have a right to hold a candidate responsible for the *major* positions he takes during a campaign but not for everything in the platform—despite his perfunctory ratification of it. And as we have already indicated, history shows that successful candidates live up to their major campaign promises from 70% to 80% of the time.[16] For political realists that is not a bad record and refutes the popular view that campaign promises are cynically made to attract votes but are promptly fogotten once the campaign is over.

The day following his acceptance speech the nominee reveals the name of his vice-presidential candidate, usually after consulting many prominent party leaders. The only recent exception to this practice was in 1956, when Adlai Stevenson let the convention select his vice-president. While almost one-third of our recent vice-presidents have become president, most are selected for something other than their presidential stature. They are picked for any number of reasons, but especially because:

1. They are good debaters who are skilled at launching verbal darts at the enemy (as were Ford's choice, Robert Dole and Eisenhower's pick, Richard Nixon)
2. They "balance the ticket" ideologically (e.g., Henry Cabot Lodge, the eastern liberal running mate of Nixon in 1960; and Hubert Humphrey, the northern liberal ticket balancer with Johnson in 1964)
3. Their selection will tend to unite the party or placate a sullen region (the reason the Democrats tapped Lyndon Johnson in 1960 and John Sparkman in 1952—to placate the south)
4. They have no political enemies (the distinction afforded Harry Truman in 1944 and Spiro Agnew in 1968)
5. They hit it off well with the nominee when being interviewed for the post (the reason "Fritz" Mondale was selected in 1976)

On the other hand, they may be chosen for reasons no one has ever been able to figure out (Goldwater's choice of William Miller in 1964).

Coming Down the Home Stretch

Between the convention and Labor Day the weary candidate and his running mate mend some political fences and plan their general election campaign strategy. Meanwhile, the American people brace themselves for the final barrage of intensive campaigning. They have already had nine months of steady political cannonading, with two more to go. (The British, in contrast, are content with less than three weeks of campaigning.) Our system is almost as hard on the public as on the candidate.

As already noted, the candidate now appeals not to the party faithful but to the independents and to wobbly party members. This means a more middling stance, as well as a more generalized appeal to widely shared public sentiments. The experimental approach continues, although within a narrower orbit; by this time both candidates have a pretty accurate picture of where their strengths lie and what thrusts will receive the warmest reception.

For several decades Democratic candidates have tried to stitch a winning coalition together by offering legislative goodies to each of a number of interest groups. By offering carrots to blacks, Chicanos, farmers, educators, western groups in need of water, the unemployed, inner-city residents, educators, small businesses, potential home owners, senior citizens, and others, they hoped to win over enough members of each group to effect a winning combination. The Republicans, on the other hand, have appealed to values that largely transcend specific group interests. As regularly as the sun, moon and stars, they have emphasized their deathless hostility to high taxes, inflation, bureaucracy, interference in people's private lives, and to high levels of federal spending. The Democratic formula may change somewhat quadrenially, but since World War II, GOP candidates have made substantially the same policy speeches. A conservative party, of course, tends to be this way.

The Democratic pattern may be changing, now that Democratic candidates, in a more conservative era, are forced to occupy much the same ground as Republicans have long held. The nation has moved to the right, and nationwide concern with inflation and antagonism to bureaucracy, federal spending, and high taxes seem to be infecting larger numbers of voters. Innovative social

Carter's home town

programs will continue to spring primarily from the Democratic party, no doubt, but there will be fewer of them and more concentration on the conservative issues that are currently fashionable. Instead of moderately liberal and moderately conservative major parties, we seem to be moving toward a conservative Republican party and a middle-of-the-road Democratic party—a considerable contrast to the party of Roosevelt (the New Deal), Truman (the Fair Deal), and Johnson (the Great Society).

Since the Democrats have been the majority party since 1933, the Democratic candidate often stresses—though with some delicacy, not wanting to offend Republicans who may be cool to their current party champion—his membership in his party and his intention to carry forward its glorious record. The names of now revered leaders like Woodrow Wilson, Franklin Roosevelt, Harry Truman, and John Kennedy are likely to be invoked to remind voters of the illustrious ancestors of their current leader. (Republicans are hard up for heroes, other than Dwight D. Eisenhower.) As leader of the minority party, the GOP candidate stresses the importance of the man rather than the party. The strategy often works, since Democratic party loyalties are less firm than are Republican loyalties.

In the general election, of course, many of the same strategies are employed as in the primaries. Candidates concentrate on the largest states with the biggest bloc of electoral votes; seek endorsements from important interest groups, from defectors from the opposing party, and from celebrities in the entertainment world; get as much free (if it's not unfavorable) media attention as possible; and keep polling to see what is on the undecided voter's mind. In the final, frenzied days TV advertising is intensified; the messages are largely devoid of substance, but those who are the last to make up their minds are the most likely to respond to personality, emotional slogans, and patriotic themes (or to a friend who urges they vote this way or that).

Getting the voters registered and to the polls is usually a major enterprise of the Democratic party. Republican voters tend to come from the more prosperous and better-educated segments of society, and they register and vote without much prodding. Democratic campaign workers, however, launch all-out drives to register lower-income and minority group citizens; the latter are likely to vote Democratic if they vote at all, but their voting propensity is weak. Seeing that potential Democratic voters go to the polls is a much more efficient way to use campaign workers than trying to convert Republicans into Democrats. For understandable reasons, then, Democrats favor proposals to simplify voter registration while Republicans resist. Of course, neither party openly acknowledges the hidden reasons for its position.

Does Propaganda Win Elections?

We have noted that, congressional primaries aside, access to the most money is rarely decisive in presidential elections. But, does superior propaganda help? Is the party that employs the best advertising agencies and uses the slickest sloganeering gimmicks and whose candidate can best strum the public heart-strings win presidential elections?

The record says rarely if ever do such efforts work, even though partisan supporters fear the worst when they see those clever ads prepared in the enemy camp. Some historical flashbacks make the point. Woodrow Wilson won in 1912 because the GOP had split between William Howard Taft and Theodore Roosevelt, not because of Wilson's superior propaganda skills. Wilson won in 1916 because he "kept us out of war," and Americans seldom rejected incumbents in those days. Warren Harding defeated James Cox because the nation had had a normal Republican electoral majority since the Civil War, and there was a hunger to "return to normalcy." A colorless Calvin Coolidge was victorious in 1924 over John W. Davis for much the same reason—plus the prosperity that prevailed at that time. Herbert Hoover, a wooden campaigner, defeated Al Smith because of continuing prosperity and because Smith, though a better campaigner, was Roman Catholic and in 1928, many Americans were still suspicious of Catholic candidates, who might do nameless but dreadful things. In 1932 almost anyone could have defeated the depression-tarred Hoover; and conversely, in 1936 a resurrected George Washington would have had trouble defeating Franklin Roosevelt. The latter won again in 1940 because Americans feared having inexperienced leadership once war had broken out in Europe; in 1944 the country was again uneasy about changing leadership in the midst of all-out war. In 1952 and 1956 no one could have defeated "Ike" (Eisenhower), whatever their propaganda genius. In 1964 Goldwater never had a ghost of a chance; likewise in 1972 for McGovern. In 1976 Ford could not overcome his pardon of Nixon and the Nixon party legacy.

Only in 1948 and 1960 could it be said that superior propaganda skills carried the day—and even that is unclear. In 1948 Truman was no great shakes as a public speaker, but his scrappy, hard-hitting attacks on the GOP, and his successful identification with common people may have been the margin of victory in an exceedingly close election. In 1960 John Kennedy's performance in the first televised presidential debate with Nixon and the millions of pamphlets sprinkled near black churches just before election reminding black voters of Kennedy's intervention on behalf of jailed Martin Luther King, Jr., could have tipped the scales. But when elections are very close any number of factors can be cited as possibly decisive. In general, both parties have sufficiently persuasive propaganda to cancel each other out, allowing more basic factors such as the state of the economy, the personality of the candidate, and fixed party loyalties to decide the election. These factors, it should be emphasized, normally determine how we vote. (Candidates' stand on specific issues like abortion and nuclear power, seem to be gaining in importance, too). This is a reassuring conclusion for those who fear that the general public is at the mercy of Madison Avenue wizards.

National politics are full of surprises, enough to cause historically minded political soothsayers to be cautious about making dogmatic predictions. All of the savvy political observers *knew* that Truman would lose in 1948—but he did not. They *knew* Nixon was washed up as a political figure after his defeat by Kennedy in 1960 and his loss in the California gubernatorial race in 1962. They *knew* that Goldwater could not be nominated for president—seven months before he was. They *knew* McGovern couldn't be nominated—seven months before he was. They *knew* no president desiring renomination could be denied that honor by a challenger within his party—until Reagan *almost* beat Ford in 1976. Journalists, commentators, and the rest of us make many cocksure statements about what will and will not happen. If we remember our history, we would make fewer of them.

Notes

1. Lester W. Milbrath and M. L. Goal, *Political Participation: How and Why Do People Get Involved in Politics?* 2nd ed. (Skokie, Ill.: Rand McNally, 1977), pp. 11–24.
2. Charles E. Lindblom, *The Policy-Making Process* (Englewood Cliffs, N. J.: Prentice-Hall, 1968), p. 45.
3. "Keep Business Cash Out of Politics?" Interview with Fred Wertheimer, *U.S. News and World Report*, April 30, 1979, p. 54.
4. Nelson W. Polsby and Aaron Wildavsky, *Presidential Elections*, 4th ed. (New York: Scribner, 1976), pp. 52-53.
5. *Congressional Quarterly*, Weekly Report, October 12, 1974, pp. 2865-2870. The money comes from voluntary check-offs on personal income tax returns.
6. Report of the Democratic Study Group of the House of Representatives, November 1971.
7. Buckley v. Valeo, 424 U.S. 1 (1976).
8. $100,000 or 8 cents for each eligible voter, for Senate primaries and $150,000 or 12 cents per eligible voter for the general election. In the House, $70,000 each for the primary and general elections.
9. The Lyndon Johnson landslide in 1964, the year in which Goldwater ran, reduced Republican membership in the House from 175 seats to 138 seats.
10. Morris P. Fiorina, *Congress, Keystone to the Washington Establishment* (New Haven, Conn.: Yale University Press, 1977), pp. 39-49.

11 "Give Us a Better Congress," *The New Republic,* November 4, 1978, pp. 7-9.
12 See Harold F. Gosnell, *Champion Campaigner Franklin D. Roosevelt* (New York: Macmillan, 1952), pp. 203-212. Presidents Dwight D. Eisenhower and Richard Nixon also resorted to this tactic when running for reelecion.
13 Polsby and Wildavsky, *Presidential Elections,* pp. 88-89, stress the point.
14 See Bernard Rubin, *Political Television* (Belmont, Calif.: Wadsworth, 1967); and Newton Minow, John Bartlow Martin, and Lee M. Mitchell, *Presidential Television* (New York: Basic Books, 1973).
15 Theodore H. White, *The Making of the President, 1960* (New York: Atheneum, 1961), pp. 294-295.
16 Michael Krukones, *Campaign Promises as Predictors of Presidential Performance* (Ph.D. diss., Miami University, 1978). Gerald M. Pomper, *Elections in America: Control and Influence in Democratic Politics* (New York: Dodd, Mead, 1968), p. 191, demonstrates that about three-fourths of national convention platform planks are at least partially fulfilled.

Not long ago, organized groups of people who tried to influence governments to do or not to do something that helped or hurt them were called "pressure groups." Journalists and others still use this term, sometimes, but political scientists do not. The latter believe "pressure groups" has a slightly sinister connotation, and since scientists like to describe empirical phenomena in an "objective" fashion, they decided to call them "interest groups" instead. Whatever they are called, their major purpose remains the same: to influence governments.

They have good reason to try. With a federal budget of over $500 billion (to say nothing of state and local budgets), and federal laws and regulations that govern Washington, (and state capitals to a lesser extent) can help or hurt groups in a major way. If people having common interests did not organize to protect those interests, they might find themselves victimized by laws and taxes that gave them less than a fair shake. Most people want not only a fair shake but a little bit more if they can get it. Interest groups behave just that way, and whatever they want seems to them indistinguishable from the public interest.

Individuals are not totally helpless in the world of politics. A very important individual, such as a leading newspaper columnist, a magazine editor, a TV commentator, a chairman of a large corporation, or a president of a national union, carries political weight. But the average citizen who writes to a senator or an editor, makes a speech, or casts a vote that adds a drop to the stream of public opinion carries some weight as well. Unfortunately, the individual actions of ordinary citizens do not amount to much, and most people know it. The way Joe Blow or Jane Blaine can maximize his or her influence on government is to join with others who share their opinions or who have similar economic interests, and then to collectively beat their drums. As we have said before, governments apply the grease to squeaky wheels, and people collectively can squeak louder and more effectively than they can as atomized individuals.

The Organized and the Unorganized

Americans love to organize. There are organizations to represent every interest from the Amalgamated Flying Saucer Clubs of America to the National Armored Car Association to the Childbirth Without Pain Education Association to the Maine Sardine Council. There are more than 10,000 national organizations—over 1,000 with headquarters in Washington, D.C.—and heaven knows how many state and local associations there are. Organizations are easy to form, and almost everyone belongs to some organization at one time in their life; in fact, surveys show that a good part of the population—40%—is *active* in one or more of them today.

Our welter of organizations reflects an educated, affluent, and advanced economy as well as a free society. The former creates the diversity that leads to a mushrooming of organizations. While this diversity is largely economic, an educated and prosperous country also spawns a growing number of organizations having ideological and moral bases—such as Common Cause, the Environmental Defense Lobby, the National Organization of Women, and organizations concerned with abortion. A free society gives our people the opportunity to freely organize and even the encouragement to do so since policy is expected to develop from a context of active public involvement. In a democracy we expect people to help make policy rather than passively await dictates from on high.

Organizational fecundity accompanied by vigorous political activity also is furthered by our decentralized political system. Federalism, a bicameral (two-house) national legislature, and separation of powers require that groups with political interests not only operate in 50 separate states (and in the municipal subdivisions, which often have considerable autonomy) but seek to persuade a succession of congressional committees and subcommittees, both houses of Congress, and the chief executive. Most important of all, oftentimes, they must then nudge administrators into using their vast discretion to make decisions that promote their well-being. A political system like this, in a democratic land, is the richest possible breeding ground for a swarm of organizations, with lobbyists running hither and yon to ensure that the government behaves as nearly as possible the way they want it to.

If we had reasonably unified, disciplined political parties controlled by a president or a cabinet, the interest group task at the national level would both be simplified and made more difficult. Instead of trying to persuade a dozen different political units, interest groups could concentrate on one power center. But at the same time, it would be much harder to pressure a powerful inner circle, responsible for overall policy formulation, than to persuade less conspicuous and more malleable subcommittee and committee chairs with narrower responsibilities and less diverse constituencies.

Finally, our decentralized political system makes it much easier for groups to *block* distasteful legislation than to push bills they want over a succession of hurdles. To do the latter often requires a massive, highly skilled, and expensive lobbying effort.

The most prominent interest groups include the National Rifle Association, American Medical Association, National Education Association, AFL-CIO, American Farm Bureau Federation, American Bar Association, Teamsters, American Petroleum Institute, "highway lobby," the so-called "Jewish lobby," "military-industrial lobby," and U.S. Chamber of Commerce. On issues that vitally affect their members, the views of these groups are treated with deference by most members of Congress.

Do powerful organized groups dominate our society? Does Congress do little more than reflect the organized pressures brought to bear upon it, rather than being a truly independent body pursuing the public interest?[1] Do rich, powerful, politically cunning private groups largely dominate our society by pressuring Congress, leaving Chicanos, Indians, migratory workers, welfare recipients, the mentally ill, and the aged, (who are poorly organized) with no say?[1] Critics of the American political system often complain bitterly that the system is unresponsive to the needs of the less fortunate groups in our society. While there is some merit in the charge, the critics often fail to recognize that the poor (and other less organized groups) have little direct political clout primarily because of their own social characteristics rather than because the system refuses to give them an equal break in the political arena.

The poor are less well-educated than other members of society; they are less articulate; they have less interest in public affairs than middle-class Americans; they have a lower voting propensity than others; they have less self-confidence, less political experience, and less political skill than others. Nor are they self-consciously a group. As a consequence of these characteristics they are much less well organized than are most other groups in our society that have a stake in public policy.

(The same is doubtless true in almost every country. Even in Russia, the peasants and unskilled workers are not only at the bottom of the prestige ladder and the income hierarchy but have less influence in party conclaves than others. It is doubtful if the poor, unskilled, and uneducated have political power proportionate to their numbers in any society in the world.)

Saul Alinsky, a colorful, aggressive, persevering, and highly imaginative figure, attempted to organize the poor for political action in the 1950s and 1960s.[2] He had a measure of success in some instances, but that success was partly attributable to his unique personal qualities. Efforts to train other leaders in order to broaden and perpetuate his work proved mainly unsuccessful, despite a training school that commanded Alinsky's best efforts. And when President Lyndon Johnson's War on Poverty programs attempted to carry out neighborhood elections, so that the poor could choose their own representatives to help direct local antipoverty programs, less than 4% of the eligible voters turned out.

If the poor were well organized, their interests undoubtedly would be better protected than they now are. But it is very difficult to organize them. While the poor have the same opportunity to organize as do other groups, their disabling political characteristics ordinarily require us to rely on the conscience of the middle class for legislation helpful to them. That conscience can be sensitized by occasional middle- or upper-class leaders (e.g., Franklin D. Roosevelt and Robert Kennedy) with a gift for dramatizing their needs and for spotlighting the obligations of the more fortunate toward them. The existence of a host of federal and local programs to improve the education, housing, health, and vocational training of the poor demonstrates that this reliance on conscience is not without fruit. On the other hand, the working, middle, and upper classes have a streak of meanness in them so far as their attitudes toward those on welfare are concerned. The almost savage hostility felt toward persons on welfare—most of whom are there for reasons beyond their control—is one of the less admirable aspects of American society.

Finally, even if the poor were well organized and politically active, it is not at all clear what major legislation benefiting them would pass that now is blocked. Important legislation, especially if it involves considerable amounts of money, would still have to be acceptable to the ever-dominant American middle class. Given current tight government budgets *and* the paucity of good ideas for helping the poor by methods compatible with American values, quite

Cesar Chavez champions migratory children

possibly no significant new legislation will follow. The problem of poverty, unfortunately, is one of the most *intellectually* baffling problems this country has ever faced. (Welfare aside, it would seem that this country is more open to criticism for tolerating an income distribution and tax system that multiplies and protects the rich than it is for callously ignoring the interests of the poor.)

As for the powerful interest groups, some of them are less powerful than is commonly thought. The business community is well organized to protect its interests, and it is usually thought to have the most formidable political power in Washington. Yet business fought most of the New Deal reforms—and lost. It lobbied against most of the numerous and expensive "welfare state" legislation that has been enacted over the past 50 years. It resisted most of our environmental protection laws. It opposed establishment of the Office of Safety and Health Administration (OSHA), and it now loathes the inspectors from that office that "harass" it on worker safety problems. It has no appetite for the entire affirmative action program aimed at eliminating job discrimination for women and minorities, now deeply entrenched in federal law. It battled unsuccessfully against various consumer protection laws.

While it is true—and significant—that business pressures have frequently been successful in watering down many of these programs and weakening their enforcement, it should be clear to all but those who will not see that Washington has not been a puppet of the business interests during most of the twentieth century. (As this book is written, however, business has gained a stronger political position than it has known for a long time.)

If business has often been a loser in Washington, labor's chief political arm, the AFL-CIO, has experienced even greater frustration. Except for Lyndon Johnson's Administration, labor has lost legislative struggles with monotonous regularity since the late 1940s. Considering its membership, wealth, and political experience, it is rather surprising, in fact, that this organization has so consistently been defeated. But while the American political climate is rarely favorable, these days, to cherished AFL-CIO goals, the organization can fight off legislation that it regards as seriously detrimental to its interests. (Political scientists Peter Bachrach and Morton Baratz have convincingly argued that organized interests are often able to prevent major issues from even being placed on the national agenda—a sobering thought.[3])

Because the American economy is so heterogeneous, it is common for competing interests to oppose each other in Congress. Railroads oppose the trucking industry, exporters battle importers, farm organizations are pitted against food processors, coal producers fight natural gas companies, corporations oppose unions, the American Medical Association jousts with the United Automobile Workers, and so forth. In some cases powerful interests clearly out-muscle less powerful ones, but many times a more even struggle enables MCs to use their own best judgment rather than merely respond to the strongest pressures bearing upon them.

However, in many instances, little organized opposition exists to discipline the activities of powerful groups. For example, there are potent organized pressures (from the Pentagon, the armed services organizations, the veterans' groups, and corporations having Pentagon contracts) to continually raise the military budget, but almost no organized pressures to reduce it. Innumerable organized groups fight to maintain indefensible tax privileges, but almost none are on hand to support serious tax reform. Any major effort to cut the federal budget activates a host of organizations prepared to fight to defend benefits currently enjoyed, but organized pressures to eliminate or reduce unjustified benefits are minimal. Both unions and corporations may oppose stiff environmental laws or support import quotas on products competitive with American industry. In these and many other ways the "countervailing power," or balancing influence, of opposing interests falls short of helping bring about a fair consideration of the issues.

As power in Congress becomes more and more decentralized, with subcommittee chairs and individual senators enjoying greater influence than ever before, interest groups are acquiring greater power over that body. A veritable

The Ingredients of Group Power

swarm of lobbyists had almost unparalleled influence on the 90th Congress, (1979–1980) usually by hacking away at a presidential program that, whatever its flaws, had attempted to put the public interest ahead of lesser interests. Political commentators fear the trend may continue.

What factors give interest groups political clout, other than the absence of potent interest groups that oppose their goals? Size is one ingredient. The larger the organization, the more respectfully its leaders are heard—at least on issues that directly and importantly affect members. The latter qualification must be borne in mind. An organization is generally assumed to reflect accurately the views of the membership on matters of great moment to its members. On issues of secondary, or peripheral, importance to members, the organization's stand may well represent the views of the leadership rather than of the rank-and-file. This is well understood by experienced politicians, who usually discount the organization's stand on these matters. (This is one reason the AFL-CIO, despite its 13 million members, so often tastes defeat.)

To digress a moment, virtually all organizations are governed by a so-called Iron Law of Oligarchy.[4] Since most organization members are too busy with their private affairs to give more than casual attention to organizational activities, only the salaried, full-time officers develop the skills and have the time to shape the organization's stance on most public issues. On matters of major significance to the general membership, they will usually attempt to ascertain and stay close to that membership's views. On other matters their experience, full-time role, control of the organizations's funds, direction of the organization's newsletters and magazines, and skill at parliamentary procedure enable them to dominate the organization and spell out its procedures and policies.

Needless to say, the degree of oligarchical domination differs from organization to organization. Always, however, a small minority is disproportionately influential because it cares more, works harder, and has the skills, time, and money to gain such influence.

Other factors as well determine interest groups' power. Prestige is one. The American Bar Association, for example, has far more prestige and hence more influence than the National Welfare Rights Organization. So does the National Conference of Mayors and the Committee for Economic Development (a group of broad-gauge business people who hire an excellent research staff to study economic problems and propose improved public policies.)

The amount of money an organization has and is willing to devote to lobbying and to persuading its members to pressure Congress also matters. So does the political sophistication, resourcefulness, and determination of its leaders.

Important, too, is an organization's political connections. If it has a powerful ally in a committee or subcommittee chair who handles legislation of concern to it, that organization has a long head start over less favored groups. Folk wisdom is correct in this case; having friends in the right places often makes a signal difference.

Finally, a group's political power is often crucially influenced by the "spirit of the times." If the prevailing currents of public opinion are running with it, or against it, those currents may be decisive. For example, because labor unions were the beneficiary of favorable public sentiment in the early New Deal period, legislation like the Wagner Act (which guaranteed the right to organize trade unions and bolstered collective bargaining) was passed in 1935. After World War II, when nationwide strikes were hampering the national effort to reconvert from wartime to peacetime production, the tide ran the other way and legislation reflected that tide. The Taft-Hartley Act, for example, cracked down on various labor union "abuses."

Consider two other examples. During the late 1950s and early 1960s public sentiment supported efforts to guarantee equal rights for blacks; the NAACP and other black organizations' legislative efforts thrived. After the urban riots of the mid-1960s, black leaders no longer ran with the wind to their back. Similarly, business organizations profited from a friendly environment of opinion in the 1920s but suffered from a much less friendly public attitude with the onset of the depression in the 1930s.

To repeat an oft-made point, the executive branch, the Congress, and even the courts try to please the majority of those who care about a particular

Vice President Mondale and labor chief Meany confer

issue. The more intensely they care, the more reluctant our government is to offend them. The controversy over federal aid to low-income mothers desiring abortions financed by Medicaid is an eloquent illustration of the principle. A minority of Americans felt so strongly that they were subsidizing what they viewed as murder with their taxes that Congress voted to stop funding a law that gave poor mothers the same opportunity to have abortions as more affluent mothers have. While the minority in this case was partially organized, it was the fervency of their objections, rather than the degree of organized pressure, that carried the day for them. Congress responds to strongly held feelings, organized or not, as was demonstrated by its reluctance to enact universal military training in the period from 1939 to 1940. Even the National Rifle Association derives much of its power from the intensity of feelings held by anti–gun control citizens in this country.

Even the most potent private groups do not get all they want from legislatures. Usually they must settle for considerably less. But the trucking industry and the Teamsters Union were long so formidable (a paralyzing nationwide trucking strike would be their ultimate and frightening weapon) that Congress gave them kid-gloves treatment. For example, the Interstate Commerce Commission (ICC) has enforced regulations that promote high transportation rates and limit competition. It has also promoted a gaggle of rules that fostered inefficient transportation by such practices as preventing trucks from carrying certain cargo on return trips from their original destination. But the trucking owners (who are making far more on their investment than the nation's manufacturing industries) and the Teamsters (who are paid very handsome wages for their work) have had such a lucrative vested interest in preserving and fighting for the status quo that Congress never thought of intervening. (Now that inflation control has such high priority, however, reforming the ICC may be a possibility.)

Similarly, the private health insurance companies, with their 500,000 employees, are so solidly entrenched in the economic scheme of things that they have thus far prevented serious consideration of any national health insurance system that does not use them as "carriers." Although experience abroad has demonstrated that a national government can administer health insurance more efficiently through its own administrative apparatus than through private corporations, the private companies here can continue to raise such a stir at the prospect of abolition that their demise cannot be seriously contemplated.

Consider another example. Economists are overwhelmingly opposed to the minimum wage, believing that it tends to reduce employment for teen-age and unskilled labor (in addition to other disadvantages). But the AFL-CIO has lobbied heavily and effectively to prevent Congress from repealing that wage or even reducing it for teenage labor.

Evidences of the negative power of major private interests are manifold. As these interests become older and more deeply entrenched and as more Americans develop self-interest attachments to them, it will become increasingly difficult to change the status quo in ways they oppose. Our economic and regulatory systems promise to become more frozen, more rigid, more resistant

Interest Groups and the Public Interest

to major reforms. As of now, reforms of a highly significant character usually take place only if some crisis has aroused a strong public demand for action. For example, the Farmington, West Virginia mine disaster killing 78 miners in 1968 made possible a major mine safety act that the mine owners strenuously opposed but the United Mine Workers Union favored. Pollution hazards alarmed enough Americans in the 1960s to enable Congress to force strongly resisted controls on the automobile industry and other polluters. The OPEC oil boycott and subsequent quintupling of oil prices made possible the elimination of an oil-depletion allowance law that had richly benefited the oil companies for years despite the opposition of most independent students of the oil industry. Finally, profound American concern over inflation since 1977 has made possible anti-inflationary reforms that stood no chance before that date.

Thus, while some reforms can be made in our economy despite the deep-lodged power of private interests, major reforms are almost impossible in the absence of disasters, crises, or anticipated crisis.

Common Cause, Ralph Nader, and Lobbying

In assessing the power of organized groups in this country, more recent political phenomena need to be taken into account. A number of public interest organizations and lobbies have recently made an appearance.

Common Cause is one such organization that has made a considerable splash in Washington.[5] This "citizens' lobby" exists, not to further the interest of any special economic group, but to promote causes it believes important to democratic, honest, and "open" government. In the past it has labored diligently and with considerable success to bring a public spotlight on campaign spending, to limit the size of private contributions, and to introduce public financing into presidential and congressional campaigns. It has pressed for legislation requiring congressional committees to open more of their meetings to the press and general public. It has fought for stronger codes of ethics for members of Congress, opposed the gerrymandering of congressional districts, battled the seniority system by which members are assigned committees and chairs are chosen, and lobbied for a federal consumer protection agency. Its impressive record is primarily due to its experienced and highly skilled leadership, supported by over 300,000 unusually well-informed, local-level activists who contribute $15 a year to the organization. These activists also constitute a formidable letter-writing brigade, which applies pressure to selected members of Congress on behalf of Common Cause goals.

Common Cause is resented or held in disdain by many members of Congress, who regard it as naively idealistic and somewhat self-righteous, but it has become one of the "movers and shakers" in Washington (and in some state capitals, too). Whether it will continue to be as effective in the future as it has been in the past is one of the more interesting political questions. Many reform organizations make a noteworthy opening effort and then either fade away or lose their crusading fervor, lapsing into bureaucratic institutions trying desperately to discover more causes that can keep the membership loyal and the bureaucracy well fed. As for Common Cause, well, we shall see.

Ralph Nader began as a one-man public interest lobby who captured pub-

Ralph Nader: champion of the consumer

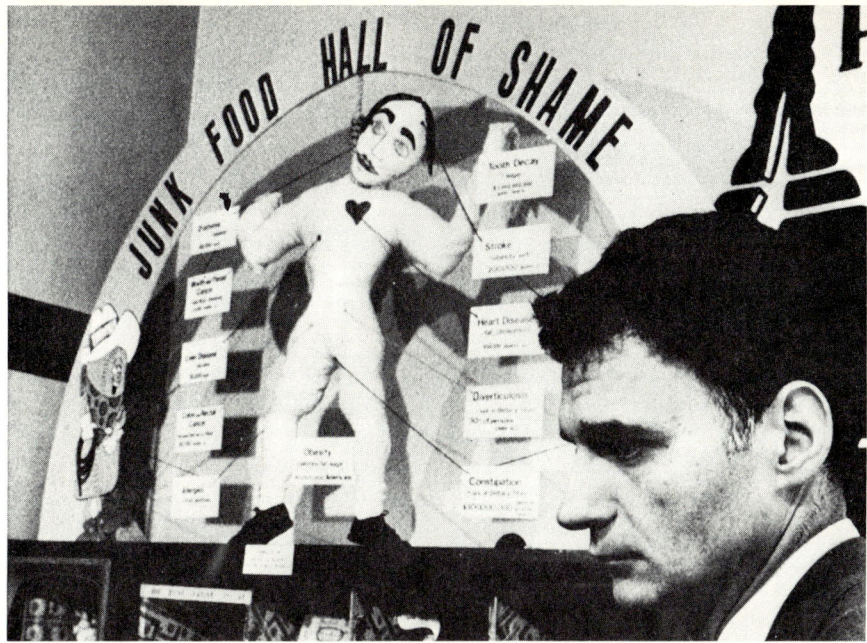

lic attention with his Sir Galahad posture and intrepid attacks both on major corporations and government agencies.[6] Nader's charges that the Corvair was *Unsafe At Any Speed* (the title of his book) so irritated General Motors that it tried to discredit him by instructing a private detective to look for something scandalous about his private life. When this invasion of privacy was discovered, the president of General Motors was obliged to apologize personally to Nader. A subsequent law suit yielded Nader over $250,000. Nader, who leads a notoriously ascetic life, promptly invested the money into various consumer-oriented activities. By mobilizing ill-paid, but enthusiastic, young college graduates, public-interest-minded lawyers, and others into a number of consumer protection agencies, Nader made himself into a household word and a feared (and often hated) gadfly to business, bureaucracy, and the Congress. Royalties from his books, from speaking engagements, and from direct-mail appeals have enabled him to finance a vast range of endeavors.

Nader is given substantial credit for the passage of such laws as the Highway Safety Act, the Wholesome Meat Act, the Federal Coal Mine Health and Safety Act, and the Radiation Control Act, to cite only a few. He has also prodded various federal regulatory agencies into taking a more aggressive stand and helps keep the major corporations on their toes by his probes and suits. Nader's strength has lain with the vigor of his efforts, the accuracy of his charges, and his utter fearlessness. Inevitably, some of his attacks have been less well founded than others, leading to some justified criticism. But because he knows that his strength lies in his credibility, his mistakes thus far have seldom been glaring.

Nader has demonstrated that knowledge is power—especially if combined with indefatigability, audacity, and a gift for capturing media attention. Not a temperate, balanced, or particularly judicious man, Nader is nonetheless one of the most remarkable political phenomena of the age. Unfortunately, he alienated many MCs in 1974 with an ill-concocted series of election profiles that contained many factual errors and distortions—the apparent result of inadequate supervision of a zealous but inexperienced group of investigators carrying out an overly hasty enterprise. Some observers think his heyday is over, but it would be premature to write him off. He remains a political force to be reckoned with, a doughty David battling our economic and political Goliaths.

Numerous environmental lobbies have also made an appreciable impact on the national legislature and on national policy. The Friends of the Earth, the Environmental Defense Fund, the Sierra Club, and others have educated, lobbied, and sued on behalf of ecological causes. Their zeal and tirelessness ensure that the interests of the general public in environmental protection will not lose out for lack of a hearing. Their power depends heavily, however, on a sufficient number of "scares" to keep the public supportive of their work. Only then will the courts and Congress pay heed to their pleas since they are usually arrayed against interests much more powerful than they.

Another aspect of today's lobbying environment is the growing number of state and local officials who regularly descend on Washington to protect or enlarge their "share" of federal funds distributed to state and local programs and agencies. About $70 billion is now funneled from Washington to state and local agencies; with this much money at stake, it is inevitable that strong efforts would be made to obtain as large a share of the federal gravy as possible. But the spectacle of public officials lobbying other public officials to obtain benefits for their clients—including the administrators of the programs involved—is a scene to which we are only slowly becoming accustomed. (Mayors and governors have been in the lobbying business since the New Deal, but lesser officials have only recently taken an active part.)

Not to be overlooked, of course, is the activity of lobbyists from federal agencies seeking more funds—or more power—from Congress. The Pentagon, for example, has hundreds of employees who publicize the functions of the Defense Department and nourish public support for a big budget, but it also has a large and highly professional staff to testify before congressional committees on behalf of that budget. The Pentagon misses no bets in cultivating key MCs on behalf of its interests. Other agencies do the same—only less skillfully and assiduously.

Applying the Pressure

Interest groups use a variety of techniques in their efforts to persuade politicians to do things their way. The most familiar device, of course, is through lobbying.[7] Early in American history lobbyists used the kind of unsavory practices that gave the label a bad name. (Lobbyists today prefer to call themselves "Washington representatives" or "legislative agents.") Lobbyists once seduced the entire Georgia legislature with fat bribes, obtaining land for one-half cent an acre, which later sold for 100 times that price (the Yazoo land fraud). During the Grant Administration bribery on a large scale led to a major railroad scandal (the Crédit Mobilier affair). Direct and indirect forms of bribery were commonplace during the post–Civil War period. But in recent years outright bribery has become quite unusual.

Today's lobbyist is usually a well-educated person, with a background in law, economics, or public relations. He or she may also be an ex-member of Congress, or a former congressional committee staff aide, or an ex-member of a federal regulatory commission. These people are well suited to lobbying because their experiences in Washington have given them a good grasp of how that city functions.

Lobbyists, of course, need to be highly knowledgeable about the levers of power in Washington and how those who control those levers can be best manipulated. Only extensive firsthand experience can provide that knowledge.

The effective lobbyist is also well informed about the organization he or she represents and the probable impact that proposed legislation will have upon its interests. Much depends, in this field, as in all others, on knowing the relevant facts and in being able to provide accurate information to legislators and administrators on matters pertinent to their mutual concerns.

Today's lobbyists, after acquiring a stock of information essential to their mission, routinely employ the "soft sell." Since any attempt to threaten or intimidate legislators would be deeply resented and prove counterproductive, they resort instead to the gentle arts of persuasion. Ignoring legislators known to be hostile to their goals, they concentrate instead on persuading the undecided and on supplying the most potent argumentative ammunition to legislators already friendly to those goals. Many MCs, incidentally, welcome being briefed by lobbyists on certain issues. After hearing lobbyists from both sides, they can be reasonably sure they have heard the major arguments at stake, thereby helping them to make informed decisions. Or, if they already intend to support or oppose a given measure, the lobbyists whose interests coincide with their stand can save them research by supplying them with materials that concisely state their case and provide rebuttals for expected counterarguments. But woe betide lobbyists who furnish MCs with inaccurate information; their welcome will be chilly indeed the next time around.

Lobbying has become a major growth industry in Washington in recent years. From 1973 to 1978 their numbers burgeoned from perhaps 8,000 to about 15,000. Although they successfully fought off efforts to force greater public disclosure of their activities (the current law is shot through with loopholes), informed observers believe it takes $1 billion a year to finance their Washington operations, with another $1 billion spent to influence public opinion at the local level.[8]

Almost every major corporation now employs one or more lobbyists. The Ford Motor Company, for instance, has a full-time staff of 40 people at the nation's capital. About 50 labor unions maintain separate lobbying offices in Washington, while the parent AFL-CIO headquarters has 300 lobbyists and supporting staff members.

Lobbyists and their staffs engage in a wide range of activities connected with the legislative process. While no single lobbyists may do all of the following in pursuit of a favorable legislative outcome, all are done by lobbyists at one time or another.

Lobbyists examine the bills introduced into Congress to see which ones affect their organization.

Lobbyists seek to discover which bills will be given a hearing. Many bills are introduced *pro forma*, to appease insistent constituents, but are not intended to be taken seriously by the committees to which they are assigned. There is no point to buttonholing legislators about bills clearly destined for committee pigeonholes.

The lobbyist may personally draft, or direct the drafting of, legislation desired by his or her employer. These are then given to friendly MCs, who obligingly introduce them into Congress. Or amendments to bills already in the legislative hopper may be drawn up for introduction during committee hearings or on the floor of the House or Senate.

Lobbyists can have maximum influence during the processing of bills in congressional committee. At this stage friendly or neutral committee members are most likely to be contacted to gain their support. Lobbyists may supply friendly MCs with tough questions to ask hostile witnesses or prepare speech drafts for later delivery on the House or Senate floor. Sometimes the most useful lobbying can be done with a senator or a representative's legislative assistant, however, since many members of Congress rely heavily on them for advice.

Lobbyists frequently discuss legislation with the staff members of congressional committees. Some staff members have considerable influence with committee chairs and members. By alerting them to the organization's stake in the legislation and "educating" them on the issue, they may facilitate the passage of a desired measure, help kill it in committee, or modify its phraseology in helpful ways. The committee staff, significantly, drafts the final committee report.

Key resource people may be asked to act. Lobbyists may, directly or through the organization's top officials, identify friends of MCs (if they agree with the organization's objectives) and urge them to write, wire, or phone their MC to support or oppose the relevant bill or amendment. A letter or call from a friend back home may well carry more weight than an appeal from an obviously self-interested lobbyist. The U.S. Chamber of Commerce, for example, maintains six regional offices that have identified key resource people known to have influence with various legislators. At critical periods these persons are urged to enlighten their congressional representative or senator about issues of importance to the chamber.[9]

Mass mailings emanating from the organization's rank-and-file are frequently employed to pressure MCs or relevant committees. The lobbyist may be charged with notifying members about what is at stake and with supplying them with pertinent facts and arguments to be used in writing their congressional representative. But members are urged to draft their own letters, phrased in their own way, rather than imitate a form letter formulated by the lobbyist. The U.S. Chamber of Commerce is able to mobilize 1,200 local Congressional Action Committees, whose 100,000 members can deluge Congress with letters, telegrams, and phone calls. In addition, chamber publications reach 7 million people, many of whom respond to a request for mail on certain issues.

Conservative organizations can call on the services of Richard Viguerie, whose carefully compiled list of 4 million conservative activists is available for a fee.[10] Viguerie's treasured, computerized list was used to generate 2.5 million letters against ratification of the Panama Canal Treaty. Senate Republican leader Senator Howard Baker was showered with about 100,000 letters originating from Viguerie's list. (The treaty passed anyway—and Senator Baker voted for its passage.)

Lobbyists try, when feasible, to combine their efforts with those of other organizations sharing their interest in certain legislation. Or they may seek to at least receive a formal endorsement of their position from organizations that may not want to play an active part in the legislative battle but are willing to provide an endorsement. (Some day the cooperating organization may want a similar favor from them.) They may also arrange for full-page ads detailing their case in either leading newspapers throughout the country or in the *New York Times* or the *Washington Post*, which are read by almost all MCs.

Lobbyists follow legislation closely throughout the long tortuous legislative process. They keep a sharp eye on the bill in subcommittees, in full committees, during floor action in both House and Senate, and during conference committee deliberations (where differences between House and Senate versions are smoothed out). They intervene at each point at which they might be influential, and particularly with those MCs whose support is most crucial at each stage. This requires a sophisticated understanding of the contours of power in Congress, and shrewd insights into the minds and psyches of individual members of Congress. Some lobbyists keep index cards on MCs—cards with information about their background, families, interests, strengths, weaknesses, prejudices, and susceptibility to different forms of flattery or entreaty. MCs are treated as unique individuals, not as stereotypes.

Once a bill has been passed, lobbyists may intervene to ensure presidential action on it. If the presidential decision is uncertain, lobbyists may seek an audience with the presidential staff member most likely to advise the president on the bill or to prepare materials for his perusal. Nothing must be left to chance.

Lobbyists follow up on distasteful bills that become law. They may advise that it be challenged in court as unconstitutional (though this is rare). More likely, they will contact the agency administering the bill.

Administrators have a great deal of power. Congress frequently hands administrative agencies broad grants of authority (e.g., to forbid unethical, unsafe, unhealthy, deceptive, discriminatory, competition-destroying practices), and these must be converted into specific regulations (Should laetrile be banned? How much coal dust per cubic feet is safe in a mine? Where must elevators be installed for the benefit of handicapped persons?). This power may affect interest groups and our daily lives more than the legislation passed by Congress. Since lobbyists know this, they spend a large part of their time testifying at public hearings on proposed administrative regulations—and in "educating" administrators in less formal settings. If lobbying with MCs receives the greatest public attention, lobbying with administrators is often much more crucial to their basic interests.

If efforts to curb enforcement fail, lobbyists can begin a fresh challenge to repugnant legislation or administrative regulations during the next congressional session. They may advocate, if not repeal, at least amendments to mitigate the damage already done. Major drives may be mounted to slash the appropriations of "hostile" agencies and hence reduce the number of employees enforcing distasteful regulations.

Friendly or potentially friendly members of Congress or candidates for Congress may be given campaign funds. This gesture, at the least, can ensure a friendly hearing and may help MCs come to a favorable decision in some cases. MCs by no means automatically vote for the interests of groups that help finance their campaigns, but they would be less than human if these funds were not a factor in making up their minds. Although many other factors are also involved, the strength of the "Jewish lobby" on issues involving Israel stems partly from the fact that Jews make disproportionately large contributions to the major political parties (especially the Democratic party) and partly because of Jewish influence within the communications industry.

Members of Congress who are "cooperative" may be invited to address an organization's national or one of its state conventions. This provides welcome "exposure" and valued publicity in the organization's magazine. Or the organization may carry a picture and a friendly write-up in one of its house organs. It may also pay a fat lecture fee to an MC who addresses one of their meetings.

Finally, when appointments are being considered to agencies that administer programs of importance to the organization, lobbyists may work to ensure the selection or defeat of potential nominees. This enterprise may involve many of the same activities used in connection with the processing of a legislative bill.

Considering the broad sweep of lobbying activities, it is not hard to understand why interest groups spend an estimated $1 billion a year to influence public policy. Given the post-Watergate weakening of the presidency (which is a less easy mark for lobbyists) and the increasingly anarchic tendencies of Congress (individual MCs are always more vulnerable to lobbyist pressures than are party leaders) the organized interests plan to get their money's worth. The presidential veto is their principal foe; fortunately, it is no mean weapon.

The Diffusion of Power

Any fair appraisal of American politics would have to concede that while political power is disproportionately lodged in formidable private economic groups, that power is also highly dispersed. Power is diffused widely within the Congress, as we shall soon see. The president has a great deal of power, as have the various bureaucracies. The Supreme Court as well as the lesser courts within our system also share in power. And so does the Federal Reserve Board, which has a major impact on our national economic policies. The Council on Foreign Affairs, Brookings Institution, and the Committee for Economic Development wield power. The editors of leading newspapers and prestige magazines[11] (e.g., the *New York Times, Washington Post, Wall Street Journal*, and of *Time, Newsweek, The New Republic, Foreign Affairs, Washington Monthly, Commentary*, and *The Public Interest*) as do leading columnists and those who program the news and prepare the documentaries and mini-documentaries for the major TV networks. Governors, mayors, and many other nonfederal public officials are listened to. So are some Catholic archbishops and cardinals, as well as some Protestant and Jewish leaders, especially on political matters with moral overtones. In brief, any effort to establish the locus of political power in the United States must deal with the incredibly complex character of power in this nation.

Organized economic power is doubtless the principal component of the power mosaic, and this component cannot only protect its legitimate interests but can often go well beyond. But when really gross abuses of power occur, the other power components are usually antagonized into bringing the offender to bay. Among those involved are likely to be other economic interests adversely affected by the flagrant behavior of the overreaching interest. Thus, a very imperfect, but still important, equilibrium of power tends to exist in this country; whatever markedly upsets this balance—once the media have put the searchlight on it—usually triggers numerous reactive and corrective forces. It is not a neat and tidy system and there are many defects, but it works with a kind of crude efficiency, given the economic premises of our society.

We have repeatedly spoken of group or private interests in this chapter. Is there such a thing as the "public interest," or do people just apply that term to policies which happen to appeal to their private value system? Many political scientists believe "public interest" cannot be accurately defined; some doubt the utility of the term.[12]

The author is less skeptical. Granted, an adequate and precise definition may prove elusive but the same is true of such useful concepts as truth, justice, and beauty. Probably the term best acquires meaning when we spell out some of its concrete applications. There *is* a public interest in maintaining a democratic way of life—that is, in supporting free speech, a free press, freedom of religion, fair trials, equality before the law, and the right of normal adults to vote in free elections. There *is* a public interest in maintaining enough honesty in government to retain the respect of the citizens. There *is* a public interest in giving affected groups a right to be heard when public policy is being formed. There *is* a public interest in giving people who want to work a chance to work and in providing consumers with protection from charlatans, shysters, and deceptive advertising. There *is* a public interest in promoting the health and developing the intelligence of our people. There *is* a public interest in protecting our environment, both for our benefit and for that of unborn generations. There *is* a public interest in avoiding stupid wars.

True, many legitimate differences of opinion arise when we apply those principles to controversial questions surrounding them. But, just because the public interest cannot be clearly discerned on numerous issues, this should not obscure the hard core of common interest that exists even as debates arise on the periphery. Of course, all concepts of value rest upon unprovable and often hidden premises, but if those concepts can survive close and uninhibited debate better than alternative concepts, they merit our confidence and allegiance. The "public interest," then, seems a valid enough concept, though its precise outlines are often, very often, obscured.

A final word about organized private interests. Whatever their useful and even essential role, they do not do two things: First, they are preoccupied with the present and rarely take long-run national needs into adequate consideration. Second, they seek their selective private ends without much regard for coordinating the total legislative product in the interests of overriding national priorities. In other words, they rarely see the "Big Picture" (as Professor David McLellan calls it). In the chapters that follow, we shall see how well our national political institutions do this important job.

Notes

1. For learned discussions of the question, see David Truman, *The Governmental Process* (New York: Knopf, 1971), chaps. 2, 9, 10, 12, and 16; Arnold M. Rose, *The Power Structure* (New York: Oxford University Press, 1967), chap. 2; and Harmon Zeigler, *Interest Groups in American Society* (Englewood Cliffs, N.J.: Prentice-Hall, 1964), chaps. 4-8.
2. See Charles E. Silberman, *Crisis in Black and White* (New York: Random House, 1964), chap. 10; and M. K. Sanders, "Saul Alinsky: Professional Radical, 1970," *Harpers Magazine*, January 1970, pp. 35-42.
3. Peter Bachrach and Morton Baratz, "Two Faces of Power," *American Political Science Review* 56 (December 1962), 947-952.
4. The classic statement was made by Robert Michels, *Political Parties* (New York: Free Press, 1962), pp. 342-356.
5. See John W. Gardner, *In Common Cause* (New York: Norton, 1972); Frank Getlein, "Conflict with Interest," *Commonwealth*, November 19, 1976, pp. 740-741; and R. M. Williams, "Rise of Middle Class Activism: Fighting City Hall," *Saturday Review*, March 8, 1975, pp. 12-15.
6. See Charles McCarry, *Citizen Nader* (New York: Saturday Review Press, 1972); "Nader: Success or Excess?" *Time*, November 14, 1977, pp. 76-81. David Ignatius, "Stages of Nader," *New York Times Magazine,* January 18, 1976, pp. 8-9; and *New York Times,* January 29, 1978, p. E3.
7. Two of the better books on interest groups and lobbying are Carol S. Greenwald, *Group Power, Lobbying and Public Policy* (New York: Praeger, 1977); and Lester W. Milbraith, *The Washington Lobbyists* (Chicago: Rand McNally, 1963). On public interest lobbies, see Jeffrey Berry, *Lobbying For The People* (Princeton, N.J., Princeton University Press, 1977).
8. *Time*, "The Swarming Lobbyists," August 8, 1978, p. 15.
9. Ibid, p 17.
10. Ibid, p 21.
11. Thomas R. Dye, "Oligarchic Tendencies in National Policy-Making: The Role of the Private Political Planning Organizations," Journal of Politics, May 1978, pp. 309-331.
12. For a disciplined analysis of the term, see Barry M. Mitnick, "A Typology of Conceptions of the Public Interest," *Administration and Society* (May, 1976), Vol. 8, pp. 5-28.

CHAPTER 10
CONGRESS: OPERATION CHAOS

The Founding Fathers made the legislature the cornerstone of their political structure. It was seen as the central political unit of a society of free men. If republican government were to flourish, it would primarily be because the legislative branch had been properly equipped to do its job. On domestic policy, then, Congress would clearly be dominant, but it would also have a strong role in foreign affairs.

Although George Washington, Thomas Jefferson, Andrew Jackson, and Abraham Lincoln flexed the executive's muscles in impressive fashion, the legislature dominated Washington through most of the nineteenth century. Woodrow Wilson's celebrated book on American government, *Congressional Government* (1888), deplored the weakness of the executive in relation to the overpowering legislature.[1] While the book reflected his post–Civil War observations, it applied to most of the pre–Civil War period as well.

Congress' dominance was challenged by Theodore Roosevelt, Woodrow Wilson, Franklin D. Roosevelt, and most of Roosevelt's successors. Yet even in the twentieth century, when stronger presidents became more common, Congress has held the upper hand in domestic affairs most of the time. The only clear-cut exceptions were during 1912–1916 (Wilson), 1933–1936 (F. D. Roosevelt), and 1964–1966 (Lyndon Johnson), which suggests that the founders succeeded in doing what they set out to do. Today's Congress remains the strongest legislative body in the world. In most democracies, the cabinet dominates the legislature as the president *cannot* dominate the Congress.

The founders' perception of the respective roles of the House and Senate were somewhat less farsighted, seen from today's perspectives. The House, with members elected biennially, was expected to reflect faithfully popular sentiment. The Senate, with members chosen for six-year terms by state legislatures, was expected to be a more elitist chamber. Its aristocratic composition would give it a more deliberative character, a more statesmanlike, broad-gauge view of the public business than that of the plebeian House. It would represent the more mature, sober, conservative opinions of the "better class of people"—the people who owned substantial property, that is, and who were better educated as well.

It worked out that way for a long time. But the passage in 1913 of the Seventeenth Amendment, requiring direct popular election of senators, fundamentally altered the senators' outlook. Like members of the House, they were now obliged to confront the voters directly; while their six-year terms made it easier to resist transient gusts of popular opinion, the inevitability of ultimate popular judgment brought them closer to the common people.

In recent decades the Senate has been the more liberal body, rather than the more conservative, apparently because rural and small-town areas (which tend to be more conservative) were heavily overrepresented in the House. When the Supreme Court changed this by its historic "one man, one vote" decision in 1964, requiring congressional districts to comprise roughly the same number of people, other explanations were sought. The best one still seems to be that many members of the House do not represent blocs of large and comparatively liberal urban constituents, while almost all senators have big cities in their states. Senators, therefore, are obliged to cater more to the needs of masses of lower-income, ethnically diverse, unemployment-prone, civil rights-conscious voters.

The more competitive character of Senate races may also be a factor. Most incumbent members of the House win reelection by thumping margins, thereby releasing them somewhat from pressures to pursue activist policies. Perhaps, too, the fact that presidentially ambitious politicians tend to come from the Senate, and that Democratic senators who want a serious shot at that office have had to be rather liberal, also has something to do with it.

The legislature today has many roles. It will not come as a stunning surprise to learn that its foremost job is to legislate. About 10,000 bills a year are introduced into Congress, and these must be winnowed and processed. A $500 billion budget must be agonized over. Charges of corruption or mismanagement in the executive branch must be investigated (with gusto, it might be added). Several thousand presidential appointments must be confirmed or rejected. And last, but far from least, Congress acts as an ombudsman for constituents who feel that the massive federal bureaucracy is not responding, or not responding properly, to their pleas for help. Many members of Congress believe their most important function is to intercede on behalf of their constituents when red tape, sluggishness, or administrative blunders (or perhaps when fair play is practiced but special favors are wanted) have created a citizen grievance. As we shall see, much congressional time is devoted to what is called "errand running."

The Committee System: Getting Down to Work

With thousands of bills to consider, covering incredibly complex problems demanding equally complex answers, Congress must organize to do its work. The *committee system* provides that organization.

The House has 22 *standing* (or permanent) *committees*, the Senate 17. Each is a specialized committee, handling a certain category of bills. Members typically stay on a committee for many years, acquiring expertise in the subject matter under its jurisdiction. Their collective experience ensures, not wisdom, but at least a measure of competence in dealing with Congress' work.

Still, since hundreds of bills rain down upon the average committee in each session of Congress, this requires more work than a single committee can collectively do. Even though only a small percentage of bills are believed worthy of serious consideration (and hearings), committees find it necessary to subdivide their work into numerous *subcommittees,* each of which is charged with a still more specialized category of bills. This puts a heavy burden of subcommittee work on senators. While each member of the 435-member House serves only on several subcommittees, senators may sit on as many as ten. That makes it all but impossible for the latter to do justice to their subcommittee work. Many subcommittees have to be shortchanged, therefore, with their work done by a very few senators, while absenteeism runs high.

The Senate's squeeze is mitigated by the fact that deliberations in House subcommittees are quite thorough, with more members actively engaged. On

The legislative gauntlet

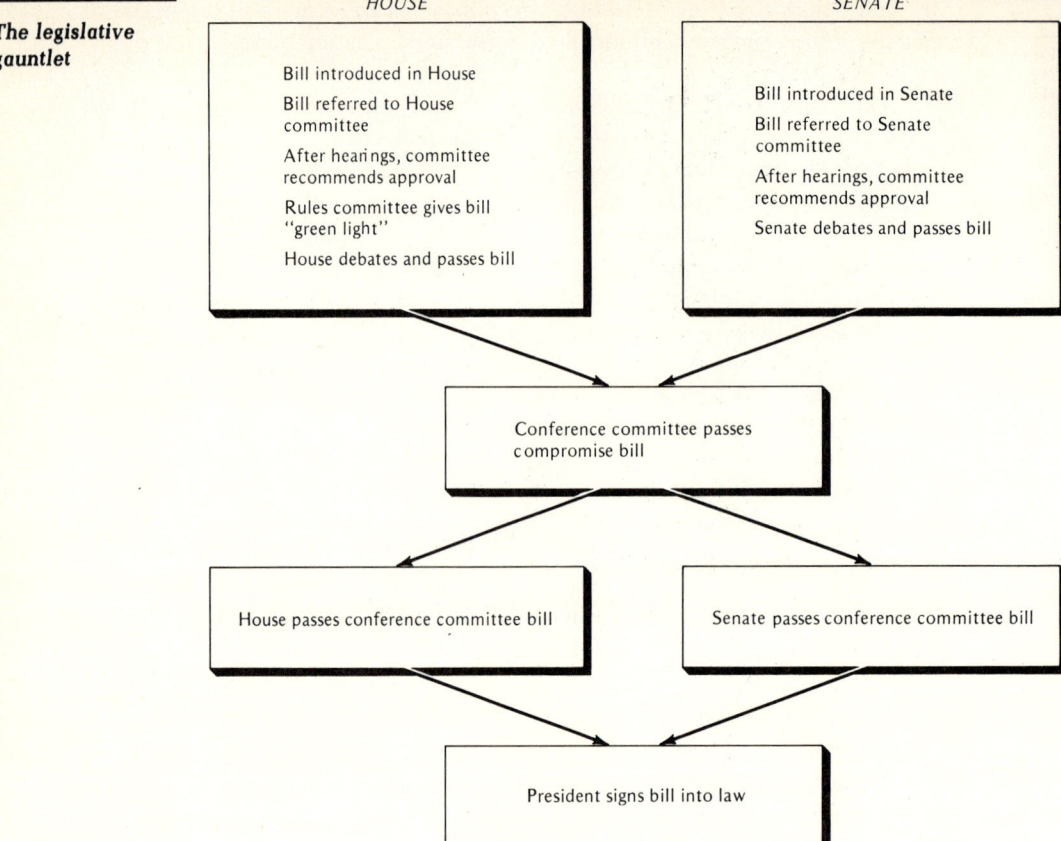

really important measures, however, more careful attention is given by Senate subcommittee members.

In considering legislation the committees and subcommittees need expert advice, which they receive from several quarters. Technical and general information is supplied by the Congressional Research Service, a body of well-paid, highly competent information specialists who do research on legislative problems not only for committees and subcommittees but also for individual MCs.

Subcommittees also draw on the knowledge and experience of the full committees' professional staffs. Each committee hires a substantial number of permanent staff members, who help provide information, arrange hearings, and write reports under the general direction of the committee or subcommittee chair. The quality of the staffs varies sharply; some committee staffs are selected on a purely "spoils system" basis; jobs are handed out in reward for political services or because of personal pressures rather than because of professional experience or ability. But increasingly, committee staffs are selected for reasons of competence; the demands of our time require it.

The principal source of expert advice is the *hearing process*. Hearings are scheduled on all significant bills. Especially qualified witnesses may be asked to testify; concerned lobbyists or persons invited by lobbyists are usually there; ordinary citizens can testify if they request the opportunity. On most bills, then, the relevant facts and arguments are brought forth by expert testimony and by the interrogation of those witnesses by committee or subcommittee members.

When the hearings are concluded, and transcripts are made available to committee members (and all interested MCs) the subcommittee reports its recommendations to the full committee for further discussion and debate. In nine cases out of ten the subcommittee's handiwork is accepted by the full committee, partly because members of other subcommittees (serving on the same full committee) want *their* subcommittee recommendations approved. A spirit of reciprocity exists: You vote for my subcommittee proposals and I'll vote for yours. The more important the bill, however, the less pronounced this tendency is. On matters that vitally concern a committee member's constituency or personal convictions, that member usually speaks out for what he or she believes should be done.

The same spirit of reciprocity prevails on the floor of the House and Senate as well. The committee recommendations are substantially accepted by the parent chamber, 90% of the time. Members of the committee reporting a bill usually have far more knowledge of the facts and the arguments involved than interested MCs who have not been on the committee—so they can usually defend their measure reasonably well during floor debate. But again, members of other committees hoping that *their* handiwork will be respected by the full House or Senate tend to defer to the judgment of the committee that processed a bill. It is a very natural and perhaps inevitable arrangement, but it does mean that a given piece of legislation is normally the work of a small number of MCs, with the great bulk of congressional members playing the role of passive and cooperative onlookers.

To avoid misunderstanding, however, the subcommittees prevail as often as they do partly because their deliberations produce a bill with provisions that do not outrage any significant proportion of the Congress. The subcommittee members are usually politicians with a good sense of what will or will not be acceptable to the Congress, the press, and the country at large. If they should fail to take a fairly accurate reading of the sentiment of these groups, the spirit of reciprocity would falter and their work would be rejected.

While on the subject of committees, several other observations should be made. New MCs apply for the committee of their choice—chosen either because of personal interest or because they believe a given committee covers work of special importance to their constituents. Thus, MCs from primarily agricultural states may want to serve on the House Agriculture Committee or the Senate Committee on Agriculture and Forestry. If from a western state, a member may wish to serve on the Committee of the Interior, which regulates public lands that are concentrated in the West. Service on such committees may enable members to perform services for their constituents that will help them be reelected. Whenever possible, the House and Senate committees that make committee assignments (guided by the Speaker of the House, majority leader of the Senate, and the minority leaders of the House and Senate) try to give MCs the committee assignments they want.

Assignments to less desirable committees is normally given to newcomers, who may hope to graduate to better committees after a few years. When more members apply for committees than seats are available, seniority in Congress normally determines the outcome (unless, that is, a MC has offended the "grand dragons" of Congress by behavior regarded as unseemly; in that case relegation to an unwanted committee may be a form of punishment, though this is uncommon).

The majority party in both House and Senate places a majority of its members on each committee. The greater the majority, the larger the proportion of its members on each committee. The same is true of subcommittee membership; but no matter how few members on any subcommittee, the opposition party is always represented.

In addition to standing committees, *special,* or *select, committees* may be temporarily created to handle special problems. Thus, the Senate created a special committee to inquire into charges growing out of the Watergate break-in. A special House committee was formed in the 1950s to investigate "grass-roots lobbying" activities. Other ad hoc committees investigated assassinations of the Kennedys and Martin Luther King, Jr.

Congressional Leadership—Sort Of

Every organization requires leadership in order to do its work. Congress is no exception.[3]

Significantly, the formal leaders of the House and Senate are sometimes less powerful than the informal leaders. The Speaker of the House, the majority and minority leaders of the House and Senate, and the party whips are often less influential than the committee and subcommittee chairs in both houses.

Committee chairs are ordinarily selected by seniority. The MCs who have the longest uninterrupted term of service on a given committee normally chair those committees—unless they are successfully challenged in the party caucus that convenes at the outset of a congressional session. The opportunity to challenge was formalized in the early 1970s; before that, seniority chairmanship was virtually absolute. But even if the senior committee member (of the majority party) must run the risk of losing his or her job by caucus action, the risk is slight. In almost every case senior MCs get the post; only if they treat other members rudely or unfairly or are ideologically poles apart from their party do they stand much chance of losing that post.

The seniority principle is defended on the ground that prolonged service on a committee yields experience, knowledge, and political savvy. If the senior members almost automatically assume the chair, this prevents a series of bruising leadership battles that would leave injured feelings and hostilities in their wake.

Although all of this is true, seniority has produced some embarrassing progeny in the past. The infamous Wisconsin Senator Joseph McCarthy won a chair through seniority and used his position to harass and demoralize the executive branch by a long succession of ill-supported charges of communist infiltration of that branch. A chairman of the Senate Foreign Relations Committee, nearing 90, could seldom hear the witnesses and often dozed off in his seat. A die-hard southern segregationist chaired a committee that examined the credentials of appointees to federal judgeships ruling on civil rights cases. Another southern segregationist used to leave Washington for prolonged periods to supervise his farm in Virginia so that his committee could not consider civil rights bills.

Developments such as these finally led to the above-mentioned caucus rules permitting a potential chair to be challenged. Many believe that the possibility of being unseated has already persuaded chairs to be less autocratic and arbitrary than in the past. They hope it has largely eliminated a problem that worried congressional observers for decades. What it will not do is alter the tendency of chairs to come from "safe districts," which have a minimum of competition in elections and hence may produce chairs less attuned to current shades of opinion than MCs who come from more hotly contested districts. Yet even here, one study shows little evidence that MCs from highly competitive districts adhere more closely to constituent opinion than those from less competitive districts.[4]

Committee chairs have many powers, although less than they had 20 years ago. They decide if bills are to be actively considered or whether they will be pigeonholed. They hire the committee staff. They appoint members of their committee to chair the subcommittees, a power of some importance. Chairs schedule committee meetings, enabling them to delay or facilitate action on bills. Prolonged delays may mean a bill cannot be adequately considered before a session ends. Chairs lead the debate on bills reported to the floor of House and Senate. They are on *conference committees*, which reconcile differences between House and Senate versions of the same bill. They are consulted by the press on matters pertaining to their committees. They are likely to meet with the president when important bills under their wing are of major concern to him.

These are formidable powers and privileges, which underlie the chairs' informal status as leading congressional figures. But a balanced view of their job requires more to be said. A strong personality can be an important leader under almost any circumstances. A weak person can convert a potentially powerful post into a feeble one. Thus, much depends on the personal qualities a chair brings to the job.

The winds of democracy have recently blown through congressional committee chambers, too. It is impossible for a chair to be the semidictator he once was. Reforms within the last decade have given most of the full committees the right to call up a bill, or schedule a meeting, whatever the chair may wish. And while committee members are usually reluctant to force through a measure distasteful to the chair, they can and will do so if the measure is important enough. Finally, subcommittees have grown in power, with subcommittee chairs exercising some of the powers once held by full committee chairs.[5]

The most successful chairs are those who are courteous and respectful to other committee members, knowledgeable about and devoted to their work, and talented enough to spot the compromise that can win majority support.[6] In other words, the successful chair is a good politician. Exploiting his or her powers to the full from time to time may still be a prerogative, but the days of the autocrat are over.

This evolution occurred partly because a spirit of rebelliousness against vested authority took place in the late 1960s. An "equality revolution" swept over this country at that time, manifesting itself in student challenges to university authority and student insistence on a larger part in decisions vitally affecting them; in the feminist movement seeking full equality for women; in the demands of lay persons for a larger voice in church matters; in public employees' demands for the right to strike; in teachers seeking to break free from excessive administrative supervision; in army draftees seeking recognition of "rights" never known before; and in a dozen other ways. Freshman senators and Members of the House, infected by the spirit of the equality revolution, were no longer willing to be as deferential and submissive to their elders as before. They wanted to be heard and to become a full part of the legislative process without going through the prolonged and meek "apprentice" period formerly prescribed for them. (The retirement of an unusually large number of very senior members helped their course along, too.)

While the committees and subcommittee chairs are among the most important leaders in Congress, the formal leadership must not be overlooked. The party caucuses that inaugurate a congressional session do more than provide an opportunity to challenge potential committee chairs. The majority party caucus selects the majority leader and party whips for the Senate—and the Speaker, majority leader, and whips in the House. The minority party caucus selects the minority leaders and party whips for both houses. These selections are then formally ratified when Congress convenes. They constitute the official leadership of the Congress.

As hinted earlier, the majority leader of the Senate and the Speaker of the House can be strong or weak leaders, depending on their personal leadership qualities. Long-time Senate Majority Leader Mike Mansfield, though universally respected as a man of decency, integrity, and intelligence, made little attempt to crack the whip over his fellow senators. This was not his style, and he refused to act out of character.

John McCormack and Carl Albert were Speakers of the House whose personal limitations never enabled them to wield the clout of stern, iron-willed Sam Rayburn in the Eisenhower era. And Rayburn, because of the times rather than of his shortcomings, had less political power than the renowned Speakers of an earlier day—"Czar" Thomas P. Reed and Joseph Cannon.

Republican Senator Robert Taft, Sr., and Democratic Senator Lyndon Johnson, on the other hand, while possessing quite different leadership skills, were able to exercise a strong unifying influence on their parties as majority leader. Taft did so by sheer intellectual horsepower and ideological conviction, combined with an ability to recognize political realities that were nevertheless repugnant to him. Johnson did it by studying the weaknesses and political needs of each senator, bullying those who could be bullied, coaxing those who could be coaxed, and by becoming the wheeler-dealer par excellence.[7]

The Senate's majority leader has few formal powers but does, in collaboration with the minority leader, determine the Senate's agenda. Like committee chairs, the majority leader can arrange the schedule so as to facilitate or impede the passage of bills. Sponsors of a bill, for example, may need more time to round up maximum support for their measure.) The majority leader also has a significant voice in making committee assignments (in conjunction with a "steering committee"). He or she is frequently interviewed by press and television and is the majority party's unofficial Senate voice.

The Speaker likewise has an important role in committee assignments in the House. He or she resolves parliamentary disputes, recognizes House members wishing to speak (sometimes a matter of consequence), and has considerable influence with the Rules Committee. Working closely with the majority leader, the Speaker plans party strategy, keeps in close touch with committee chairs, and generally keeps the House running smoothly. Like the Senate majority leader, the Speaker also receives a good deal of media attention.

Minority leaders are consulted by the majority party leaders, as a matter of courtesy, on scheduling and some other matters. Usually a spirit of comity exists among leaders of both parties; it is regarded as improper, for example, to spring a surprise vote on the opposition in an effort to catch it off guard. And since the majority party leaders may become the minority party leaders in the next session, respect for legitimate minority interests will bring reciprocal treatment if the tables are turned.[8]

In both House and Senate, an air of exaggerated courtesy marks the legislative process. MCs frequently address opponents on the floor as "honorable" and "distinguished" even if they regard them with loathing. That is no doubt hypocritical, but it helps maintain an air of civility when feelings run high. One of the most cherished folkways of Congress is the practice, when hotly disagreeing in floor debate, of keeping that debate impersonal and of retaining good personal relations after the controversy has ended.

Shooting the Legislative Rapids

The organization of Congress and the involved legislative procedures have a major consequence. They make it extraordinarily difficult to pass legislation since at so many points legislation can be blocked, with potentially hostile legislators manning the ramparts at each of these points.

To become law, a bill must (usually) be approved by a subcommittee in the House. Failure to win majority support there normally dooms it. Then it must obtain full committee approval. From there, the bill goes to the House Rules Committee, which can strangle a bill on the spot or send it to the floor under rules that promote or hamper its passage. The Rules Committee limits the period of debate (not vitally important, since few House members are swayed by formal debate) and rules whether a bill may be amended. The latter is often a most important decision. A bill that has been carefully crafted in committee, embodying a judicious series of compromises designed to hold a fragile majority coalition together, can fall apart through the passage of one or a series of floor amendments.

While members understandably find it exasperating to vote a bill up or down, without being able to offer an amendment, experienced politicians know this is often the only way to get a highly controversial measure passed. A majority may favor a given amendment that infuriates one minority, a different majority may support a second amendment that angers yet another minority, and before long a negative majority of alienated minorities has arisen. In committee, delicate and painstaking accommodations to appease various sensitive groups have been worked out, and heavy-handed floor actions can wreck this handiwork. On the other hand, if the Rules Committee *wants* to see a bill killed, granting the right to amend may be the best way to do it.

After a bill has survived a subcommittee, full committee, and the Rules Committee, it must win majority approval by the full House. Then it must get past a Senate subcommittee and committee and the full Senate—and face the risk of being waylaid by a filibuster, or unlimited debate.

Numerous bills have been talked to death during the twentieth century. While rules issued by the House Rules Committee prevent unlimited debate in the House, debate can proceed *ad nauseam* in the Senate unless 60 senators vote to curtail it. Such a vote (called *cloture*) is hard to obtain, partly because the Senate cherishes its tradition of unlimited debate and partly because those who dislike filibusters nonetheless fear the time may come when they will want to kill an odious bill with a filibuster of their own.

Filibusters were used by southern senators for several decades to block civil rights bills they opposed. But liberals have used them on many occasions, too.

A single senator can delay Senate action by talking all day (the record is 23 hours), and a handful of Senators can keep a filibuster going indefinitely by asking questions of the key speaker—questions that turn into long speeches. If those opposed to the filibuster try to wear them down by all-night sessions, the filibustering minority can retaliate by frequent quorum calls, forcing weary and exasperated senators to trudge back and forth to the Senate chamber to create a quorum and avoid adjournment. (A quorum is the smallest number of members legally permitted to transact business.) Since votes on a bill can only be called by unanimous consent or after cloture (which limits each Senator to one hour of debate), the filibustering senators have been in a strong position. Over the past decade, however, cloture has become easier to obtain.

An alternative form of filibuster involves submitting a host of amendments to a bill, each of which can delay action still further—(although such amendments cannot consume more than 100 hours after cloture occurs). Prolonged filibusters that do not encounter cloture lead to either a compromise acceptable to the intransigent minority or the defeat of a bill altogther. Even the threat of a filibuster can often extract concessions from those eager to avoid that calamity. That threat is often just as potent as the filibuster itself.

If a bill has survived all the pitfalls mentioned, it still must gain majority assent in the full Senate, plus the approval of a conference committee. The latter is not required if a bill has passed both House and Senate in identical form, but on major bills this rarely happens. To reconcile differences between House and Senate versions of the same bill, a conference committee—composed of senior majority and minority members of committees that handled the bill in each house—is formed. Once it has reached agreement, the final bill must be approved, without further amendments, by both House and Senate. Then, the President must add his signature before the bill becomes law.

This is not the end since many bills require funds before they can be carried out. The entire process must be duplicated in the passage of an appropriations bill; it is not uncommon for a program to be gutted during this phase of the legislative struggle.

If party leaders led a disciplined party, shooting the legislative rapids would be a much less treacherous enterprise than it is. But since party leaders have no major penalties to impose—such as the denial of committee chairs, campaign funds, or the privilege of using the party label—their power to coerce is minimal. And since MCs—especially senators—glory in their independence and feel far more obligation to their constituents than to their party, the path to legislative fruition is a rocky one, with legislative "muggers" stationed all along the way. All that opponents need do is block the legislation at only one point in order to succeed; the affirmative must prevail at a dozen points. It is a marvel, then, that Congress does its work at all.

There are limits to the capacity of a few persons to obstruct, however. If a

Prominent Democratic Party leaders (L–R) Al Ullman, Russell Long, Gaylord Nelson, A. A. Ribicoff, and Daniel Moynihan

subcommittee refuses to forward a bill, the full committee can override and hold its own hearings. If a full committee balks at reporting a bill that a House majority wants to pass, a discharge petition signed by a majority of House members can wrest that bill from the committee—or from an obstructive Rules Committee. The Senate can suspend the rules by a two-thirds vote and consider any bill it pleases. Cloture can be invoked to curb a filibuster.

All of these can be done, but they rarely are. So committed are MCs to the prerogatives of committees and to unlimited debate in the Senate that overriding the ordinary procedures is done rarely and with great reluctance.

The principal reason small minorities do not tie up Congress in perpetual knots is that Congress is composed of people who must live with each other. A small minority that abuses its powers too grossly violates the unwritten rules of political comity. That minority will be frowned upon; its subsequent legislative enterprises will languish in an atmosphere that has quietly become inhospitable to its goals. Or the formal powers to override will finally be exercised. In brief, unpleasant things happen to MCs who carry their power too far. They may temporarily prevail—but though the mills of Congress grind slowly, they grind exceedingly fine.

Thus, abuses have a way of creating their own antidote. But having said this, one must return to perhaps the central fact about Congress—the lack of a leadership armed with the tools to lead and the existence of a labyrinthine legislative process strewn with obstacles, each of which can prove fatal. The system gives minorities far more power than they enjoy in any other legislative system in the world. If they cannot kill a bill outright, they can usually exact a price before permitting it to survive. In parliamentary systems, with strong party discipline enfolding those who guard (fewer) hurdles, their power would be far less.

Part of the minority's power lies in our vigorous bicameral system. In most parliamentary systems the second house has withered into minor importance, having been shorn of most of its aristocratic power by the steady ascent of the more democratic chamber. This is not the case in the United States. Since the Senate remains as potent as ever, our full-blown bicameral system gives minorities twice as many opportunities to kill, mutilate, or modify a bill as exists in most democracies. (Some argue that we do not need two chambers, as evidenced by city councils, Nebraska's legislature, and those of numerous democracies—all of which are unicameral. But regardless of the merits of this argument, bicameralism is frozen forever into our Constitution and into our customary modes of thought.)

The House and the Senate may have roughly equal power, but they are quite different bodies. The Senate is a more individualistic, easygoing, free-wheeling chamber in which each senator, if capable, can make his or her mark. The House is a more tightly controlled organization, with debate strictly limited, the leadership enjoying greater influence, and with neophyte MCs still consigned to relative obscurity and impotence.

Relations between House and Senate are rarely cordial. The Senate thinks of itself as the more elite and prestigious body—though members must be careful not to let this show. To corral a Senator for a Washington party is cause for more hostess rejoicing than to net three members of the House. Members of the House often run for Senate seats, not the other way around. Senators, not representatives, are potential presidential candidates. (Morris Udall, able representative from Arizona, was one of the rare exceptions.)

Although presidents have rarely dominated the Congress throughout American history, presidents largely establish the agenda for Congress. The latter prefers not to even consider legislation in an area of any importance until the president has submitted his program. It is normally the president's bill on which hearings are held rather than the bill drafted by an individual MC. (However, MCs do formally introduce administration bills.)

When the president is a member of a party that does not control Congress, the latter, of course, pays less attention to his recommendations. But although such a president's proposals may be treated rudely, he largely decides what issues are to receive major attention. And if the president belongs to the party holding the most congressional seats, that party is more strongly inclined to accept his legislative leadership. Note, however, the word "inclined." Most members of the majority party are normally sympathetic to their party leader and his program, but individual MCs will not yield their convictions to him nor sacrifice the interest of their constituents (as they see it) to his perceptions of the national interest. On most matters of substance the president must try to put together a bipartisan majority on each controversial bill. He has no reliable built-in majority such as a prime minister can command in a parliamentary system.

Members of Congress: A Close-up View

Having looked at Congress as a collective body, it is now time to take a closer look at the individual Members of Congress. MCs differ from the general electorate in many respects. They are usually considerably more affluent, although their congressional salaries are much lower than that of persons with comparable work loads and responsibilities in private enterprise. (Major corporate vice-presidents, for example, usually have much higher salaries than MCs.) They are better educated. Their income and education usually place them in the upper-middle class, if not a rank higher. In 1978, 17 senators were millionaires and one-third owned property worth over $500,000.[9] More than half of MCs are lawyers, with business and banking as the next most frequent occupational background. Blue-collar workers and lower-income people in general are rarely found in Congress.

This does not mean necessarily that the latter are poorly represented in Washington. The question is not so much whether various income groups, ethnic groups, age groups, religious groups, and so forth are represented in proper mathematical proportions in Congress; since there are so many different ways of classifying people, this could never be done anyway. Instead, the issue is how well the *interests* of the various groups in our polyglot country are represented. Many wealthy MCs have shown more concern for this nation's poor than those with much less wealth. White MCs led the civil rights battle in the 1950s and 1960s with all the fervor black voters could wish. That a reasonable sprinkling of persons from various significant social and ethnic groups is desirable, few would contest. But the crucial matter is the legislative output itself. Even if minorities were numerically well represented in Congress, they would be minorities still. Justice basically depends on the sympathies, insights, and spirit of fair play that are present in a legislative body, whatever its demographic composition. And upon MCs' perception of a minority's role in deciding a close election.

This raises the question of whether all significant interests and points of view are heard from in Congress and how MCs make up their minds to vote as they do. The committee hearing process, enabling witnesses from every organized group in the nation to express their views, gives reasonable assurance that an adequate diversity of opinions will at least be heard. Inevitably, the opinions of the better organized and more powerful interest groups are heard more frequently, forcibly, and persuasively than those of other groups. There may be no feasible way, under our Constitution and political system, to avoid this.

Greater assurance of adequate attention for all interest groups grows out of the fact that each person's vote counts for as much as any other's at the polls. The vote of the mother on welfare counts as heavily as the millionaire's ballot. And since the overriding concern of almost all MCs is being reelected, they cannot afford to ignore the interests of any group, however inarticulate the members of that group may be. Since there are far more blue-collar workers than upper-class professional people, offending the former can be more dangerous than displeasing the latter. On the other hand, lower-class people have a lower voting propensity than more prosperous and educated classes and less awareness of their class interests. Doubtless this militates against their receiving as much consideration as they would otherwise receive.

MCs are perpetually alert to any evidence that their votes are promoting or injuring their reelection prospects. Often such evidence is very scanty. Not only are half of their constituents ignorant of MCs' names, but the average voter does not even know how his or her MC voted on a single issue during the last session of Congress. Those who write to their representative tend to be those who agree with him or her. If citizens are interested in an issue and request MC support for, or opposition to, it, they seldom follow up to find out how he or she voted. If they did, a confusing picture would present itself to them.

The bill that did or did not pass probably contained many provisions that most voters know nothing about and that might change their minds if they did know. They would need to know how an MC voted on numerous amendments to accurately understand where he or she really stood. The MC also might have voted for a bill in committee only because he or she knew that the Rules Committee would kill it. Members of the House might vote for a bill they oppose because they understood the Senate would kill it or the conference committee would extract an obnoxious provision. MCs sometimes vote for bills they oppose only because they know it will not win a majority vote anyway. Or they may vote for a crippling amendment and when that loses, vote for the bill itself, further confusing the vote. These other subterfuges are employed to placate clamorous minorities by appearing to agree with them, although the MC has no real intention of helping their cause along. But the key point is that few constituents know how MCs vote, thus giving the latter a great deal of freedom in casting their votes.

That MCs need not become neurotic about how they vote is demonstrated by the astounding regularity with which incumbents are reelected—and reelected by increasingly comfortable margins. Since World War II, 90% of incumbents who sought reelection have won. And only about one-fourth of the winners won by less than 60%.[10]

Incumbents win so easily partly because campaign funds flow freely to them, whereas challengers find money harder to get. But primarily incumbents' easy victories are attributable to name recognition and constituent services.[11] As incumbents, their pictures appear in the papers and on local TV news programs. They respond to constituent letters, faithfully performing every possible service for them—from helping them win government contracts to accelerating action on a pending agency decision to helping social security pensioners receive their overdue checks. These days they have a much larger staff to help them perform these services and more branch offices within their state or district to facilitate the doing of favors. More use is being made of the congressional frank—to send (postage-free) public relations materials to constituents. More tax dollars are available for weekend trips to visit their constituents—trips during which MCs ask, "What can I do for you?" For many MCs, helping their constituents with problems relating to the federal bureaucracy is their first responsibility—more important than legislating and far more important in terms of winning reelection, which is their supreme goal. The more favors members of Congress can do for the voters, the more favorably they will be known to a larger number of them.

Name recognition and a positive image come from other activities, too. When federal projects are approved for their district, MCs make the announcements and get their names in the paper (that is, if they are members of the majority party). They prepare TV newsclips for use by the local TV stations, with their own roles prominently featured. They send out newsletters to their constituents and perhaps have an occasional column in the local weekly newspaper discussing their work and views. As a result the public comes to know their names better than that of their opponents, and name recognition—especially when associated with a helpful image—is the single most important factor in winning reelection. Faced with several names at the polling booth, voters usually choose either their party's nominee or the name they recognize (unless it has recently been associated with a scandal).

The diligent performance of constituent favors has an important result: MCs become freer to vote the way they want to without fearing defeat at the polls. It is safer for them to adopt a "trustee" role—voting their personal convictions rather than merely reflecting local sentiment—since voter loyalty grows more out of personal services than out of MCs' voting pattern.

But if the careers of Members of Congress seem less dependent on their voting patterns than might be thought, this has less effect on that pattern than might be expected. MCs are a cautious breed, fearful that *this* time the "wrong" vote may trigger an angry reaction that sends them back to Paducah. MCs chronically "run scared," even if the pollsters give them a safe edge and even if they regularly receive 60% to 65% of the vote. So they usually vote *as if* the public were staring over their shoulders, ready to visit vengeance on them if they stray from the course that local sentiment requires.

Casting the "safe" vote, as we have said, means voting in accordance with those who care most about the issue at hand. That is determined by interest group pressures, by letters from the home state or district, by newspaper editorials, by polls, and sometimes by hunch. Public opinion polls may not always reveal intensity of opinion, but they at least show the general drift of opinion.

On many issues, however, the various indicators of public opinion either are inconclusive or register so faintly that MCs must look further for advice on how to vote. In such cases (which are very frequent), MCs have a number of options:

1. They may consult their state congressional colleagues to see how they plan to vote.
2. The bill may have an ideological component that strongly disposes them to cast a "liberal" or a "conservative" vote along with most members of their party.
3. They may talk it over with a number of congressional friends whose judgment they trust.
4. They may go along with the majority or minority report of the committee that processed the bill.
5. They may take the advice of a party leader after a 30-second conversation in the House or Senate chamber.
6. They may be guided by a trusted member of their staff.
7. They may yield to the pleas of the White House (usually conveyed by one of the president's legislative liaison staff), if the president belongs to the MC's party.
8. MCs may vote on the basis of a personal conviction that a yea or nay vote is the "right" thing to do.

John Kingdon (remember him from the first chapter?) found that MCs are primarily influenced by other MCs they trust, with constituent opinion coming second, followed by staff influences, interest group pressures, with party leaders requests and presidential pleas bringing up the rear.[12]

The point is that MCs vote as they do for any number of reasons. Voting sometimes turns out to be as complex and mysterious a decision as are many of the decisions each of us makes in our personal lives. Sometimes the *real* reason MCs vote as they do (and we decide as we do) is not clear even to them (or to us). There are so many pros and cons, both substantive and political, and the advice is so contradictory that the factor that finally settles an issue is lodged deep within the psyche, inaccessible to even one's own introspection.

One thing seems quite clear, however. *If* MCs believe a given vote will promote their reelection prospects, they will nearly always vote that way, however they arrive at that conclusion.

There is nothing really new about this, although preoccupation with re-election may be even more pronounced than in the past. Morton Kondracke, the brilliant executive editor of the *New Republic*, shook his head over the "new breed of representative" he saw in the 1978 election. He observed that "there is little sense that [they] stand for anything except what will best insure reelection. They are not liberals or conservatives, or deeply committed any-things."[3] We can only hope that time will prove him wrong. Otherwise, winning *has* become everything.

A Day on Capitol Hill

Besides looking at their voting records, it is instructive to follow MCs in their daily routine. Consider a typical MC's day. (We will assume, this time, the MC is a he.) He probably begins the day (after feeding the cat) by scanning the *Washington Post* or the *Washington Star* (or both) and perhaps the *New York Times* and *Wall Street Journal*. He may watch one of the morning TV news programs. Arriving at the office, he may peruse the newpapers from his state or congressional district (which may have items of special interest to him underlined by an aide). Another aide has probably read the *Congressional Record* (containing a roughly verbatim account of yesterday's House and Senate floor debates and actions) and has marked those passages he may want to read. (Reading the entire voluminous document would take far too long; most of the speeches were delivered for the benefit of interest groups back home anyway. Copies may be sent to interest group leaders or other concerned constituents to demonstrate that the MC is battling for their cause.)

The MC may then attend his first committee meeting. (These meetings occupy perhaps one-fourth of his working hours.) If he cannot attend, he usually sends an aide to the session to observe and report upon what happened. He may then exchange scuttlebutt with other MCs, catching up with the latest political gossip and being filled in on the floor action scheduled for that day—perhaps by a party whip.

Returning to his office, he may spend some time with lobbyists, with constituents who have come to see him, or with newspaper reporters wishing to interview him. He may then look over his mail. Most of it is routine and will be routinely answered by his staff. If there is a lot of mail on a particular subject, he will either dictate a form-letter response or edit such a letter prepared by an aide. Only a few of the more interesting or informative letters usually come to his desk—plus letters from VIPs. (If he were to personally read and personally answer his mail—which, for senators, may be thousands of letters a day—he would not only have no time to do anything else, but require six heads and twelve hands to do even that!)

As we have said before, the MC is likely to be very scrupulous about seeing that requests for information or for help from his constituents are honored.[14] That scrupulosity is brought to bear whether it is straightening out a social security error, helping a constituent find information about a goverment contract, facilitating entry into the United States of a constituent's relative from abroad, getting information about postal employment for someone, helping a vet obtain admission to a Veterans Administration hospital, getting

A Congressional
office scene

prompt action on a long-delayed decision from the Small Business Administration on someone's loan application, providing information about the capital for a high-school student writing a theme, or answering a request for some dirt from the White House lawn! (In answering this request, an MC dispatched an assistant to the White House, "instructing him not to knock on the front door ... but to reach through the back fence and dig some dirt into an envelope.")

The MC wants to be sure that his or her staff gives the desired help promptly and may do it himself or herself if personal intervention seems necessary. MCs are a very diverse lot, and their operational styles differ enormously. But on constituent services, they are of one mind: Do them, do them well, and do them now.

Unhappily, hard and skillful work within committees wins respect from colleagues but few votes from back home. Similarly, the invaluable talent and time-consuming efforts needed to build a coalition that can pass important legislation enhances one's reputation among one's colleagues but yields few political dividends at home. This is one of the genuine tragedies about congressional life, a tragedy for which the press bears heavy responsibility for not reporting such efforts better.

Part of the MC's time may be spent revising ghostwritten speeches for delivery on the House or Senate floor or before constituent audiences. He may also prepare taped radio or TV statements for local stations using the special radio-TV facilities Congress provides for the convenience of its members.

Cynical observers sometimes say MCs lie awake nights trying to think of ways to get their names in the paper or on TV. It is often true, both because politicians have healthy egos and because getting their names in front of their constituents reminds busy citizens that they have a representative who is doing something. As one politician observed, "Politics is 80% getting credit." How it is gotten often matters less than getting it.

It may be somewhat deceptive to talk about a "typical MC's day" because there are no typical MCs. They can be classified in many different ways.[15] Some are showboats, exhibitionists, the cruder kind of demagogues. Some take their committee work very seriously and try hard to solve the problems that come their way. Others take little interest in legislation, preferring to concentrate on errand running and trips back home to "meet the folks." Some relish the political game of devising strategy, cultivating key people, mastering parliamentary procedure, and putting together a successful coalition. A few do as little as possible, hoping to get along by staying out of the line of fire and avoiding trouble. Some are highly ideological; more are highly pragmatic. Some are party loyalists, while others are mavericks. In sum, MCs are as diverse as people in general, and they run the gamut from the most admirable to the most despicable types. But it is a fair generalization that most MCs work very hard, want to do a good job, are fairly good at judging public opinion, and try to serve the public interest as they see it. MCs with unsavory records often get the most media attention, but dishonorable MCs are a very small minority. (Many people don't seem to believe this but it's still true, the author said doggedly!)

Congress: A Rudderless Ship?

Political scientists who criticize Congress frequently focus on the weakness of the leadership. With each committee and subcommittee operating as a relatively autonomous unit, considering each bill in isolation without general guidelines or criteria, the decision-making process is so decentralized as to border on anarchy. As Lance Morrow put it, "Congress now has all the discipline of a five-year-old's birthday party."[15] The capacity and tendency of each committee to go its own merry way—whatever the contradictions and incongruities between its product and that of other committees considering related aspects of the broader problem—and the resulting absence of an integrated policy overview, is perhaps Congress' most conspicuous deficiency. In other words, the legislative output is not effectively guided and coordinated by a leadership that has a reasonably clear vision of where it thinks the nation should go. Rather, Congress operates much as Adam Smith prescribed for the economic world: If each committee does its thing, the total product—by some mysterious alchemy—will work together for good. This is a wildly optimistic assumption, the critics would say.

Fortunately, although this semiorganized chaos *is* perhaps the most important truth about Congress, it is not the whole truth. Congress does work on proposals submitted by the chief executive, who *sometimes* has a broader and clearer vision of where the nation should be going and who often does a better job of coordinating his various legislative recommendations.

And, after failing in an earlier attempt, Congress itself is making a serious effort to coordinate some of its policies, relating to taxation and spending, in the interests of better economic policy. Formerly, the total amount of congressional spending depended on the largely independent outputs of each of a dozen appropriations subcommittees in the House and in the Senate. Each subcommittee acted as a law unto itself, and no one knew what the overall appropriations would be. Meanwhile, the Senate Finance Committee and House Ways and Means Committee formulated tax policy without knowing how their revenue acts would mesh with the appropriations acts. Thus, the size of the federal deficit or (rarely) surplus was guesswork, even though the amount of surplus or deficit was crucial to the performance of the economy. It was a helterskelter, dipsy-doodle way to run a railroad, but that is the way Congress did it.

In 1974, however, Congress resolved to reform its budget practices. The details need not concern us, but the Congressional Budget Reform Act established a system for setting spending ceilings, which the various appropriations subcommittees must bear in mind. The tax committees devise their tax bills in the light of these ceilings, enabling a degree of coordination and centralized economic planning that never existed before. We are not at all sure how long or how well the system will work, but it is a noble try. While this does not coordinate the *substance* of nonfiscal bills (a coordination that remains badly needed), it is a long step toward a more rational legislative process.

A final word must be added in mitigation of congressional chaos. It is not at all clear that *any* planning group—in the White House, in Congress, or elsewhere—is smart enough to provide the overall coordination and direction we have talked about. For example, minimum-wage laws, manpower training laws, public service job laws, Federal Reserve Board credit policies, antipollution laws, investment tax credit laws, federal mortgage interest rates for housing, energy policy, the volume of budgetary deficit (or surplus), our international trade policies, multinational corporation investment decisions, and half a dozen other policy matters materially affect our inflation-employment picture. With economists wrong almost as often as they are right, and with the complexity of the economy beyond the capacity of the most brilliant minds to master, we should not expect that a supreme headquarters of political planners could bring predictably constructive and well-coordinated results out of their plans.

Having conceded this, it still makes sense to *try* to coordinate policy toward certain agreed ends. If then we fail, we have at least failed intelligently! For the most part, Congress does not even try.

Notes

1. Woodrow Wilson, *Congressional Government* (New York: New American Library [Meridian Books], 1956).
2. For general treatments of congressional committees, see Richard F. Fenno, *Congressmen in Committees* (Boston: Little, Brown, 1973); and George Goodwin, *The Little Legislatures; Committees of Congress* (Amherst: University of Massachusetts Press, 1970).
3. Leading studies of congressional leadership include Randall B. Ripley, *Majority Party Leadership in Congress* (Boston: Little, Brown, 1969); and Robert L. Peabody, *Leadership in Congress; Stability, Succession, and Change* (Boston: Little, Brown, 1976).
4. Morris P. Fiorina, "Electoral Margins, Constituency Influence and Policy Moderation: A Critical Assessment," *American Politics Quarterly* (October 1973), vol. 1, pp. 479-498; and Robert S. Erikson, "Is There Such a Thing as a Safe Seat?" *Polity* (Summer 1976).
5. On congressional subcommittees, see Goodwin, *The Little Legislatures*; and Norman J. Ornstein, ed., *Congress in Change* (New York: Praeger, 1975), pp. 88-114.
6. A useful case study illustrating the point is is John F. Manley, "Wilbur D. Mills: A Study in Congressional Influence," *American Political Science Review* 63 (June 1969), 442-464.
7. See "Johnson's Leadership," *New Republic*, March 9, 1959, p. 2; "Master Tactician," *Reporter*, January 23, 1958, pp. 2-5, and Cabell Phillips, "The Way Lyndon Johnson Does It," *New York Times Magazine*, July 26, 1959, pp. 9ff.
8. Both parties also have policy committees and steering committees, which fully deserve the inattention we give them here.
9. "Why the Senate is Called A Rich Man's Club", *U. S. News and World Report*, May 29, 1978. p. 30.
10. Morris P. Fiorina, *Congress; Keystone of the Washington Establishment* (New Haven, Conn.: Yale University Press, 1977), p. 53.
11. See Lewis Perdue, "The Million Dollar Advantage of Incumbency," *Washington Monthly*, March 1977, pp. 50-54.
12. John W. Kingdon, *Congressmen's Voting Decisions* (New York: Harper Row, 1973), pp. 20-21.
13. Morton Kondracke, "Freshman Orientation," *New Republic*, December 16, 1978, p. 12.

14 Fiorina, *Congress*, pp. 58–60.
15 See Roger H. Davidson, *The Role of the Congressman* (New York: Pegasus, 1969); and Donald Matthews, *U.S. Senators and Their World* (Chapel Hill: University of North Carolina Press, 1960).
16 Lance Morrow, "The Decline of the Parties", *Time*, November 20, 1978, p. 42.

CHAPTER 11

THE PRESIDENCY—
THE VITAL CENTER

The American political system reaches a peak on the presidency. It is the political fulcrum, the intelligence center, the "bully pulpit," the point toward which all eyes turn when national leadership is needed. Even when the moral authority and political power of the office was sapped by Watergate, the Vietnam fiasco, and a resurgent Congress, the nation learned anew that leadership comes from the White House or it does not come at all.

The Founding Fathers foresaw the need for a strong executive when they drew up the Constitution. The executive power had been exercised by a series of legislative committees during the Articles of Confederation, and this had proved inadequate. Particularly in foreign policy they wanted an executive with the power to "take charge" and to command the respect of other nations. They also wanted a chief executive capable of dealing with domestic disorder. But mindful of the popular distaste for royal governors and King George III, historically aware of the tendency of monarchs to abuse their power, and instructed by Montesquieu's *The Spirit of the Laws* that safety and freedom require separation of powers, they constructed an office limited by a powerful legislature and by impeachment, with the courts to play a significant but largely undefined role.

Although the comparative powers of Congress and of the executive have alternately waxed and waned, the calculated balance was generally well maintained for the first 150 years. Congress usually held the upper hand on domestic policy, and the president usually prevailed on foreign policy—as the founders intended. Thomas Jefferson, Andrew Jackson, Abraham Lincoln, Theodore Roosevelt, and Woodrow Wilson temporarily strengthened the executive power, but their successors were unable to hold the ground they gained.

Events were conspiring to alter this equilibrium, however. Not only in the United States but in countries around the world, executives were outdistancing legislatures in the ceaseless struggle for power. The reasons why it happened in this nation need to be briefly explored.

The Swelling of the Presidency

The constitutional language that deals with the chief executive is vague. Article I states: "The Executive power shall be vested in a president"; and "The president shall be commander in chief of the army and navy." These clauses lend themselves to broad interpretation by ambitious presidents. Concerning the first clause, one writer declared, "In all the annals of politics, there may never have been written a critical proposition more direct in sound and more cryptic in substance."[1]

Historically, the chief executive of almost every country has had vast powers over foreign policy, over matters of war and peace, and in times of national emergency. Did the clause concerning "Executive power" assume that some of the historic powers of executives in other countries were to be vested in this country's executive? Did it include what John Locke called "the royal prerogative"—"the power to act according to discretion for the public good, without the prescription of law and sometimes even against it"?[2]

Lucius Wilmerding, who has studied the question of the Founding Fathers' views of the "royal prerogative," concluded that they believed that a grave emergency might indeed require presidents to act beyond the law for the common good—but that presidents who acted thusly should not contend that they were behaving in accordance with the Constitution but should go to the people, explain their reasons, and beg the forgiveness of the people because of the goodness of their motives.[3]

At various periods in American history, however, Thomas Jefferson, Abraham Lincoln, Theodore Roosevelt, Franklin Roosevelt, and Richard Nixon seemed to believe that national emergencies somehow empowered them to transcend the law in doing what they believed the national security or the national interest required. But they did not concede the illegality of their behavior, relying instead upon their interpretations of the "Executive power" or the "commander in chief" clauses to justify what they did. Theodore Roosevelt constructed a "stewardship" doctrine, which held that it was the president's "duty to do anything that the needs of the nation demanded unless such action was forbidden by the constitution or the laws."[4] In other words, even if he could not point to a specific empowering clause in Article I, he could still act if he believed it necessary. He used this theory in building the Panama Canal and in settling a major coal strike in 1902.

The president's power and prestige is enhanced by his responsibility as chief of state as well as of chief executive. In Britain the queen (or king) is the symbolic head of state, while the prime minister is the chief executive. In France and Germany the president and chancellor are heads of state, with the prime minister as chief executive. Fusing these two roles has given an extra measure of dignity and symbolic importance to our president. As historian Clinton Rossiter put it, "Whether or not he enjoys the role, no president can fail to realize that all his powers are invigorated, indeed are given a new dimension of authority, because he is the symbol of our sovereignty, continuity and grandeur."[5] (Rossiter, writing before Watergate, Vietnam, and knowledge of CIA excesses, can perhaps be forgiven the term "grandeur.")

The presidency expanded because societies seem to yearn for a single leader. There is something vaguely unsatisfying about collective leadership—especially if that collectivity is a milling throng of squabbling legislators.

Writing in 1813, Henry Lockwood declared:

The tendency of all people is to elevate a single person to the position or ruler. The idea is simple. It appeals to all orders of intellects. It can be understood by all. Around this centre all nationality and patriotism are grouped. A nation comes to know the characteristics and nature of an individual. It learns to believe in the man. . . . He is the chief officer of the nation. He stands alone. He is a separate power in himself. The lines with which we attempt to mark the limits of his power are shadowy and ill-defined. . . . The sentiment of hero-worship, which to a great extent prevails among the American people, will endorse him.[6]

A single leader can personify the nation; in time of danger, especially, people seek reassurance in the presence of the strong leader who can unite the nation and give it security. The tendency, then, has been to magnify the president's allegedly heroic qualities during troubled times (can a legislature ever appear heroic?) and attribute special and superhuman virtues to him.

Expansion of the presidency also took place because of the democratization of the office. Initially nominated, in effect, by a congressional caucus and selected by an electoral college, this semiaristocratic selection process soon gave way to nomination by popular convention and election by the people (with the electoral college merely ratifying the popular choice). This process made the president (and vice-president) the only nationally elected officer in the land, enabling him to capitalize on his status as the only official who represents *all* the people.

The development of political parties, with the president as leader of his party, expanded his powers. Our parties, as we have seen, are decentralized to an almost chaotic degree. Only the president (or the presidential nominee) can bring some semblance of unity to his party. Thus, although our parties are normally not unified and not subject to firm party discipline, MCs give their party leader the benefit of the doubt on many policy stands. The president can count on a much higher degree of support from his own party than from the opposition party. From time to time, the president can also draw upon a measure of political backing from mayors and governors of his party. Like his role as chief of state, then, the president's position as party leader adds a significant dimension to his overall power.

The nation has learned that Congress requires strong presidential leadership if it is to function well. Legislatures seem incapable of generating adequate internal leadership. They are too large, too cumbersome, too undisciplined, too faction-ridden, and too vulnerable to parliamentary stalling tactics. Its members also have too parochial an outlook.

As the press of legislative business grows in urban, industrial societies, in which heavy demands are made on the government, the need for able legislative leadership increases—a leadership only the executive seems able to supply. And since much modern legislation involves highly technical matters, legislatures find themselves delegating vast authority to the executive branch. Legislative power thus ebbs away, seeping year by year into the executive departments.

The presidency grew because of reluctance by the Supreme Court to challenge executive expansion of powers during periods of national peril.[7] It takes time for cases to reach the Supreme Court; when they do, the Court has been extraordinarily skittish about challenging a presidential act taken in the name of national security. To some degree this may reflect the Court's powerlessness to enforce its verdict; partly, too, the Court feels that the political—not the judicial—power should govern during emergencies. The Court on several occasions has rebuked presidential power *after* the emergency ended (e.g., Lincoln's suspension of the writ of habeas corpus during the Civil War, and Franklin Roosevelt's unjustified exercise of martial law in Hawaii during World War II); however, the closest it has come to immediate interference in even a limited sort of emergency was to deny President Harry Truman the right to seize the nation's steel mills when a strike endangered the production of military supplies needed for the Korean War.

The development of electronic communications has also enhanced executive power. In the first place, it has shrunk our world, making international crises more dramatically visible and action seemingly more urgent. The president is expected to point the way when such occasions arise. But the electronic media serve the president's power in quite another way, too. The media find it more convenient and profitable to train their cameras, microphones, and reporters on the executive than upon a swarm of legislators. The public is far more interested in what the president says or does than in what a less glamorous legislator says or does. Hence the president's activities receive disproportionate attention, which indirectly leads him to be seen as a political giant among the political pygmies in the legislature. Perhaps equally important, radio and TV enable the president to address the people directly, on all major networks, a privilege rarely granted other political figures. His ability to shape public opinion, if he uses these media skillfully, is thus greatly enhanced.

The Anatomy of Presidential Power

Let us look in some detail at the powers and responsibilities of the presidential office. The president's major function, as usually seen, is to enforce the laws of the land. This may seem to be a prosaic task, more a thankless duty than an important power. But Congress passes a great deal of legislation in broadly worded language, partly because members lack the expertise to be more specific, partly because flexibility of interpretation is genuinely needed, partly because it is easier to get agreement on vaguely phrased statutes. These laws must then be interpreted. The executive establishment has the first word in interpreting the laws, with the judiciary having the last although definitive opportunity to do so. But most executive interpretations are never brought to the courts. Hence, converting malleable language into living law is primarily the executive department's privilege. When Congress forbids "unfair trade practices," or discrimination based on sex or race it is crucially important to know just what is unfair or just what a discriminatory practice against women or blacks might be. The executive provides most of the answers.

The president can only single out a few areas of interpretation on which to put his personal stamp, since laws are voluminous, his responsibilities are many, and his time limited. He can do something else, however, of perhaps greater moment. He can enforce certain laws either with vigor or in a perfunctory manner. Some presidents have enforced the antitrust laws with enthusiasm; others have let them gather dust. Some have actively enforced civil rights statutes; others have done so with restraint. Some have emphasized the importance of curtailing drug trafficking; others have given law-enforcement priority to other matters. The capacity to apply the accelerator or the brakes when enforcing the law is a power that counts.

The president's power to appoint, with the consent of the Senate, remains of very great significance. The president can appoint members to the regulatory commissions (e.g., the Federal Trade Commission, Interstate Commerce

Commission, and Securities and Exchange Commission), with a probusiness bias or a proconsumer bias. The entire tone of our vast regulatory establishment depends on the kind of people a president nominates. The appointments to the Supreme Court are indisputably of great importance, also. Whether he nominates absurdities like Nixon's choice of Harold Carrswell, or sub-mediocrities as Truman did, or judicial giants like Hughes, Cardozo, Brandeis or Stone, is no trivial matter. In addition, presidential appointments to the Federal Reserve Board, the Federal Bureau of Investigation, and the Central Intelligence Agency make a major impact on the country, to say nothing of all the cabinet nominations. Selecting the secretaries of state, defense, treasury, transportation, agriculture, labor, interior, energy, HUD (Housing & Urban Development), HEW (Health, Education and Welfare), and the attorney general—along with his other appointments—can make a clear imprint on our government. Since the president himself can only do a tiny part of the executive work, his appointments may be the most important part of his job—decisions on war or peace excepted.

Although portions of the president's budget are often treated rudely by the Congress, its preparation does more to shape the detailed priorities of the government than any other activity. The president, acting upon the advice of the director of the Office of Management and Budget (who responds to the president's personal priorities, however) proposes budgetary ceilings for each of the several thousand federal agencies. Most of these are respected by Congress. Moreover, the president is in a position to veto appropriations he regards as excessive; normally it is difficult to muster the two-thirds majority necessary to override the veto. (The Congress, however, can lump various appropriations into a single bill, forcing the president to veto provisions he badly wants in order to reject what he does not want.)

Of particular importance is the president's military budget. Congress may add or subtract a few billions, but when the president—backed by his secretary of defense, the chairman of the Joint Chiefs of Staff, and the technical experts in the Pentagon—says this is what we need, it is not easy for Congress to say nay. Congress often makes a grandstand play in some area of the military budget to indicate its fierce determination to keep ahead of the Russians, but when all is said and done, the chief executive largely has his way. With the military budget constituting about 25% of the federal budget, this is an impressive power.

Economics is not a sufficiently exact science to enable presidents to finetune the economy, but the president is expected to take the lead in keeping unemployment and inflation at tolerable levels and to keep our international balance of payments (money flowing out of the country) from poisoning the economic system. The president's taxing and spending recommendations are his principal instrument toward this end, but pressures on the independent (but often responsive) Federal Reserve Board, the acceleration or deceleration of spending on highways and federal projects, proposals to make available more or less mortgage money for housing construction, recommendations to increase public service jobs or employment training programs, to impose wage and price controls or provide fiscal incentives to keep wages and prices down—these are among the actions a president can take to cope with the economy. Congress must cooperate to bring most of these into operation, but the initiative belongs to the president.

Presidents are authorized, by the Constitution, to recommend legislative proposals to the Congress and our earliest presidents acted accordingly. After Andrew Jackson's tumultuous presidency, the Whigs decided it was time to take the presidency down a few pegs. Their philosophy was perfectly exemplified by a statement of William Henry Harrison in 1840:

> *It is preposterous to suppose... for a moment that the President, placed at the capitol, in the center of the country, could better understand the wants and wishes of the people than their own immediate representatives who spend a part of every year among them... and [are] bound to them by the triple tie of interest, duty and affection.*[8]

But subsequent presidents often reverted to the Washington-Jefferson active leadership model. In the twentieth century we have tended to judge presidents by their legislative proposals and their skill in shepherding these through Congress. Although it may not be the best criterion for evaluating a president, that measure is tenaciously employed by the media and by many president watchers.

Even if we exaggerate its importance, a president's ability to move his bills through Congress is of major consequence. Congress is a plodding creature and unless it is pressured and sweet talked into action it can be exasperatingly laggard. Only the president, it seems, can harness Congress and bring some measure of discipline into its performance.

But if only a president can do this, not many have done it well. Only George Washington (through Alexander Hamilton's maneuvers), Thomas Jefferson, William McKinley, Woodrow Wilson, Franklin Roosevelt (during his first term), and Lyndon Johnson (from 1964 to 1966) have kept the Congress largely under control. About 85% of the time, then, Congress has largely gone its own way at its own speed—meaning not very far and not very fast.

If a president is to be an effective leader of Congress, he or she needs to obey ten political commandments.[9]

A president needs to understand the congressional "power structure" to know who counts, who must be cultivated, and how they can be persuaded to cooperate. To have a good "feel" for the Washington political milieu is essential. Jimmy Carter, one of our most intelligent presidents, quickly learned that native intelligence alone is not enough. He had to be initiated, painfully, into the realities of Washington politics before he was able to partially cope with Congress. Even then he often found that body to be unmanageable.

A president needs to be a master of political timing—to know when to lead and when to pause. There have been times (during the depths of the Great Depression and after John F. Kennedy's assassination) when the nation was eager for action. At other times (after World War I and when Eisenhower became president in 1953), the nation yearned for peace and tranquillity. Domestic disasters or heightened national fears (major mine catastrophes, the thalidomide drug horrors in the 1960s resulting in deformed babies, fears of air and water pollution in the 1960s) have paved the way for strong action in certain legislative areas. A president needs to be attuned to national moods which are usually faithfully reflected in Congress.

The president should consult fully with his party's congressional leaders before launching major domestic or foreign policy initiatives. These leaders can give invaluable advice, from their years of experience and their close connections with the congressional rank-and-file, about what Congress will and will not accept. They may also be more willing to promote the passage of the president's program if they have had a hand in its development.

The most disastrous presidential decisions of modern times have occurred when presidents failed to consult with their party leaders in Congress. Franklin Roosevelt's attempt to "pack" the Supreme Court in 1937 (which scarred his second term in office), Johnson's stealthy acceleration of the Vietnam War, Nixon's concealment of his cover-up role in the Watergate affair, Ford's pardon of Nixon—all occurred in the absence of collaboration with congressional leaders. These leaders do not always give sound advice, but history suggests a president is foolish not to listen to them.

The president should clarify priorities and proceed accordingly. An activist president always wants Congress to do more than it is able or willing to do. The president, therefore, should select a few proposals that matter most and give them primary attention. Harry S. Truman violated this rule by handing Congress a long and largely indigestible list of proposals and failing to indicate where his priorities lay. Jimmy Carter made the same mistake in his first year as chief executive.

An adequate follow-through is indispensable not only to success in sports but also in presidential politics. It is not enough to hand Congress a platter of proposals and hope for the best. The president must keep a sharp eye on the legislation at every point in the long and tortuous obstacle course that our bicameral system represents. The president must show that he or she really *cares* and is willing to take the time required to nurse a bill along and wheedle, coax, and cajole as the occasion requires. Important legislation is rarely easy to pass; a score of hurdles and political land mines block the way. A president must be vigilant, tireless, and resourceful if he or she is to prevail.

At the same time a president can pressure the Congress only so much. If ridden too hard, for too long, Congress usually bridles and balks. That is another reason a president should have priorities in order and concentrate on the crucial issues.

The president needs a good congressional liaison staff. There are limits to the time a president can devote to nursing the Congress, and a limit to the MCs he can personally contact. Liaison personnel are needed who have good rapport with the members of Congress, have the clout that comes from being close to the president, and can make an accurate count of who is for a bill, who is against, and who is undecided. The latter is most important since the president's pleas must be confined to those who are undecided, and the congressional leadership needs to schedule the vote when there is the best possible chance of success. Only if the administration is a few votes short of passage should the president personally buttonhole members of Congress in an effort to win them over; overuse of this tactic diminishes its effectiveness. The president must know when prevote interventions may carry the day, and a good liaison staff (working closely with congressional whips) can provide this intelligence.

Since most legislation needs bipartisan support in order to pass, the president should not overlook potential votes from opposition party members. The proprieties of partisan politics require that cultivation of the opposition be done unobtrusively and with finesse. But presidents can play the quid pro quo game with them—giving a quiet push to legislation *they* may be interested in, yielding to amendments they may favor, not campaigning against them in congressional elections.

A president must show deference to Congress as a coequal institution and respect the motives of those who oppose him or her (even if those motives are indeed suspect). Congress is very touchy about its coequal status and quick to resent presidential words or actions that it regards as disparaging or disrespectful. That resentment can manifest itself in behavior costly to the president.

As for courteous treatment of his adversaries, a president must remember that coalitions constantly form, dissolve, and reform; enemies on one issue may be friends on another—unless they have been antagonized by remarks that they construe as belittling or insulting. Politics is working with people, and Members of Congress are just as capable of reacting to friendliness or hostility as are other people. The temptation to lash out at one's temporary foes is often powerful, but wise presidents bite their tongues.

A president must be willing to compromise and be able to do so skillfully. Some presidents have developed streaks of stubbornness that have cost them dearly (e.g., Woodrow Wilson on the League of Nations, Herbert Hoover in his confrontations with a Democratic Congress in 1931–1932, Lyndon Johnson on the Vietnam War). An overweening faith in the total righteousness of their cause and a conviction about the total malevolence of their opponents can produce a rigidity that leads to disaster.

Knowing when to compromise and what kind of compromise to strike—one that nobody is quite happy about but a majority can live with—is the essence of the political art. If the president is seen as a pushover, Congress will repeatedly push him or her over. If the president delays too long or compromises too late, others may take the decision out of the president's hands. A president needs wise counsel on this matter from people intimately acquainted with the complexities, the personalities, and the interests involved.

No matter how operationally astute a president may be, Congress cannot be effectively led unless it is offered a well-formulated program. If the president's proposals have been poorly researched and poorly crafted, Congress will treat them roughly. There is no substitute for doing one's homework well, and a president who shirks this task should not be surprised if the Congress does not take his or her work seriously.

All this does not suggest that there is a magic formula by which any president can successfully direct the Congress. Able leadership is always a somewhat mysterious quality, composed of imponderables as well as of recognized behavior patterns. But if no set of rules can guarantee success, violation of these rules can ensure unnecessary difficulties.

The President and Foreign Policy

While the chief executive was probably intended to be the senior partner in foreign policymaking, a leading constitutional scholar once termed the Constitution's provisions "an invitation [for Congress and the president] to struggle for the privilege of directing American foreign policy."[10]

The president ordinarily has the greatest impact on foreign policy but as we shall see, Congress has the means and the will to strongly assert itself from time to time.

The president's foreign policy tools and prerogatives are formidable. He is the sole spokesman in the conduct of international affairs; it is illegal for anyone but the president, or his assistants, to conduct diplomatic negotiations or carry on formal diplomatic correspondence with other governments.

Thus, the privilege of taking the initiative in foreign affairs rests with the president. A few examples illustrate the importance of this power. The Monroe Doctrine, warning European countries not to meddle in this hemisphere, was proclaimed by President James Monroe in 1823. Theodore Roosevelt modified the Monroe Doctrine with the so-called Roosevelt Corollary, which announced that while European powers should keep their hands out of Latin American affairs, this country *could* intervene if nations in this hemisphere did not conduct themselves properly (as interpreted by the United States). Thus if they did not pay their debts or did not protect American lives or property within their country, the president could step in—by force if necessary—to ensure that they behaved in a manner acceptable to him.

Franklin D. Roosevelt took the initiative before World War II by prodding Congress to modify various Neutrality Acts (designed to maintain our isolationist position) in order to permit the sale and transportation of arms and other military equipment to Great Britain. Harry Truman fostered the Marshall Plan (to help restore the war-ravaged economies of Europe after World War II) and took a variety of other measures to resist communist expansion (e.g., the Berlin airlift, the Greek-Turkish aid plan, and the creation of the North Atlantic Treaty Organization). Richard Nixon made a celebrated trip to the People's Republic of China in order to unfreeze long-frozen relations with the world's most populous nation. These and many others that could be cited demonstrate how vitally important is the president's prerogative of seizing the initiative on foreign affairs whenever and wherever he chooses. Congress played a significant supporting role in many of these actions but it was just that—a supporting role. The president was the main actor.

Similarly, the president alone can negotiate treaties. Again, a few examples illustrate the importance of this power. The controversial Jay Treaty, settling various prickly issues with Great Britain growing out of the Revolutionary War, was negotiated by Secretary of State John Jay under President

Washington's direction. Although the Versailles Treaty, at the conclusion of World War I, was not ratified by the Senate, President Woodrow Wilson was this nation's representative at the postwar peace conference, and his role at that conference was crucial. One of John Kennedy's major triumphs was the successful negotiation of the Test Ban Treaty in 1962, in which the United States and the Soviet Union agreed to discontinue nuclear tests in outer space—tests creating fallout that was poisoning the atmosphere. The Panama Canal Treaty in 1978 grew out of years of executive branch consultation with Panama and provided for ultimate Panamanian control of the canal.

Finally, the various Strategic Arms Limitation Talks (SALT) are major undertakings, and while the Senate must ratify the treaties growing out of these talks, their formulation is in the hands of the chief executive and his counterparts in Russia. If the arms race is not to terminate in global catastrophe, it is widely believed, the SALT negotiators will have to reach agreements that limit that race.

But the president is not confined, where international agreements are concerned, to treaties. He may make "executive agreements," which are as binding and sometimes as consequential as treaties. International agreements involving such matters as postal and fishing regulations, or such larger matters as the demilitarization of the Great Lakes (an agreement made in 1824 with Canada) or the Yalta accords (involving post–World War II agreements with the Soviet Union and Great Britain concerning the status of Poland, Berlin, China, and other areas) have been made by the president on his own authority as president. Other international agreements of historic moment, such as the annexation of Hawaii and Texas (after treaties had failed), required the approval of only a majority of the members of both House and Senate. Usually it is easier to win majority approval of both houses of Congress than to get two-thirds approval from the Senate, and it is not at all clear when the president must resort to treaties and when he may seek the same objective by executive agreement.[11] (The mood of the Senate is often conclusive; if it will be sufficiently outraged by the submission of an executive agreement instead of a treaty, that prospective reaction may make up the president's mind.)

Finally, the president is constitutionally authorized to receive foreign ambassadors, which in effect gives him the right to formally recognize or refuse to recognize newly formed governments abroad. Washington's recognition of the revolutionary French government in 1790, Wilson's refusal to recognize an unfriendly Mexican government following a coup in 1914, Franklin Roosevelt's recognition of the Soviet Union after 25 years of nonrecognition, and Jimmy Carter's recognition of the People's Republic of China testify to the importance of this power.

Congress and the American people are usually willing to give the president considerable latitude in conducting foreign affairs because of the "inside information" supposedly available only to the president. He receives regular reports from his ambassadors in every country in the world, supplemented by daily communications from the CIA, from such special envoys as he may appoint to investigate special problems, and from occasional direct contacts with heads of state abroad. He has the formidable resources of the State Department at his disposal, resources that include career experts on every region and all of the major countries of the world. He can also call upon the National Security Council—composed of the Secretary of State, the Secretary of the Treasury, the Secretary of Defense, the chairman of the Joint Chiefs of Staff, the director of the CIA, plus such experts as the president may designate from time to time—to help him formulate policy. These resources, which cannot be matched by Congress, combined with the speed with which the chief executive can act when speed is demanded, and protected by the mantle of secrecy that is sometimes required, provide advantages that have strengthened the president's status over the years as the senior partner in foreign affairs.

But if the president ordinarily has the greatest impact on foreign policy, Congress is far from a cipher in this area. Many of the president's foreign policies require supporting appropriations; Congress can refuse to cooperate or can cooperate on its own terms. Thus the foreign aid budget's size depends on congressional satisfaction with the way the previous budgets have been spent and with the results achieved. And the appropriations for that budget are normally accompanied by a long series of restrictions on what the money may or may not be spent for.

Congress can investigate the president's foreign policy and is prone to do so if things are not going well. Senator William Fulbright, when chairing the Senate Foreign Relations Committee, invited a succession of academic experts to testify concerning the Vietnam War, experts who questioned not only the conduct of the war but its underlying rationale as well. Later, Senator Frank Church's investigations into the CIA exposed the kinds of abuses that forced the administration to establish new guidelines for CIA activities and that made it more cautious in undertaking CIA missions around the world.

From time to time, Congress may pass joint resolutions expressing the "sense of the Senate" (or the House) on some foreign policy issue. Although these resolutions are not legally binding, a president ignores them at his peril. If he disregards Congress' advice, he is likely to find himself in serious trouble when he needs congressional cooperation on other matters.

Since treaties must be approved by two thirds of the Senate, that body has a powerful voice in many crucial foreign policy decisions. To win two-thirds approval, the president often must make important concessions to potential treaty opponents, just as Congress often must make concessions to the president to avoid a veto on bills it is passing. This was conspicuously evident when President Carter was seeking ratification of the Panama Canal Treaty. Much earlier, the Senate's rejection of the Versailles Treaty at the conclusion of World War I had a highly significant effect on this nation's international role between the two great wars.

Finally, Congress has enacted many pieces of legislation that have limited presidential discretion in foreign affairs, some of which have created severe problems for him. Statutes strictly limiting the immigration of persons from the Orient, after World War I, exacerbated relations with Japan and China. These countries understandably regarded the acts as discriminatory and insulting—

which indeed they were since far larger quotas of immigrants were permitted from other countries.

The Neutrality Acts in the 1930s, designed to prevent the United States from being drawn into another European conflict by forbidding the president to sell war materials to nations at war or make loans to them, were enacted despite the displeasure of President Roosevelt. On the other hand, heavy loans were forced upon the administration by Congress to help Chiang Kai-shek resist communism in China, although President Truman felt it was already a lost cause. In the 1950s Congress limited the strategic materials that could be sent to any communist country, despite administration pleas that it be given an opportunity to distinguish between the Soviet Union and such communist countries as Poland and Yugoslavia. When Americans became disillusioned with the Vietnam War, Congress forbade the use of ground troops in Laos and Cambodia and banned bombing in Cambodia after a certain date. A few years later it declined to permit President Gerald Ford to become involved in a civil war in Angola in which one side had communist support. It also forced the president to terminate arms sales to Turkey when the latter intervened in a civil war in Cyprus, using American arms illegally for that purpose.

Thus, while it remains true that the president usually has the upper hand in foreign affairs, it is a mistake to underestimate the ability of Congress to intervene when it chooses to do so.

Presidents usually devote increasing attention to foreign affairs as their term of office lengthens. As President Kennedy once said, domestic policy can defeat you, but foreign policy can kill you. Moreover, domestic policy is so frustrating and nerve-frazzling that presidents often turn to foreign policy, where they have more elbow room. Trips abroad and meetings with heads of state produce vast amounts of television and press attention, which frequently improves the president's standing in the polls. Playing the role of the international statesman is also an ego-gratifying experience; one seems to be doing "big things," making decisions that affect the country's security and exercising leadership on an international scale. Summit meetings are rarely productive, but face-to-face talks with Nikita Khrushchev, Charles de Gaulle, and Mao Tse-tung in the past, and Leonid Brezhnev, Anwar Sadat, and Menachem Begin, in the present, put the president in publicity-rich settings that few presidents have been able to resist.

The President as Commander in Chief

The president's role as commander in chief of the armed forces is the presidential power that has enjoyed the greatest inflation since 1787.[12] By 1972 Congress had lost most of the power that the Constitution had conferred upon it in this area.

As originally intended, Congress' power to declare war was designed to give that body the power to *make* military policy. The president, as commander in chief, was supposed to *carry out* the policy developed by Congress. But whereas Jefferson would not even permit, without congressional approval, retaliatory naval attacks upon Tripoli pirates who attacked American ships, and whereas the Senate, in 1810, regarded a resolution authorizing the president to protect American shipping against foreign raiders to be an unconstitutional delegation of congressional authority, this scrupulous attitude gradually gave way to increasing executive boldness in employing the armed forces as the president saw fit. President James Polk took unilateral action in sending American troops into disputed Mexican territory, in 1846, virtually guaranteeing war with Mexico. (Abraham Lincoln vigorously protested this usurpation of congressional power.) President William McKinley sent 5000 troops to China to help put down the Boxer Rebellion in 1900 without bothering to first consult Congress. Wilson took it upon himself to blockade Vera Cruz during World War I, to prevent German supplies from reaching a Mexican government unfriendly to the United States. Franklin Roosevelt did not ask for congressional consent when he ordered our fleet to fire upon enemy submarines that menaced American ships transporting military supplies to Great Britain—months before Pearl Harbor. Historian Samuel Eliot Morrison said that from this date (April 9, 1941) "the U.S. was engaged in a de facto naval war with Germany on the Atlantic Ocean."[13] Truman initially acted without congressional consultation or consent when he dispatched troops to help South Korea resist a North Korean attack in 1950; he ordered American forces into action even before the United Nations Security Council had requested U.N. members to give military assistance to South Korea.[14]

During these years, however, the American people tended to adopt a tolerant and even an approving attitude when presidents encroached upon Congress' constitutional power to make war policy. They did so, in part, because historians and political scientists eulogized the "strong president" who had broadened presidential power by bold initiatives—whether in the area of military policy or in domestic affairs. If the president's action was deemed successful, he was praised. Indeed, a possible explanation of President Nixon's disdain for congressional attempts to limit his war-making power was his reading of history: illustrious presidents seemed free to brush aside constitutional restraints and aggrandize their power to "protect the national interest."

Until recent years, then, events and their interpreters have conspired to greatly enlarge presidential power and to diminish Congress. Three developments brought this period to at least a temporary halt, however.

First, awareness spread that President Johnson, less than candidly and without appropriate congressional collaboration, led us into a Vietnamese Civil War in which American security interests were minimal. When we were ultimately obliged to withdraw and the North Vietnamese promptly overran a well-equipped South Vietnamese army that refused to fight, it was all too clear that we had sacrificed 50,000 lives and over $100 billion in a senseless enterprise for which presidents bore major responsibility.

Second, President Nixon's behavior during the Vietnam War furthered the fears that the presidency was getting out of control. Nixon did not consult congressional leaders when he and Secretary of State Henry Kissinger decided to prolong American withdrawal from Vietnam for four long years—with the end of that withdrawal curiously coinciding with the president's reelection

A president resigns in disgrace

campaign. Nor did he consult those leaders when, out of the blue, he invaded Cambodia in 1970. Earlier, neither Congress nor the secretaries of state and the Air Force knew that the president was secretly bombing Cambodia for 13 months while assuring the nation he was respecting Cambodian neutrality. Later, he sent South Vietnam President Nguyen Van Thieu a private message promising to resume this nation's military role—despite the withdrawal of American forces and despite Congress' desire to wash its hands of the war—*if* Hanoi should attack again.

In the words of distinguished historian Arthur Schlesinger, Jr., Nixon made the claim "that inherent and exclusive presidential authority, unaccompanied by emergencies threatening the life of the nation, unaccompanied by the authorization of Congress or the blessing of an international organization, permitted a President to order troops into battle at his unilateral pleasure."[15] He added, "By 1973 the American president had become, on issues of war and peace, the most absolute monarch (with the possible exception of Mao) among the great powers of the world."[16] The inability to control presidential war, he said, revealed a great failure in the Constitution.

The third factor that tended to halt expansion of the executive's power was President Nixon's long list of culpable acts—including income tax fraud; the spending of large sums of public money on his personal property; the authorization of a "dirty tricks" campaign against his political opponents; the raising of millions of campaign dollars by illegal means and unethical pressures; the creation of a private police force to carry out burglaries, wiretapping, and other illegal activities; the obstruction of justice by a wide-ranging cover-up of the Watergate burglary; the impounding (i.e., the refusal to spend) billions of congressional appropriations even after his veto had been overridden; and a claim of executive privilege (the alleged right to withhold information from Congress), which made him the sole judge of what information in the executive branch would be made available to Congress. Abuses of this magnitude were so shocking that it was no longer possible to perceive presidential power as almost inevitably benign. Our constitutional system was itself at stake; the naive belief, so long held, that the office automatically conferred a sober sense of responsibility on its occupant was no longer tenable.

(Some Americans still believe other presidents have committed offenses as grievous as Nixon's but that he was singled out for persecution by vengeful media and a partisan Congress. Interestingly, this is precisely the explanation that the Soviet Union provided its newspaper readers.[17] But in fact no predecessor came close to engaging in as wide a range of unethical or illegal actions, or carried abuses of power so far, although other presidents *have* been guilty of some offenses of a similar order. Certainly no other president was involved in the kind of criminal obstruction of justice of which Nixon was manifestly guilty.)

Reacting to all of these events, Congress was emboldened to assert itself and resist the president on all fronts. It pressed ahead with an impeachment proceedings that terminated in the president's resignation. It passed the War Powers Act of 1973, requiring the president to consult with Congress "whenever possible" before sending troops into action overseas and limiting his use of such troops to 60 days unless Congress had specifically approved his military course. (Thirty additional days were granted if needed to make a safe troop withdrawal.) Thereafter, Congress must give its consent every six months to the continued use of troops in this military venture.[18]

Congress passed other legislation enabling the president to impound appropriated funds only with the consent of Congress. Nixon had impounded about $15 billion that Congress had appropriated for various purposes, contending that spending this money would be inflationary. This was a direct and deadly blow at our constitutional system, since it challenged congressional control over the purse. If a president can refuse to spend money that Congress has appropriated, and even passed over his veto, the president is not only refusing to "execute the laws of the land" but is disemboweling Congress' legislative power. What good does it do Congress to pass a law funding an agency or program if the president, by refusing to spend the money, nullifies congressional action? Such an action constitutes, in effect, an absolute veto—a veto that has never been constitutionally granted the president.

How Powerful—Really?

We have broadly surveyed the role of the president, noting the powers and limitations of his office and concluding with a survey of recent abuses of power that have diminished popular respect for the office. A congressional renaissance, moreover, has clipped the president's wings. How much power, then, does the president really have at this point in our history? Is the presidency an institution which enables Great Men to make a deep imprint on history? Or is the office at the mercy of powerful political currents and sharply limited by competing political groups?

One school of thought holds that the presidency is not nearly as powerful an office as is popularly believed. This school would argue that Congress has more to do with the final outcome of domestic policy than the president. By the time two sets of subcommittees and full committees have worked on a bill, and floor amendments have taken their toll, and conference committees have pawed over it, it often bears little resemblance to the brightly minted measure that emerged from the White House. With rare exceptions domestic policy is "Congress country," as most presidents quickly learn.

The president's limited tether in this area is most evident if he tries to alter long-entrenched programs. Usually he will not even try because he knows that once benefits begin flowing to an interest group, it is next to impossible to turn off the spigot. Thus, most of the federal budget is beyond the president's control.

In addition, as will be noted more extensively in the final chapter, most of our serious domestic problems are so deep-rooted and intractable that neither Congress nor the president can do much about them. They currently defy solution because of hard-rock public attitudes or because even our finest minds are baffled by them.

The president has a greater impact on foreign policy but not as much as in bygone days. Foreign policy is remarkably stable, in its larger outlines, and this stability stems mainly from the difficulties a president will have with Congress if he veers off course very much. Our national interests, antagonisms, and goals change only slowly, and this massive fact sharply limits a president's freedom of action. As one of our shrewdest and most experienced political observers, Eli Ginsberg, has noted, "Having served the past seven presidents, I am impressed with one point: the continuity of national policy. It changes slowly and only at the margins. The president does not have the power to do much, except in times of war or a [military] crisis."[19]

Presidents make many important appointments, but they also commonly complain that their appointees develop a departmental orientation that reduces the president's capacity to impose his priorities on them. No gripe is heard more frequently from presidents than their sense of frustration and helplessness in dealing with the bureaucracy. Harry Truman said of incoming President (and former General) Dwight D. Eisenhower, "He will sit here and he'll say, 'Do this! Do that!' And nothing will happen. Poor Ike—it won't be a bit like the army. He'll find it very frustrating."[20] Cabinet members, not long after their appointments, are hemmed in by career bureaucrats, by congressional committees, and by interest groups with a stake in departmental programs. The president faces stiff competition in his efforts to keep his cabinet secretaries in line.

Major reorganizations in the executive establishment are almost impossible, as Jimmy Carter rapidly learned. Too many powerful people and groups feel they have too much to lose if the lines of influence they have developed with the bureaucracy are disturbed. They have an almost absolute veto over reorganization proposals.

A president's popularity, upon which much of his power rests, is almost inevitably eroded by the media's obsession with bad news. The media like nothing better than to dwell on whatever alleged weaknesses, blunders, and conflicts may exist in any administration, and their ceaseless preoccupation with whatever may discredit a president is bound to take a heavy toll. The media love red meat, and they snatch for it at every opportunity. Presidents are likely to age rapidly under this onslaught, partly beacause there is nothing a president can do that cannot be attacked by someone with a different idea. That attack will appear on the evening news.

But while the other school of thought largely concedes the truth of these charges, they contend it is only part of the truth. They say that the president does set the agenda for both Congress and the nation.[21] He largely decides what Congress shall devote its energies to and what the media (and hence the public) shall focus their substantive attention upon.

The political mood of the nation derives considerably from the president. Theodore Roosevelt's lustiness and strutting masculinity, Franklin Roosevelt's buoyance and energy, Eisenhower's prudence and steadiness, Kennedy's wit and zest, Carter's down-home quality left their mark on the nation. Something about the essential spirit of certain presidents finds its way into the spirit of the nation. The point should not be overdrawn, but it should also not be overlooked.

Presidential appointments do face the pressures that have been mentioned, but there is no way to accurately belittle the importance of appointments to the Supreme Court, the FBI, the CIA, the Federal Reserve Board, and the regulatory commissions should not be underestimated. While the Senate will not confirm appointees whose views and goals are too far off-center, the competence of these appointees and their capacity to make as constructive an impact as possible depends on the president's appointive wisdom.

We have already stressed the presidential initiative in foreign policy; that initiative must respect the traditions, values, and prejudices of the people, but if wisely undertaken, it can shift national attitudes to a significant degree and change the nation's course in important ways. And while the president can only commit American troops to action for 60 days, without congressional approval, action during that 60 days can create a *fait accompli*, giving the Congress little choice but to back the president. The tendency to support the president on his military decisions is strong; only if he clearly blunders or his military enterprise encounters heavy weather will Congress and the country block his path. Even if presidents act in an unconstitutional manner, if they do so *successfully*, we are disinclined to fault them for their lack of constitutional fastidiousness. If it works, that's good enough.

In times of crisis, as even the other school of thought agrees, the nation is willing to give the president extraordinary power to meet the economic or military emergencies that threaten the nation. At that time, as Woodrow Wilson once put it, the president is at liberty to be as big a man as he can be.[22]

If the president also happens to be an energetic activist, is attuned to the mood of the nation, is skillful in dealing with Congress (that is, he has read and follows my ten principles listed above!), is able to use television effectively, and avoids delusions of grandeur, he will be a potent figure throughout his term. Admittedly, not many presidents have this combination of qualities. But if they have, they are formidable political figures throughout their administrations; if they lack such qualities, they will not have (and do not deserve) the preeminence of their more talented presidential brethren.

The President's Hired Hands

With almost 3 million members in the executive establishment (not including the armed forces) and over $500 billion to spend, the president's task is the biggest managerial job around.[23] He needs help in making the multitude of decisions that come to his desk.

Of course, his cabinet secretaries shoulder much of his administrative burden. Usually administration of their departments becomes their main task because the president's initial intention to use his cabinet as a policy advisory group almost invariably fades as his experience lengthens. He soon comes to prefer working with a smaller group that is more expert on the issue at hand. Cabinet meetings tend to become more infrequent and to be used less and less for broadly advisory purposes.

The president needs a large personal staff to help him get the information he needs, to help coordinate executive actions, to keep an eye on the bureaucracy, to help him make intelligent decisions, and to help ensure those decisions are carried out. The White House staff exceeded 500 persons under Richard Nixon (although Jimmy Carter has reduced that number appreciably). Many of these are clerical personnel, of course, but perhaps 50 have posts of importance. A president needs to restrict the size of the staff reporting personally to him; one expert thinks eight staff members is as many as a president can properly oversee on a direct, day-to-day basis. But presidents have a hard time holding to this rule.

Every president needs someone to supervise the answering of White House mail. That person will oversee the largest number of employees in the White House office since a huge volume of mail daily pours into the White

House. These vary from thoughtful, heavyweight letters from prominent intellectuals, to letters from children expressing whatever happens to be on their minds. Here, for example, were some children's letters to President Kennedy:

Dear Mr. Kennedy: How are you? What are you doing in Washington? Your pal, Harry Slocum.

Dear President Kennedy, I would like to have your opinion on the subject of animals. Do they have brains? Dorothy Eyre. P.S. Please answer. Thanks.

Dear Mr. President: I told my sister that I wanted to be the president of the U.S. in the future. When I said this she laughed and said I could not because to become president you have to know all the capitals of the states. Which I do not. Do you have to know all of them before you can be president? Do you know them? Yours truly, Jane Mercado.

Dear Mr. Kennedy: I did not watch when you became Pres. nor did we vote for you and we didn't like you cause you were too young. But today guess you do as much as any other President would do. My brother and sister don't like you that much. I like you so cheerup. A week from now I am going to school. Well gotta leave now. Joyce O'Boyle.

Dear Mr. Kennedy. Please answer this question for me. What are Presidents for? Thank you. Yours truly, Richard Sinclair.

Dear Mr. Kennedy: I have heard some of your speeches and I liked them. How are you and your family? I'm ok. Do you have any pets? I have one stupid cat that is afraid of the vacuum cleaner. Say hello to Caroline and your wife for me. Love, Mickey Gargan.

Dear Mr. President, The boys on my street are so rough and rowdy that something must be done. Larry Johnson is their leader of them. He is also mean. I know you have problems about Cuba and Berlin but will you stop them? Sincerely Mary O'Toole.

Dear Mr. President I saw a picture of you on vacation at Hyannis Port. In the picture I see that you are crossing in the middle of the street. In the future I hope you will cross at the cross walk. Respectfully yours, Marsha Lefcourt.

Dear Mr. President, I would like to make reservations about coming to see you and meet you in the White House. What days do you got off from work so I can see you. Truly, Francis Stubbs.

Someone must arrange the president's appointments calendar; far more people want to see the president face to face than time will permit. Someone else needs to make the necessary travel arrangements for the president and the substantial staff that accompanies him on his domestic and foreign trips. The chief executive needs a talent scout to comb through *Who's Who,* the more prestigious universities, the great national foundations (Brookings, Ford, Rockefeller, Hudson, etc), and the flood of applications and recommended applicants for jobs. Several thousand top positions must be filled, and since appointees leave these posts from time to time, this means a perpetual talent hunt—including assurance that there are no skeletons in the closet which Jack Anderson or Senate sleuths will rattle when the Senate holds confirmation hearings.

Since the president is called upon to make numerous speeches, he needs

213

The President's Hired Hands

a speechwriter (who in turn needs half a dozen assistants). He also needs someone to prepare a daily summary of what is appearing in prominent newspapers and magazines that might be of interest to him. (This can be an invaluable source of information and of new ideas for him.)

Since Franklin D. Roosevelt all presidents have had press secretaries, who provide information to the press and answer questions from the White House correspondents. Some of these men (e.g., James Hagerty for Eisenhower, Bill Moyers for Lyndon Johnson, Jody Powell for Carter) are important advisors to the president. They help groom the presidents for press conferences, too, by suggesting the questions he will probably be asked and helping prepare answers for highly sensitive ones.

From all of the memoranda, reports, letters, cables, and telegrams that flood into the White House from both inside and outside the government, someone needs to decide which merit a busy president's personal attention. The responsibility is weighty; whoever decides what the president shall and shall not see profoundly affects the president's decision-making duties. A president can be overwhelmed by more material than he can ever digest; on the other hand, he can be deprived of material that would give him information, insights, and proposals he needs to know about. Not an avid reader, President Eisenhower wanted staff memos reduced to a single page. Alas, many decisions require information that cannot be condensed that briefly, even by the most succinct of writers.

President Carter and Press Secretary Powell

As already stated, one of the president's principal aides is the person in charge of legislative liaison activities. If this person has good relations with members of Congress and is trusted by them, he can help break logjams that block the president's legislative program.

Presidents need someone to oversee the development of their domestic policy programs, since there is no institutional equivalent to the state department in the domestic realm. These persons are among the most valuable presidential assistants, as the names of Ted Sorensen (for Kennedy), Joe Califano (for Lyndon Johnson), Clark Clifford (for Truman), and Stuart Eizenstat (for Carter) indicate. Not only do they have to ensure that proposals have been thoroughly researched and possible weaknesses identified and dealt with; they must also be sure that the various departments concerned have all had a chance to comment on them. If they do their job well, these persons can save the president countless headaches. (Strong presidents, of course, make the major substantive decisions about the final content of their proposals.)

It is becoming increasingly common for presidents to have a general counsel—to provide legal advice and, in practice, other advice as well, a person to handle intergovernmental relations with mayors and governors, a science advisor, and someone who acts as liaison with the "intellectual community." More significantly, presidents have a foreign policy advisor and a military policy advisor. The latter may seem unnecessary since the secretary of state and the secretary of defense are already on hand to give counsel in these areas. But presidents may not wish to be dependent too exclusively on one major source of advice. Multiple advisors help ensure that a president will have diverse and conflicting advice, enabling him to choose the policy he prefers rather than merely ratify (or reject) what his principal advisor in a given area recommends. "Preserving his options," in brief, enables a president to actually *be* the chief decision maker rather than merely appear to be that person. President Eisenhower was widely criticized for rather routinely approving the recommendations of his foremost advisors. Since Eisenhower, however, presidents have demanded staff-prepared alternative policies, each of which has been carefully researched, with pros and cons laid out for the president's perusal. (President Carter asked that policy proposals also include a statement on what congressional consultation had taken place while the proposal was gestating.)

Some of the president's foreign policy advisors have been persons of first-rank importance. Henry Kissinger was the de facto secretary of state although William Rogers bore that title under President Nixon; McGeorge Bundy was as powerful as Secretary of State Dean Rusk for President Johnson, and Zbigniew Brzezinski rivaled Cyrus Vance for influence in the Carter Administration.

Some presidents have chosen to coordinate the work of staff members under a chief of staff, and others have not. Among modern presidents Franklin Roosevelt did not have a chief of staff, choosing to personally supervise his staff instead. Eisenhower, acting in accordance with his military experience and his penchant for logical and orderly procedures and organization, chose

New Hampshire Governor Sherman Adams as his chief of staff (with the title "assistant to the President"). He exercised such extraordinary power that a popular line in Washington was, "What would happen if Adams died and Eisenhower became president?" (Adams *was* forced out of office by a minor scandal; when he and powerful Secretary of State John Foster Dulles left the government, Eisenhower *did* become a stronger president.)

Kennedy had no chief of staff, preferring the Roosevelt concept of the administrative "wheel" (with many staffers reporting directly to him rather than reporting through a chief of staff) to the pyramidal or hierarchical arrangement of Eisenhower.[24] Johnson did the same, although Joseph Califano came close to being a chief of staff for domestic affairs. Nixon used H.R. Haldeman as his chief of staff. Ford used Donald Rumsfeld as a de facto chief of staff; but Carter initially opposed giving anyone this position. Confusion, disorder, and inefficiency marked the first year of the Carter staff operation, with the president never quite making Hamilton Jordan his chief of staff.

Some observers believe a president needs a chief of staff who can perform these duties:

1. Keeping track of what the other members of the staff are doing
2. Coordinating staff activities where these impinge on a problem affecting several groups and/or departments or agencies
3. Deciding which staff problems and interdepartmental disputes should be bucked to the president and which should be handled at a lower level
4. Passing on the president's latest instructions and decisions to the staff.

Some would add, perhaps, that the president needs a "hatchet man" to fire unsatisfactory people (a nasty job), to talk bluntly to others, and to say "no" to people who will be outraged at such action. The chief of staff can thus become the presidential lightning rod and fall guy.

Defenders of the chief-of-staff system contend that there is no reason why that person needs to guard the portals to the presidential Oval Office so strictly that he isolates the president from people he needs to see; the president can lay down his instructions on that score. Nor need a chief of staff deprive the president of the policy options he requires in order to be the master of his house. He is, after all, the president's appointee, and he will follow the president's orders on these matters.

But the president's advisory and managerial aides extend well beyond the White House office and the cabinet secretaries. The executive office of the president encompasses about 5000 additional persons. A high proportion of these is in the Office of Management and Budget, which tries to improve managerial efficiency in the executive establishment and keeps a sharp eye on expenditures while drawing up its annual agency-by-agency budget recommendations. But the executive office also includes the Council of Economic Advisers, which, with the aid of a substantial staff, prepares economic reports and counsels the president on his crucially important economic decisions. The Council on Environmental Quality advise him on antipollution policy, and the National Security Council (NSC) staff helps the president integrate domestic, foreign and military policies relating to national security. The NSC is usually

Executive office of the president

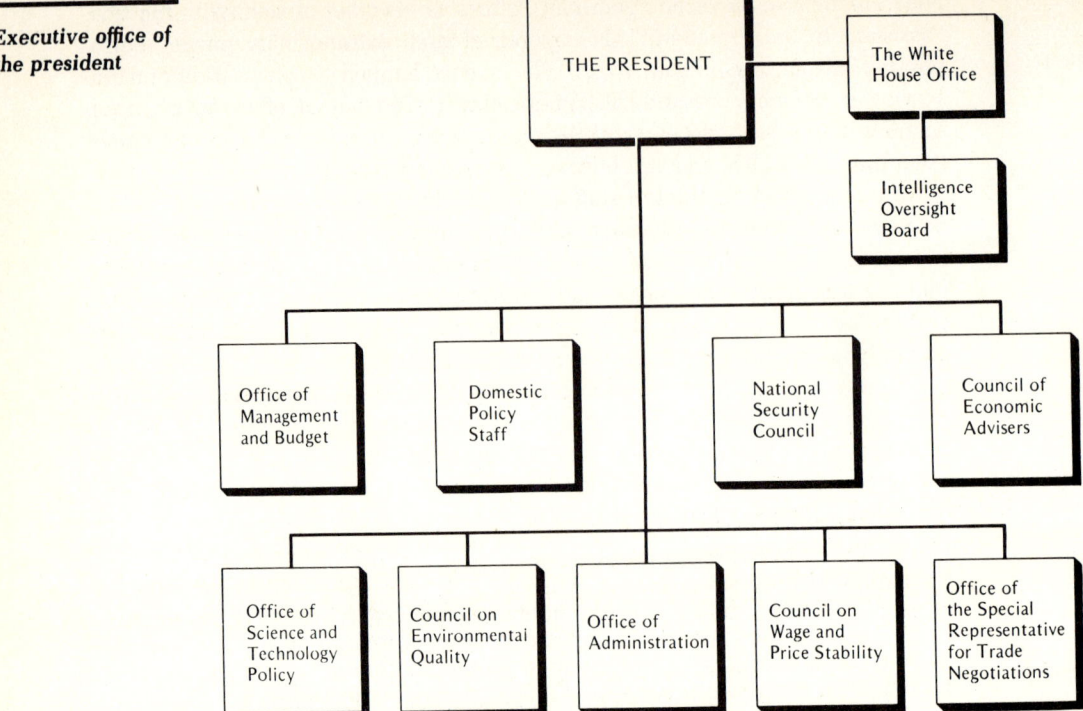

composed of the president, vice-president, the secretary of state, of defense, of the treasury, the chairman of the Joint Chiefs of Staff, the director of the Central Intelligence Agency, and such other officials as the president chooses to assign on a permanent or ad hoc basis. Some presidents have employed the NSC as a major advisory body; others have tended to by-pass it.

President Carter utilized the services of the National Security Council considerably, but like many presidents he also arrived at foreign policy decisions through meetings with smaller groups—usually including the secretary of state, the secretary of defense, the vice-president, Zbigniew Brzezinski (learn to spell his name and impress your prof!) and Hamilton Jordan.[25] Each president tends to rely on a smaller number of trusted foreign policy (and domestic policy) advisors as his administration lengthens.

Concluding Notes

In conclusion, few historians subscribe to the "Great Man" theory of history—that great men and women markedly change the course of human events. More fundamental forces—economic and technological, especially—are usually credited or blamed for major developments of historic import. Still, it is hard to believe that history would not have been considerably different if men like Napoleon, V. I. Lenin, Adolf Hitler, Joseph Stalin, Abraham Lincoln, Franklin D. Roosevelt, Winston Churchill, Charles de Gaulle, and Mahatma Gandhi had not appeared when and where they did.

In any case, one need not belong to the "Great Men" school of thought to believe that the ability and values of our chief executive are the most significant political factors in the way we respond to the challenges of each decade. There are severe limits to what he can achieve (fewer limits to the damage he can do), but he usually leaves a much deeper imprint than anyone else in government. The nation makes no decision more important than who shall inhabit 1600 Pennsylvania Avenue.

Is there any way for the public to improve its batting average in choosing among presidential aspirants? Professor James David Barber thinks so.[26] He believes that paying close attention to a candidate's early life experiences can be helpful. Did the candidate have a secure and loving family environment, so that he grew to be self-confident and emotionally healthy? Does he have energy reserves sufficient to enable him to conduct an active presidency? Does he enjoy politics (without being obsessive about it), rather than look upon political activity as a duty, an onerous chore, something to be endured? Has he a sense of humor and a sense of perspective rather than being a solemn, intense, driven person who is out to overcome his self-doubts about his mettle and virtue by performing extraordinary feats of military valor? Is he more interested in achievement for its own sake than in having people love him? If we can ascertain the truth about a candidate's character, defined in this way, we can have greater assurance that we are choosing wisely.

Whether journalists will give us this information early enough, by evidence that can be trusted, is another matter. Many political scientists doubt that there is any reliable formula for screening out probable failures and identifying the probably successful. Would Washington and Lincoln have failed Barber's test? Probably. Is life so complex and the requirements of the presidency so varied at different periods in our history that we must inevitably grope in semidarkness for the person best qualified to lead us? Probably. Can the mind always find reasons for doing what our hearts desire? Assuredly. But Barber's criteria, although far from infallible, are worth considering nonetheless (along with a candidate's values and priorities). They may not give us greatness, but they might save us from disaster.

Notes

1. Emmet John Hughes, *The Living Presidency* (New York: Coward, McCann and Geoghegan, 1973), p. 40.
2. Cited in Arthur M. Schlesinger, Jr., *The Imperial Presidency* (New York: Popular Library, 1974), p. 8.
3. Ibid, p. 151.
4. Theodore Roosevelt, in one of his speeches. (Some footnote!)
5. Clinton Rossiter, *The American Presidency*, rev. ed. (New York: Harcourt Brace Jovanovich, 1960), p. 18.
6. Edward S. Corwin, *The President: Office and Powers* (New York University Press, 1957), pp. 25–26.
7. Rossiter, *The American Presidency*, p. 57.
8. William Henry Harrison, quoted in Wilfred Binkley, *President and Congress* (New York: Knopf, 1947), p. 90.
9. Reo M. Christenson, "Presidential Leadership of Congress," *Presidential Studies Quarterly* (Summer 1978), Vol. 8, pp. 257–267.

10. Corwin, *The President*, p. 71.
11. Wallace McClure, *International Executive Agreements* (New York: Columbia University Press, 1941), p. 364.
12. Schlesinger, *The Imperial Presidency*, is the best source on this development.
13. Samuel Eliot Morison, *The Battle of the Atlantic, 1939-1943*, cited by Merlo Pusey, *The Way We Go to War* (Boston: Houghton Mifflin, 1969), p. 3.
14. Schlesinger, *The Imperial Presidency*, p. 135.
15. Ibid., pp. 191-192.
16. Ibid., p. 11.
17. "Kremlin Cover Up on Watergate." *Time*, August 26, 1974, p. 41.
18. For a good analysis of the War Powers Act, see Graham T. Allison, "Making War: The President and Congress," in *The Presidency Reappraised*, eds. Thomas E. Cronin and Rexford Tugwell (New York: Praeger, 1977), pp. 228-247.
19. Eli Ginzberg, "Planning Full Employment," *Society*, May-June, 1976, p. 62.
20. Quoted in Richard Neustadt, *Presidential Power* (New York: New American Library (Mentor Books), 1960), p. 22.
21. "Dear Mr. President," *McCalls*, January 1962.
22. William F. Mullen, *Presidential Power and Politics* (New York: St. Martin's Press, 1976), p. 144.
22. Quoted in Hughes, *The Living Presidency*, p. 59.
23. See Stephen Hess, *Organizing the Presidency* (Washington, D.C.: Brookings Institute, 1976).
24. Ibid., p. 78.
25. Richard Burt, "Zbig Makes It Big," *New York Times Magazine*, July 30, 1978, pp. 8-10.
26. James David Barber, *The Presidential Character, Predicting Performance in the White House*, 2nd ed. (Englewood Cliffs, N.J.: Prentice-Hall, 1977).

CHAPTER 12
THE BUREAUCRACY AND ITS CRITICS

Bureaucracy! The images that term evokes! Millions of faceless people lapping up our taxes, regulating our lives, and exercising their power with incompetence, slothfulness, and an insolent disdain for the human needs they are supposed to serve. People who treat others like numbers, people who see life in terms of forms, reports, and red tape. People who, when asked for help, refer you to someone else. People who pry into your life. People who rigidly adhere to rules that make no sense. People who take pleasure in saying "no." People who cannot be fired, and act accordingly. People who spend their lives waiting for 5 o'clock to come.

For millions of Americans—maybe most—this is the picture which "bureaucracy" brings to mind. But strangely enough, while this stereotype applies to "bureaucracy" in general, it usually does not apply to the "bureaucrats" we actually deal with. A major study reported in *Psychology Today* revealed a striking contrast between American attitudes toward bureaucrats in general and the bureaucrats they have known. Over 70% of those who had dealt with bureaucrats found their problems adequately handled, 80% thought they were treated fairly, and almost 80% believed they were treated with courtesy. At the same time, only 30% believed government agencies do their work well, only 42% thought those agencies treat people fairly, and about 40% believed they treat people considerately.[1]

Bureaucracy Versus Efficiency?

No one really knows if the federal bureaucracy is inefficient or not. As the Frenchman replied, when asked if he loved his wife—"Compared to what?" You simply cannot compare governmental functions to private enterprise because they are different ball games. Business is out to make a profit and government isn't. They play by different rules and seek different ends.

Government operates under civil service rules and internal regulations designed to promote equal job opportunities, equal treatment before the law, to protect minorities, prevent corruption and misuse of power, and ensure that sufficient records are kept to enable Congress and the Office of Management and Budget to evaluate their work. These rules and regulations may not promote efficiency, by business standards, but they do promote fair play and the proper exercise of power by democratic standards. Is it inefficient to carry out the rules which democratic criteria require? Or are we comparing apples and oranges?

Moreover, since there are several thousand government agencies, no one has ever made a sufficiently intensive study of a sufficiently large cross-section of government employees to accurately generalize about the overall "efficiency" of government. (Which doesn't deter government critics one whit, of course!)

One thing is certain. Those government agencies that carry on operations of a businesslike nature do so either because business was unable to make a profit or because a natural monopoly made it hazardous to leave the function up to persons whose only goal is profit. For example, the railroads have been unable to make money carrying passengers but find freight hauling to be quite lucrative. So what do we do? We let them haul freight and turn passenger ser-

Bureaucracy Versus Efficiency?

vice over to the government. Then we wag our heads because Amtrak doesn't make a profit!

Municipal transportation is another case in point. Only when private groups find it unprofitable to carry passengers do municipalities take over the job—and of course they run deficits on those operations. Experiments to run public services like businesses have generally failed. Given autonomous status so that it could deliver the mail on a businesslike basis, the post office has not pleased the public any more than before.

This chapter is concerned not with bureaucrats in general but with the federal bureaucracy and those who control it. The former number less than 3 million, compared to about 13 million who work for state and local governments. Over 85% of federal bureaucrats, associated with about 2000 agencies, live outside of Washington, since federal agencies have regional, state, and local offices scattered throughout the nation. (Two-thirds of these work for the military, the post office, and the Veterans Administration.) They administer a budget of over $500 billion, which pays almost 50 million checks a month to persons who qualify under one or more of roughly a thousand federal aid programs. They give to state and local governments, in accordance with federal law, about one-fourth of all the money these governments spend. One-third of the nation's land (mostly in the West) owned by Washington falls under their control. And they administer federal regulations that blanket the land and are steadily expanding in number year by year.

While some people think of federal bureaucrats as clerks and routine paper-shufflers, over 500,000 are engineers, architects, accountants, budget specialists, doctors, and other health specialists, natural scientists, social scientists, psychologists, lawyers, and librarians.

Almost all federal bureaucrats have won their jobs through competitive exams or by decisions based on a comparative evaluation of applicants' education, training, and experience. Veterans, however, receive special preference when their examination grades are computed. On a scale of 100, 5 points are added to veterans' grades and 10 points are added for disabled veterans. Applicants who graduate in the top tenth of their college class or have had a grade-point average of 3.5 or above get their PACE (Professional Administrative Career Examination—GS 5–7) scores raised because of this record. The examinations are usually conducted by the Office of Personnel Management (formerly the Civil Service Commission) although many agencies (like the TVA, the FBI, and the CIA) have their own systems for evaluating the comparative merits of job applicants.

The OPM prepares registers of those who pass the examinations for various jobs at a grade of 70 or above. When a federal administrator has a vacancy to fill, he or she asks the OPM for help. The latter supplies the administrator with the names of the 3 highest-ranking candidates, from which a selection is made. (Under exceptional circumstances the OPM permits the administrator to waive the rule—but not the criterion of competence.)

Federal jobs are classified by ranks, which correspond to the levels of work difficulty and/or experience and training required to do those jobs.

These begin at GS 1 and move up the scale to GS 18. Pay for jobs is supposed to be comparable to that for similar work in private enterprise, but when pensions and other fringe benefits are considered, the lower levels are compensated more liberally. At the upper levels they may be paid less than persons of comparable skill and experience in nongovernmental positions. (GS 18 paid $47,500 a year in 1978.)

The process of selecting federal employees on the basis of competitive exams rather than by administrators' discretion reflects the belief that everyone should have an equal chance to secure federal jobs. Prior to the establishment of the current system, elected officials usually gave federal jobs to those who contributed cash or personal services to their election campaign. This so-called *patronage* (or *spoils*) system was attacked by those who believed appointments should be based on merit rather than on partisan activities. It was further argued that administrative expertise would be promoted if employees could hold their jobs permanently rather than be subject to dismissal because of a shift in party fortunes. Experience normally enables people to do better work, yet the spoils system ignored this prime qualification for job competence. The prospect of arbitrary dismissal, regardless of how well work is done, discouraged able people from entering the federal service. Since there is no Republican or Democratic way to do most jobs, partisan affiliation or activities ought to be unrelated to hiring and firing, it was said. Accordingly, the Pendleton Act was passed in 1883, requiring competitive exams for many federal jobs. Congress extended the new *merit system* from time to time until it covered almost the entire federal service.

The principle has not been extended, however, to more than 2000 jobs at the apex of the federal bureaucracy. The president appoints persons to these positions with the consent of the Senate. The jobs include cabinet positions (as well as positions as agency heads), top aide posts, and less important jobs of a "confidential" nature.

Some observers today think we have carried the merit system too far and that department and agency heads should be able to appoint more of their subordinates according to their personal standards.[2] These might or might not involve partisan criteria, but since the administrator is held responsible for the performance of his or her department or agency, he or she should be able to hire *and* fire those who hold the most responsible jobs in the agency. Those whose responsibility is weighty extend farther down the administrative hierarchy than the civil service system acknowledges, it is said.

Much of the discontent with the current system reflects the imperfections of the selection process, automatic pay increases, and the difficulty of firing those appointed under the merit system. The attempt at "objectivity" in rating applicants often slights qualities of critical importance to effective long-run administrative performance—compatibility, for example, as well as drive, initiative, flexibility, originality, the ability to take criticism, and emotional maturity. OPM rules do not exclude the consideration of these factors, but they weigh less heavily than critics believe they should.

Pay increases are supposed to be based on merit, but over 99% of federal employees regularly receive them. This suggests that seniority is almost the only basis for these increases, with "merit" as window dressing only. (President Carter has tried to reduce this tendency in the upper levels of the bureaucracy, with uncertain results.)

New appointees are required to successfully pass a probationary period of one year before they win permanent status. If they look like poor risks during this period, dismissal is possible with a minimum of fuss. But just as persons can conceal certain disagreeable qualities when they are in the marriage market, some employees can conceal certain weaknesses during their probationary period. Or, prolonged work experience may bring out latent or dimly perceived personal weaknesses that eventually cause a once acceptable employee to become a liability. There is no doubt that it has become extremely difficult to discharge federal employees who have achieved tenure, whatever the quality of their work.

Fire Them—If You Can!

The *Washington Monthly* gives us a horrendous example of the tribulations that may accompany the firing of a tenured bureaucrat. (This occurred before President Carter's civil service reform bill sought to simplify and facilitate the firing process.)

> A federal executive, a woman, describes what is involved in trying to dismiss a typist who has become impossible to work with:
>
> She had been unsatisfactory for close to a year.... She was extremely moody and temperamental. Her attendance was terribly spotty. She did not take criticism of any sort. You never knew when she was going to blow. And during a long period when I took no notes—it was not yet even in my mind to start an adverse action—she would come into my office and ream me up one side and down the other. She would make the most outlandish accusations about my relations with other people in the division. It would happen, usually, when I called her in to discuss her attendance. She was hot-tempered, she had a foul mouth, and you could hear her all the way down the corridor when she laced off.
>
> The straw that broke the camel's back was her rather sudden refusal to carry out one clerical function which was a necessary part of her duties. She flatly refused. She just stopped doing it. When I realized that other people on the staff were having to do this [person's] job I knew I had to take a hand. I went in and told her that I expected her to perform that function and complete it by four o'clock that afternoon. She was typing and she didn't reply. She went on typing and I asked her if she'd heard me. Without looking up, she said, "I heard you." And I said, "Are you going to do it?" She said, "We'll see."
>
> She went home that day without having done it. I believe that was when I realized that drastic measures would have to be taken. I consulted with a great number of people in the administrative area of our agency. I got all the books and received verbal advice on how you initiate an adverse action. And I carried everything out to the letter. I spent a good part of the next two months documenting [this person's] performance on the job. I wrote an extensive evaluation of her work, which I gave to her, and followed this with a memo to her requesting improvement in the deficient areas. She wrote a memo to me asking for "specifics." I asked her supervisor to reply by memo, giving more

specifics. You would be astonished at the number of memos which flowed back and forth between me and various elements of the agency on this one case. Finally I was in a position to write [this person] a formal letter telling her that I was initiating action to have her dismissed. I had the letter looked at by the people who know about this kind of thing and, on their instruction, gave it to her in the presence of a witness.

The [employee] asked for a formal agency hearing on the charges, which is her right, and she got the union to represent her. The agency appointed a lawyer to represent me. More months went by and lots more paperwork. A hearing examiner was assigned. He wrote telling us the requirements for the hearing—you have to set the room up exactly the way they want it. The tables have to be set up in certain ways, you have to rent a tape recorder and hire two operators to take down the proceedings—that alone, and the subsequent transcriptions, ended up costing the agency something like $2,000.

When the hearings finally did take place, six months had elapsed since I had decided to take action. The hearings lasted three days. By the rules of the game [the employee] was there the whole time, I was only permitted in while actually giving my own testimony; I couldn't even be there when witnesses on my own side were testifying.

Anyway, another month or so elapsed while the recordings of the proceedings were transcribed and relevant portions sent to all concerned parties for their comments or corrections. Then, after the transcripts were returned to the examiner and he was pondering his recommendation, [this person] found another job and quit. Otherwise, it might still be going on.

The system is actually geared, in my mind, to the incompetent. You really have to do something heinous for your supervisor to take any action because it's so damn much trouble. And it is a lot of trouble. I was warned it was a lot of trouble. And I found it occupying, and I'm not kidding, five-eighths of my day toward the end. And 100 per cent of my mind. The system and the rule book are geared to making you think 50 times before you start. The system assumes a supervisor has nothing else to do; the paperwork is unbelievable. My assistant, call her the office manager for this particular episode, and my secretary, the two of them were spending 50 per cent of their time—that's one person, 100 per cent—typing up reports with umpteen copies. A copy of everything, incidentally, had to go to [this person's] representative. We couldn't hold a meeting to discuss the case and what we were going to do without either her or her representative being present. That's all in the rules and regulations.

While President Carter made a major effort to simplify and streamline the process of firing incompetent federal employees, experienced Washington observer John Herkers wrote that "... Mr. Carter's efforts ... still leave a formidable array of procedures that will have to be exhausted before an incompetent can be fired. Time is on the side of the government worker; the civil service has a way of waiting out and wearing down every reform effort." ("Washington, An Insider's Game," *New York Times Magazine*, April 22, 1979, p. 86.)

If you want to find some rather cold comfort in all this, you might reflect on this point of view. If disagreeable or inefficient employees *were* fired, they would either be disagreeable or inefficient in some other job. Or they would go on welfare, to be supported by your tax dollars. Would that be much better? Are there a certain percentage of people who will always be a pain in the neck—and *someone* has to put up with them? (But, you say, if they *knew* they had to either shape up or ship out, they'd shape up. Well, maybe. Some of them. But a lot of them will be inefficient or disagreeable no matter what we do. Maybe we need to become more philosophical about intractable problems? Which is easy, unless *we* are the ones who have to deal with these people!)

Fortunately, there are devious ways to deal with incompetents, including harassment until they resign, reassignment to an unsuspecting agency, an internal reorganization that eliminates the job, or assigning the offender to a job where little work is required and hence little damage is done.

Critics of the present system also point to a "bureaucratic mentality" that allegedly comes to afflict those who have long served in any bureaucracy. These critics complain about a tendency among bureaucrats to lose sight of the policy ends to be sought—helping people with their problems—in their obsession with the tyranny of paper; a tendency to treat people as if they were objects rather than flesh-and-blood human beings; a propensity to get in ruts, to become so accustomed to doing something in a routine manner that there is strong resistance to change. Among high-ranking career civil servants an especially pronounced tendency develops to see the world wholly from an agency perspective, to equate what is good for the agency as good for the country, and to identify progress with more appropriations, more employees, and more functions. This is true of bureaucrats in private enterprise, too, but private bureaucrats do not enjoy the same job security as those in public service.

Red Tape: A Necessary Evil

Critics also rail endlessly against "red tape"—for reasons both good and bad. It is a favorite object of head shaking by disgruntled citizens of every political stripe. But Herbert Kaufman, author of the splendid little book, *Red Tape*, maintains that government personnel usually dislike red tape as much as ordinary citizens:

> *They would like to get on with their missions as they see them, to pursue their program goals energetically, efficiently, speedily. They chafe at the obstacles placed in their way, the restraints imposed on them, the boundaries they must observe, the procedures they must follow. Nobody is more critical of red tape than they. To them, it is ironic that they should be blamed for it.*[4]

Kaufman adds that government leaders are equally frustrated:

> *Political superiors find administrative agencies less responsive to them than they would like because the agencies are bound by generations of accumulated obligations and restraints. Leaders therefore cannot do as they would like to shape administrative action to the image of their own philosophies or to the demands of their allies and constituents. They are also angry and embarrassed by their apparent inability to eliminate the red tape that everyone complains about; the persistence of red tape makes them seem unresponsive or powerless. Unable to get their own way or to do favors for their friends whenever they want, the highest*

government officials are frequently as enraged by the vast corpus of constraints embodied in official documents as any of their subordinates and as any private citizen. They are among the loudest and most intense critics.[5]

If the public, lower-level bureaucrats, and top-level bureaucrats as well hate red tape, why then, do we have it? The answer is that the public appears to want it, partly for the sake of order, partly because our democratic ethics demand it.

Some regulations are necessary to the orderly functioning of any enterprise. Employees need to know what to do, how to do it and what not to do. The heavier the responsibilities and the more complex the organization, the more red tape is involved. A business owned by one person needs no formal rules, but General Motors and the Department of Health, Education, and Welfare require a host of them. Someone once said that "red tape involves that part of my job you know nothing about." In addition to complex interrelationships requiring rules, the necessity for impartial administration of government services, benefits, and penalties requires red tape.

If, for example, we left it up to each welfare administrator within a state to authorize welfare payments on the basis of "need" at his or her own discretion, we would often encounter gross discrimination and shocking disparities. Some administrators would discriminate against blacks or Chicanos, others against mothers with illegitimate children, and still others against able-bodied men. Some would require a person to be flat broke, with no assets, before qualifying for welfare benefits. Others would be more liberal. Some would pay $100 a month to a family of four, others might pay $500. Some would require an exhaustive itemization of their financial status; others might ask for a simple sworn statement of need. Some would demand that a welfare mother with five children be sterilized before getting further payments; others would regard such a requirement as outrageous. In brief, fairly detailed rules and regulations applying to all welfare administrators ensure rough equality of treatment and prevent flagrant inequities in the granting or withholding of benefits. As Herbert Kaufman puts it, "One person's red tape is another person's sacred protection."[6]

Furthermore, every time an abuse occurs (whether through misuse of the remaining administrative discretion, the appearance of official corruption, or because of innovative ingenuities by cheating clients), a new regulation will probably be created to prevent its recurrence. And since new regulations almost invariably require clarification when applied to unexpected situations, still more rules to explain the earlier ones are needed. Thus, the longer an agency exists, the longer the list of rules and regulations.

Each person having a claim upon the government for some service or benefit feels his or her case is unique (which it often is) and believes the administrator should bend the rules to accommodate that uniqueness. When the citizen is not granted special consideration, always in the direction of greater generosity or permissibility, he or she complains bitterly about "bureaucracy" and its hardheartedness.

Employment Development Office

Admittedly, there are times when rules should be bent to adjust to special circumstances—or perhaps even waived entirely. But inevitably, people will differ in interpreting the need for such action. Some persons are legalists and literalists who feel more secure living up to the letter of the law. Others believe rules are made to be bent or broken for good reason—and act accordingly. But these variations are products of ineradicable individual differences, and bureaucracies (public or private) will always have both types in their midst. Critics can fault each group for either "flouting the rules" or for "undue rigidity." If citizens realized that these conditions are an inevitable and normal part of life, they might be less prone to generalized complaining.

In short, bureaucrats probably do about as good or as bad work and demonstrate about as good or bad judgment as the rest of us. That does not mean that certain bureaucratic tendencies should not be resisted, or that strenuous efforts should not be made to improve performance or reduce unnecessary regulations. Congress and the executive branch might perform a public service by stopping the creation of new programs and the issuing of new rules for a year. They could then devote themselves almost exclusively to improving and streamlining existing laws and regulations so that programs could be more efficiently administered and so that marginal or counterproductive programs

Income tax forms ready for shipment

could be identified and phased out. It might be a great idea—but don't hold your breath!

Bureaucrats: Drunk with Power?

Aside from questions of efficiency and impartiality, federal administrators have a great deal of political power. One may think administrators only carry out policy made by legislatures, but in fact administrators often make policy just as much as legislatures do. The laws Congress passes must be interpreted since their precise meaning as applied to specific circumstances is often unclear. A shrewd person once said, "I care not who writes the laws so long as I can interpret them." Although courts may be the final interpreters, most interpretations of what a law means are made by administrators, with only a tiny percentage of their decisions being appealed to the courts.

Even when laws are written with great precision, questions of interpretation inevitably arise from time to time. But Congress often deliberately passes legislation that is ambiguously worded since ambiguities can be interpreted differently by those having contradictory goals. Vague language often makes majority coalitions possible, coalitions that would fall apart if the law was worded so precisely that different elements saw their diverse hopes dashed. (Another sage has noted that people will die for their principles, if only they are sufficiently vague.)

Many times, however, Congress passes legislation in broad, general terms because it lacks the expertise to spell out the statute in finely drawn language. Legislators will express a general goal ("regulate in the public interest," "forbid unfair trade practices," "insure a fair rate of return") and leave it to administrators to reach their goal by rules appropriate to a highly complex and rapidly changing situation. A federal agency that focuses exclusively on the regulation of a given industry (e.g., mining,) can develop sufficient knowledge of the coal industry to issue detailed safety regulations that a harassed and overworked Congress could never do.

Similarly, Congress may enact legislation forbidding federal grants to institutions receiving federal funds that discriminate against females. But such legislation raises many questions. Does this mean that such institutions must hire as many men as women? Are quotas to be established as administrative "goals"? Must the institution compensate for past discrimination by giving female job applicants a preference until a certain percentage of employees are female? If a smaller percentage of women have the technical training certain jobs require, what effect does that have? Does availability of skilled female labor involve only the local labor market or the national labor market? In universities, must as much money be spent on women's athletics as men's athletics—if spectators prefer watching male football, basketball, and baseball teams? If layoffs become necessary and the seniority principle governs, does this illegally discriminate against the last persons hired—who may be women? The administrators of the law must decide all these questions.

The upshot is that when administrators (bureaucrats) put flesh on the bones of a vaguely worded statute by issuing numerous clarifying regulations, they are "legislating" just as much as if the legislature were writing these regulations into the law. Indeed, these regulations become law, enforceable in the courts, and are published daily in the *Federal Register*—which publishes over 50,000 pages annually of regulations and proposed regulations. It is important to remember, then, that Congress legislates, administrators legislate, and the courts legislate—only at different stages in the larger, overall legislative process.

In recent years we have become acutely aware that many problems are not solved just by passing laws, even if those laws are intelligently drafted. The passage of legislation is, at best, only the first step. Only if laws are effectively administered do they stand much chance of achieving their ends. Quality administration, moreover, is not commonplace; good administrators are no more abundant than good mechanics, electricians, professors, or third basemen. Excellence is always in short supply.

As the chief executive, the president is ultimately responsible for the administrative operations of the far-flung national government. The Constitution enjoins him to "take care that the laws be faithfully executed." With 2.80 million federal civilian employees and over 2 million members of the armed forces, that is a crushing burden to undertake.

The president's principal tool in seeking the faithful (and efficient) execution of the laws is his appointing power. His selection of cabinet members and other agency and commission heads represent his most important contribution to the quality of administration during his presidency. Unfortunately, cabinet members are often selected not because of their administrative ability but because they supported the president's campaign, are backed by powerful interests, will give representation to various groups (blacks, women, Jews), bring geographical balance to the cabinet, or are personal friends of the president. If they also happen to be good administrators, that is usually no more than a happy accident.

Presidents complain bitterly that the bureaucracy does not respond to presidential orders. Presidents Franklin Roosevelt, Harry Truman, John Kennedy, and Richard Nixon grumbled about the sluggishness of the bureaucracy or its resistance to their directives—and the other presidents would doubtless say the same if exhumed and interrogated.

To a considerable degree, Congress wants it this way. It established a number of so-called *independent regulatory commissions* to handle some of the most important functions of our government. These include the Federal Communications Commission (regulating radio and TV), the Interstate Commerce Commission (controlling railroads, trucking, and interstate waterways), the Federal Trade Commission (responsible for identifying and preventing unfair business practices), the Federal Power Commission (formerly in charge of natural gas and hydroelectric-power pricing and distribution), the Securities and Exchange Commission (overseeing the stock market and of the issuance of securities), and the National Labor Relations Board (empowered to enforce national labor laws). These agencies are "independent" in that the president cannot dictate policy to them nor can he fire commission members whose policy stances displease him. Because they issue a host of regulations under the broad authority entrusted to them by Congress and because they sit in judgment when business or labor interests are accused of violating their rules, they were given a degree of independence not permitted the Departments of Defense, Treasury, Commerce, and the like. Partly, too, Congress did not want to give the president too much power, which it feared supervisory authority over these agencies would bring. A number of government corporations, such as the TVA and the post office, have also been given considerable autonomy. Thus, a substantial chunk of administrative authority that might have flowed to the president was withheld from him.

As for the cabinet departments their alleged "unresponsiveness" is attributable to many factors. The president may hope his hand-picked cabinet members will be able to impose the presidential perspective and priorities on their respective departments, but frequently this does not happen. Cabinet secretaries usually enter upon their duties with a very limited knowledge of the operations of their departments—or its problems. The civil servants who have ascended to the top rank of the departments' career ladder know their department's work well; they have had many years to acquire familiarity with its activities. It is only natural that they would take the incoming secretary in tow. In the course of "educating" him or her to new responsibilities, they also orient the secretary to see things their way. They explain why things are done in a certain way, why alternative courses are unfeasible, and perhaps why the views "outsiders" (like the president?) have of the department's work do not fit the operational realities. Since the secretary is expected to represent the interests of the department when its objectives and problems receive presidential attention, he or she may become the department's advocate as much as the president's appointee. Since he or she sees the president rarely and circulates daily among the upper-echelon figures in the department, attachment to the latter tends to grow. John Ehrlichman, one of President Nixon's right-hand men, put it this way: "The secretaries run off and marry the natives."[7]

Thus, when the president wants something done that conflicts with a department's evaluation of the proper course, the secretary has ambivalent feelings. He or she may try to implement the president's instructions, only to face quiet resistance from the department's staff. As professionals, these career civil servants believe they know what should be done. Since they are almost never fired, they expect to outlast both secretary and president. Frequently, they can count on support from the organized interests served by the department (farm organizations may back the Department of Agriculture, business organizations the Department of Commerce, and labor unions the Department of Labor) if the president is trying to prune away funds previously allotted to department programs, to withdraw previously available services, or to impose tougher regulations on interest groups. Not only are the career civil servants likely to have interest group support in these cases, but their foot dragging may also be encouraged by the congressional committees that handle legislation and appropriations affecting them. The committee and subcommittee chairs frequently establish close relations with these administrators, supporting their powers and appropriations in return for department favors to their constituents. When the president, therefore, seeks to pull departmental administrative policy in directions a department does not wish to go, the president may face a less than enthusiastic secretary surrounded by resistant aides, who in turn are backed by powerful interest groups sustained by formidable figures in Congress.[8]

Even if the president got full cooperation from his cabinet secretary and top career people, many orders issued at the top of an administrative hierarchy have a disconcerting way of losing force and effect as they move down the ladder to the civil servants who directly encounter the affected public. If these "line" personnel are not sympathetic with the president's policy, they can sabotage it in quiet ways—perhaps with no upper-echelon officials being the wiser. The greater the distance from those who give orders to those who carry them out, the greater the loss of authoritative potency.

Efforts to gain greater presidential control by reorganizing departments, agencies, boards, and commissions into more manageable (and rationally related) units also meet stubborn and usually insuperable obstacles. Congress can reject reorganization plans by a majority of either house, and it usually does if major reorganizations are undertaken. As we have noted, many MCs (especially committee and subcommittee chairs) have established close ties over a period of years with officials in various agencies. Each has done favors for the other, and each "knows the ropes" and knows who to see and how to get things done. These MCs normally fight any reorganization that alters the existing "power structure" and disrupts lines of communication and lines of authority in ways threatening to current comfortable arrangements.[9] If the reorganization "downgrades" a governmental unit, reduces its independence, or places it under the control of an agency believed less sympathetic to its powers and functions, the affected officials will do all in their power to mobilize opposition from the constituencies they serve and the MCs with whom they are allied. Ordinarily the political support they can generate is more potent than that which a president can generate from people less directly affected by the proposed reorganization. In brief, whenever groups are threatened with the loss of power, privileges, dollars, or prestige, they will utilize every available means to protect themselves. This holds true both inside government and out. High and noble principles will always be invoked to justify the struggle, with the self-interest discreetly concealed. In struggles of this nature, as in our private lives, there are usually two reasons for human behavior: one is the reason that is given, the other is the real reason.

Finally, bureaucracies retain power because presidents have far too much on their minds to give much attention to administrative problems. Most of their time is devoted to foreign affairs and national security. After they have sweated over appointments, wrangled with Congress, prepared for press conferences, answered their mail, met with important people, read the newspapers, studied official reports and staff memoranda, traveled here and there, met their ceremonial obligations, gotten some exercise (hopefully), and waved at their wives, there is precious little time for mastering administrative complexities, making decisions about them, and following up to ensure decisions are carried out. If they do focus on a few administrative problems, 100 others are necessarily neglected. The sheer lack of time guarantees that the bureaucracy will largely remain the same no matter who is president.

Is this presidential impotence necessarily deplorable? Some say yes, but others dissent. Few people find desirable an all-powerful executive, whose every administrative desire is obediently carried out by the career officials and top-level appointees who run our vast executive establishment. No president is so wise that his will should automatically be translated into administrative policy throughout the bureaucracy. Perhaps, then the capacity of bureaucrats to resist all but the most skillful and persistent of presidential pressures is a source of stability to the nation and a protection against sometimes arbitrary or headstrong presidents. When we elect a president we give him a mandate to *try* to put his program through Congress, to *try* to make foreign policy, and to *try* to control the bureaucracy. But not to snap his fingers and have the bureaucracy come to heel. Wasn't it a good thing that the IRS and the FBI did *not* yield to improper pressures from President Nixon and his staff? Most observers believe that the president, Congress, and the courts all have a role in directing and controlling the bureaucracy—not just the president alone. In this they are surely right although the president, as chief executive, *is* entrusted with a special responsibility to "see that the laws shall be faithfully executed."

The Taming of Bureaucrats

We do not want a bureaucracy that is headless or that lacks accountability, directly or indirectly, to elected officials. A career bureaucracy that was "out of control," subject to no oversight by persons responsible to the people, would be a danger to our liberties and an obstacle to effective and efficient administration. What controls, then, do we have?

In addition to a president's appointees, who can make such impact as their abilities permit, the Office of Management and Budget (OMB) annually and closely examines agency budget requests. The agencies ask for a given amount of funds, broken down into various categories. The OMB scrutinizes these closely (especially new or enlarged requests) and asks searching questions about the necessity for various fund requests. Bent upon paring down budget requests, the OMB's "budget examiners" are not easily satisfied, and worried agency budget officials need to be able to make a detailed and cogent defense of their budgets. They are also questioned about management practices that may suggest waste or inefficiency.

Since the OMB keeps a skeptical eye on the administration of all federal programs and advises the president of its findings, it is very much feared. The director of the OMB, if a highly competent person, may be the most powerful appointee in the executive branch.

The General Accounting Office (GAO), an "independent" agency directly accountable to Congress, also issues reports from time to time criticizing waste and mismanagement. Its examination of accounts and auditing of expenditures are often accompanied by penetrating investigations of agency activities. Congressional appropriations committees and subcommittees sometimes subject agency budgets to searching examination before approving them. (Some committees, of course, are much more thorough than others.)[10] So, given an assumption that existing programs will continue, agency budgets are given a double and sometimes triple investigation. Unfortunately, whether a given program deserves to continue is a question rarely raised by the bureaucracy, the Congress, or the GAO.

President Carter attempted to introduce *zero-based budgeting* as a means of bringing more effective evaluative techniques to bear on federal programs. This required each department, bureau, or agency to rationally justify each of its numerous programs annually and rank them according to their comparative value. The OMB and the president would thereby be able to identify the least defensible programs and apply the ax accordingly. The idea sounds plausible enough, but as seasoned Washingtonians predicted, little came of it.[11] Bureaucracies are much too skillful at defending their terrain to be outwitted by a device such as this. They know, too, that whatever the logic of a presidential pruning operation, Congress with its own priorities, would have the last word.

As for proposed federal *sunset laws*, which would automatically phase out programs every five years or so, forcing their administrators to adequately explain why these programs deserved continuation, these are no more promising. No one can devise criteria for judging the substantive and comparative merits of programs that will persuade both the president and Congress to terminate programs commanding strong vocal support from their beneficiaries. Sunset laws would doubtless prove no more workable on the national level than they have in state governments where they have been adopted.[12]

Lyndon Johnson's administration made an ambitious attempt to bring more scientific practices into program evaluation. An experiment with a so-called Planning, Programming, and Budgeting System (PPBS) attempted to force agencies to explain more precisely just what they were trying to accomplish so that the OMB could decide if they were achieving their goals. The PPBS would also "search for alternative means of reaching (national) goals most effectively at the least cost ... to insure a dollar's worth of service for each dollar spent."[13]

But in actual operation, the PPBS created a torrent of paperwork, proved unable to properly assess indirect program costs, was unable to put a dollar amount on benefits, and led to a great deal of dubious and self-serving data by agencies eager to justify their programs and their established ways of doing things.[14] In 1971 the PPBS had given up the ghost, and was replaced by a managerial emphasis on Management by Objective (MBO). The latter is a more realistic, and commonsense approach that requires program directors to ascertain what needs to be done, how, when, and at what cost. It also seeks more precise indicators of satisfactory performance, better methods of measuring the progress achieved by a program, and guidelines for taking the corrective action called for by results when they come in. Because it is not very different from what good administrators were already doing, it is not likely to have striking results.[15] Unfortunately, there are no sure-fire formulas for eliminating waste in government—there are only solemn gimmicks. Plus the occasional fruits of exceptionally able and vigorous administrators who are able to bring about some, though very limited, economies in their agencies.

Congress may launch formal investigations into department or agency activities, but these are rare and seldom occur unless charges of corruption are made by people who cannot be ignored. Members of Congress like to investigate only if headlines are in sight. Investigations into inefficiency per se arouse little public interest and hence command little congressional attention.

From time to time, persons within the bureaucracy may see examples of mismanagement (or corruption) that exceed the normal range of tolerance. Telling superiors that they are making egregious blunders—or worse—is not the recommended formula for winning their favor. Thus, while those who witness these misdeeds have an obligation to bring their evidence to the attention of the proper authorities, the risks in doing so can be very great; witnesses usually grumble in private and let it go at that.

Some of them, however, may write to columnist Jack Anderson and spill the beans—if assured of anonymity. A few may go so far as to publicly reveal what they regard as shocking offenses against the public interest. In most cases these "whistle blowers" receive a very cold shoulder thereafter; they may be fired or transferred to a less important post as punishment for their sin.

An effort was made by the Carter Administration to protect whistle blowers from reprisals, but writing appropriate protective legislation has proved to be a most difficult task. Not all of these seemingly noble characters are as virtuous as they may seem. As *Newsweek* columnist Meg Greenfield once pointed out:

> *One man's whistle blower is another man's informer... or faceless accuser... or malcontent... or disgruntled employee... or bad loser... or just plain sorehead. A whistle blower, if we are... honest about it, is someone who exposes a government policy or practice or agency or official you don't like.*[16]

Whether a way will be found to protect responsible whistle blowers without encouraging the kind of informing that can demoralize agencies and involve them in a maze of procedural red tape remains to be seen. Still, the effort seems well worth making.

If bureaucracies are alleged to misinterpret the law, or exercise powers not clearly entrusted to them by Congress, they can be sued by injured parties. The courts thus are an important part of the network of controls that keep the bureaucracy under some control. The courts, however, can do nothing about agency inefficiency or lack of responsiveness.

The responsiveness of agencies to the public's needs rather than private interests has long been questioned. A widely held theory maintains that the independent regulatory commissions are created to control the antisocial practices of the big corporations, begin their work with a burst of public-spirited zeal, but gradually lose that zeal as bureaucratic tendencies begin to assert themselves. Before long, they fall under the control of the very industries they are supposed to regulate and end up nursing those industries with protective interpretations of the law. Thus regulation, which begins as a laudable pursuit of the public interest, becomes subverted on behalf of private ends because public administrators are simply no match for powerful private interests that bear down on them constantly without countervailing public interest pressures. Significantly, too, the private interests open up lucrative jobs for the regulators when they retire from their agency—if they have been "cooperative."

Critics further allege that the regulatory agencies hold on to their delegated powers with the utmost tenacity, unwilling to yield any ground that may reduce their budgets or their personnel. In the past there was considerable evidence to sustain these accusations.

But under the Carter Administration, the Civil Aeronautics Board confounded these critics by a successful effort to deregulate the airlines—an effort that promptly led to lower passenger rates at a time when other prices were rising rapidly. The Interstate Commerce Commission also demonstrated a willingness to relax its authority over the trucking and railroad industries' contrary to previous expectations. There *was* something new under the sun, after all!

The newer regulatory agencies (the Office of Safety and Health Administration, the Environmental Protection Agency, the Consumer Product Safety Commission, the National Highway Transportation Safety Board, and the Equal Employment Opportunity Commission) certainly have not been "captured" by big business, although it could be argued that they have not been around long enough for this allegedly evolutionary development to manifest itself.[17] Some observers believe that the tendency of agencies not to oppose the interests of those they regulate, while doubtless a danger requiring constant public vigilance, can be resisted if presidential appointees are strong personalities with firm convictions about the public responsibilities of the agencies they head. It is noted, too, that whereas some of the earlier agencies (the Interstate Commerce Commission, the Civil Aeronautics Board and the Federal Trade Commission, e.g.) were initially perceived by the regulated industries as agencies which could be quietly harnessed to the task of reducing "excessive" competition, the newer agencies were never welcomed as potential allies but rather were resented by business.

The newer regulatory agencies also differ from some of the older ones in that they regulate all industries, rather than particular ones, which can more readily impose their point of view on the administrators. They also operate under much more specific and detailed regulations than did the old-line agencies, thus leaving them with less discretionary authority for business to indirectly subvert.[18]

Liberal defenders insist that critics of regulatory commissions often overlook the very real public services that regulatory agencies have performed in protecting our food and drugs, in reducing air and water pollution, in keeping telephone rates in check, holding down natural gas prices, cutting coal mining accidents in half, making our cars more safe, facilitating opportunities for the handicapped, requiring the networks to give equal time to opposing viewpoints, and preventing power plays by corporations seeking monopolistic status or other unfair advantages.[19] These services would not be provided by a free market. Special agencies were created because of serious offenses against the public interest—either of commission or omission—offenses that would multiply if the government took a total hands-off policy, according to liberal thinkers. The law of the economic jungle does not give us the freely competitive, consumer-governed Utopia that business people and political conservatives like to picture for us.

Government can overregulate, but it can also underregulate, as the history of the last two centuries so abundantly declares. Wisdom consists in finding the right balance between the two, not in making broadside blasts at bureaucratic stupidity. The liberals admit that reform of individual agencies is sometimes necessary, but such reform must be done with a scalpel, not an ax.

But many people believe the reform should be much more drastic. The federal bureaucracy is much too large, they claim, with far too many employees feeding at the federal trough. For the most part people who feel this way are expressing no more than a generalized hostility toward "too much government." If asked to give a factual and moderately detailed explanation of why

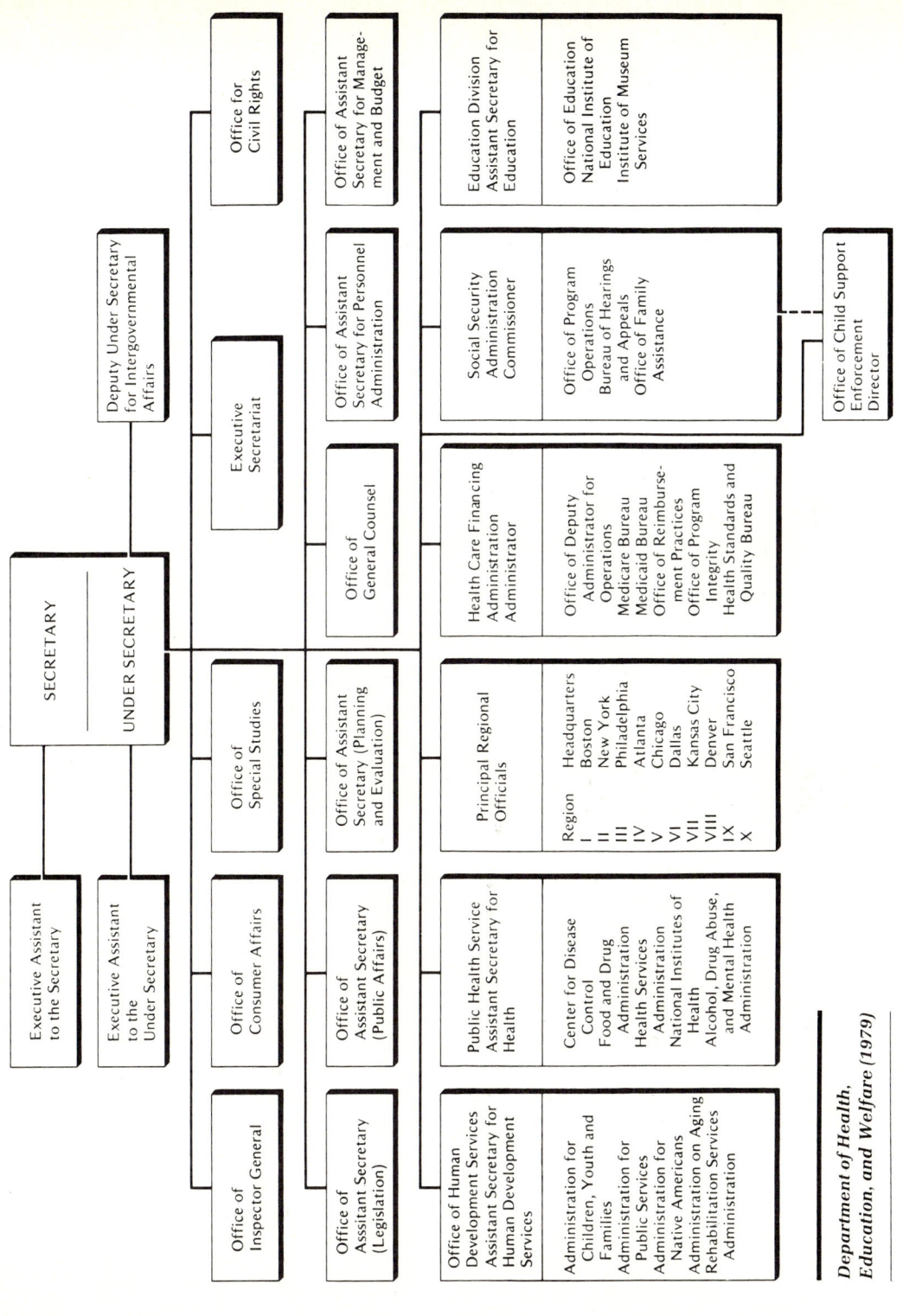

Department of Health, Education, and Welfare (1979)

Pollution: challenge to bureaucracy and to us

they believe as they do, they would hastily retreat into a cloud of generalities.

As it happens, the number of federal employees has remained virtually stationary since 1968, while the congressional staff has almost doubled during that time and state and local payrolls have risen from 5.3 million employees in 1957 to about 13 million today. This is somewhat misleading, however, since the number of people who work for state and local governments but are subsidized by Washington runs into the millions.[20] The federal civilian payroll thus is considerably larger than the number that is usually cited.

Doubtless there are "too many" bureaucrats in the sense that almost any organization, public or private, has more employees than the perfect administrator would need. Doubtless, too, the federal milieu with its automatic pay raises and job security, does not stimulate maximum efficiency. But if there are too many federal bureaucrats, it is primarily because Congress and the president are trying to do too much. It is essential to remember, in this connection, that almost every federal program was established because pressure from a segment of the American people—wanting some special consideration—was stronger than opposition pressure from the rest of the people. To repeat what has been previously emphasized, Congress responds to the majority of those who care and make themselves heard on a given issue. And programs are continued for the same reason they are created. The American people's generalized hostility toward "too much government" is no match for the intensive, closely focused support that a minority of Americans give to any particular program that benefits them. It is also true that those who complain loudly about "too much government" almost always make exceptions for programs that benefit them. It's the programs which benefit the other guy which ought to be eliminated! So if we want to know why taxes seem too high, look in the mirror. That's the person who's to blame.

We probably will not make any material inroads into the size of the federal bureaucracy until someone organizes a public interest lobby with a large membership that will noisily support efforts to assassinate indefensible programs. It must support them by making an unholy racket—writing more letters than those who defend the programs do and lobbying just as vigorously as they do. Real economies will then be possible and the bureaucracy will shrink. But no such organization is now in sight. On the contrary, pressures persist to establish still more programs, which will add to the bureaucracy and become just as tenaciously rooted as the programs we now have. Politically related organizations in this country are overwhelmingly devoted to promoting the self-interest of specialized groups, not the broad interests of society as a whole. Even groups like Common Cause do not focus attention on "whether a program is really needed." Until an important organization is formed to ask this question—an organization whose leadership is neither clearly liberal nor conservative—and is backed by significant numbers of active, articulate members, efforts to prune away unnecessary programs will accomplish very little.

A postscript on bureaucracy might be added here, relating to the question discussed in Chapter 9 on who runs this country. Recall that some people believe that a political elite (usually thought to involve high-ranking corporation officials, Pentagon brass, and leading national politicians, drawn from affluent, upper-level social strata and sharing common values and goals) really runs this nation despite surface appearances to the contrary.

As you now know, this writer rejects this theory as failing to do justice to the incredible dispersion of political power in America and failing to recognize that our governments almost always respond to the *majority of those who care* and make themselves heard on a given issue. But there is another theory, already hinted at in this chapter, that should be briefly mentioned: the theory that ours is a political system in which ultimately nobody is really in charge. The system is largely out of control, with public policy made in such a chaotic, helter-skelter fashion by so many groups and institutions that it is virtually impossible for the public to know how to master it. The bureaucracy has grown so large, encompasses so many aspects of American life, and is so impervious to central direction that no one or no group is now in charge. If an elite were actually running things, it would be possible for discontented elements (reformers) to concentrate pressure on that "control center" and perhaps move policy in a given direction.

But, so goes the countertheory, if anyone runs this country, it is the bureaucracy, and the bureaucracy has no "control center." It is not even a self-conscious political force with a self-selected high command and unified goals and policies. Rather, it sprawls shapelessly, all over the map, like a giant dinosaur with a thousand nerve centers instead of a single nervous system that can respond in a coordinated fashion to stimulus from its environment.[21]

This is an intriguing and disturbing theory, which is more true to life than the elitist theories. To the extent that it is true (how true is it?), it again suggests that citizens can make only small political changes—and make these by focusing on particular problems in particular places. As for larger political concerns, of broad national importance, we can expect major changes here only if there is a crisis of staggering proportions. Only then is a major shakeup possible because only then is the public willing to follow leadership (the president) that puts overriding national needs ahead of our special interests.

Notes

1 Robert L. Kahn et al., "Americans Love Their Bureaucrats," *Psychology Today*, June 1975, pp. 66-75. See also Glenn R. Parker and Roger H. Davidson, "Who Do Americans Love their Congressmen So Much More Than Their Congress," *Legislative Studies* Quarterly, Feb. 1979, pp. 53-61.
2 Nicholas Lemann, "The Case for Political Patronage," *Washington Monthly*, December 1977, pp. 8-17; and Peter Ognibene, "Is Civil Service Strangling the Government?", *Saturday Review*, November 11, 1978, pp.
3 Leonard Reed, "Firing a Federal Employee: The Impossible Dream," *The Washington Monthly*, July-August 1977, pp. 21-23. Reprinted with permission from *The Washington Monthly*. Copyright 1977 by the Washington Monthly Co., 1028 Connecticut Ave., N.W., Washington, D.C. 20036.
4 Herbert Kaufman, *Red Tape* (Washington, D.C.: Brookings Institute, 1977), p. 20.
5 *Ibid.*, p. 27.
6 *Ibid.*, p. 61.
7 Stephen Hess, *Organizing the Presidency* (Washington D.C., Brookings Institution, 1976), p. 199. Hess provides an incomplete quote of Ehrlichman's full statement.
8 Thomas E. Cronin, *The State of the Presidency* (Boston: Little, Brown, 1975), pp. 167-169.
9 *Ibid.*, p. 61.
10 Two useful studies on congressional oversight are Seymour Scher, "Conditions for Legislative Control," *Journal of Politics* (Aug., 1963); and John Bibby, "Committee Characteristics and Legislative Oversight," *Midwest Journal of Political Science* (Feb., 1966).
11 Apparently it had not worked very well when tried by the U.S. Department of Agriculture in 1962 and by Governor Jimmy Carter in Georgia. See George C. Edwards, III, and Ira Sharkansky, *The Policy Predicament* (San Francisco: Freeman, 1978), p. 274.
12 See Robert D. Brehm, "The False Dawn of the Sunset Laws," *The Public Interest*, Fall, 1977; "Sunset Laws: One More Brave Idea That's Gone Awry?" *U.S. News and World Report*, May 29, 1978, p. 45.
13 Fred A. Kramer, *Dynamics of Public Bureaucracy* (Cambridge, Mass.: Winthrop, 1977), p. 189.
14 *Ibid.*, pp. 189-190, 230-233.
15 *Ibid.*, pp. 234-242.

16. Meg Greenfield, "Blowing the Whistle," *Newsweek*, September 24, 1978, p. 112.
17. Paul H. Weaver, "Regulation, Social Policy and Class Conflict," *The Public Interest*, Winter 1978, pp. 50-51.
18. *Ibid.*
19. Steven Kelman, "Regulation that Works," *New Republic*, November 25, 1978, pp. 16-19. and David L. Sudhalter, "The Case For Government Regulation," *The New Englander*, October 1977.
20. Charles Peters, "Tilting at Windmills," *Washington Monthly*, September 1978, p. 8.
21. See Kenneth Smorsten, *A Preface to Action* (Pacific Palisades, Calif.: Goodyear, 1976), pp. 41-43 and John Herbers, "Washington: An Insider's Drama," *N.Y. Times Magazine*, April 22, 1979, p. 86.

CHAPTER 13

THE SUPREME COURT: NINE POLITICIANS AT WORK

Congress, we have said, is the most powerful legislative branch in the world. Not to be outdone, the Supreme Court is also the most powerful court in the world. The magnitude of its role astonishes foreign observers of the American political scene. Elsewhere, courts are secondary governmental units, not institutions that play a major part in establishing public policy.

The story of how the Supreme Court achieved its eminence, the factors contributing toward its rise, and the controversies over its status are among the most fascinating aspects of the American political experience. They warrant a close look.

The Founding Fathers had a somewhat fuzzy view of the Supreme Court's place in our political constellation. Their discussions of the Court's role were skimpy and inconclusive; they did not, with any clarity, assign it the definitive role of interpreting the Constitution. The latter says that "the judicial Power shall extend to all Cases, in Law and Equity, arising under this Constitution, the Laws of the United States, and Treaties made, or which shall be made, under their Authority." (The Fathers were brilliant men but they didn't know much about capitalizing words!) Although constitutional scholars insist that a majority of the delegates in 1787 expected the Supreme Court to exercise *judicial review*—that is, determine whether national or state laws are constitutional—this power is not explicitly conferred to the Court. In our early history, in fact, many believed that state legislatures had the right to interpret those portions of the Constitution that affected the division of powers between the national and the state governments. Others believed the state courts had this authority. Presidents believed *they* had a right to interpret constitutional phrases pertaining to the executive branch. And political celebrities like Daniel Webster, Henry Clay, and John Calhoun regarded themselves as the foremost interpreters of that famous document. Not until after the Civil War did the nation come to accept the Supreme Court as the institution having the last word on what the Constitution really means.

Maybe it never would have won this position if outgoing Secretary of State John Marshall had mailed a letter before midnight, instead of leaving it signed, sealed, but undelivered. This letter, appointing William Marbury justice of the peace in the District of Columbia, was discovered on his desk by incoming Secretary of State James Madison—who refused to mail it because of President Thomas Jefferson's order to that effect. Marbury, learning that he was to be denied this post on the seemingly flimsy ground that the appointment was not officially consummated until it was mailed, sued in the Supreme Court for his commission. Although Marshall, now the new Chief Justice of the Supreme Court, was so directly involved in the case that he should have stepped aside as an interested party, he not only presided over the case but delivered the verdict of the Court.

The case turned out to be crucial because the constitutionality of a federal law was at stake. The Judiciary Act of 1789 authorized the Supreme Court to issue writs of mandamus "to persons holding office under the authority of the U.S." A *writ of mandamus* is a judicial instrument requiring a public official to carry out a prescribed duty that he or she allegedly refuses to perform. Marbury asked the Supreme Court to issue a writ of mandamus compelling Madison to give him the commission as justice of the peace. The Court, however, declared that while the appointment was valid and Jefferson should have honored it, Article III of the Constitution gave the Court *original* jurisdiction only in cases where an ambassador or foreign minister was affected, or in which a state was involved. Since Marbury's case came to the Court not on appeal but on original jurisdiction, and since Marbury brought the suit to the Court because Section 13 of the Judiciary Act of 1789 said he could do so, Section 13 was unconstitutional, the Court found. (Actually Section 13 did *not* specifically prescribe that writs of mandamus could reach the Court in original jurisdiction, but Marshall interpreted it in this manner so that he could make his point.) Marshall then reasoned that since the Constitution is law, judges are the proper persons to interpret law. And since the Constitution is the highest law of the land, lesser laws in conflict with its provisions should not be enforced. Thus, in a dubious case that has caused head-shaking by constitutional lawyers ever since, the doctrine of judicial review was born.[1]

Marbury v. *Madison* was decided in 1803. Not until 1857 was another federal law declared unconstitutional. If that fateful letter had been mailed, and the Court had not staked out its claim to exercise judicial review until 1857 (involving another dubious case, that of Dred Scott),[2] would the Court have been able to make good its claim to such power? No one knows; it is one of history's more intriguing questions.

The Controversial Court

The Supreme Court chambers are a place of deceptive calm; Justice Oliver Wendell Holmes once said, "We are very quiet here but it is the quiet of a storm center."[3] A brief recital of its most controversial periods and decisions will demonstrate how often the Court has antagonized major segments of our people and precipitated raging battles over the meaning of the Constitution.

Marbury v. *Madison* infuriated Jefferson and his Republican supporters. They not only rejected the conclusion but felt Marshall had gone out of his way to reprimand Jefferson for not delivering the commission to Marbury. Marshall's long tenure as Chief Justice produced a succession of decisions strengthening the power of the national government at the expense of the states; these came at a time when most people were pro-states' rights. Although now regarded as one of our greatest Chief Justices, Marshall was highly unpopular in his day. His only really popular decision was *Gibbons* v. *Ogden* (1824), in which he struck down a steamboat monopoly.[4]

The Court tended to sidestep slavery questions during most of the pre-Civil War period. But in the celebrated Dred Scott case mentioned above, the Court declared that Negroes could not become American citizens and that Congress lacked authority to forbid the spread of slavery to the territories. This touched off a towering debate—and was not accepted by most northerners as a valid expression of Court authority.

The constitutional scene calmed down after the Civil War; the Court's position as the authoritative interpreter of the Constitution became more firmly established. Its decision in *Plessy* v. *Ferguson* (1896), holding that the equal protection clause of the Fourteenth Amendment was satisfied if blacks were given "separate but equal," schools and other facilities, was accepted without much dissent.[5] Even its approval of antitrust prosecutions of major trusts (e.g., Standard Oil, the American Tobacco Company, the "Sugar Trust") stirred up less controversy than might have been expected.

In the late nineteenth and early twentieth centuries, however, as we saw in Chapter 15, the Court's decisions limiting the regulatory power of Washington over industry on matters affecting the interests of the working people caused much grumbling in Populist and liberal circles. When the Court interpreted the Fourteenth Amendment's rendering of "person" ("nor shall any state deprive any person of life, liberty or property without due process of law") to include "corporations," and went on to say that due process of law meant "reasonable" law (reasonable as seen by the Court, that is),[6] the Court's rulings incensed those who rightly saw them as shielding powerful corporations in their struggles against state regulation. For the most part the Court, from 1865 to 1933, was a conservative body, partial to the propertied interests of the country. Naturally, this posture was often displeasing to persons and groups critical of the status quo.

When the Supreme Court took aim at Franklin Roosevelt's New Deal and toppled half a dozen prominent New Deal measures by narrow margins, groups partisan to Roosevelt were dismayed. They railed at the "Nine Old Men" who were blocking progress and spoke angrily of "judicial usurpation" and "judicial tyranny." The Court was acting as a "superlegislature" rather than a judicial body, they charged.[7]

Franklin Roosevelt responded with his so-called court-packing plan, which would add a justice to the Court for each justice over 70 who did not retire (up to a maximum of 15). But the press and the public, after an initial period of uncertainty, turned against the proposal.

One of the factors in this rejection, however, was a turnabout by the Court. After making his plea for reorganizing the Court, the latter made its "switch in time that saved nine;" it began narrowly ruling *in favor* of the constitutionality of controversial New Deal laws. When a number of conservative justices retired, Roosevelt was able to appoint his own men to the Court. Eventually, the "Roosevelt Court" gave Congress a virtually free hand to enact economic regulation and social welfare measures—leading to conservative charges that "the Constitution is gone" and that the Court had become the spineless puppet of a power-hungry president.

Conservative bitterness over the Court's conversion was intensified after Earl Warren became Chief Justice. Warren, appointed by Dwight Eisenhower as a presumed "moderate," turned out to be one of the most liberal Chief Justices in American history. (Eisenhower privately termed his appointment of Warren "the biggest damfool mistake I ever made."[8]) A series of decisions upholding the constitutional rights of American Communist party member in 1957 so angered Congress that it came close to withdrawing the Court's jurisdiction over national security cases.[9] The "one man, one vote" decisions, ensuring that members of the state legislatures—and also of the U.S. House of

Representatives—were chosen from election districts having roughly equal population, produced a hail of complaints from rural areas and small towns that had long enjoyed overrepresentation. Spokesmen for these groups sought a constitutional amendment to overthrow that decision, but to no avail.

Miranda v. *Arizona,* excluding from court any confessions made in the absence of police reminders of the suspect's constitutional rights, also aroused hostility in conservative quarters,[10] as did the Court's very permissive attitude toward pornography and its prohibiting of religious exercises (Bible reading and prayers, specifically) in the public schools.

But none of these unleashed anything like the tidal wave of criticism that washed over the Court when, in *Brown* v. *Board of Education of Topeka, Kansas* (1954),[11] it outlawed racial segregation in public schools. Although polls showed the majority of Americans approved this decision, the minority displayed a sense of outrage rarely witnessed in public affairs. When the Court sanctioned public busing, to accelerate the desegregation of schools in the North as well as the South, the feeling among many northerners rivaled that of white southerners during the late 1950s.

The Court led by Chief Justice Warren Burger has displeased liberals with its drift toward the right. None of its decisions, however, brought more vociferous protests than *Roe* v. *Wade* (1973), which strictly limited the right of states

The Warren Court had warm friends and ardent foes

to interfere with abortion during the first six months of pregnancy.[12] Again, objectors sought—unsuccessfully—a constitutional amendment to override the Court.

In sum, the Supreme Court has repeatedly alienated first this, then that, geographical or ideological portion of the country. During the Warren Era, the ultra-right-wing John Birch Society even promoted "Impeach Earl Warren" bumper stickers and billboards. But for liberals Warren was a candidate for sainthood.

The Court as Policymaker

Why has the Court become such a potent body? And why does it decide so many "political" questions—defining public policy on desegregated schools, capital punishment, abortion, and so forth—which would ordinarily be handled by legislatures?

Part of the reason is that the Congress tends to shy away from inflammatory issues that, however, resolved, leave the losers bitter about the outcome. MCs like to offend as few people as possible; rather than come directly to grips with "no win" issues, they wriggle away from them whenever possible. This invites aggrieved parties to bring cases before the Court.

Another reason is that the Bill of Rights and especially the "equal protection of the laws" and "due process" clauses of the Fourteenth Amendment are subject to sufficiently elastic interpretation to give the Court wide discretion on a vast range of cases. In an age when people are prone to convert political grievances into issues of human rights, the courts are the natural beneficiaries of this trend. People do what they can when they feel strongly about an issue; if they cannot win in the legislature, they turn to the courts. When they do, they have a right to be heard and the Court has an obligation to decide. So, partly the Court's power has been handed to it—a power not distasteful to it, one might add.

Finally, since the Supreme Court has largely abandoned the effort to oversee congressional regulation of the economy, it perhaps naturally is more willing to hear noneconomic cases. If it were not, the overall role of the Court would wither.

At this point it may be well to establish the fact that the Supreme Court is, to a very large extent, a "political" arm of government. That is, the Court makes policy choices based on largely subjective factors rather than being strictly constrained by the stern necessities of the law to reach objective legal conclusions. It could be regarded as a narrowly "judicial" branch if, in the words of the Court in 1936, "the judicial branch of the government has only one duty—to lay the article of Constitution which is invoked beside the statute which is challenged and to decide whether the latter squares with the former."[13] This naive concept of judicial review, once so widely held, reduces judges to legal technicians whose job is to "find" the law and apply it to the case at hand. The reasons for rejecting this view and for recognizing how much political choice is available to judges are twofold.

First, the language of the Constitution is often so imprecise that it can be interpreted rationally in different ways, especially in a world that is technologically light-years removed from that of 1787. For example, Congress has the power "to regulate commerce among the several states." Does commerce include criminals crossing state lines? Radio and television waves beamed from state to state? The sale of insurance across state boundaries? Does "regulate commerce" mean regulating strikes that affect interstate commerce? Intrastate commerce in competition with interstate commerce? Goods made with child labor? Factory smoke that drifts across state lines?

One can meditate (transcendentally or otherwise) upon the Constitutional language as long as one wishes without the "true meaning" of the Constitution breaking through. The Court must invent a meaning for "regulate commerce among the several states" in these cases rather than apply a "dark room" legalistic formula that brings out the "hidden meaning" within that clause.

"Due process of law" is a noble phrase that usually means different things to different people since it embodies the concept of fair procedures. But what is fair to one person is not fair to another. Two of our most distinguished justices once became involved in such a furious debate over the meaning of this phrase that they finally agreed it should be tossed overboard. Probably a ten-foot shelf of books has been written about the meaning of that phrase as applied to specific cases and problems.

Does "equal protection of the laws" mean that members of racial minorities can receive preference in obtaining admission to institutions of higher learning in order to compensate for past discrimination? Or does it require equal treatment of all applicants without regard to race? Does it permit or forbid racial quotas from becoming "goals" that admissions officers take into account in making their decisions?

The vagueness of constitutional phraseology is the principal reason why the concept of *strict construction,* the notion that judges must interpret the Constitution very literally, is largely meaningless. How can you "strictly construe" language that gives little or no guidance when applied to situations the drafters of the Constitution never dreamed of? When politicians like Richard Nixon spoke gravely of wanting to nominate "strict constructionists" to the Court, that was only a code phrase signifying the desire to nominate Justices who would make decisions pleasing to conservatives. When former Chief Justice Charles Evans Hughes realistically said, "We are under a Constitution but the Constitution is what the judges say it is,"[14] he was recognizing the broad political discretion available to the Court as well as reminding us that the Court has no serious competition when it comes to interpreting the Constitution.

(Conservative Senator Sam Ervin's classic complaint seems relevant to the issue: "Everyone will concede," he said, "that the Constitution is written in words. If these words have no fixed meaning, they make the Constitution conform to Mark Twain's description of the dictionary. He said the dictionary has a wonderful vocabulary but no plot."[15])

Alternative ways of interpreting the Constitution widen the court's area of political choice. For example, should the justices try to put themselves inside the skin of the Founding Fathers, to discern how *they* would apply those phrases? Or should the language of the Constitution be interpreted in the light of today's world, according to today's views of democracy, justice, and fairness? Should they see the Constitution as a living, growing, evolving instrument or as a document that should change by constitutional amendment rather than flexible judicial interpretation? The premises from which they operate often lead to different results.

If provisions of the Constitution seem to conflict, at a given historical moment on a given issue, which provision should prevail? Congress has the power to raise armies and declare war, which presumably also implies the power to "wage war effectively." The First Amendment also protects freedom of speech and press. Does this mean speech and press are as free in wartime as in peacetime? Similarly, Congress has the power to "lay and collect taxes to ... provide for ... the general welfare of the United States," but it also is forbidden to "make any law respecting the establishment of religion." Does aid for parochial schools promote the general welfare or violate the "establishment" clause? And, Congress can regulate commerce, but it is also supposed to respect the "reserved rights" of the states. When these are in conflict, which gets priority?

Political choice is often maintained rather than reduced by the Court's attempt to apply the rule of *stare decisis*. This rule requires the Court to apply relevant principles of the past to cases before it in order to give stability and predictability to the law. But in the course of settling thousands of cases since 1787, the Court has amassed such a host of precedents that it can often choose between one group of precedents that point one way or another group that point another way.

Since cases brought before the Court are seldom quite the same as cases previously decided, it is always possible to "distinguish" between one case and the early case (or cases) urged as a precedent. Since no precedent fits perfectly, judges can select the precedent(s) they like to justify whatever decision they prefer. Justice William O. Douglas once said there were "plenty of precedents to go around."[16] (The first Justice John Marshall Harlan said roughly the same thing.)

Finally, the Supreme Court only hears the tough cases. If the application of the Constitution, or the available precedents, quite clearly points to a given decision, parties rarely take their cases to the Supreme Court because the odds are against them. Thus, the Court generally passes judgment only on the difficult cases on which reasonable persons can disagree. Historian Arthur Schlesinger, Jr., wrote:

> Any judge chooses his results and reasons backwards. The resources of legal artifice, the ambiguities of precedents, the range of applicable doctrines, are all so extensive that in most cases in which there is a reasonable difference of opinion a judge can come out on either side without straining the fabric of legal logic. A naive judge does this unconsciously and conceives himself to be the objective interpreter of the law. A wise judge knows that political choice is inevitable; he makes no false pretenses of objectivity and consciously exercises the judicial power with an eye to the social results.[17]

Schlesinger overstates his case, most judicial experts would probably say. Many examples can be cited of Justices who have come to conclusions distasteful to them because the weight of relevant evidence seemed so compelling that judicial integrity seemed to require a decision they disliked. And in many cases justices may have no strong predilections toward a given outcome, thus freeing them to favor the side presenting the most cogent evidence.[18] Moreover, when it comes to *interpreting* federal law, many justices do make a serious effort to ascertain what the legislature's *intent* was, rather than substituting their personal judgment of what they want the law to mean.

But Schlesinger's statement contains a vast amount of truth, nonetheless—truth that bulwarks the belief that the judiciary is essentially a political body, making public policy through choices essentially similar to those made by legislative bodies. As one writer has noted, "Judicial decision-making involves, at bottom, a choice between competing values by fallible, pragmatic and, at times, non-rational men engaged in a highly complex process in a very human setting."[19] This sounds very much like the old-fashioned political process.

Besides the imprecision of the Constitution's language, the second reason for the "political" nature of the Court is the political process by which Justices are selected. Presidents have always taken an interest in appointing the "right" people to the Court. As previously noted the Court radically changed its view of the Constitution after Franklin Roosevelt placed his choices on the Court. He made sure that conservatives were not appointed. Richard Nixon, on the other hand, reserved his nominations for lawyers with conservative ideologies. Very early in our history the Federalists were scrupulous to appoint only Federalists to the Court, knowing the Constitution would mean something different if Federalists interpreted the Constitution than if Jeffersonian Republicans did so. The consistent interest of presidents in the ideology of their appointees eloquently attests to the significance of personal political attitudes in determining what the Constitution means. The Constitution means what the Supreme Court says it means, and what it says depends heavily on who is doing the saying. As Max Lerner once said, "Judicial decisions are not babies brought by constitutional storks."[20]

We can see, then, how naive is the view that interpreting the Constitution is a simple, straightforward matter of looking at a law, checking the relevant part of the Constitution, and deciding if the two are compatible. It is, instead, a painfully complicated business, often with only the vaguest (and sometimes conflicting) constitutional guidelines, and with value judgments inevitably intruding into the process. In the broader sense it is a profoundly political operation.

There are many other similarities between the "judicial" process and the undisguised, traditionally recognized "political" process. The Court hears both sides of an issue, just as legislatures schedule committee hearings that take testimony from opponents and proponents of a bill. In the Court, interested parties—including individuals, interest groups, and government agencies—not immediately involved in the outcome submit *amici curiae* ("friends of the court") briefs setting forth their reasons for favoring a given decision, just as interest groups indirectly affected by a bill testify before congressional committees. It takes money to hire the services of lawyers to pursue a case to the Supreme Court's level, just as it takes money to hire lobbyists to advance one's cause in the legislature. Considering the inevitable appeals made by disappointed litigants of lower court decisions, years may elapse before a final decision is reached by the Supreme Court, just as bills often take years to pass through the legislative catacombs. The appeals process usually follows a route from federal district courts to federal circuit courts to Supreme Court, constituting a triple hurdle roughly corresponding to the various hurdles in the legislature. Liberal and conservative factions on the Supreme Court correspond to liberal and conservative factions in a legislature. Finally, judges make decisions with an eye to how those decisions will be received by other judges, the legal community in general, their friends, the media, and—to some extent—the public. Legislators also worry about what the Washington community, their friends, voters, and the media will think about their votes.

The Court Versus Congress: History's Verdict

We have argued, then, that the Court is more properly termed a "political" body than a narrowly judicial one. If so, the judges are a species of politicians—but politicians who wear black robes, solemn expressions, and are enshrouded in a mist of tradition, deference, and public misperception that disguises their political character. But if Supreme Court Justices *are* politicians, how wise have their political judgments been *when they have challenged Congress' political judgments*? When Congress passes a major statute, believing it to be constitutional, and the Court strikes it down as unconstitutional, does history tend to vindicate the Court or the Congress? Let us take a nonselective review of major federal laws invalidated by the Supreme Court, and see what conclusion emerges.

In 1857 the Court overthrew the Missouri Compromise in the Dred Scott case; the statute at stake had forbidden slavery to be established in territories north of 36° 30'. The Court's decision is thought of as infamous today. After the Civil War the Court leveled a law permitting paper money to be used as legal tender for the payment of all debts. Several years later it reversed itself. All nations now use paper money as legal tender.

The Court in 1883 overturned the Civil Rights Act of 1875, guaranteeing Negroes equal access to public accommodations.[21] Statesmanship? In 1895 it turned a baleful eye on the nation's first peacetime income tax, forcing the nation to adopt the Sixteenth Amendment, which specifically permits the installation of such a tax.[22] Students of constitutional law regard the decision as poorly reasoned and as an unwarranted restriction not required by the original Constitution.[23] As for sound public policy, most people today believe that taxes should be imposed in accordance with the ability to pay.

In 1895 the Court in effect gutted the Sherman Antitrust Act by limiting its application to monopolies in the field of transportation.[24] Manufacturing monopolies were thus excluded from national control. A few years later the Court repented of its sin and reversed itself.

In 1908 the Court invalidated a federal law prohibiting so-called yellow dog contracts.[25] This decision virtually stripped workers of the right to join unions if the employer objcted. Workers desperate for a job were thus coerced into giving up their right to freely join organizations of their choice—hardly a decision to be proud of, and one that a later Court repudiated.

Federal law forbidding employers to sell goods in interstate commerce that were made with child labor next fell under the Court's ax.[26] A similar law imposing a substantial federal tax on such goods was also guillotined.[27]

The Court struck down federal laws establishing old-age pensions for railroad workers[28] as well as a federal workman's compensation law.[29] But in a few years the Court changed its mind and decided such laws were constitutional after all.

Minimum wage laws? Unconstitutional, said the Court,[30] only to experience a change of heart one year later.

Can Washington regulate the coal industry, even if the industry is in deep distress in the midst of the worst depression in history? Absolutely not, said the Court.[31] Could the national government regulate agricultural production at a time when surpluses drove farm prices down to levels that were forcing tens of thousands of farmers into bankruptcy?[32] No, said the Court sternly. But in a few years it backed away and found regulation of both coal mining and of agriculture to be constitutionally permissible.[33]

The National Recovery Act (NRA) by which Franklin Roosevelt sought to restore a stricken nation to economic health was also struck down by the Court.[34]

In each of these cases (with one possible exception), plausible constitutional arguments could have been advanced on either side of the issue. That the Court decided as it did was largely attributable to the ideological preferences of the judges, with retirements and new appointments leading to the many reversals we have seen. The Court's political preferences, compared to those of Congress, are seen in retrospect to have been less progressive than those of Congress. The only exceptions, in the light of today's best judgment, were the NRA case—since the NRA was never very successful and was badly drafted in the first place—and perhaps the minimum-wage case. Overall, the Court's record when it challenges Congress does not suggest that judicial review has spared us from headlong or reckless abuse of power by Congress or represents a farsighted wisdom exceeding that of Congress.

There was a time (mostly in the 1930s) when judicial review of federal legislation was hotly debated, with critics citing the Court's dismal record and adding other arguments for good measure.[35] Why should major political decisions—for political they are—be made by a handful of (usually) old men who are neither elected by the people nor removable by them? If major court decisions are indeed political decisions, why should those decisions not be made by elected representatives of the people in Congress? If Congress errs from time to time, it can correct itself; besides, it seems to err less than the Court. It is fundamentally undemocratic, so the argument went, for lifetime appointees to exercise such power over public affairs. In a government run by an elite, this might be acceptable, but not in a government of, by, and for the people.

Critics (mostly from 1920 to 1940) suggested many reforms. Since many congressional statutes were overthrown by 5 to 4 decisions, some reformers suggested that no federal law be declared unconstitutional unless at least two-thirds of the Court concurred. Others would let Congress override a dubious decision by a two-thirds vote. Some members of the Progressive Movement (a neo-Populist movement led by Sen. Robert LaFollette of Wis.) thought the voters should be empowered to overrule the Court by popular referendum. Others would permit the people to elect Supreme Court Justices rather than have them appointed by the president and confirmed by the Senate. Finally, more moderate critics counseled the Court to exercise greater self-restraint, declaring laws unconstitutional only if the evidence overwhelmingly led to this conclusion.

Defenders of the Court fought back with vigor and even with passion.[36] Certainly judicial review is necessary so far as state laws are concerned, to ensure that the Constitution means the same in all 50 states. (There is general agreement on this point.) Although it is exceedingly difficult—perhaps impossible—to argue that the Court's historical record, when it clashed with Congress, is admirable, we do not know what legislation Congress *would* have passed had it not known the Court was keeping a sharp eye on its work, the defenders maintain. (Opponents, would retort that Congress may in fact act more carelessly, because it lets the Court worry about constitutionality.) But, the defenders ask, why have a government of limited powers, if Congress or the executive can interpret its own powers and stretch them as far as it pleases? Is it not better for the Constitution to be interpreted by judges who *do* have life tenure and hence need not worry about fitful, shortsighted, self-interested public opinion?

Far from looking upon the Court as undemocratic, the general public *wants* the Court to exercise judicial review and would be furious if that power were removed! (Because they've been brainwashed to believe that way, and know almost nothing about the Court's real record??) How can it be undemocratic to retain a political process the people so strongly approve? Even if their judgment is wrong, they have a right to be wrong!

Moreover, democracy means more than majority rule, expressed through representative government. It means minority and individual rights, and these are protected by the Court. According to its defenders, the Court is really only a superficially undemocratic body that staunchly defends democratic rights.

Actually the Court's record of defending individual rights has also been less than inspiring. It upheld the Fugitive Slave Laws,[37] made the Dred Scott decision, overthrew the Civil Rights Act of 1875, upheld "separate but equal" public facilities in 1896, sanctioned the internment of the Japanese-Americans in World War II,[34] accepted the constitutionality of imprisoning Socialist party leader Eugene Debs in World War I for verbally oppposing that war,[39] was slow to recognize the right to organize, took a timid stance during the "Red Scare" of the 1920s, and was hardly a bastion of courage during the McCarthy anticommunist hysteria after World War II.

But the Court defenders have another potentially strong argument. Most of the Court blunders recited on the previous pages were committed before the Court sobered up and virtually swore off trying to override Congress on economic and social welfare legislation. Historians believe the Court tacitly accepted the indictment made against it in this area. The Court now recognizes that it has no special expertise on economic legislation or policies designed to reduce personal insecurity and is no longer eager to chaperone Congress in this field. The commerce clause can be stretched (and *how* it has been stretched!) to give Congress almost carte blanche here. But having renounced its former role in this area, the Court has acquired a special incentive to safeguard the Bill of Rights. Unless it does this, its general role will sharply shrink, and few institutions are interested in promoting their own attrition. We can reasonably hope, therefore, that the Court will cherish a role as "keeper of the nation's conscience," with custodianship of the Bill of Rights as its major responsibility. It may not always perform this role as liberals or conservatives wish, but the odds are that, over the years, it will keep the first Ten Amendments—plus the Fourteenth—in a better state of preservation than if judicial review were abolished. If it upholds congressional legislation that infringes on valid human rights, we are not much worse off than if judicial review did not exist. But if it is *more* solicitous of human rights than Congress, that is a net gain.

To the writer, this is a persuasive argument. History, however, is so full of surprises that no one can know what the future holds, and conservatives and liberals often interpret the Bill of Rights quite differently, each side sure that *it* has the only defensible view. But if the Court pinpoints civil liberty issues, sharpens the focus, and precipitates nationwide debates on them, that is a valuable service in itself. In a democracy public opinion will finally prevail—but we want it to be an educated opinion that has matured from intense and prolonged discussion of the real issues involved. That opinion may still be wrong, but the process of arriving at it is our best hope. The Court is a vital part of that process.

It is important to remember that by far the largest part of the Court's work does *not* involve testing the constitutionality of federal legislation. Most of it concerns *interpretation* of the Constitution or federal law. It decides not on constitutionality but on what the Constitution or federal law means. Most of the major Supreme Court decisions of recent years—the desegregation decisions (including *Brown v. the Board of Education*); one man, one vote (*Baker v. Carr*[40]); notifying criminal suspects of their constitutional rights (*Miranda v. Arizona*); the abortion decision (*Roe v. Wade*); the prayer and Bible reading cases (*Engel v. Vitale*)[41] and *School District of Abington Township v. Schempp*[42]); the busing decisions, and the capital punishment cases—have been of this kind. Thus, even if judicial review were abolished, the Court's interpretive function would still give it almost as weighty a role as it enjoys today.

A second point to bear in mind is that while the Supreme Court's decisions may seem final, this is not really the case. On burning issues Americans do not necessarily accept a Supreme Court decision as the correct and authoritative interpretation of a given provision of the Constitution. Disappointed persons may seek a constitutional amendment with which to override the Court. Thus, the Fourteenth Amendment nullified the Dred Scott decision, and the Sixteenth Amendment reversed the Court's decision against an income tax.

Numerous attempts have failed, of course, to reverse a repugnant Court ruling. In that case disgruntled persons may simply decline to obey the Court. Many refused to accept the Court's approval of the Fugitive Slave Act; the famous "underground railroad" was the result. The white South strenuously resisted *Brown* v. *Board of Education,* finally yielding only after resorting to every obstructive and delaying tactic that the ingenious minds of determined people could devise. And particularly in the South, but here and there throughout the land, schools have openly defied the Court's edict on Bible reading and prayers in the public schools.[43]

In several instances, public hostility to Supreme Court decisions has been expressed so intensely—through public meetings, letters to editors and to members of Congress, organizational resolutions, and the like—that the Court has backed away from its provocative decision(s). This apparently happened in 1937, when the Court feared that its anti–New Deal rulings might jeopardize its institutional position by feeding public support of Roosevelt's court-packing plan. And in 1958 belligerent public reaction to its decisions upholding the constitutional rights of Communist party members led to a succession of closely related cases in which the Court qualified its previous decisions by pulling back from its most politically vulnerable positions.[44] (It held to its central principle, however; Communists could advocate violent overthrow in an abstract manner.[45])

Congressional displeasure with the Court may lead that body to strip the Court of some of its authority. Article III of the Constitution gives Congress the power to limit the appellate jurisdiction of the Court. Congress has come close to using this power on several occasions but has never carried through with the threat. Just how far it could go is unclear since the fundamental work of the Court would be eroded if Congress limited its jurisdiction too narrowly.

Finally, unpopular decisions have been reversed by the Court itself after Justices retired and their replacements had a chance to vote on similar cases. Presidents appoint new justices every 1.7 years, on the average, and this process keeps the Court from stagnating and from adhering indefinitely to outmoded positions.

A third point to consider in judging the Court's position is that most of the time the Court does *not* overturn federal or state laws as unconstitutional. Instead, it upholds those laws, thereby conferring a kind of legitimacy upon them that has a stabilizing effect on the country. On the *most* divisive issues this effect may not be present, but in general people are more willing to accept the authority of law if controversial laws or administrative actions have been taken to the courts and the latter have found them constitutional.

How people feel about the power of the Supreme Court ultimately depends on whether they approve of the general drift of the Court's decisions—that is, whether those decisions are generally supportive of or antagonistic to their private value systems. People rarely put it so bluntly, but not only does this attitude prevail but it is also logical that it should. If people believe that, on the most important issues, the Court will usually further their value priorities, of course they will be sympathetic to *judicial activism*; if the contrary is true, they will favor a policy of *judicial restraint*. In judicial activism, the Court acts boldly to express its views on major issues which might otherwise be left to the legislature and the executive; judicial restraint, on the other hand, seeks to reduce the Court's role on controversial issues, giving the more openly political branches an opportunity to deal with them.

While defenders of judicial activism usually defend it on the ground that the Court's activism furthers their value goals, some persons additionally argue that only the Court, sometimes, has the courage and capacity to act. The legislature may duck issues that, however decided, will anger many constituents, in order to avoid risk. The desegregation, abortion, prayers in public schools, and one man, one vote cases were issues of this character. Having a governmental body that will grasp the nettle and make a decision—be it good or bad—is sometimes looked on with favor. Generally, however, defenders raise this argument only if they approve of what the Court does. Otherwise, they stress the point that "political" decisions ought to be made by the "political" arms of government, and not by "judicial imperialism."

The Court at Work

Cases involving two states or between a state and the Federal government may come directly to the Supreme Court rather than on appeal from state or lower federal courts. Where appeals are involved, the Court has discretion as to whether it will hear such cases at all. It tries to confine its work to cases that involve important questions of constitutionality or of interpretation of federal law, questions that will significantly affect more persons or groups than those immediately involved in the case. Law clerks who work for the Justices peruse the thousands of cases appealed to the Supreme Court and identify those they regard as the most important. From these the individual Justices select a smaller number that they believe should be heard. If four Justices agree that a case should come before the Court, it goes on the docket. While only a small percentage of appeals finally reaches the court, the Court still rules on perhaps 200 cases a year. Few people work harder than Justices on the Supreme Court; even when on vacation, many of them continue to struggle with preparations for next term's work load.

When cases are scheduled for Court consideration, written briefs (which are often not brief at all) are submitted by both sides to the dispute, setting forth the arguments that they hope will persuade the Court. As we have noted, *amicus* briefs are often presented to the Court by outside parties with a keen interest in the outcome. Later, the Court schedules an hour or two for oral arguments, a proceeding that brings together some of the nation's outstanding lawyers, demonstrating their finest lawyerly talents before the Court. Arguing before the Supreme Court is like playing in the World Series for members of the legal community. Here is where reputations are made or tarnished.

The oral presentations are tightly reasoned but without the emotional ap-

How cases reach the Supreme Court

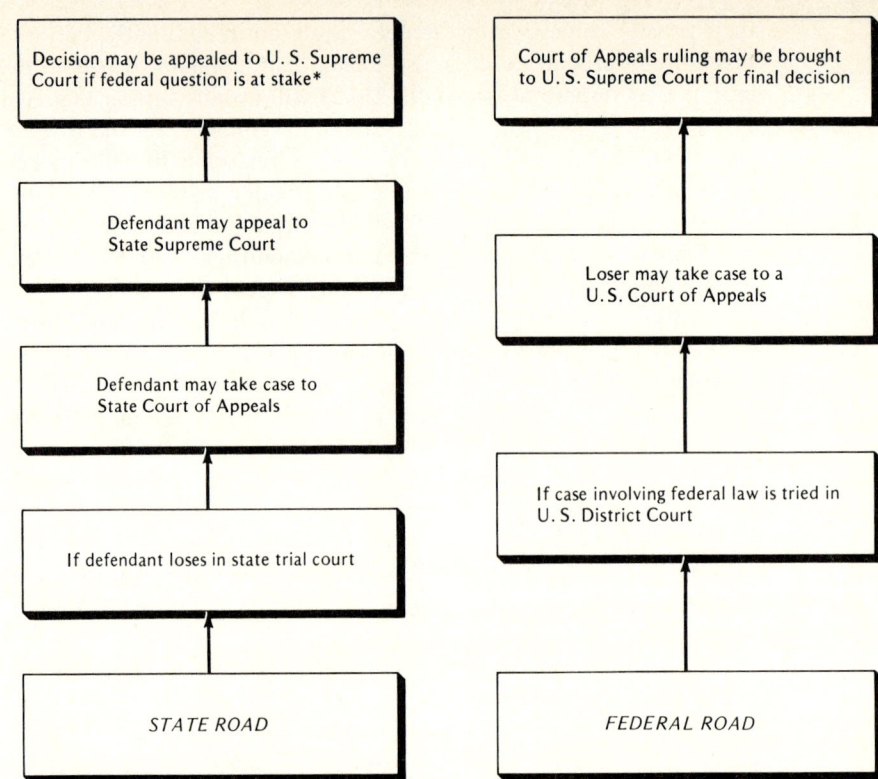

*It becomes a federal question if the interpretation of the U.S. Constitution, a national law, or a treaty of the U.S. is at stake.

peals that enliven the proceedings in lower courts. Justices frequently interrupt the combatant lawyers with penetrating questions designed to clarify important matters or to get to the heart of the issue. Justice Harlan Fiske Stone has stated that "when an argument begins, all the trappings and ceremony seem to fade and the scene takes on extraordinary intimacy. In the most informal way, altogether without pomp, Court and counsel converse. It is conversation—as direct, unpretentious and focused discussion as can be found anywhere in Washington."[46] But it is also drama, externally low key but intensely absorbing to those involved.

After the Justices have been given time to brood over the written briefs and oral examinations, they meet to discuss their views of the case(s) and to cast their votes. When they do so, the fact that judges are very, very human often becomes clear. Putting on black robes does not alter a person's basic characteristics or temperament. Animosities spring up between judges, tempers sometimes flare and harsh words are spoken. Sometimes the formal majority or minority opinions of the court chastise the other side for its failure to recognize the plain facts and to miss the perfectly obvious conclusions that should be drawn. When strong feelings are held on important issues, this is probably inevitable. For the most part, however, the Justices strive to be as civilized as possible and to keep sharp words within the family.

The tentative voting is not the end of the decision-making process. The majority opinion is composed only after written opinions are circulated among the members, commented on by them, redrafted to meet certain objections, re-circulated, further commented on, and then further modified to take account of editorial and substantive suggestions by members of the potential majority. It is one thing to get a majority to agree on the decision and something else to get a majority to agree to the reasoning employed and terminology used in support of that decision. The bargaining process that goes on is closely akin to that which occurs in legislative committee sessions. Although most decisions involve a divided vote, this internal bargaining sometimes seeks the largest possible majority. On highly important cases unamimity is earnestly sought though seldom achieved. Obviously a unanimous opinion (which was gained in *Brown* v. *Board of Education* and in *U.S.* v. *Nixon* [1974]—requiring the president to turn over his tape recordings to a federal district court[47]) carries more weight than a 5 to 4 decision. But judges have various ideologies and an independent turn of mind; the issues are complex; the reasoning is ingenious; and dissenting opinions are therefore common.

Individual dissenting opinions are often more stinging and more quotable than majority opinions since the latter represent a consensus that necessitates

The Burger court (L–R) foreground: Byron R. White, William J. Brennan, Jr., Chief Justice Warren R. Burger, Potter Stewart, Thurgood Marshall Background: William H. Rehnquist, Harry A. Blackmun, Lewis F. Powell, and John P. Stevens

more muted tones and a softening of sharp edges. Dissenters can always express themselves in a more freewheeling and pungent manner than those who speak for majority coalitions, and Court dissenters are no exception. Some dissenting opinions foreshadow majority opinions of the future, although far more do not. Some of the most eloquent judicial language in history is found in the dissenting opinions of Justices Oliver Wendell Holmes, Louis Brandeis, Benjamin Cardozo, Felix Frankfurter, William O. Douglas, and Hugo Black.

The Supreme Court is the apex of a federal judicial system, which includes 92 district courts; the larger states have several of these courts. One rung higher on the ladder are eleven federal circuit courts of appeal. Whereas district courts normally consist of single judges, circuit courts usually find three justices collectively hearing cases. All of these judges are nominated by the president and confirmed by the Senate. Ordinarily appointments are made on a partisan basis, and the recommendations of U.S. senators (if from the president's party) are often crucial to federal district court choices.

In recent years the federal district courts have been flooded with cases involving disputes of a uniquely contemporary character. The passage of civil rights acts and affirmative action laws, to prevent discrimination by reason of race or sex, has led to numerous administrative orders and rulings that are intensely controversial. They involve questions concerning quotas, seniority, busing, and the like that generate strong feelings and hence are frequently appealed to the courts. Cases involving the Environmental Protection Agency and the Office of Safety and Health Administration also pour into the courts; disgruntled business people complain bitterly about many of these rulings, feeling that the administrators have exceeded their authority under the law. The importance of many of these cases, and the incapacity of the Supreme Court to hear more than a small fraction of cases appealed to it, is giving federal district (and circuit) courts a more significant role than they have known before.

Just how litigious a society we wish to become—and how many public policy decisions we wish to make in the courts—may well become one of the major issues confronting our nation in the years ahead.

Notes

1 See Alfred H. Kelly and Winfred A. Harbison, *The American Constitution: Its Origins and Development*, 5th ed. (New York: Norton, 1976), pp. 214–218.
2 Dred Scott v. Sanford, 19 Howard 393 (1857).
3 James M. Burns and Jack Peltason, *Government by the People* (4th ed.) (Englewood Cliffs, N.J., Prentice-Hall, 1960) p. 500.
4 Gibbons v. Ogden, 9 Wheaton 1 (1824).
5 Plessy v. Ferguson, 163 U.S. 537 (1896).
6 Kelly and Harbison, *The American Constitution*, chap. 19.
7 Robert H. Jackson, *The Struggle for Judicial Supremacy* (New York: Knopf, 1941), pp. 177–196.
8 William E. Leuchtenberg, *The Troubled Feast* (Boston: Little Brown, 1979), rev., p. 99.
9 Kelly and Harbison, *The American Constitution*, pp. 915–930.

10 Miranda v. Arizona, 377 U.S. 201 (1966).
11 Brown v. Board of Education of Topeka, Kansas, 347 U.S. 483 (1954).
12 Roe v. Wade, 410 U.S. 113 (1973).
13 United States v. Butler, 297 U.S. 1 (1936).
14 Merlo Pusey, *Charles Evans Hughes* (New York, Macmillan, 1952), p. 204.
15 Former Sen. Sam Ervin of N.C. confirmed that he said this in a letter dated May 25, 1979. Neither of us knew where the quotation appeared in print.
16 William O. Douglas, "Stare Decisis," *Columbia Law Review* 32 (1949), pp. 735–755.
17 Arthur M. Schlesinger, Jr., "The Supreme Court: 1947," *Fortune*, January 1947, p. 201. Courtesy of *Fortune*.
18 See Walter F. Murphy and C. Herman Pritchett, *Courts, Judges, and Politics* (New York: Random House, 1974).
19 Nina Totenberg, "Behind the Marble, Beneath the Robes," *New York Times Magazine*, March 15, 1975, p. 58.
20 James M. Burns and Jack W. Peltason, *Government by the People* (Englewood Cliffs, N.J.: Prentice-Hall 1960) 4th ed., p. 530.
21 Civil Rights Cases 109 U.S. 3 (1883).
22 Pollock v. Farmers' Loan and Trust Co., 157 U.S. 429 (1895).
23 Kelly and Harbison, *The American Constitution*, pp. 531–41.
23 United States v. E. C. Knight Co., 156 U.S. 1 (1895).
25 Adair v. United States, 208 U.S. 161 (1908).
26 Hammer v. Dagenhart, 247 U.S. 251 (1918).
27 Bailey v. Drexel Furniture Co., 259 U.S. 20 (1922).
28 Retirement Board v. Alton Railroad Co., 295 U.S. 330 (1935).
29 New York Central R.R. Co. v. White, 243 U.S. 188 (1917).
30 Morehead v. New York ex. rel. Tipaldo, 298 U.S. 587 (1936).
31 Carter v. Carter Coal Company, 298 U.S. 238 (1936).
32 United States v. Butler, 297 U.S. 1 (1936).
33 Sunshine Anthracite Coal Co. v. Adkins, 310 U.S. 381 (1940).
34 Schechter v. United States, 297 U.S. 495 (1935).
35 Leonard Baker, *Back to Back: The Duel Between FDR and the Supreme Court* (New York: Macmillan, 1967); and William E. Leuchtenburg, *Franklin D. Roosevelt and the New Deal: 1932–1940* (New York: Harper & Row, 1963), pp. 231–238.
36 William F. Swindler, *Court and Constitution in the Twentieth Century: The Old Legality, 1889–1932* (Indianapolis: Bobbs-Merrill, 1969); and George E. Mowry, *Theodore Roosevelt and the Progressive Movement* (Madison: The University of Wisconsin Press, 1946).
37 Ableman v. Booth, 21 Howard 506 (1859).
38 Korematsu v. United States, 323 U.S. 214 (1944). Ex parte Endo, 323 U.S. 283 (1944).
39 In re Debs, 158 U.S. 564 (1895).
40 Baker v. Carr, 359 U.S. 186 (1962).
41 Engle v. Vitale, 370 U.S. 421 (1962).
42 School District of Abington Township v. Schempp, 374 U.S. 203 (1963).
43 See, for example, Frank Sorauf, "Zorach v. Clauson: The Impact of a Supreme Court Decision," *American Political Science Review*, 53 (1959), 777–791; and Robert H. Berkby, "The Supreme Court and the Bible Belt: Tennessee's Reaction to the 'Schempp' Decision," *Midwest Journal of Political Science*, 10 (1966), pp. 304–319.
44 See Barenblatt v. United States, 360 U.S. 109 (1959); Uphaus v. Wyman, 360 U.S. 72 (1959); Wilkinson v. United States, 365 U.S. 399 (1961);

Braden v. United States, 365 U.S. 431 (1961); and Hutcheson v. United States, 365 U.S. 599 (1962).
45 Yates v. United States, 355 U.S. 66 (1957).
46 Quoted in Anthony Lewis, *Gideon's Trumpet* (New York: Random House [Vintage Books], 1964), p. 167.
47 United States v. Nixon, 418 U.S. 683 (1974).

CHAPTER 14

THE BILL OF RIGHTS: SIMPLE RULES AND COMPLEX CASES

One of the Supreme Court's preeminent functions, as indicated in the previous chapter, is interpreting and protecting the Bill of Rights. It could not ask for a more solemn or significant task. The Bill of Rights is the most cherished part of our Constitution—and well it might be. The personal freedoms that lie at the heart of a democratic society rest in the first ten amendments to the Constitution. Many parts of our political system are optional matters, unrelated to the essentials of democracy. For example, whether or not we have bicameralism, the electoral college, or treaty ratification by two-thirds of the Senate are not relevant to the democratic idea. But unless we have free speech, a free press, freedom of assembly, and freedom of religion, we are not a free people. This chapter, then, will dwell primarily (though not exclusively) upon the First Amendment.

Strangely, the Constitutional Convention adjourned in 1787 without formally guaranteeing our most fundamental freedoms. It did so believing that the Congress was limited to the exercise of delegated powers, and no powers were thought to have been delegated that would interfere with these liberties. The states, presumably the primary guardians of the people's rights, had provisions in their own constitutions that protected the freedom of their people.

Before they were willing to accept the Constitution, however, prominent spokesmen in the states insisted on a Bill of Rights, to ensure more fully that Washington would not invade the rights of their citizens. Their views were heeded, and the ten amendments were added.

The Bill of Rights initially operated as a restraint only upon Washington, not upon the states. The latter were restrained only by their own constitutions, insofar as most human rights were concerned. This condition persisted until well into the twentieth century, when the states proved to be less scrupulous about protecting the rights of their citizens than many freedom-loving people wished. The Supreme Court came to the rescue. Since the Fourteenth Amendment specified that no *state* could deprive its people of "life, liberty or property without due process of law," the Court interpreted that "liberty" to include the four First Amendment freedoms—speech, press, assembly, religion. If the states, henceforth, took action that seemingly jeopardized these basic freedoms, the aggrieved citizens could seek redress in either state or federal courts. Sometimes the latter would be more responsive to citizen complaints.

Step by step, the Court selected other provisions of the Bill of Rights that the states must respect. They must not, for example, engage in unreasonable searches and seizures (the Fourth Amendment). They may not seize private property without paying just compensation (the Fifth Amendment). Nor may they require a defendant to testify against himself (the Fifth Amendment's self-incrimination clause) or deny an accused a fair trial (the Sixth Amendment again).

The Supreme Court, however, has not demanded that *every* provision of the Bill of Rights be applied to the states. The latter may indict a suspect by "information" (that is, the prosecuting attorney can draw up the indictment) rather than by grand jury, as federal courts are required to do (by the Fifth Amendment). Judges rather than juries may sit in judgment in civil cases, state

The First Amendment in U.S. History

juries may consist of less than 12 members, and the jury finding need not be unanimous—all of which are commonly adhered to in federal cases. But for the most part, the Bill of Rights now constrains both the national and the state governments.

The First Amendment states categorically that "Congress shall make no law ... abridging the freedom of speech, or of the press." This is about as direct, straightforward, and unequivocal a declaration as one could ask. It would seem to leave little room for argument; "no law" would appear to mean "no law." But although some students of the Constitution have held that the First Amendment means what it says, their views have not prevailed. It turns out not to be such a simple, stark, undebatable provision after all.

In more than a score of ways Washington and the states have limited speech and press. And in the overwhelming majority of instances even the most devoted civil libertarians have gone along. For example, statutes or federal regulations forbid perjury, contempt of court, or recital by the prosecution of the past convictions of a criminal defendant—all of which are forms of expression. Other laws forbid libel, slander, plagiarism, fraudulent advertisements, the offering of bribes to do something illegal, obscene and threatening phone calls, threats to kill the president, cigarette ads on television, private correspondence with officials of foreign countries in an attempt to influence foreign policy, the sale or exhibition of obscene materials, the divulgence of military secrets, the advocacy of strikes by federal employees, jokes about hijacking in airports, and disrespectful language towards one's commanding officer. Still other laws limit the time and place in which speeches may be made. (Speeches at 3 A.M. in a public square or in hospital zones are frowned upon, as is falsely shouting "fire" in a crowded theatre.) Nor may anyone use speech to "incite to violence" (to be discussed later). Federal employees (as well as state employees whose activities are partially or wholly financed by Washington) may not give partisan speeches during campaigns. Television stations must adhere to a "fairness doctrine" (allowing equal time to opponents) when controversial political views are aired on those stations.[1] Picketing, while ordinarily a form of protected expression, may be forbidden when it takes place "in a context of violence." Finally, the First Amendment itself limits free expression; as interpreted by the courts, the "establishment of religion" clause forbids teachers in public schools to use the classroom as a platform for advancing their religious views.

The history of interpretation of the First Amendment really says that Congress shall make no *unreasonable* law abridging the freedom of speech or of the press. But it also says much more, namely, that neither the national nor state governments may pass laws that forbid the advocacy of any heretical expression. No opinion, however obnoxious it may be to the overwhelming majority of people, may be constitutionally denied the right of expression. That is the crucial core of the "free speech, free press" portion of the First Amendment. When we tamper with that, we imperil the most precious element of our democratic heritage.

A brief history of our experience with freedom of speech and press may be instructive. Our ancestors did not come to this country because of their commitment to freedom of either religion, speech, or the press. They wanted religious freedom for themselves but not for members of religions they despised. Members of minority sects (such as the Quakers and the Catholics), or heretical members within their own denomination were often subjected to discrimination and even legal punishment by the Puritans. During the Revolutionary War Tories (those with pro-British sentiments) were denied the privilege of expressing their opposition to the war. (In one instance they were even forbidden to publicly pray for the British cause.) The Alien and Sedition Acts were enacted by the Federalists in 1798 over furious opposition by Jeffersonian forces; these infamous laws forbade false, "scandalous," or "malicious" statements designed to bring the national government or its officers into "disrepute" or "to incite against them the hatred of the good people of the United States." (Presumably bad people could be incited?) Since strong criticism of the government could be regarded as "malicious" and could bring its members into "disrepute," the law was subject to the kind of abusive interpretations that could sharply reduce free speech. Many editors were fined or jailed for statements that today we would regard as wholly legitimate; fortunately, the incoming Jefferson Administration pardoned the editors and the laws were promptly repealed.

Opponents of slavery were denied, in some cases by law but most effectively by fear, the privilege of expressing their views on that abomination. About 300 whites were lynched prior to the Civil War because of actual or alleged hostility to slavery. In the North abolitionists were free from legal restraints, but a number of abolitionist presses were destroyed by partisans of slavery. Prior to the Civil War both blacks and whites were intimidated by every conceivable means against publicly opposing slavery—and later, from challenging the system of white supremacy that followed the elimination of slavery. Only within the last 25 years have blacks known what freedom of speech and press really mean.

During the Civil War Abraham Lincoln suppressed newspapers that were sympathetic with the rebels. Private letters were opened, and "treasonable correspondence" led to fines or jail sentences.

Throughout our history universities have intermittently punished certain kinds of utterances. In many institutions of higher learning it was once dangerous for professors to support socialism (even outside the classroom), including the advocacy of public ownership of private utilities. Support for the theory of evolution led to the dismissal of some professors, as did the espousal of pacifism. In one instance research demonstrating that oleomargarine was nutritionally equivalent to butter led to the dismissal of several professors. The advocacy of unorthodox views on sexual behavior has often been a hazardous enterprise on campus. Criticism of the college administrative hierarchy has led to reprisals, although the subsequent dismissals or penalties were invariably attributed to other factors.

Parenthetically, colleges today are not quite the bastions of free speech that many people (including the colleges) believe they are. In a formal sense reputable public universities *do* protect both faculty and students in the expression of highly unorthodox views. But the social atmosphere in most colleges is incredibly inhospitable to the expression of views that challenge whatever may be the prevailing intellectual orthodoxy. Both students and professors are afraid to advocate views regarded as "unenlightened" or philistine. In most public universities, "unenlightened" is typically defined by the liberals, with conservatives feeling the brunt of the social pressure to avoid statements that will stigmatize them as benighted. In the last two decades, many campus conservatives were afraid to defend Barry Goldwater's bid for the presidency in 1964. Or to defend the Vietnam war, in its later stages. Or to defend Richard Nixon during the impeachment controversy. Or to advocate pre-marital virginity, to attack the smoking of pot, to criticize the raggedy clothes of the 1966–1973 period, to defend the censorship of pornography, to oppose the feminist movement or the Equal Rights Amendment, to condemn or criticize homosexuality, or to publicly dissent from whatever powerfully dominant feeling happens to prevail on the campus at any given time.

It should be added that liberal or radical professors, on many campuses, are afraid to challenge the college administration on issues important to it. They know that while the administration will never retaliate on overt grounds of resenting criticism, unpleasant things can happen to the critics that will be attributed to other causes, or to misdeeds which are either fictitious or would be otherwise overlooked.

Teaching fellows and professors or instructors who do not yet have tenure are also cautious—sometimes very, *very* cautious—about expressing opinions that might offend those who may write letters of recommendation for them or recommend tenure for them. (Ask your professor or teaching fellow about the state of free speech on your campus.)

It is not that college campuses are unique in the coercive social atmosphere that abridges freedom of expression. Teachers usually feel obliged to adopt a cautious conformity in high-school and grade-school environments. Pastors and priests yield to similar pressures in their environments. The climate of every institution—be it labor union, church, fraternity, corporation, or Nader research group—has its own unwritten code concerning what one must say and may not say to be a member in good standing. I have focused on universities because I know them best and because they regard themselves as the great strongholds of free expression—which they aren't so far as conservative students are concerned. And are blissfully unaware that they aren't.

If restraints on freedom of expression exist today, they mirror historical realities. During World War I a sedition law forbade criticism of the flag, the Constitution, our form of government, and the armed forces. And it forbade giving aid or comfort to the enemy by *word* or deed. Many Americans were jailed or otherwise punished for dissenting from the wisdom of our participation in that conflict; those of Germanic ancestry found it prudent to be extremely circumspect in their conversations. (The United States had a much better record during World War II, partly because it was a popular war.)

During the 1950s when Wis. Senator Joseph R. McCarthy "raised our consciousness" about the spectre of a domestic communist threat and recklessly accused various public figures of either being Communist Party members or "soft on communism," or "fellow-travellers," his crusade was both hotly opposed and fervently supported by various organizations.[2] The American Legion attacked the *New York Times*, the *New York Herald Tribune* (one of New York's then leading newspapers—and a conservative one at that), and the *Saturday Review* for carrying pro-Communist book reviews. The Boston Public Library was criticized for permitting Soviet-produced books and journals to be on open shelves. The San Antonio Minute Women demanded that all library books written *or illustrated* by persons accused (not proved, just accused) of being procommunist should be removed from the shelves. A bill almost passed the Texas legislature banning school books that "unfairly hold up to public scorn or ridicule American or Texas history and parts played therein by patriotic Americans or Texans." In Indiana a campaign was launched to protect the students from Robin Hood—who was guilty of harboring socialistic ideas—and to eliminate references to Quakers (who are pacifists) from school books. Literature that presented the United Nations in a favorable light was excoriated in many cities by right-wing groups (because communist countries were members of the United Nations). Many students avoided meetings addressed by "leftists" and kept their distance from organizations accused of being leftist. They were reluctant to subscribe to periodicals attacked by pro-McCarthy forces and loathe to criticize the House Un-American Activities Committee that McCarthy headed, lest this become known to the FBI and jeopardize their prospects for federal employment or otherwise imperil their

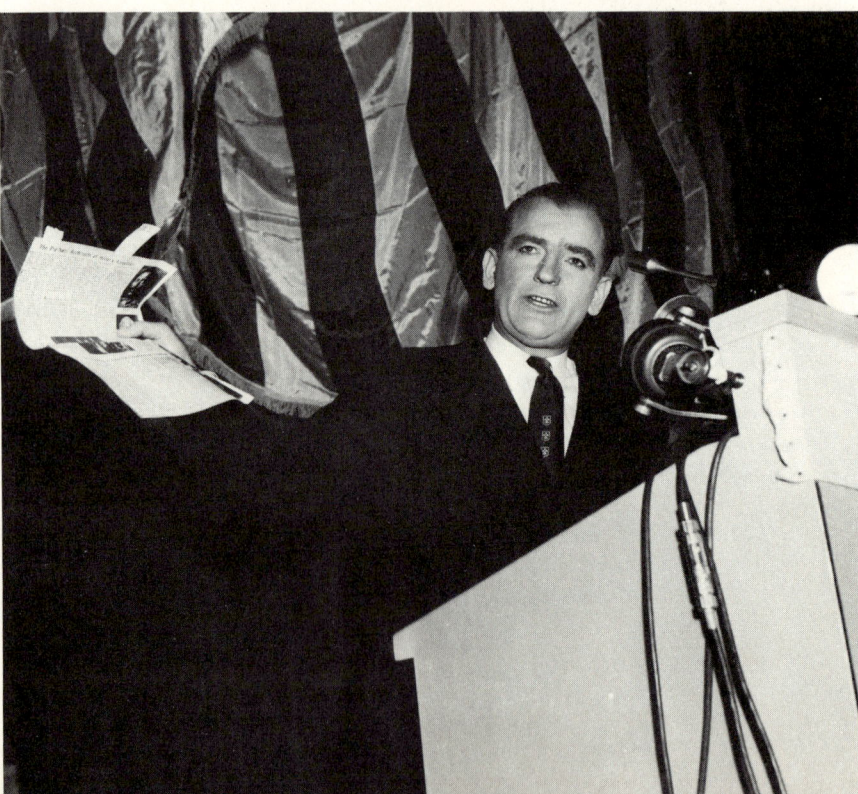

Senator Joseph McCarthy warns of "Communist Peril"

career. Writers and artists were blacklisted for years because of accusations about their political sympathies. Throughout the nation people became ultracautious about their political activities and statements—not an atmosphere very appropriate for a self-confident, politically robust, mature nation deeply committed to freedom.

During the Vietnam War prowar speakers were often hooted, jeered, and booed to the point they were unable to speak on college campuses. And in some of the nation's leading universities, too! Professors holding unpopular views on racial issues (especially genetic theories) have been denied platforms at major universities as a result of student protests.

Freedom of speech and press, then, have often been endangered during American history. That they will be endangered again can be taken for granted. Perhaps this brief recital of the major (and some minor) challenges to that freedom will help remind us that when we become frightened, we often overreact to the "threat" in ways that we later regret. Knowing this, we may be able to react more sanely the next time our security seems threatened.

John Stuart Mill and Free Speech Tested

College students intolerant of opinions they deplore need exposure to British philosopher John Stuart Mill's *On Liberty*. In this classic defense of free speech Mill argued that ideas we detest might be accepted as true by later generations. For example, the belief that popular government was feasible and desirable was long thought to be an absurd and dangerous form of subversive thought. Women's suffrage was believed to be not only ridiculous but destructive to the well-being of home and family. The concept of equal rights for blacks was rejected by virtually all "right-thinking" whites for most of Western history. Those who dared dissent from religious orthodoxy were believed for centuries to be a menace to society by the overwhelming majority of Europeans. Even Marcus Aurelius, the most enlightened of Roman emperors and a philosopher whose works are widely admired today, concluded that freedom of religious expression and practice for Christians was more than the Roman Empire could tolerate. And English poet John Milton, whose *Areopagitica* is almost as much of a classic as *On Liberty,* fervently defended freedom of speech and press—except for atheists, Catholics, and social revolutionaries. So, warned Mill, we can never be sure that the idea we now detest may not some day prove to be sounder than we think.

Even if time may not fully vindicate an idea, Mill went on, it may prove to be partly right. History is replete with opinions that, initially seen as alien and subversive, were later found to bear important elements of truth. Marxism clearly overstates the importance of economic factors as historical determinants, but that they are far more significant than pre-Marxists believed is now widely acknowledged. Sigmund Freud doubtless overstated the role of sexual drives in human affairs, but those drives are much more influential than pre-Freudians believed. The overstatement of truths often creates intense resistance to new doctrines, but society eventually separates the kernel of truth from the hull of error—and profits from the experience.

But suppose, Mill proceeded, that an idea is just as wrong as we believe it to be. Even so, he argued, that idea has as much right to be heard as the truth itself. The reason is that the expression of error makes the truth stand out. The contrast between a defensible truth and an indefensible error gives a clarity and a strength to truth that it might otherwise lack. We appreciate truths far more if they are attacked than if they are passed along, unchallenged—and hence, not really understood. Ideas tend to be enfeebled, to be accepted passively and rather indifferently, unless they are pitted against contradictory views and forced to defend themselves. Ideas become vital, alive, and meaningful only if they become accepted after a period of struggle and challenge. Mill added a final observation:

> Nor is it enough that he [the student] should hear the arguments of adversaries from his own teachers, presented as stated, and accompanied by what they offer as refutations. That is not the way to do justice to the arguments, or bring them into real contact with his own mind. He must be able to hear them from persons who actually believe them; who defend them in earnest, and do their very utmost for them. He must know them in their most plausible and persuasive form; he must feel the whole force of the difficulty which the true view of the subject has to encounter and dispose of; else he will never really possess himself of the portion of truth which meets and removes that difficulty.[3]

It would be interesting to hear college students, or anyone else who would deny an audience to speakers whose views they hate, come to grips with Mill's arguments. For many believers in democracy, they represent the strongest case for freedom of speech and press that has ever been presented.

The major free speech issue that confronted the courts in the last 30 years involved the Communist party and other left-wing groups. The story is worth telling. During World War I an antiwar agitator distributed pamphlets urging resistance to the draft on the ground that the war was ultimately being fought for capitalistic purposes. Was this activity protected by the First Amendment?

The Supreme Court said no. Freedom of speech is not without its limits, declared the Court; circumstances may be such that certain kinds of expression may be forbidden. In addition to citing the "shouting fire in the theatre" example, the majority opinion declared, "The question in every case is whether the words used are used in such circumstances and are of such a nature as to create a clear and present danger that they will bring about the substantive evils that Congress has a right to prevent."[4] The key words were "clear and present danger" and "the substantive evils that Congress has a right to prevent." In other words, since Congress has the right to declare war, and by implication to draft persons into the army, it also has a right to prevent activities that interfere with the draft. If speeches and pamphlets constitute a "clear and present danger" that resistance to the draft will grow, then the nation can properly forbid those forms of expression. Balancing the right to free speech against the right to effectively prosecute the war, the Court gave priority to the latter.

Although the "clear and present danger" test was thus used to restrict free speech, its broader implications became apparent in the minority opinion in a case that followed shortly. Another dissenter had distributed literature protesting U.S. and allied military intervention against the Bolsheviks (Communists) in Murmansk and Vladivostok (Russia)—and had called for a general strike so that no munitions could be sent there. While the majority of the Court upheld his conviction, Justices Oliver Wendell Holmes and Louis D. Brandeis did some dissenting themselves. They thought that the "surreptitious publishing of a silly leaflet" was no clear and present danger to the foreign policy objectives of the government. Justice Holmes warned, "We should be eternally vigilant against attempts to check the expression of opinions that we loathe and believe to be fraught with death, *unless they so imminently threaten immediate interference* with the lawful and pressing purposes of the law that an immediate check is required to save the country."[5] (Emphasis supplied.)

In a still later case Brandeis' minority opinion urged that "no danger flowing from speech can be deemed clear and present unless the incidence of the evil apprehended is so imminent that it may befall before there is opportunity for full discussion."[6] That is, the remedy for potentially destructive speech is more speech, so that truth can refute error and wisdom can overcome folly. But if there is not time for the benefits of full discussion to be felt, and a legitimate government activity is imperiled, then restraint may be constitutional.

A few years before this, however, the Court had adopted a very loose standard known as the "bad tendency" test. A communist who had distributed "revolutionary and inflammatory" literature advocating the use of violence against the state was charged with violating a state law that forbade such advocacy. Rejecting the "imminency" test, the Court majority upheld the conviction by declaring that this material constituted a "bad tendency" to "incite to crime and disturb the public peace."[7] We need not wait for a conflagration before we put out a fire, the Court said; it is all right to quench the spark that may lead to the conflagration.[8] As the Court had declared in another case, the state can "kill the serpent in the egg."[9]

The "bad tendency" test was regarded by most constitutional authorities as a dangerous departure from the "clear and present danger" criterion—a departure that opened the way for the suppression of many forms of legitimate expression. Any serious criticism of our Constitution, of the government, or even of our country could be interpreted as having a "bad tendency" to lead to loss of confidence in our system, thus preparing the way for advocates of violence to capitalize on growing public distrust of the government. So elastic are the possible interpretations of this doctrine that free speech would have been gravely threatened had this principle long prevailed.

After the fears precipitated by the Bolshevik Revolution in Russia in 1917 had subsided, supplanted by the greater fears of economic collapse, the Court returned to the "clear and present danger" test during the period of the Roosevelt Court (after 1937). The court reinforced this trend by announcing that the freedoms of the First Amendment had a "preferred status";[10] that is, while federal and state laws bearing on other matters are given the benefit of the doubt if their unconstitutionality is alleged, statutes that impinge upon the rights guaranteed in the First Amendment enjoy no such privilege. On the contrary, a presumption of unconstitutionality adheres to such laws, to be overcome only by clear evidence of a public need for the limitations imposed.

Communists and Free Speech

In 1940 Congress passed the Smith Act, which forbade the advocacy of violence, conspiring to advocate violence, or joining an organization that advocates violence. The legislation, enacted just prior to this country's entry into World War II, was designed to discourage domestic participation in both communist and fascist organizations.

After World War II over 80 Communist party members were jailed under the Smith Act. Was it constitutional to forbid the advocacy of violence, or a conspiracy to advocate violence, in view of the First Amendment's protection of free speech and press? The issue was hotly debated; a conviction of prominent Communist party leaders for conspiring to advocate violence was brought before the Supreme Court, which upheld the constitutionality of the legislation in *Dennis* v. *U.S.* (1951).[11]

The majority opinion held that even though no "clear and present danger" existed that the defendant's activities would lead to a violent overthrow of the government, even an *attempted* overthrow would be a sufficiently serious matter to warrant preventive action. The Communists would attempt such an overthrow at the earliest possible moment—and the government need not await the arrival of the revolutionary outbreak before taking appropriate protective action.

Nor were party members, said the Court, an insignificant minority, which could be disregarded because of their small numbers. They were a disciplined, dedicated, conspiratorial element that was part of a worldwide revolutionary movement bent on the destruction of capitalist governments. Rather than being a legitimate political party, seeking political goals by acceptable democratic methods, Communist party members were essentially agents of a foreign power seeking to subvert our political system.

Supporters of the Court declared that the Communists were employing freedom for the purpose of destroying the capitalist system, once the opportunity arose. And they warned that a minority can create a revolution; indeed, revolutions are ordinarily made by minorities. Governments have no obligation to indulgently condone the activities of those who spurn the democratic process and prepare for the day when they can violently seize power and suppress all opposition to their totalitarian system.

Finally, it was charged that the Communists often concealed their subversive intentions by posing as liberals or democratic socialists whose only goal was the elimination of injustice in this nation. By masquerading under false labels, they attract recruits who would shy away from them if they showed their true colors. Once recruited, they can be drawn little by little into the revolutionary ideology.

The Smith Act and the Court decision put John Stuart Mill's beliefs to the sternest test in our history. Were Mill's ideas valid when groups were advocating the violent overthrow of the government? Were Communists (and Nazis) an exception to an otherwise valid principle protecting free speech and press even for hated minority groups?

Political liberals, joined by some conservatives, argued vehemently against the Court's decision.[12] There case went something like this.

Communists and Free Speech

Freedom of speech is a reality *only* if it protects the advocacy of ideas we fear and believe dangerous. Every nation tolerates speech that is no threat to the security of the state or the power of its rulers. It is only when we protect speech challenging what we hold dear that we demonstrate our true commitment to free speech. This is the supreme test of our faith in the democratic idea.

Suppression of any form of free speech, it was argued, denies the public the right to *hear* what a minority wants to say. The right to hear is also a precious right, and it affects the freedom of all. Freedom to speak and freedom to hear are opposite sides of the same coin.

If we deny Communist party members the full benefits of free speech, because that speech may be dangerous to the security of our country, should we not purge our libraries of the works of Marx, Lenin, and other such writers? But would this not, in fact, be an outrageous act that would expose us to ridicule throughout the world as well as expose the hollowness and hypocrisy of our claims to believe in freedom of the mind?

Although their propaganda was sometimes masked under false labels, ideas should be judged on their own merits, not by the labels attached to them, the argument continued. To judge an idea as true or false by the respectability or ill repute of its sponsor is to default on intellectual independence. A valid idea is not less valid because it comes from a despised group; a defective belief is no better because it emerges from a respected source. As for a group presenting its most attractive face to potential recruits, reserving its less immediately appealing features for later examination, that is a characteristic common to many religious groups during their proselytizing activities.

Critics of the Court insisted that the Communists were not advocating violent revolution by a minority—a Leninist doctrine. Instead, they were advocating the Marxist brand of revolution. The latter (in most interpretations of Marx) predicted that disillusioned workers would initially seek the peaceful control of the government. Denied this right because of the government's refusal to yield power, the workers (now a majority) would have no choice but to resort to armed revolution. This philosophy of revolution is not much different from that of Jefferson—and of democrats in general. Most Americans would agree that if most voters were forcibly denied the fruits of an electoral victory, they would be justified in seeking control by armed rebellion.

Perhaps the Communists, given the opportunity, would follow the Leninist doctrine that a Communist party, however small, should seize power whenever this was possible—but this is not what the jailed Marxists were advocating. They should not be judged in the courts by speculations about their possible intentions.

But suppose the Communists *did* advocate the Leninist view of revolution? Would that be permissible, especially if they were enjoying full democratic rights in seeking support for their political program? Yes, said the critics. That would be the best way for them to discredit their movement since Americans would overwhelmingly reject that doctrine. By giving the Communists full freedom to expound their views, we would enable them to expose their

Communists on trial (clockwise) Jacob Stachel, Irving Potash, Carl Winter, Benjamin F. Davis, Jr., John Gates, Gilbert Green, John B. Williamson, Gus Hall, Eugene Dennis, Henry Winston, and Robert G. Thompson

warts and blemishes and be better able to appraise their true character. During the 1930s and early 1940s, the *Communist Daily Worker's* twisting and turning to follow the latest Moscow party line was a valuable education for American observers, as they witnessed the robot submissiveness of American Communists to the policy dictates of Moscow.

Agreeing with the minority opinion of the Supreme Court in the Dennis case, critics contended that the time to take action against the Communists would be when they began collecting arms and ammunition, trained their members in the physical techniques of violence and sabotage, or practiced espionage—in brief, when they were engaged in illegal action rather than merely talking. Such restraint would be fully consistent with a democratic society and in no way a violation of the Constitution.

While a small revolutionary group *can* sometimes effect a coup d'état, this can only be done if the majority of the population is either supportive of their action or politically indifferent. Neither condition remotely describes the United States, which is one of the most anticommunist nations in the world.

Finally, it was stressed that denial of free speech and press for Communists would show a lack of faith in the capacity of democratic ideas to stand up in open discussion. Surely the Communist party philosophy is not so cogent that democratic views cannot risk an open encounter with them. In fact the contrary is the case. Communist countries have zealously barred democratic ideas from infiltrating their countries. Are they not fearful because they know full well how attractive the prospect of freedom would be to their people?

Let us, it was said, make the distinction between democracy and communism as sharp as possible. We expect the communist nations to suppress democratic literature and jail its advocates; let us not imitate them by following the same repressive practices. If we do, how are we better than they? If fear of communism causes us to betray our democratic principles, Moscow will have succeeded in subverting democracy without firing a shot. They will have won by proving that we do not really believe in democracy after all.

The dissenters from the Dennis decision, and the supporters of John Stuart Mill, make an eloquent case. Whether or not the intense national debate that followed that decision led the Supreme Court to alter its stance is uncertain. But in 1957, the Court shifted ground, and in the Yates case declared that the *abstract* advocacy of violence *was* a constitutional right.[13] So long as the views expressed were of a purely theoretical nature and did not call upon the audience to engage in specific acts of violence, that expression was protected by the First Amendment. Mill would have beamed!

The First Amendment and the Press

Since the days of the Alien and Sedition Acts, newspaper and magazine editors have had few occasions to seriously complain about governmental threats to their freedom. Reporters who refuse to reveal confidential sources to prosecutors have sometimes been jailed. The issue is a difficult one, in which the reporter's right to conceal the names of informants (since future news sources would decline to talk unless their identity was hidden) collides with the court's right to require witnesses to reveal information necessary for determining a defendant's guilt or innocence.[14] When constitutional rights collide, the courts agonize, the public debates, and a tug of war takes place. No definitive transcending principle has yet been devised for resolving these disputes involving a free press versus a fair trial.

Similarly, newspapers may reveal classified information that the national government believes is detrimental to national security but that the press believes is legitimate public information. In the *Pentagon Papers* case, publication by the *New York Times* of the government's own historical account of its decisional processes in the Vietnam War was challenged by the government as an unacceptable breach of national security.[15] The Supreme Court, however, did not agree that national security had been materially injured and refused to support the government.

In some future case it is entirely conceivable that the Court will rule against the press since the resolution of the issue of a free press versus national security will not always vindicate the judgment of the press. Cases will be decided on their individual merits, as a court majority sees them, in the light of the public opinion that develops in each case. The Constitution gives us no guidelines that can settle the tough cases when legitimate interests must be balanced against one another.

The press won a noteworthy victory when the Court ruled that press criticism of public officials was permissible, no matter how inaccurate that criticism might be, unless it could be shown that falsehoods partook of malice. In other words, what might be libelous if said of a private citizen would not be libelous if said of a politician unless it could be demonstrated that the press knowingly printed a libelous statement about that politician.[16]

Finally, a long, drawn-out, and highly emotional struggle has been going on for decades over the right of the press to publish obscene material.[17] The courts have never established a constitutional right to print obscene literature, but the battle over the interpretation of what is obscene has been furious and indecisive. For many years the Supreme Court moved toward a more permissive view, culminating in the Warren Court decisions, which made prosecution extremely difficult. Material had to be "utterly without redeeming social importance" in order to be condemned, and there were always experts who could find some redeemimg social importance in almost anything. But the Burger Court established a more restrictive definition of obscenity, ruling that movies, pictures, or literature could be condemned if "the average person, applying contemporary community standards would find that the work, taken as a whole, appeals to the prurient interest . . . or if the work depicts or describes in a patently offensive way, sexual conduct specifically defined by the applicable state law and the work, taken as a whole, lacks serious literary, artistic, political or scientific value."[18]

The Court ruling that "community standards" should be used by juries rather than a national standard has made possible successful prosecutions that might otherwise have gone the other way. Both sides in the continuing battle over this form of censorship have strong arguments to make; we can assume that the struggle will go on for many years to come.

That Leaky Wall of Separation

The First Amendment states that "Congress shall make no law respecting the establishment of religion or denying the free exercise thereof." This simple and seemingly unequivocal statement has bred a host of controversies during this century.[19]

Although it may appear as if this statement ensures *total* religious freedom, it does not. The Supreme Court has interpreted the due-process clause to forbid violation of the First Amendment religious guarantees by the states, but some of the latter have forbidden snake-handling religious services by cults believing this practice demonstrated that God will protect them from poisonous snakes if they have faith in Him. Because such snakes have sometimes bitten members of the worship service, these states have outlawed the practice. The Supreme Court has not overturned their prohibitions.

Mormons were forbidden to practice polygamy in spite of church teachings that it was a permissible practice. Utah was denied admission to the Union until its constitution prohibited polygamy. Jehovah's Witnesses have been restrained from certain kinds of aggressive proselytizing that interferes with the right of privacy in people's homes. Christian Scientists have opposed vaccination and water fluoridation as "compulsory medication" in violation of their religious tenets, but states and localities may make both mandatory. Doctors may order blood transfusions for children of Jehovah's Witnesses, despite the religious objections of the parents, who regard this as contrary to Old Testament warnings against "eating blood." If any church wanted to practice human sacrifice, the states would say no (despite the television possibilities of such rites!!)

On the other hand, school requirements that all children salute the flag (which Jehovah's Witnesses believe to be a form of idolatry) were once sustained by the Supreme Court (though they were later overthrown as unconstitutional).[20] And the Amish have succeeded in limiting the education of their children to eight years, despite state and local efforts to require compulsory school attendance through high school.[21]

The First Amendment has been construed to invalidate laws requiring all students to go to *public* schools. But though parochial and private schools thus have constitutional protection, the question of how much public financial aid may be given them has proved a thorny one.

What does the Constitution mean by "establishment of religion"?[22] In Europe "established" churches were those bearing official governmental approval, an approval that might involve tax support. In 1787 three states gave some public aid to all Protestant churches, three others aided all Christian religions, and three more had abolished provisions that formerly conferred "establishment" status on some religions. Four states had never had such provisions.

As for aid to church schools, in much of the nineteenth century, public aid was given to church-supported colleges and lower-level parochial schools. Most of this was eliminated, however, when anti-Catholic agitation arose during the 1830s and free public education began to flourish.

Was aid to parochial schools constitutionally acceptable if given impartially? Or may it be given at all? Can public schools practice any form of religious activity or cooperate with churches in their efforts to instruct the young? The Court has been wrestling with these questions for the past fifty years.

In 1925 the Supreme Court upheld the state of Louisiana when it gave free textbooks to students in parochial schools; the issue was not framed in First Amendment terms, however, but concerned the question of whether such expenditures were or were not "for a public purpose."[23] It was 1947 before the Court directly confronted the issue of whether aid for parochial schools violates the establishment of religion clause, and if so, whether it applies to *all* forms of aid. In *Everson v. Board of Education* (1947), the Court announced:

> *Neither a state nor the Federal Government can set up a church. Neither can pass laws that aid one religion, aid all religions, or prefer one religion over another. Neither can force nor influence a person to go to or remain away from church ... or force him to profess a belief or a disbelief in any religion.... No tax in any amount, large or small, can be levied to support any religious activities or institutions, whatever they may be called, or whatever form they may adopt to teach or practice religion.... In the words of Jefferson, the clause against establishment of religion by law was intended to erect "a wall of separation between Church and State."*[24]

But in this same case the Court approved public busing of parochial students, contending that this was aid to pupils, not to churches. Many students of constitutional law were puzzled by the apparently sweeping nature of the Court's stricture against parochial school aid, combined with its acceptance of what seemed to them an important aspect of that aid.

A year later the Court outlawed a state plan that permitted religious instruction to take place on school premises under a "released time" provision, which enabled students to attend either classes of religious instruction taught by nonfaculty members or secular classes, depending on parental choice.[25] The Court rejected the plan not only on the ground that religious instruction was taking place in tax-supported public school buildings but also because the churches were able to utilize the state's "compulsory public school machinery" for recruiting students to their classes.

But in 1952 the Court permitted public schools to release students for voluntary church instruction in nearby areas. The majority opinion saw significant differences between this case and the preceding case and argued that "we find no constitutional requirement which makes it necessary for government to be hostile to religion and to throw its weight against efforts to widen the effective scope of religious influence."[26] The minority opinion, on the other hand, said this was "not separation but combination of Church and State."

In *Engel* v. *Vitale* (1962), the Court turned thumbs down on a New York State school law that authorized, but did not require, the recitation by pupils of a nondenominational prayer composed by the New York State Board of Regents.[27] This was clearly a religious activity, said the Court, and "it is no part of the business of government to compose official prayers for any group of the American people to recite as part of a religious program carried on by the government." Critics of the Court contended that it was adopting an "antireligion" posture, although the Court majority argued that its "wall of separation" was in the best interests of the churches. Government involvement in religious matters would ultimately be a threat to religious freedom, it contended.

The Engel decision foreshadowed the Court's banning of Bible reading in the public schools and of the voluntary recitation of the Lord's Prayer in them.[28] Polls revealed that a heavy majority of Americans disapproved of this decision, and a movement for a constitutional amendment overriding the Court decision was begun. This movement, however, encountered the opposition not only of secular organizations but of many religious leaders as well. The latter agreed that the government should not engage in or sponsor religious activities in the schools, both for constitutional and practical reasons. They argued that this protects the community from divisive and rancorous disputes, and it is doubtful that perfunctory and rather superficial religious exercises are very meaningful. These exercises allegedly trivialized religion and were unfair to those with no religion or those whose religious beliefs did not support the particular kind of religious exercise that would be undertaken. But opponents of the Court objected strongly to "excluding God from the classroom" and creating the presumption (they said) that religion was too insignificant to warrant attention in the schools.

The battle to prevent state involvement in religious activities involving the public schools seems to have been won, although the Court refuses to carry this doctrine to its ultimate limit. It remains willing for the Pledge of Allegiance to the flag to contain the words "under God;" to permit "in God we trust" to remain on coins; to allow chaplains paid from tax funds to conduct military services; to exempt ministers, priests, and rabbis from any military draft; and to exempt church property from taxation.[29] Moreover, veterans who opt for college using aid from the GI Bill can attend parochial colleges if they wish.

The effort to ascertain what aid can be given parochial schools has not been settled. It is an exceptionally difficult question.[30] Even the strongest supporters of the "wall of separation" theory agree that police and fire departments should give protection to parochial school property. And the Court has approved busing of parochial school students.

But the Court has rejected partial payment for instructors teaching nonreligious subjects in parochial school, arguing that this would involve "excessive entanglement" with religion and was a form of assistance to religion, even if indirect. Still, free school lunches for parochial students were ruled permissible. And federal law giving aid to *all* elementary and secondary schools, the amount depending upon the proportion of children from low-income families in each school, has been upheld. This permits, interestingly enough, sending specially qualified teachers from public schools into private schools during regular school hours to teach disadvantaged children.

On the other hand, public grants for the maintenance and repair of a private school's buildings and for testing and record keeping have been disallowed, as has aid for counseling, remedial speech, hearing therapy, and for instructional equipment like maps, records, films, tape recorders, and projectors. And direct tuition grants for parents of *all* schoolchildren within the state have been forbidden since some of this money would go for paying tuition to parochial schools.

A law requiring public schools to *lend* textbooks to students in private schools was approved, again on the theory that students were being helped, not churches. And aid for the construction of academic buildings for all colleges—religious and secular alike—has been upheld. Salary supplement programs, however, are impermissible.

Trying to find the true constitutional meaning of the "establishment of religion" clause has obviously involved the Court in difficulties the Founding Fathers never remotely imagined. Nor can scholars discern from the often contradictory statements of persons like James Madison, Thomas Jefferson, and others just what the drafters of the Constitution would have done if faced with these questions. In any case, the Constitution must be addressed in the light of today, and not just in the light of an age that reflected different experiences and that had different attitudes. The question is not so much one of what the Constitution permits; that question is enveloped in a mist of uncertainty. (See Daniel P. Moynihan, "Social Science and the Courts," *The Public Interest*, Winter, 1979, p. 24). It is a question of what is in the public interest. Those who support parochial school aid can make a strong case that the Court has been unsympathetic with their needs and has adopted a legal posture not required by the Constitution. Those who oppose parochial school aid can make an equally strong defense of the Court. But beneath the legal argumentation lie hidden value systems that usually dictate which side of the issue one comes out on.

The public policy dispute brings out arguments that provide adequate comfort to each side. Those who favor parochial school aid on a larger scale insist that parents of parochial school students pay taxes to support schools but benefit little from those taxes. They are financially punished for the offense of wanting their children to have religious training. Well-to-do parents may be able to send their children to parochial schools, but poorer parents often cannot; this discrimination against lower-income parents ought to be eliminated so that they have the same freedom of choice that more affluent parents have. The parochial schools are rendering a public service since most of their classes are secular. They should be reimbursed for at least that proportion of their expenditure. It is important for all children to have the best possible education, and it is in the national interest for them to have it.

Opponents of such aid respond as follows: Public schools are available for all children to attend; if parents are not satisfied with what it offers, they should be willing to pay for schooling that they regard as superior. Any significant assistance to parochial schools *does* represent assistance to the churches sponsoring those schools; they would not conduct such schools if they did not believe they would strengthen student attachment to those churches. It is wrong to compel people, through taxes, to support indirectly religious beliefs that they reject. Even ostensibly nonreligious parochial school should not receive aid. Their classes often use religious illustrations or are infused with a vaguely religious tone, since devout believers reject the notion that religion should be confined to church and religious classes. They believe religion should be part of the whole of life, not restricted to narrowly "religious" times and activities, and therefore intersperse religion throughout the school program. Opponents stress that major aid to parochial schools may create such turmoil and discord in states and communities that churches are well advised to appreciate the more harmonious conditions that now prevails. Finally, aid to parochial schools may lead to the splintering of our school system, with more and more churches reaching for the available aid to establish their own parochial schools. The steady shrinkage and deterioration of public schools in recent years is not, they believe, in the public interest, and anything that accelerates that trend is to be deplored.

Privacy and Due Process

Before closing this chapter a few of the other provisions of the Bill of Rights deserve comment. The Second Amendment reads, "A well regulated Militia, being necessary to the security of a free state, the right of the people to keep and bear Arms shall not be infringed." While gun enthusiasts often argue that this forbids federal efforts to outlaw handguns or restrict private ownership of guns in general, constitutional lawyers disagree. The latter contend that this amendment refers only to a militia, not to private ownership of firearms. It may or may not be wise for Washington to restrict private ownership of guns, but it is not unconstitutional to do so.[31]

The Eighth Amendment forbids "excessive bail." Excessive bail is whatever the courts may deem to be more than necessary to assure that someone charged with a crime will appear in court when ordered to do so. This amendment also forbids "cruel and unusual punishment." At a minimum this outlaws the use of physical torture or other barbaric treatment in dealing with criminals. It has also been interpreted to forbid making alcoholism a crime (though drunkenness in public can be made a criminal offense). The death penalty is not a "cruel and unusual punishment" if it is properly imposed in a nondiscriminatory way. But legislators may not require that everyone convicted of a given offense shall receive the death penalty; opportunity for mitigating circumstances to be taken into account must be given. It now appears that the death penalty can be constitutionally applied only if the crime involved resulted in the victim's death.[32]

A "right of privacy" is not specifically guaranteed in the Bill of Rights or in any subsequent amendment. But the Court has pieced together the language and implications of the First, Fourth, Fifth, and Ninth Amendments and concluded that such a right is implicit from their collective admonitions. This newly discovered right first appeared when the Court forbade a state from interfering with the dissemination of contraceptive information or materials.[33] Constitutional scholars believe it may have a much wider application, such as protecting the public from unnecessary governmental surveillance and snooping into private lives, but the Court has not yet clarified the range of this concept. (It has applied the "privacy" interpretation to abortion, however).

But if the "right of privacy" is still embryonic, the Bill of Rights has specifically forbidden "unreasonable searches and seizures." The constitutional language of the Fourth Amendment reads as follows:

> *The right of the people to be secure in their persons, houses, papers, and effects, against unreasonable searches and seizures, shall not be violated, and no Warrants shall issue, but upon probable cause, supported by Oath or affirmation, and particularly describing the place to be searched, and the persons or things to be seized.*

What is "unreasonable"?[34] A long series of cases have attempted to spell out what law enforcement officers may or may not do, consonant with this amendment. The Court has not followed a consistent course; its decisions seem to depend from term to term on the comparative liberalism or conservatism of its membership, as well as upon the public mood. The Court does permit the police to make arrests without a warrant if they have probable cause (not mere suspicion) to believe that someone has committed a crime or is on the verge of committing one. Drawing the line between mere suspicion and probable cause is sometimes difficult for both the police and the courts to do.

As for searches, the police do not need a warrant in order to stop and "frisk" a suspect for concealed weapons if they have sufficient reason to believe that person is armed and dangerous. The courts are not prepared, in other words, to deny police the right to protect themselves from weapons that reasonable prudence suggests might be used against them. If the search reveals no weapon but does turn up evidence of criminal behavior, a full warrantless search may then be made. Police may not, however, search a person or a car on grounds of mere suspicion.

When making a proper arrest, the police may search the suspect fully as well as the immediately surrounding area. They may also search a suspect's automobile if it is believed to harbor incriminating evidence or if it is being used to facilitate the commission of a crime.

These, however, are exceptions to the general rule that the police should obtain search warrants from a magistrate before engaging in searches and seizures. The magistrate is not supposed to issue the warrant unless the police can show there is "probable cause" to believe that criminal evidence will be found. The police must also indicate with some precision just what they are looking for and where they propose to find it; a general "fishing expedition" is out of bounds.

When the issue was first raised, the Supreme Court did not regard wiretapping as unconstitutional since nothing was being literally searched or seized. Forty years later the Court changed its mind and decided that electronic eavesdropping *was* an invasion of privacy within the meaning of the Fourth Amendment. However, Congress enacted legislation shortly thereafter authorizing the attorney general to obtain permission from a federal judge for federal officers to engage in wiretapping or electronic "bugging" while investigating the commission of certain serious crimes. But the Court ruled out these investigative techniques when applied to persons suspected of domestic subversion.

To discourage violation of the Constitution's search and seizure clause, the Court has held that evidence illegally seized may not be introduced into court as evidence of a defendant's guilt. The *exclusionary rule,* as it is called, is one of the most debated of the Court's positions;[35] many critics accuse the Court of tilting unduly in favor of defendants at the expense of public safety. They would punish police for illegal searches and seizures while permitting the evidence acquired thereby to be considered by a court and jury. The Supreme Court's defenders, however, do not regard this as a sufficiently effective way to deter overzealous police from invading legitimate citizen privacy.

The exclusionary rule is related to another constitutional amendment as well. The Fifth Amendment declares, in part, that no one "shall be compelled in any criminal case to be a witness against himself." This prohibition against compulsory self-incrimination was, as we have seen, only recently held to be a restriction on the states as well as on the federal government. The Fifth Amendment also declares that no one shall be "deprived of life, liberty, or property without due process of law." Basically, due process of law requires that procedures fair to a defendant shall be followed during the prosecution of a criminal case. What is fair? Thousands of cases have grappled with this question since the Court is unable to give a precise definition of what the phrase means. But in *Miranda* v. *Arizona* (1966), the Court ruled that suspects cannot be interrogated unless they have been told they may remain silent, that anything they say may be used against them in Court, that they have a right to the services of a lawyer (supplied by the state if the defendant cannot afford one), and that if an interrogation follows these reminders, it can be terminated at the defendant's pleasure.[36] If a suspect is questioned before the defendant has been informed of his or her rights, any confession or incriminating evidence that he or she supplies cannot be brought before the Court. This ruling, too, has been challenged, but it seems to be successfully withstanding its critics.

A famous Supreme Court Justice, Felix Frankfurter, once declared, "The history of liberty has largely been the history of observance of procedural safeguards."[37] These safeguards are largely set forth in the Sixth Amendment, which guarantees a defendant a "speedy and public trial" before an "impartial jury" with the right to be "informed of the nature and cause of the accusation" plus the privilege "to be confronted with the witnesses against him" and the right "to have compulsory process for obtaining witnesses in his favor and to have the Assistance of Counsel for his defense."

The right to counsel was once a right dependent on one's financial ability to hire a lawyer. In recent years the Supreme Court has ruled that counsel must be provided free (where conviction could carry imprisonment) by the federal government or by the states if a defendant is unable to pay for this service. These "public defenders," unfortunately, are often relatively inexperienced young lawyers who may give the indigent defendant poorer quality legal assistance than that received by more affluent accused persons. No one has yet devised a practicable way to correct this inequity.

The due-process clause in the Fifth Amendment is of central importance to the "procedural safeguards" Justice Frankfurter spoke about. The "liberty" cited in that amendment, says the Court, includes:

> *the right of the individual to contract, to engage in any of the common occupations of life, to marry, to establish a home and bring up children, to worship God according to the dictates of his own conscience, and generally to enjoy those common law privileges long recognized as essential to the orderly pursuit of happiness by free men.*[38] (Free women, too?)

These rights are guaranteed unreservedly; the amendment simply ensures that people shall not be deprived of them without due process of law—that is, unless they have violated a constitutional law and have been found guilty in a fair trial.

A constitutional law regulating human behavior is one that the Supreme Court finds compatible with the Constitution's provisions, one that imposes restraints in language sufficiently clear to be understood by "men of common intelligence," and one that does not impose arbitrary or unreasonable restraints on one's liberty.[39] The Court used to find laws unconstitutional if they unduly interfered with the freedom of business people.[40] It has largely abandoned this line of interpretation, but it still determines what is unreasonable in some other areas. For example, it has forbidden schools to fire teachers just because they are pregnant and states to outlaw abortions during the first three months of a pregnancy. (The state may regulate abortions during the second three months, if the health of mother and fetus is jeopardized and may forbid abortions in the third "trimester" unless necessary to protect a mother's life or health.)

Initially, the procedural guarantees of the due-process clause were confined to law enforcement activities. More recently, the clause has been interpreted to extend procedural protection to persons whose eligibility for welfare payments has been denied, to students facing punishment or expulsion, to prisoners whose alleged misbehavior in jail exposes them to additional punishment, to lawyers threatened with the loss of the right to practice law, and to persons whose drivers' licenses may be revoked. Fair procedures must be followed in these cases, too; at a minimum this means the accused has the right to be informed of the basis for an adverse decision and an opportunity to be heard.

While the "equal protection" clause of the Fourteenth Amendment ("No state shall ... deny to any person within its jurisdiction the equal protection of the laws") is not a formal part of the Bill of Rights and does not directly apply to the federal government, the Court has indirectly held that the "due process" clause of the Fifth Amendment incorporates the principle of equal protection of the laws.

The equal protection clause has spawned a formidable body of litigation over the last three decades.[41] Most of it has involved alleged state impairment of human rights, but some has had federal application. The long struggle to ensure the democratic rights of black citizens has drawn heavily upon the equal protection clause.[42] It has been used to invalidate restrictions that limit black voting; to outlaw "Jim Crow" laws that segregated blacks and whites in trains, theatres, schools, restrooms, and so forth; and to nullify laws denying blacks equal access to public accommodations like restaurants, hotels, and motels. It has also been used to strike down rules and practices that discriminate against blacks (and other minorities) in obtaining equal access to public schools, colleges, and graduate schools; in buying houses wherever they wished; and in employment. Wherever minorities can demonstrate that some public policy that disadvantages them grew out of a racially discriminatory purpose, that policy can be challenged under the equal protection clause.

The clause does not forbid reasonable classifications that are free from racial taint. It does permit a graduated income tax, zoning laws (unless those laws can be shown to have been designed to discriminate against minorities), and laws limiting the age at which persons may legally drink or marry. It also permits race to be taken into consideration in establishing public policies relevant to racial progress. Thus while the Court, in the famous Bakke case,[43] outlawed the establishment of racial quotas that were strictly reserved for minority applicants to medical school, it did not negate "affirmative action" programs that take race into account as one factor among others to be considered in making admissions or other personnel decisions. Many federal programs incorporate affirmative action principles, requiring beneficiaries of federal contracts or funds to demonstrate that they are acting to ensure minority groups fair treatment (or even preferential treatment, critics charge). Private firms may also give some degree of preference to minorities without incurring Supreme Court disapproval of "reverse discrimination." We can expect further Supreme Court decisions explaining just what that body believes is permissible and impermissible in this tricky field.

Concerning laws that use sexual classifications, these are apparently not always in violation of the equal protection clause, at least as long as the Equal Rights Amendment has not been ratified.[44] All classifications based on race are automatically "suspect", that is, the presumption is that they are illegal unless a good case can be made that they are designed to overcome the effects of past discrimination against nonwhites. But the Supreme Court has not yet assigned sex a "suspect" classification. Although almost all cases involving alleged discrimination against women have been resolved in a manner approved by feminists, the Court has not gone quite as far as the latter would wish. It has not, for example, banned insurance programs that treat pregnancy differently from other "disabilities," nor does it regard a state policy of reserving guard jobs in maximum-security prisons for men as an unreasonable classification.

The Court has also held that sex may be reasonably taken into account insofar as creating property-tax exemptions for widows but not widowers. It was not thought unreasonable, our society being what it is, to assume that widows might face more financial hardships than widowers.[45] In general, however, sexual classifications are seen as constitutionally permissible only if a rational case can be made that such classification is based on reasonable purposes and not on "the role-typing society has long imposed upon women," or upon "archaic . . . generalizations."[46]

As we have previously stated, the liberties embodied in the Bill of Rights are being constantly reexamined. New rights are being discovered and older ones modified as the courts wrestle with the never-ending question of what rights are implicit in "equal protection of the laws," "due process of law," and other provisions of the Constitution. The Supreme Court is inevitably influenced by the climate of opinion in intellectual circles and in the general public's wider circle. Its innovations usually draw upon the former, but it is careful not to drift too far from the opinions held by the majority of concerned citizens. The prestige of the Court depends, in part, on the general public's respect for its work. That respect requires that the Court not flout public opinion too recklessly when it hands down its decisions. Ultimately, the people have the last word on personal freedom issues that matter deeply to them.

Notes

1 Jerome A. Barron, *Freedom of the Press, for Whom?* (Bloomington: Indiana University Press, 1973).
2 See Leroy Gore, *Joe Must Go* (New York: Messner, 1954); and Jack Anderson and Ronald W. May, *McCarthy, the Man, the Senator, the 'Ism'* (Boston: Beacon Press, 1952).
3 John Stuart Mill, *On Liberty*, ed. David Spitz (Chicago: Regnery, 1955) pp. 52–53.

4. Quoted in Henry J. Abraham, *Freedom and the Court*, 3rd ed. (New York: Oxford University Press, 1977), pp. 228–229.
5. Quoted in Felix Frankfurter, *Justice Holmes and the Supreme Court* (Cambridge, Mass.: Harvard University Press, 1938), pp. 54–55.
6. Quoted in Abraham, *Freedom and the Court*, p. 237.
7. Gitlow v. N.Y. 268 U.S. 652 (1925).
8. *Ibid.*
9. I can't locate the case but as J. Carter used to say, "Trust me."
10. Abraham, *Freedom and the Court*, p. 238.
11. Dennis v. United States, 341 U.S. 494 (1951).
12. Alfred H. Kelly and Winfred Harbison, *The American Constitution; Its Origins and Development*, 5th ed. (New York: Norton, 1976), p. 830.
13. Yates v. United States, 355 U.S. 66 (1957).
14. For contrasting views, see Theodore White, "Why the Jailing of Forbes Terrifies Me," *New York Times Magazine*, November 26, 1978; and Robert M. Knaus, "The Constitution, the Press and the Rest of Us," *Washington Monthly*, November 1978.
15. New York Times Co. v. United States, 403 U.S. 713 (1971).
16. New York Times Co. v. Sullivan, 376 U.S. 254 (1964).
17. See *The Report of the Commission on Pornography and Obscenity* (New York; Bantam Books, 1970); and Reo M. Christenson, *Challenge and Decision: Political Issues of Our Time*, 5th ed. (New York: Harper & Row, 1976), chap. 9.
18. Miller v. Calif. (1973).
19. See Abraham, *Freedom and the Court*, chap. 6.
20. West Virginia State Board of Education v. Barnette, 319 U.S. 628 (1943); Minersville School District v. Gobitis, 310 U.S. 586 (1940); and Taylor v. Mississippi, 319 U.S. 536 (1943).
21. Abraham, *Freedom and the Court*, pp. 283, 325.
22. See Michael R. Smith and Joseph E. Bryson, *Church-State Relations: The Legality of Using Public Funds for Religious Schools* (National Organization on Legal Problems of Education, 1972); and Leonard Levy, "School Prayers and the Founding Fathers," *Commentary*, September 1962.
23. Cox v. Louisiana, 379 U.S. 536 (1925).
24. Everson v. Board of Education, 330 U.S. 1 (1947).
25. McCollum v. Board of Education, 333 U.S. 203 (1948).
26. Zorach v. Clauson, 343 U.S. 306 (1952).
27. Engel v. Vitale, 370 U.S. 421 (1962).
28. School District of Abington Township v. Schempp, 374 U.S. 203 (1963).
29. Abraham, *Freedom and the Court*, p. 308.
30. See Ibid., chap. 6; and Christenson, *Challenge and Decision*, 3rd ed. (1970), chap. 7.
31. Edward S. Corwin, *The Constitution and What It Means Today*, rev. ed. by Harold W. Chase and Craig R. Ducat (Princeton University Press, 1973), pp. 306–307.
32. Abraham, *Freedom and the Court*, p. 75. See also Erwin N. Griswold, *Search and Seizure: A Dilemma of the Supreme Court* (Lincoln: University of Nebraska Press, 1975).
33. Griswold v. Connecticut, 381 U.S. 479 (1965).
34. Abraham, *Freedom and the Court*, pp. 156–169.
35. See, for example, Albert M. and Julia C. Rosenblatt, "A Legal House of Cards," *Harpers*, July 1977, pp.00; and Charles Peters, "Tilting at Windmills," *Washington Monthly*, May 1977, pp. 5–6.
36. Miranda v. Arizona, 377 U.S. 201 (1966).

37 McNabb v. United States, 318 U.S. 332 (1943).
38 Abraham, *Freedom and the Court*, pp. 108–109.
39 Connally v. General Construction Co., 269 U.S. 385 (1926).
40 For an excellent discussion of the evolution of due process of law, see Kelly and Harbison, *The American Constitution*, chap. 19.
40 Ibid., chaps. 19-20.
41 A good brief account of the Supreme Court's interpretation of the equal protection clause is found in Henry I. Abraham, *The Judiciary* (4th ed.) (Boston: Allyn and Bacon, 1977), pp. 117–145.
42 See Abraham, *Freedom and the Court*, chapter VII, and Kelly, *The American Constitution*, chap. 33.
43 The Government of U. of California v. Bakke, 98 *Small Court Reporter* 2733 (1978).
44 Frontiero v. Richardson, 411 U.S. 677 (1973).
45 Reed v. Reed, 404 U.S. 71 (1971).
46 Kahn v. Shevin, 416 U.S. 351 (1974).

CHAPTER 15

PUBLIC POLICY: CHANGE AND RESISTANCE TO CHANGE

The Bible says, "Of making many books there is no end." In the United States it can be said that "of making many laws there is no end." Laws and governmental regulations keep tumbling forth, year after year, in cascade proportions. Each year Congress passes hundreds of them, mostly of minor consequence but many having major importance. The web of federal regulations grows ever wider, penetrating ever more deeply into American life. And the array of legislation designed to help aggrieved groups grows likewise. Some people wonder where it will end, and whether law will become so pervasive, so intrusive, so stifling—and so costly to administer—that society will become the worse for all our efforts to improve it. A national mood of hostility toward bigger and more costly government seems to be gaining strength, with ultimate effects no one can know.

What are the factors that fertilize this volume of legislative and administrative activity—and that, therefore, accelerate social change? And what are the resistances to these forces? We need to know both before we can evaluate this phenomenon and decide what to do about it.

The Impetus to Legislate

The first and by all odds the most significant trigger of legislation and social change—technology—comes as no surprise. The industrial resolution in the last century and all the so-called post-industrial revolutions have conspired to create a seemingly irresistible demand for bigger government. By making it possible for people to leave the farms and live in massive metropolitan complexes, technology created problems without end—including unemployment, transportation jams, increased crime, air and water pollution, ethnic collisions, and inner-city blight. Almost every facet of law today owes its origin or its multiplication to urbanization and industrialization. The by-products of those two social phenomena are the ultimate explanation for most of what concerns modern Americans. Because technology's inherent momentum carries us onward, almost willy-nilly, to new vistas and new problems, there is no end in sight to the growth of government.

A second and closely related factor is the optimism that technology has generated—an optimism that has long affected almost every aspect of life. We support technology because we believe it will improve human welfare; we support new legislation because we believe it will do likewise. It was not always so. For most of history, people were essentially fatalistic. Frustrations, scarcities, and sufferings were regarded as a normal and inevitable part of human existence. They had always been with us and would always be with us; an attitude of resignation was appropriate, therefore. The modern-day faith that we can, by technology and experiment, either eliminate many problems technology has brought us or at least ameliorate human sufferings was an outgrowth of the industrial revolution. Without this spirit of optimism, our legislative outpouring would not have occurred.

Third, while technology per se has spawned as many problems as it has solved, human greed has added to them. In their perpetual effort to outdistance others, entrepreneurs have frequently resorted to unethical practices that have angered segments of the general public. The latter's indignation culminates in the cry, "There ought to be a law." Congress responds.

This seems to be a logical sequence, but new legislation is not the only option available to us. Conservatives usually believe that most economic problems are self-correcting, given time, in a basically free enterprise, freely competitive society. People who cheat the consumer or take unfair advantage of their competitors will eventually outsmart themselves, it is believed, by opening the way for more responsible competitors to better serve the public. When these competitors appear, the sleazy, ruthless, quick-buck artists will get their comeuppance, since the public will soon patronize the more upright, reliable, and efficient producer or merchandiser. Even monopolists eventually overreach themselves and pave the way for competitors who will displace them or force them to behave more responsibly. So far as the economy is concerned, government should permit the economy to correct its own maladies or, at most, rigorously enforce antitrust laws.[1] Liberals, of course, have less faith in the market and more faith in law.

There is another alternative to which insufficient attention has been paid. Instead of a new law for each new abuse, government could seek to protect the citizenry by a greater reliance on surveillance and publicity. "Pitiless publicity," to use Woodrow Wilson's phrase, can often be an effective regulator in itself. If governmental investigations, armed with the powers of subpoena and "contempt of Congress" citations, were to publicly expose the more egregious types of market misbehavior, the shame that would befall its perpetrators and the adverse publicity that would surround the guilty firm or firms could have a chastening and salutary effect. (The often dramatic results of the TV program, "60 minutes" suggests something of the potential involved.) Of course, this could only apply to large corporations, but they are the ones least disciplined by competitive market forces. Only if this failed to produce reformed behavior would government need to resort to new legislation. This option avoids the creation of new administrative bureaucracies, as well as of rules and regulations that may be clumsy, destructive of efficiency, and capable of being evaded.

Indeed, one of the by-products of new legislation is the certainty that it will prove inadequate. Tax legislation, for example, usually contains loopholes that clever lawyers and unscrupulous taxpayers discover and exploit, thus frustrating the reformers. This leads to more corrective legislation, which again proves porous and requires yet more legislation ad infinitum. If some of the more ingenious lawyers were hung at dawn and taken down at dusk for their part in all this, the problem might be less severe.

Fourth, much modern legislation stems from our efforts to avoid economic insecurities and improve economic opportunities for less fortunate people. In addition to trying to iron out the economic cycle, government is called on to provide workmen's compensation, old-age pensions, disability pensions, health insurance, disaster relief, and many other protections against penury. It is also called upon to provide more equal economic opportunities, via voca-

The federal budget (1980)

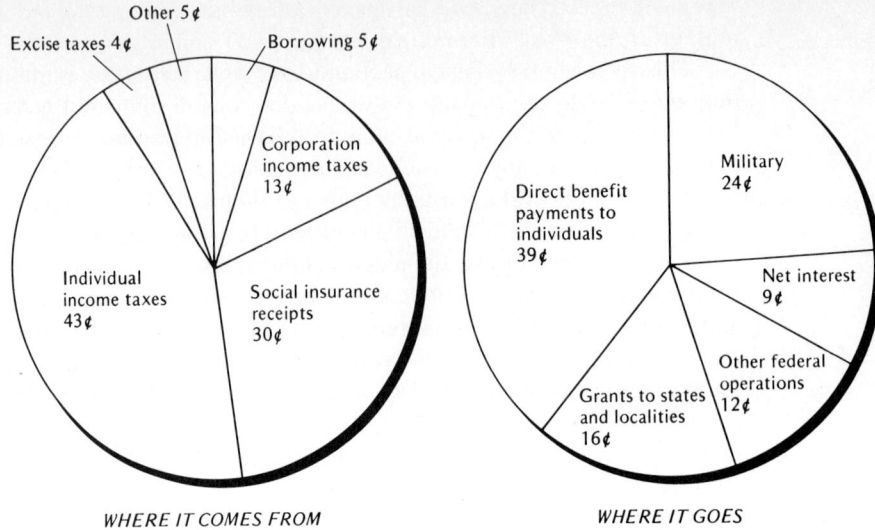

WHERE IT COMES FROM　　　WHERE IT GOES

tional training services, aid for the handicapped, educational subsidies for the poorer states, antidiscrimination laws, and the like. Humane reformers ceaselessly seek to improve the lot of the less fortunate by such laws and by others designed, for example, to provide better education for migrant workers' children, bring free or cheaper legal assistance for the poor, and improve the welfare system. As long as there are injustices, alleged injustices, or any distress that government might possible relieve, people demand that it deal with these problems. And since grievances never end, the legislative flood tends to go on and on.

Fifth, we get a good deal of legislation because Congress' job is believed to be that of legislation. (Woodrow Wilson said its first job was "informing"—a shrewd insight—but this has never prevailed.) Congress is expected to churn out a large volume of laws each session; if it fails to, the press and the president berate it for not doing its job. Its prestige, never very high, threatens to fall still further, so Congress hitches up its britches and hustles bills along.

Each congressional house, it should be remembered, has about a score of committees and over a hundred subcommittees. These subcommittees (with a few exceptions) feel they are shirking their duty unless they give birth to new laws. So they legislate, and then legislate some more. There are always plausible arguments for correcting an endless succession of evils.

The president, likewise, is excoriated by the press unless he presents Congress with a wide-ranging legislative program to meet our endless array of problems. This is regarded as his first responsibility, and he is judged in considerable measure by his diligence and skill in promoting that program. Once it is presented to Congress, the president is expected to dig his spurs into the lumbering creature to see that the program is enacted. If bills are stalled, the press castigates both president and Congress for not getting on with their job.

Conceivably, both Congress and the president could be judged by their ability to un-legislate—that is, to eliminate or scale down dubious programs, subsidies, and controls. This, however, would involve a major shift in the way we perceive government. That shift may be beginning, judging by recent developments, but powerful bureaucratic forces and special interests militate against it.

Administrators create new rules and regulations because that, too, is seen as a major part of their job. In the course of administering the laws in their domain, numerous questions of interpretation arise that are answered with clarifying rules (or, sometimes, with obfuscating rules since the language of bureaucratese is not usually that clear). Or the passage of time reveals that unexpected abuses or problems have appeared, within the purview of their authority, that call for corrective rules. Again, administrators seldom think in terms of un-legislating, of reducing unnecessary regulations. They think instead of *more* rules to "improve" those now on the books or to meet new problems that administrative experience has disclosed.

Finally, the media play a part in promoting more legislation, too. They are always on the alert for something new. The writer with an innovative proposal for coping with a social problem is not only published but invited over to NBC to be interviewed about it. The media are geared to pay attention to people who tell us how bad things are and how unconscionable it is for us to tolerate the continuance of the misbehavior or stupidity they bring before us. Writers who contend that problems are being handled about as well as can be expected are courting oblivion. Who is interested in hearing that? The public wants *bad* news, news that tells us how abominably someone or some group is behaving—behavior that, of course, ought to be met by a new law.

Until recently new and costly legislation has been facilitated by this country's economic growth. As per man-hour output expanded and the standard of living improved, expanding tax resources made new revenues available for new programs. When Congress can spend more without taxing more, it has been irresistibly tempted to go ahead with new laws and expensive programs designed to mitigate the latest media-focused problem.

Why Change Comes Hard

It might seem that the forces listed above would give us such a torrent of new legislation that society would be in a constant state of turmoil over the rapid rate of governmentally promoted change. Indeed, modern society *is* characterized by rates of change that not only contrast sharply with those of medieval, ancient, and primitive societies but that also place a heavy psychological burden on our ability to adapt to change. As we have noted, technology is the principal actor in this drama, with government primarily engaged in trying to cope with the problems technology creates. But an equally long list of factors tends to resist change.

Change can be refreshing, adding interest, excitement, and novelty to our lives. One part of us welcomes diversion from the commonplace. But another part of us likes the familiar—familiar people, places, and things. We are comfortable with the familiar; it is often reassuring, tension-reducing, and it makes fewer demands on our overworked adjustive mechanisms. We know how to deal with the familiar.

This satisfaction with the familiar (combined with fears of the unknown dangers or discomforts change may bring) tends to make societies conservative and hence resistant to change.

All societies tend to be somewhat conservative, to see major change as threatening and disruptive. Even during the depths of the Great Depression, when discontent and suffering were at a peak, Franklin D. Roosevelt was welcomed largely because his New Deal programs were seen as shoring up the familiar system, making it work better rather than fundamentally altering it. Socialists and communists made gains during that depression but remarkably few, considering the gravity of the crisis.

Ours is an affluent society and affluent societies have special reasons to fear change. Since most people already have a good life, materially speaking, they do not want to jeopardize their status. In a predominantly middle-class society such as ours, people own their homes, cars, and myriad personal belongings; they are usually more fearful that *major* change will worsen things than hopeful that it will better their circumstances. They are less than ecstatic at legislation that would redistribute income from them to poorer groups in society. The altruistic streak in most of us may accept some income redistribution, if it is accomplished rather invisibly, with no sense of current or impending deprivation on our part. But if we believe it will enhance the poor's standard of living while reducing ours, this altruism takes flight amidst various conservative rationalizations.

(Primitive, rural, and semirural societies are conservative, too—insufferably so, reformers often believe. Anyone who tries to get farmers in India to change their ways of farming, to adopt birth control measures, to institute new sanitation practices, to do anything that differs from age-old customs encounters incredibly stubborn resistance. These people are deeply attached to the old ways and are very suspicious and skeptical of anything new. The same is true of many other societies in Africa, South America, and elsewhere.)

Historically aware people expect even so-called revolutionary societies to rapidly revert to conservatism. Their early "reforms" become sacrosanct and rooted in reinforced concrete. To question them is to be branded a heretic or traitor. And the political leaders of some modern "revolutionary" societies exercise the same kind of despotic powers that dictators have used from time immemorial. The techniques of coercion are more sophisticated, because modern technology has been adapted to that end, but the general repression is much the same. No society deals more ruthlessly with would-be reformers than do "revolutionary" regimes.

But to return to our own society, other factors work to reduce the rate of change here. The wealthy can appeal to widely shared conservative values and use them to protect their interests and frustrate reforms. They prevent the establishment of a truly progressive tax system by arguing that capital accumulation (by them) is necessary to provide investment capital, and investment capital is needed to create jobs for all. We should, therefore, treat rich people's money tenderly, they argue; taxing it will ultimately hurt the poor worker. The appeal has worked beautifully for years.

Similarly, the wealthy have managed to keep effective rates of inheritance taxes at remarkably low levels by invoking the almost universal desire of parents to pass on an inheritance to their children. The rich—and conservatives in general—smoothly gloss over the fact that it is one thing to pass on small sums to help one's children get a good start in life and quite another to pass on enough to enable them to live in idleness and luxury.[2] That thought somehow does not enter their mind or is dismissed as unimportant.

Large corporations often effectively oppose government regulation by exploiting the common belief that government equals bureaucracy and bureaucracy is allegedly wasteful, inefficient, bungling, and stupid, in addition to being too bloated already. Since bureaucracies botch whatever they do, why give them still greater opportunity to commit mischief? The American people's tendency to respect the "hard-working, enterprising, productive" business person and to look down their noses at bureaucrats is a powerful conservative force in this country.

Interestingly, bureaucracies themselves become highly resistant to change, even though a new bureaucracy may regulate with gusto for a few years until the reforming fervor dies down and a comfortable routine is established. Disturbing that routine is then firmly resisted, by all the various means people use to avoid doing what they do not want to do. Laws which restrict their power or turf are also usually opposed.

The poor have the greatest stake in change—but the least power to bring it about. As previously noted, they have a poorer education, are less articulate, lack political savvy, and have little self-confidence. They vote less often and are less well informed when they do. They have a sense of futility and hoplessness about their lot, believing it is impossible to "fight City Hall." This militates against the formation of a political bloc designed to advance their interests. That we transfer some $50 billion a year from the more affluent to the less affluent[3] by social welfare programs is due not to the political activities of the poor but to the spirit of decency and compassion that is present in many of the nonpoor. The latter have applied the principal pressure for reforms that aid the less privileged groups.

Within the past decade a number of relatively new developments and insights have strengthened opposition to governmentally induced change (i.e., to major new programs). Foremost among these have been the disappointments associated with many liberal programs that were launched with great enthusiasm in the 1950s and 1960s. Federal aid for education has not improved students' educational performance. The war on poverty, although partially successful, was unable to cope with the stubborn roots of poverty, leaving a hard-core poverty population beyond the effective reach of corrective programs. Busing programs have not materially benefitted the education of black students. Urban renewal programs, once highly touted, proved disillusioning. Public housing projects often deteriorated prematurely and became havens for drunks, drug addicts, criminal elements, and irresponsible persons in general—instead of giving new hope and courage to their inhabitants. Prisoner rehabilitation programs have failed. Foreign economic aid frequently enriched bureaucrats, politicians, speculators, and big landlords instead of helping the poor abroad, as had been hoped. "Affirmative action" programs may have yielded as many losses as gains.

The latter, as applied to blacks, was discussed by black economist Thomas Sowell. After noting that blacks themselves repeatedly reject "preferential treatment" over "ability as determined by test scores" in obtaining jobs or college admissions, he observed that black income, relative to white income, has actually declined since these programs took effect. Moreover, black-white relations have sometimes worsened because of hostilities engendered by them. And the policy of "preferential admissions," for example, has had adverse consequences. Black students are admitted to prestigious colleges and universities for which they are not adequately prepared so that these institutions can boast a better "student mix" and can demonstrate their lack of prejudice. But the competition is so stiff that a high percentage of failures results. These were good students, moreover, who would have done well at other colleges to which they would otherwise have been admitted. Sowell then notes:

> *When the top institutions reach further down to get minority students, then academic institutions at the next level are forced to reach still further down, so they too will end up with a minority body count high enough to escape criticism and avoid trouble with the government and other donors. Each academic level, therefore, ends up with minority students underqualified for that level, though, usually perfectly qualified for some other level.*[4]

Sowell further observes that preferential admission inevitably impairs some other person's chances of attending college. Not the children of the rich and privileged, he says, but those of struggling whites seeking to make their way up the ladder. And the blacks that are supposedly advantaged are not those with poor opportunities but those from "the top of the minority distribution," those who least need special treatment. Thus, he declares, "The past is a great unchangeable fact. *Nothing* is going to undo its sufferings and injustices. . . . Neither the sins nor the sufferings of those now dead are within our power to change."[5]

He goes on to point out the widely acknowledged failure of forced school busing to improve either the education of black students or relations between the races and concludes:

> *"However futile the various numerical approaches have been in their avowed goal of advancing minorities, their impact has been strongly felt in other ways. The message that comes through loud and clear is that minorities are losers who will never have anything unless someone gives it to them. The destructiveness of this message—on society in general and minority youth in particular—outweighs any trivial gains that may occur here and there.*[6]

Sowell has every confidence that minorities can achieve economic equality—if they are treated as equals rather than as people who need preferential treatment in order to achieve their potential.

The point is not that Sowell is necessarily right; many writers would take strong exception to his conclusions. But when so many people—including many liberals—find much truth in what he says, and in what critics of similar well-intentioned programs have to say, the prospects for further legislation of a similar nature are reduced.

It was once believed that social science would provide us with reliable guidance in establishing and evaluating social programs. Instead of devising programs by guess and by gosh, trusting to hunch and speculation, empirical studies would give us more trustworthy leads in formulating or at least in assessing the merits of social programs. Much of this confidence has evaporated. We have learned that for every expert opinion, there is an expert counteropinion. For every study that defends busing, the negative income tax, the censorship of pornography, the television industry's use of violence, affirmative action programs, slum clearance, or whatever—another ponderous, methodologically impressive study draws the opposite conclusion. It is rare indeed, on issues heavily freighted with ideological significance, that social scientists ever come to agreement. Somehow or other, their biases seem to be reflected in the "scientific" conclusions they reach.[7]

Social scientists' incapacity to predict how new programs will develop, what side effects will be generated, or what their overall consequences are likely to be is not seriously questioned. The heart of social science is its predictive capacity, but in a world as changing and complex as ours, social science is quite incapable of giving us advance knowledge of how myriad impinging factors will affect the outcome of a social experiment. (Whether the current emphasis on "public policy analysis" will yield more gratifying results remains to be seen.)

One thing we have learned, however, is that programs that begin on a modest scale with modest costs often balloon into monsters whose dimensions alarm us. As the population grows, and the program is gradually modified to embrace new groups clamoring for aid to which they are "entitled," Congress and the nation sometimes find they have a tiger by the tail.

Similarly, there is increasing awareness that although individual programs may seem separately justified, the cumulative effect of all these programs imposes a burden of cost and controls that can become collectively injurious. Whether this consciousness will actually affect the viability of specific programs remains to be seen, but the political climate is surely affected by this awareness.

Currently the nation is caught in the throes of a nationwide "tax revolt," spurred by a successful referendum in California that cut property taxes by over 50%. Both Republicans and Democrats are rushing to identify with the popular clamor against "outrageously" high taxes. This movement, sometimes demagogically exploited by members of both parties, is unaffected by the fact that while U.S. taxes are more than 30% of our gross national product, much higher tax rates (from 32% to 51%) are present in Western Europe.[8] Some would wryly note, too, that it is a bit incongruous for middle-class families with several fine cars, television sets, an expensive stereo, attractive and well-furnished air-conditioned homes, anything they wish to eat, good clothes, Eu-

A modern tax revolt

ropean vacations, and heavy budgets for alcohol to bewail the "crushing" burden of taxes (to say nothing of the effrontery of complaints from upper-income families who already enjoy tax breaks not available to less affluent families).

The "tax revolt" was appreciably fueled by the fact that inflation automatically elevates taxpayers into higher income-tax brackets and partly by the fact that this country is nearing the end of a long era during which standards of living steadily rose. As inflation and economic slowdown take their toll, people are having difficulty adjusting to the likelihood that the nation has reached a stationary economic level, and they are becoming ever more critical of big government—at least in the abstract.

In any case, the drive for lower taxes can only have a depressing effect on legislative initiatives. With less money to spend, less can be done.

There is always the possibility, of course, that Congress will yield to the demand for lower taxes but will not make corresponding reductions in federal spending, which, under normal circumstances, would be an inflationary development. As is often noted, Congress finds it much easier to vote tax cuts than spending cuts. The former face little if any organized opposition, whereas spending cuts invariably bring a hail of protests from affected groups. The almost total incapacity of Congress to establish priorities among the host of federal programs means that there is often no realistic alternative to across-the-board cuts. But this involves cutting benefits or subsidies to groups like veterans, the aged, and the disabled or handicapped, which understandably gives Members of Congress pain. Even conservatives often balk at making cuts in these areas. But once exceptions start to be made, the list becomes endless and no one knows where to stop. Congress has not begun to master the fine art of budget cutting. In yearning for tax cuts but shying away from equivalent spending reductions, Congress reflects the confused attitudes of the American people. They want "waste" eliminated, but waste is defined as spending on programs that affect *other* people.

Of course there *is* waste in government, which theoretically could be weeded out without impairing the substance of worthwhile programs. But waste is everywhere, not just in government. It exists in churches, in philanthropic and charitable institutions, in business firms (as witnessed by energy profligacy before energy prices skyrocketed, and lavish executive expense accounts), in labor union headquarters, and above all, in higher education (where poorly taught courses are offered that add almost nothing to students' education but cannot be eliminated). Higher education may well be the most wasteful enterprise in America, with the possible exception of advertising. And there are countless homes whose family budgets could not withstand a close examination for waste. The author's blood pressure admittedly soars to medically hazardous levels when government waste is singled out as if it were a unique phenomenon. Unique? In a pig's eye!

But we digress. And while digressing, another comment. While we do seem to face inundation by laws and administrative rules, it is amazing how lightly this web of government rests on the shoulders of the average American. Although businessmen's work is greatly complicated by government regulations, and almost everyone is annoyed by the complexity of income tax computations, the average American's day is lived with little or no conscious awareness of government's so-called "heavy hand." He and she get up, eat breakfast, go to factory or office (or care for home and kids), come home, do this and that, watch the evening news, engage in their favorite form of relaxation, and go to bed. Throughout the day, our zillion laws and regulations silently condition our lives in innumerable ways but the "burdens" and "stifling constraints" of government are scarcely felt at all. When we think about it, it is difficult to bleed profusely when John or Jane Doe deplore how dreadful life has become because of Big Government and its omnipresent and baneful influence. Heaven knows government needs constant critical examination and improvement but most Americans aren't really suffering that much. (On the other hand, if cursing the government and blaming it for most of our troubles has a therapeutic effect, it is inexpensive therapy.)

One other force may be added to those that tend to counterbalance the pressures for more government. Will Durant, who has made a lifetime study of history, describes that force this way:

> Out of every hundred new ideas, ninety-nine or more will probably be inferior to the traditional responses which they propose to replace....
> So the conservative who resists change is as valuable as the radical who proposes it—perhaps as much more valuable as roots are more vital than grafts.

However, Durant wisely adds:

> It is good that new ideas should be heard, for the sake of the few that can be used; but it is also good that new ideas should be compelled to go through the mill of objection, opposition and contumely; this is the trial heat which innovations must survive before being allowed to enter the human race. It is good that the old should resist the young and that the young should prod the old; out of this tension, as out of the strife of the sexes and the classes, comes a creative tensile strength, a stimulated development, a secret and basic uniting and movement of the whole.[9]

Incrementalism—Thinking Small

In the United States (and in most countries) policy change normally comes about by a process sometimes called *incrementalism*—that is, by small, piecemeal reforms rather than drastic, revolutionary changes. Incrementalists do not envision some ideal state or ideal solution to a vexing problem and promptly launch forth to reach that goal. They restrict their goals to the means at hand, regarding the politically practicable as the foremost consideration to bear in mind. Only alternatives that seem politically feasible receive their attention. These are usually modest ones, which do not fundamentally alter the status quo; rather, their choices are for small improvements that ameliorate rather than cure.

Incrementalists usually doubt that there is any single "right" solution to a problem; every alternative involves gains and losses, making intelligent decisions difficult. They are dubious of the grand schemes for human betterment, believing that history casts doubt on their workability and beneficence. They would agree with Stephen Marcus that "the most important consequences of any [governmental] intervention almost always turn out to be those that were not intended . . . or could not have been calculated beforehand."[10] The consequences of moderate measures are more predictable; if they prove to be more deleterious than planned, corrections can also be more easily made. It is best, then, to seek remedial, short-run approaches to pressing problems.

Raising basic questions of principle that call for reevaluating the foundations of our system or of long-established policies stimulates passionate and highly divisive debates, which diminish the spirit of compromise and accommodation needed if bills are to pass. Utopian debates may be exhilarating and emotionally cathartic, but they are terribly time consuming, unsettling, and noisy, and they usually produce little but exhaustion and long-lasting wounds.

For the incrementalist, then, the watchwords are pragmatism, practicability, realism, compromise, and down-to-earth sensibility. Their approach, they believe, promotes social stability and domestic tranquillity, and it is compatible with our system of limited government and checks and balances.

The incrementalists are also convinced that this is the only way the nation *does* move forward—except in times of crisis. In the wake of a great depression, a runaway inflation, atomic war, the possession of nuclear weapons by terrorists or mad dictators, the arrival of a plague, or some other dire threat, then the nation can set aside its normally cautious stance and follow a bold and pioneering leader. But in other circumstances Congress prefers to build upon, not subvert, our foundations; to extend existing practices, not invent new ones; to improve present institutions, not create new ones. A proposal's prospects are enhanced if precedents can be cited and if its novelty can be discounted. Congress is as fearful of major change as a dog is of thunder. It likes to tinker, to putter, and to graft on, but genuine innovations of substance send it into a panic. Even when minor innovations are approved, they are hedged by safeguards (like detailed statutory restrictions, judicial appeals, and committee oversight), which ensure that nothing too shocking occurs. But this attitude, it should be emphasized, faithfully reflects the will of the people.

Incrementalists would add that Congress acts not only moderately but slowly as well. From the time that a major new legislative proposal first appears in the *New Republic* or the *New York Times*, to when it receives serious attention in intellectual circles, is mentioned in *Time* and *Newsweek* and later by the evening newscasts, is considered by committees in Congress, and ultimately passes through the elaborate congressional gauntlet, years may have passed. The resistances to significant change, in terms of both public conservatism and congressional checkpoints, are such that rapid legislative change rarely occurs. Congress dislikes ratifying major innovations until the interested public has had a chance to get used to the ideas involved, to overcome its initial skepticism, and finally to diminish its opposition or provide persistent support. If impatient people find this exasperating, that is understandable. But a society that readily accepted the latest reasonably plausible proposal for change might be one we would not welcome, either. We love

The Planners— Thinking Big

change, if it is *our* brand, but are appalled at the next person's notion of the kind of change we need. A reasonable degree of legislative caution is not unwise, according to the incrementalists.

Another school of thought finds this outlook depressing, evasive, and intellectually shabby, however. It believes that incrementalism is beautifully adapted to serve the interests of those who profit from the status quo. Incrementalism ducks the hidden premises that underlie the present system—premises that are far more favorable to some groups than to others. Basic questions of justice and power are bypassed by minor adjustments to a system that promotes the interests of well-organized, selfish private groups at the expense of the larger public good. Incrementalism's greatest sin, this school believes, is its tendency to prevent a root-and-branch examination of who has the power, who gets the goods, how they get it, and whether the outcome is really fair. Until the shrouded and often harsh facts about power, its roots, and its fruits are brought to light, the public cannot really know if it approves the system or the major policies that proceed from it. Only a searching and unsparing social analysis of the political and economic realities can enable us to recognize the real issues and consider the sweeping changes needed if social realities are to correspond to our democratic rhetoric and supposed principles.

Marxists belong to this school of critics, as do the democratic socialists (who may or may not consider themselves Marxists). The democratic socialists, who believe in government by consent and are deeply committed to the protection of personal freedoms, believe that a master plan is needed to establish our major economic and political goals and then to integrate public policy toward that end.

Michael Harrington, for example, wrote a book deploring our "accidental century."[11] He believes that our tendency to let the economy evolve haphazardly and then hope that public needs will be met fortuitously is tragically mistaken. We cannot count on the accidents of the marketplace plus Band-Aid legislation to give us the housing, jobs, health care facilities, educational institutions, day-care centers, recreational facilities, pure air and water, and other programs that the nation needs. Instead we get what the consumer's dollar demands—and the dollars of the more affluent classes will not demand what the poorer classes need or what a proper concern for the "quality of life" may require. We may get plenty of yachts, hang gliders, and Givenchy clothes but a shortage of public libraries, national parks, vocational education, and facilities for the aged.[12] Only if we consciously plan to provide for society's real needs are we likely to have those needs fulfilled; that plan must be long range, and it can only be made by government.

The "incrementalists" disagree. They believe no group is wise enough to establish national goals for many years ahead or persuasive enough to mobilize the Congress for consistent support of those goals. The nation is too complex, too many unpredictables appear, public priorities are constantly changing, and long-range plans will be rendered obsolete by the curious twists and

Energy crisis challenges planners

turns of history. Those plans will either become a strait jacket, or they will be outdated before the goals are reached.

The best we can do, say the incrementalists, is to meet problems as they arise, move one step at a time, feel our way forward in a cautious and prudent manner, and adjust our short-range plans as circumstances dictate. It would be nice if we were farsighted enough to make ambitious long-range plans that worked as well as their sponsors wish, but we are not. So, let us fashion our drawing boards in accordance with our limitations. We are also more likely to remain a free people that way; grandiose master plans that are resolutely carried out are appropriate for authoritarian societies only.[13]

For the most part, this book sides with the incrementalists. The author is highly skeptical of the long-range projections of social scientists—and of planners in general. Political realities (crises aside) seem to require moderate measures if the political activist wants to succeed.

But still—is there not a middle way which is wiser than either? A middle way that concedes the fallibility of our vision— even that of our most brilliant minds—but that recognizes that in an age of potential nuclear destruction, of declining natural resources, and of massive chemical pollution, we need to look farther than we are prone to do.

People once believed, with Adam Smith's *The Wealth of Nations*, that if each individual pursued his or her self-interest, the good of all would follow. We have learned better. Is there any greater likelihood that the broader public interest will emerge from the self-serving struggles of private interest groups and from the stunted vision of MCs with eyes fixed on errand running and the next election than from Adam Smith's naive dream?

A legislature-dominated society, it would seem, can never meet the minimal planning needs of this age. This is especially true of the current Congress, which is as atomized and unruly as any in history. Only the president can provide the leadership that can place policy debate on higher ground, turn our eyes beyond the immediate and comfortable present, and bring out the best of which we are capable. Only the president can persuade us to focus attention on our need to look beyond tomorrow and make the long-range plans that reasonable prudence requires. Those plans may turn out to be misconceived; true. But to face foreseeable future perils without applying the best intelligence we can muster is to be unconscionably irresponsible. We may fail but we must try. And try with courage and resolution as well as intelligence. If we do, it will be because we have presidents gifted and courageous enough to lead. Not many of them are.

The Utility and Ethics of Violence

What part has violence played in bringing about social change in this country? At the outset it should be observed that most social reforms in American history have been achieved with little or no violence. The major regulatory acts and our principal measures to promote individual economic security were not the product of violence. Woodrow Wilson's program to achieve the "New Freedom," Franklin Roosevelt's New Deal, Lyndon Johnson's "Great Society" reforms owed little to violence. The belief, sometimes held by radicals, that violence alone brings significant change finds little support from American experience.

If a clear majority wants major reforms, it will usually have no difficulty in getting them without resort to violence. But does violence when committed by a relatively small and determined minority force a complacent or reluctant majority to recognize the legitimacy of the minority's grievance and bring about reforms that would otherwise fail? Again, American history provides more refutation than support for such a claim.[14] The Indian uprisings did not prevent the exploitation and repression of these native Americans, no matter how just their cause would seem. Shays' Rebellion—a debtor protest—helped produce a Constitution that forbade the government interfering with the obligation of contract rather than providing relief for debtors. John Brown's raid and other black uprisings did not ameliorate the lot of the black people in the pre–Civil War period. The Irish riots during the Civil War did not end the hated draft. Nor did labor union violence promote union success. As historian Richard Hofstadter notes, "In the main, the outstandingly violent episodes in industrial conflicts were tragic defeats for labor...."[15]

The black riots in the 1960s are another case in point. Instead of bringing sweeping reforms and massive supporting appropriations, they strengthened the presidential ambitions of segregationist George Wallace, and brought about growing pleas for "law and order," a hardening of resistance to black demands and a growing mood of national and congressional conservatism. Urban violence helped make bigotry respectable again in parts of the nation, delighting the "rednecks," the champions of white supremacy, and those who had said all along that we were "moving too fast" in the area of race.

The student violence (and non-violent protests) in the late 1960s and early 1970s apparently did help bring about some desired reforms—such as more "credit, no credit" courses, fewer compulsory academic requirements, student representation on university governing bodies, and relaxed social regulations. How many of these would have come about, even in the absence of violence, because the permissive atmosphere of the times was propitious for their introduction, is impossible to say, but some of them doubtless would. Furthermore, the tide has turned against these innovations to a large degree. Student violence unquestionably produced something else—a public attitude of growing hostility to higher education and stricter state laws designed to make sure it did not happen again. On the whole the American educational system was not appreciably altered by these violent outbreaks.

Hofstadter observes that violence has seldom served the interests of the Left, "except in that rarest of rare circumstances, the truly revolutionary situation. Under normal circumstances, violence has more characteristically served domineering capitalists or trigger-happy police, peremptory sergeants or fascist hoodlums."[16]

Terrorism has not proved to be a politically successful tactic, either. Walter Laqueur, a foremost student of this phenomenon, says, "On the whole, terrorism has not been effective. Of course, there are exceptions. But even where the terrorists have appeared successful initially, their methods often have proved self-defeating in the end."[17]

What about the ethics of violence? Many political scientists would regard the question as out of their domain. This one dissents, believing that a discussion of this crucial question is entirely appropriate for an introductory textbook.

Besides being unproductive in many instances, violence may be questioned on a moral basis. To many philosophers and historians, the idea that good ends do not justify immoral means is the most important lesson human reason and experience have given us. The insistence that ends should be achieved only by means that respect the rights and dignity of others is regarded as the cornerstone of civilization. It is the heart of the democratic idea. The principal difference between authoritarian communism and liberal democracy lies in their different attitudes toward this principle. Because they believe their system will ultimately produce the greatest abundance and justice for all, communists typically hold that whatever means are successful in hastening the inauguration and development of communism are justified. Specifically, whatever promotes the interests of the Communist party—since the Party promotes the best interests of the people—is by that very fact moral. Democracy, on the other hand, rejects shortcuts that purport to seek noble ends but that deprive minorities (or even majorities) of basic human rights. Progress must come by peaceful persuasion, not by tossing opponents of a particular policy in jail or by denying their right to mobilize opposition to that policy. No democracy adheres undeviatingly to this principle under every circumstance, but violation always provokes protests; sooner or later the protesters are likely to find their claims vindicated.

The use of cruelty and violence gradually corrupts those who engage in it. The individual cannot employ violence without its leaving a subtle but indelible mark upon that person. Above all, the use of violence tends to corrupt the cause it seeks to advance. The original nobility of purpose that may have been present (though such nobility is never as pure as the crusader likes to believe) tends to degenerate as the practitioners of violence get caught up in the spirit of the struggle. Violence begets counterviolence; both heighten the seeming importance of the struggle; the world divides ever more clearly between the deliverers and the damned; and the cause acquires such supreme moral significance that virtually anything seems justified in order to ensure the triumph of righteousness and virtue and the defeat of enemies. At that point, the means can become an end in themselves. History speaks all too eloquently on this theme.

Once the process of rationalizing the use of illegal force is begun, a course is undertaken that knows no limit. If unethical means are not only permissible but also laudable because they alone enable justice to prevail, why should Joseph Stalin not have starved resisting landowners so that agricultural collectivism could bring more abundance for all Russians? Why should Communist China not have used ruthless brainwashing to purge the nation of decadent bourgeois, capitalist, reactionary ideas? Why should Joseph McCarthy not employ lies and half-truths to prevent communists from infiltrating ever more deeply into the government? Why should antiwar protesters have refrained from assassinating Lyndon Johnson to bring the Vietnam War to a halt sooner? Was the president's life worth more than all the Americans and Vietnamese who died because of his stubborn support of that war?

These are not far-fetched questions; they lie at the very heart of the ends–means controversy. Once it is decided that the normal ethical and social restraints must be sacrificed for a larger good, the road leads with inexorable logic to just such questions.

There are other questions, too. Everyone is convinced that his or her cause is just. If it is proper for one group to employ force or violence because its cause is "right," one can hardly blame others, equally convinced of their righteousness, from drawing the same conclusions. Thus, once illegal violence is morally legitimized for one group, the door to violence is opened for all.

The use of violence as an instrument of social change violates the democratic idea of the dignity and worth of each individual and violates the doctrine that no person should be considered a means to another's end. If each person is an end in himself or herself, as Western civilization has long assumed, each person must respect others' rights just as that individual would want his or her rights respected.

Alternatives to Violence

Fortunately for those who feel deeply frustrated and despair that conventional political activity offers no hope that their grievances will receive serious attention, methods short of violence are available for dramatizing their cause and forcing society to pay them heed.[18]

Some examples that might be cited include the sit-in strikes of the 1930s, in which auto workers simply refused to leave their jobs at the end of the workday to protest management's refusal to recognize their union and to bargain collectively with them. These strikes did not involve violence, but they prevented "scab" labor from taking the workers' places, and they compelled management to accede to their requests. (That they were successful, however, was partly due to a measure of public sympathy for them at a time when business prestige was at a low ebb and by public resentment of the violence visited upon the workers.)

Similarly, the famous sit-in demonstrations of the 1960s helped advance the cause of American blacks. By peacefully sitting at counters formerly reserved for whites and refusing to budge until they were served, black youth vividly dramatized their complaints in a manner designed to maximize public sympathy. Their illegal acts were pinpointed to bear on specific grievances and were directed against specific individuals responsible for those grievances—a far cry from random acts of protest violence. The "freedom rides" in the South, by which northern sympathizers demonstrated their solidarity with southern blacks deprived of civil rights, are another example.

Street marches and demonstrations, in which substantial numbers of people carry placards capsulizing their cause, are other ways to draw public attention to the plight of an indignant group. While the authorities can regulate the manner and place in which these are held, they are generally protected by the First Amendment. Their effectiveness depends on many factors, including general public attitudes toward the group involved, the timing of these activities, the behavior of participants, their degree of interference with other activities people wish to engage in, and the frequency with which demonstrations occur. Much also depends on the willingness of television to cover these events and upon the kind of treatment television chooses to give them.

Tax strikes can be used to express the intensity of people's sentiment against a governmental policy that they oppose, such as the Vietnam War. Although the government can withdraw funds from a protester's bank account—plus a penalty for nonpayment—or place a lien on his or her property, it remains a form of protest which protects the individual's conscience while expressing his or her satisfaction in a pointed form. Or people can disobey a law in order to have its constitutionality tested in court, boycott a product produced by an industry that has an offensive policy, or take out a full page ad in a respected newspaper protesting some alleged outrage.

Our System and Its Critics

The American political system has been strenuously attacked by numerous political critics and assailed for its failure to achieve objectives favored by those critics. Usually the criticism focuses on the fact that the system, overlaying a capitalist economy, has not eliminated poverty—despite our national wealth—or that it abets racism or sexism, inadequately protects the interests of minorities, gives the Pentagon and the great corporations far too much power, and responds too slowly or too feebly to the problems it faces.

The substance of these charges is advanced year after year, not only in books that supplement introductory political science texts but in many college classes as well. The criticism comes mainly from the left, but it is not confined to the left. The minority of political scientists who accept the critique as valid either argue for sweeping changes in our politico-economic system or throw up their hands in despair at the hopelessness of such change. In either case they are convinced that our present system, stripped of the comfortable myths that surround and protect it, deplorably fails to meet the criteria of a humane, enlightened, and progressive society.

The author is by no means content with our political system; as previous chapters reveal, he favors numerous reforms in the system. But he believes the more severe critics of our system usually fail to face reality in appraising it. They may be quite accurate in reciting its shortcomings but quite misleading when explaining the cause of our failures.

Are our failures really attributable to "the system" or to something else? To answer this question, let us look at the most serious problems that plague our society.

Who knows how, in a democratic society, to eliminate unemployment while controlling inflation? The best economists in the world are baffled by this dilemma.

Who knows how to *rapidly* eliminate the three-year learning gap between black and white high-school seniors? The best educators in the United States have no answer.

Who knows how to *rapidly* eliminate the income gap between black and white families? Because of fewer skills, less adequate education, and (sometimes) unstable black family backgrounds, the problem admits of no quick answer, whatever the system.

Similarly, who has a *workable* plan for the economic revival of the inner city? And who, in any system that involves government by consent, can persuade suburbanites to permit the poorer classes (black or white) to live amongst them and share their pleasant environment?

Who has a plan to eliminate poverty that will persuade middleclass Americans—in an age of inflation—to make the sacrifices necessary to achieve that end?

Who knows how to effectively curb rocketing health care costs, and to do so in a way that a cautious and skeptical electorate will approve?

Granted that income distribution in the U.S. is appallingly unjust (by many people's standards), how can a people who admire millionaires and want a system that allows them to strike it rich, be persuaded to support the kind of public policy that would reduce the gross inequalities which now exist? George McGovern wanted to tax wealthy inheritances more heavily, but *blue-collar* resistance persuaded him to back away from his proposal.

Who has designed a politically practicable formula for converting the television industry into a more constructive social force, and for reducing the vastly excessive volume of advertising in this country?

The arms race, and our gargantuan military budget, are a species of madness. But how can people be convinced to take risks for peace when they are determined that this country shall remain number one? Any politician recommending major cuts in the arms budget would be slaughtered at the polls.

And who can politically survive while arguing for a slower rate of growth in order to conserve our resources and enable effective antipollution measures to prevail?

It is the author's contention, then, that most of the grave problems in our society are not being solved because we either do not know how to solve them or because the public will not accept their solution. Until those dissatisfied with our system can offer plausible reasons why another system—which is still based on the principle of democratic consent—can solve or greatly ameliorate these problems, their indictments of our system carry little weight. Nothing is easier than to point out inequities and failures in any institution, governmental or nongovernmental, and then to wail about how disgraceful this is. But until reformers of the American political system come to grips with the stubborn facts of specific, down-to-earth problems and explain why another system could handle these problems better, they will fail to command serious attention.

Sweeping moral condemnations and vague prescriptions are always in vogue among certain intellectuals. They are, indeed, a form of pathology endemic in some academic circles—one which grows out of unwillingness to examine specific problems in sufficient detail to appreciate their complexity and the difficulty of their resolution. It is easy to fly high among rarefied abstractions but the going is slow when one's feet are on the ground, amidst the mud, stones, and pot-holes of reality. Many academics need to take the earthbound trip.

This is not a plea for complacency, or an attempt to persuade students that nothing can be done to improve the political landscape. It is a plea for maturity—enough maturity to recognize that progress comes slowly, painfully, and uncertainly. Modest successes are as much as we should hope for.

In this connection nothing is more predictable than that 99 percent of our programs will work out less well than their supporters initially hoped. One of two developments normally occurs in the course of pushing a program through Congress. Either it is so eroded by amendments that its sponsors lose most of their enthusiasm for it by the time the misshapen, bruised, and battered product staggers from the legislative hall; or the euphoric proponents believe a giant step has been taken toward human betterment. Once the program has been put into effect, it is administered by people of average ability (meaning, not very efficiently), confronted by people seeking to either evade or exploit it, and faced with difficulties no one had anticipated. Overpriced and underproductive, it ends up being a small step forward—if that.

Still, this should not diminish the efforts of people of good will to do what they can to improve our country. If great things cannot be accomplished, worthwhile things can. If they can, they deserve our best efforts.

One might add that major change comes hard everywhere—not just in government. Ask those who seek major reforms within their college or university, within their church, within their corporation or labor union, or, for that matter, within themselves. We should hardly be surprised if society is resistant to our proposals for changing it.

British poet and critic Samuel Johnson once wrote, "How little of all that human hearts endure, the part which kings or laws cause or cure." This is an important truth for political scientists and those who study politics to bear in mind. It helps keep government in perspective, to be reminded that for most people, most of the time, public policy has far less impact on their lives than personal fortunes or misfortunes and the personal value system they use to confront life. If there were no television, radio, newpapers, or magazines to tell us what Washington was doing, we would scarcely know the difference between life under one administration and life under another. Our sense of well-being is overwhelmingly dominated not by what a given administration does, but by our health, our experiences on the job, our relations with our spouse, the well-being of our children, our recreations, our friends, the state of our conscience, our religious faith or lack thereof, and our temperament. Government is largely peripheral to our central concerns.

But having absorbed this truth, we just recognize that it is not the whole truth. Were government to cease doing most of the multitudinous things it now does, we would be shocked into awareness of how much the quality of our life owes to government. If there were no police, firefighters, people to safeguard our food and water, repair our streets, work in our courtrooms, provide our social security checks, license our doctors, run our schools, and do innumerable other things, we would soon learn how impoverished and insecure our world would be without government. Government alone makes an orderly and civilized society possible.

In addition, government policy has an enormous effect on the state of our economy, going far to determine whether prosperity or depression befalls us. Governmental policy on civil liberties and civil rights determines whether or not we are free men and women. And government decisions on war and peace have an importance, in the nuclear age, that cannot be overestimated.

Although governmental policy and services sometimes seem peripheral, then, their substance goes farther than we realize to shape the quality of our lives—and even the duration of our lives. Good government deserves our best efforts, and those in power who serve us well should be among the most honored of our people. Good politicians are indispensable to the good society. They should be treasured for making democracy—and a better life—possible.

Notes

1. Some of the most prominent spokesmen for a relatively free market are Milton Friedman, *Capitalism and Freedom* (University of Chicago Press, 1962); Friedrick Hayek, *The Road to Serfdom* (University of Chicago Press, 1944); Robert Nozick, *Anarchy, State and Utopia* (New York; Basic Books, 1974); and William Simon, *A Time for Truth* (New York; McGraw-Hill (Reader's Digest Press), 1978).
2. A provocative view of taxation and inheritances is found in Lester Thurow, "Tax Wealth, Not Income," *New York Times Magazine*, April 11, 1976, pp. 32-33.
3. Robert J. Lampman, "What Does It Do for the Poor?—A New Test for National Policy," *The Public Interest*, Winter 1974, pp. 66-82. I have revised his statistics upward because of inflation.
4. Thomas Sowell, "Are Quotas Good for Blacks?" *Commentary*, June 1978, p. 41. Courtesy of *Commentary*.
5. Ibid., p.42.
6. Ibid., p. 43.
7. James Q. Wilson, "On Pettigrew and Armor: An Afterword," *The Public Interest*, Winter 1973, pp. 132-136; and Wayne Sage, "Update/The Loaded School Bus," *Human Behavior*, March 1978, pp. 18-27. Also see Daniel P. Moynihan, "Social Science and the Courts," *The Public Interest*, Winter 1979, pp. 12-31.
8. Milton Friedman, "A Progress Report," *Newsweek*, April 10, 1978, p. 80.
9. Willard Aviel Durant, *The Lessons of History* (New York: Simon & Schuster, 1968), p. 36.
10. Steven Marcus (with Willard Gaylin, Ira Glasser, and David Rothman), *Doing Good: The Limits of Benevolence* (New York: Pantheon Books, 1978), p. 66.
11. Michael Harrington, *The Accidental Century* (New York: Macmillan, 1965), p. 16.
12. John Kenneth Galbraith made the point memorably in *The Affluent Society* (Boston: Houghton Mifflin, 1958), pp. 251-253.
13. A good discussion of incrementalism is contained in George C. Edwards, III, and Ira Sharkansky, *The Policy Predicament* (San Francisco: Freeman, 1978), pp. 265ff; and in Charles Lindblom, "The Science of Muddling Through," *Public Administration Review*, Spring 1959, pp. 79-88.
14. Richard Hofstadter, "The Future of American Violence," *Harper's*, April 1970, p. 47.
15. Ibid., p. 51.
16. Ibid., p. 47.
17. Walter Laqueur, interviewed by *U.S. News and World Report*, May 22, 1978, p. 35.
18. A good brief discussion of "Change and Violence in American Politics" appears in Raymond E. Wolfinger, Martin Shapiro, and Fred J. Greenstein, *Dynamics of American Politics* (Englewood Cliffs, N.J.: Prentice-Hall, 1976), ch. 16.

PRESIDENTIAL ELECTIONS 1789–1976

Year	Candidates	Party	Popular vote	Electoral vote
1789	**George Washington**			69
	John Adams			34
	Others			35
1792	**George Washington**			132
	John Adams			77
	George Clinton			50
	Others			5
1796	**John Adams**	Federalist		71
	Thomas Jefferson	Democratic-Republican		68
	Thomas Pinckney	Federalist		59
	Aaron Burr	Democratic-Republican		30
	Others			48
1800	**Thomas Jefferson**	Democratic-Republican		73
	Aaron Burr	Democratic-Republican		73
	John Adams	Federalist		65
	Charles C. Pinckney	Federalist		64
1804	**Thomas Jefferson**	Democratic-Republican		162
	Charles C. Pinckney	Federalist		14
1808	**James Madison**	Democratic-Republican		122
	Charles C. Pinckney	Federalist		47
	George Clinton	Independent-Republican		6
1812	**James Madison**	Democratic-Republican		128
	DeWitt Clinton	Federalist		89
1816	**James Monroe**	Democratic-Republican		183
	Rufus King	Federalist		34
1820	**James Monroe**	Democratic-Republican		231
	John Quincy Adams	Independent-Republican		1
1824	**John Quincy Adams**	Democratic-Republican	108,740 (30.5%)	84
	Andrew Jackson	Democratic-Republican	153,544 (43.1%)	99
	Henry Clay	Democratic-Republican	47,136 (13.2%)	37
	William H. Crawford	Democratic-Republican	46,618 (13.1%)	41
1828	**Andrew Jackson**	Democratic	647,231 (56.0%)	178
	John Quincy Adams	National Republican	509,097 (44.0%)	83
1832	**Andrew Jackson**	Democratic	687,502 (55.0%)	219
	Henry Clay	National Republican	530,189 (42.4%)	49
	William Wirt	Anti-Masonic		7
	John Floyd	National Republican	33,108 (2.6%)	11
1836	**Martin Van Buren**	Democratic	761,549 (50.9%)	170
	William H. Harrison	Whig	549,567 (36.7%)	73
	Hugh L. White	Whig	145,396 (9.7%)	26
	Daniel Webster	Whig	41,287 (2.7%)	14
1840	**William H. Harrison** (John Tyler, 1841)	Whig	1,275,017 (53.1%)	234
	Martin Van Buren	Democratic	1,128,702 (46.9%)	60
1844	**James K. Polk**	Democratic	1,337,243 (49.6%)	170
	Henry Clay	Whig	1,299,068 (48.1%)	105
	James G. Birney	Liberty	62,300 (2.3%)	

Year	Candidates	Party	Popular vote	Electoral vote
1848	**Zachary Taylor** (Millard Fillmore, 1850)	Whig	1,360,101 (47.4%)	163
	Lewis Cass	Democratic	1,220,544 (42.5%)	127
	Martin Van Buren	Free Soil	291,263 (10.1%)	
1852	**Franklin Pierce**	Democratic	1,601,474 (50.9%)	254
	Winfield Scott	Whig	1,386,578 (44.1%)	42
1856	**James Buchanan**	Democratic	1,838,169 (45.4%)	174
	John C. Fremont	Republican	1,335,264 (33.0%)	114
	Millard Fillmore	American	874,534 (21.6%)	8
1860	**Abraham Lincoln**	Republican	1,865,593 (39.8%)	180
	Stephen A. Douglas	Democratic	1,382,713 (29.5%)	12
	John C. Breckenridge	Democratic	848,356 (18.1%)	72
	John Bell	Constitutional Union	592,906 (12.6%)	39
1864	**Abraham Lincoln** (Andrew Johnson, 1865)	Republican	2,206,938 (55.0%)	212
	George B. McClellan	Democratic	1,803,787 (45.0%)	21
1868	**Ulysses S. Grant**	Republican	3,013,421 (52.7%)	214
	Horatio Seymour	Democratic	2,706,829 (47.3%)	80
1872	**Ulysses S. Grant**	Republican	3,596,745 (55.6%)	286
	Horace Greeley	Democratic	2,843,446 (43.9%)	66
1876	**Rutherford B. Hayes**	Republican	4,036,572 (48.0%)	185
	Samuel J. Tilden	Democratic	4,284,020 (51.0%)	184
1880	**James A. Garfield** (Chester A. Arthur, 1881)	Republican	4,449,053 (48.3%)	214
	Winfield S. Hancock	Democratic	4,442,035 (48.2%)	155
	James B. Weaver	Greenback-Labor	308,578 (3.4%)	
1884	**Grover Cleveland**	Democratic	4,874,986 (48.5%)	219
	James G. Blaine	Republican	4,851,981 (48.2%)	182
	Benjamin F. Butler	Greenback-Labor	175,370 (1.8%)	
1888	**Benjamin Harrison**	Republican	5,444,337 (47.8%)	233
	Grover Cleveland	Democratic	5,540,050 (48.6%)	168
1892	**Grover Cleveland**	Democratic	5,554,414 (46.0%)	277
	Benjamin Harrison	Republican	5,190,802 (43.0%)	145
	James B. Weaver	People's	1,027,329 (8.5%)	22
1896	**William McKinley**	Republican	7,035,638 (50.8%)	271
	William J. Bryan	Democratic: Populist	6,467,946 (46.7%)	176
1900	**William McKinley** (Theodore Roosevelt, 1901)	Republican	7,219,530 (51.7%)	292
	William J. Bryan	Democratic: Populist	6,356,734 (45.5%)	155
1904	**Theodore Roosevelt**	Republican	7,628,834 (56.4%)	336
	Alton B. Parker	Democratic	5,084,401 (37.6%)	140
	Eugene V. Debs	Socialist	402,460 (3.0%)	
1908	**William H. Taft**	Republican	7,679,006 (51.6%)	321
	William J. Bryan	Democratic	6,409,106 (43.1%)	162
	Eugene V. Debs	Socialist	420,820 (2.8%)	
1912	**Woodrow Wilson**	Democratic	6,286,820 (41.8%)	430
	Theodore Roosevelt	Progressive	4,126,020 (27.4%)	88
	William H. Taft	Republican	3,483,922 (23.2%)	8
	Eugene V. Debs	Socialist	897,011 (6.0%)	
1916	**Woodrow Wilson**	Democratic	9,129,606 (49.3%)	277
	Charles E. Hughes	Republican	8,538,221 (46.1%)	254

Year	Candidates	Party	Popular vote	Electoral vote
1920	**Warren G. Harding** (Calvin Coolidge, 1923)	Republican	16,152,200 (61.0%)	404
	James M. Cox	Democratic	9.147,353 (34.6%)	127
	Eugene V. Debs	Socialist	919,799 (3.5%)	
1924	**Calvin Coolidge**	Republican	15,725,016 (54.1%)	382
	John W. Davis	Democratic	8,385,586 (28.8%)	136
	Robert M. La Follette	Progressive	4,822,856 (16.6%)	13
1928	**Herbert C. Hoover**	Republican	21,392,190 (58.2%)	444
	Alfred E. Smith	Democratic	15,016,443 (40.8%)	87
1932	**Franklin D. Roosevelt**	Democratic	22,809,638 (57.3%)	472
	Herbert C. Hoover	Republican	15,758,901 (39.6%)	59
	Norman Thomas	Socialist	881,951 (2.2%)	
1936	**Franklin D. Roosevelt**	Democratic	27,751,612 (60.7%)	523
	Alfred M. Landon	Republican	16,681,913 (36.4%)	8
	William Lemke	Union	891,858 (1.9%)	
1940	**Franklin D. Roosevelt**	Democratic	27,243,466 (54.7%)	449
	Wendell L. Willkie	Republican	22,304,755 (44.8%)	82
1944	**Franklin D. Roosevelt** (Harry S Truman, 1945)	Democratic	25,602,505 (52.8%)	432
	Thomas E. Dewey	Republican	22,006,278 (44.5%)	99
1948	**Harry S Truman**	Democratic	24,105,812 (49.5%)	303
	Thomas E. Dewey	Republican	21,970,065 (45.1%)	189
	J. Strom Thurmond	States' Rights	1,169,063 (2.4%)	39
	Henry A. Wallace	Progressive	1,157,172 (2.4%)	
1952	**Dwight D. Eisenhower**	Republican	33,936,234 (55.2%)	442
	Adlai E. Stevenson	Democratic	27,314,992 (44.5%)	89
1956	**Dwight D. Eisenhower**	Republican	35,590,472 (57.4%)	457
	Adlai E. Stevenson	Democratic	26,022,752 (42.0%)	73
1960	**John F. Kennedy** (Lyndon B. Johnson, 1963)	Democratic	34,227,096 (49.9%)	303
	Richard M. Nixon	Republican	34,108,546 (49.6%)	219
1964	**Lyndon B. Johnson**	Democratic	43,126,233 (61.1%)	486
	Barry M. Goldwater	Republican	27,174,989 (38.5%)	52
1968	**Richard M. Nixon**	Republican	31,783,783 (43.4%)	301
	Hubert H. Humphrey	Democratic	31,271,839 (42.7%)	191
	George C. Wallace	American Independent	9,899,557 (13.5%)	46
1972	**Richard M. Nixon** (Gerald Ford, 1974)	Republican	46,631,189 (61.3%)	521
	George McGovern	Democratic	28,422,015 (37.3%)	17
1976	**James E. Carter**	Democratic	40,828,587 (50.1%)	297
	Gerald Ford	Republican	39,147,613 (48%)	240
	Eugene McCarthy	Independent	700,000 (0.9%)	

Note: Because only the leading candidates are listed, popular-vote percentages do not always total 100. The elections of 1800 and 1824, in which no candidate received an electoral-vote majority, were decided in the House of Representatives.

CONSTITUTION OF THE UNITED STATES

WE THE PEOPLE of the United States, in Order to form a more perfect Union, establish Justice, insure domestic Tranquility, provide for the common defence, promote the general Welfare, and secure the Blessings of Liberty to ourselves and our Posterity, do ordain and establish this CONSTITUTION for the United States of Anerica.

Article 1

Section 1. All legislative Powers herein granted shall be vested in a Congress of the United States, which shall consist of a Senate and House of Representatives.

Section 2. ¹ The House of Representatives shall be composed of Members chosen every second Year by the People of the several States, and the Electors in each State shall have the Qualifications requisite for Electors of the most numerous Branch of the State Legislature.

² No Person shall be a Representative who shall not have attained to the Age of twenty-five Years, and been seven Years a Citizen of the United States, and who shall not, when elected, be an Inhabitant of that State in which he shall be chosen.

³* [Representatives and direct Taxes shall be apportioned among the several States which may be included within this Union, according to their respective Numbers, which shall be determined by adding to the whole Number of free Persons, including those bound to Service for a Term of Years, and excluding Indians not taxed, three fifths of all other Persons.] The actual Enumeration shall be made within three Years after the first Meeting of the Congress of the United States, and within every subsequent Term of ten Years, in such Manner as they shall by Law direct. The Number of Representatives shall not exceed one for every thirty Thousand, but each State shall have at Least one Representative; and until such enumeration shall be made, the State of New Hampshire shall be entitled to chuse three, Massachusetts eight, Rhode-Island and Providence Plantations one, Connecticut five, New-York six, New Jersey four, Pennsylvania eight, Delaware one, Maryland six, Virginia ten, North Carolina five, South Carolina five, and Georgia three.

⁴ When vacancies happen in the Representation from any State, the Executive Authority thereof shall issue Writs of Election to fill such vacancies.

⁵ The House of Representatives shall chuse their Speaker and other Officers; and shall have the sole Power of Impeachment.

¹ **Section 3.** ** The Senate of the United States shall be composed of two Senators from each State, [chosen by the Legislature] thereof, for six Years; and each Senator shall have one Vote.

² Immediately after they shall be assembled in Consequence of the first Election, they shall be divided as equally as may be into three Classes. The Seats of the Senators of the first Class shall be vacated at the Expiration of the Second Year, of the second Class at the Expiration of the fourth Year, and of the third Class at the Expiration of the sixth Year, so that one third may be chosen every second Year; [and if Vacancies happen by Resignation, or otherwise, during the Recess of the Legislature of any State, the Executive thereof may make temporary Appointments until the next Meeting of the Legislature, which shall then fill such Vacancies].***

³ No Person shall be a Senator who shall not have attained to the Age of thirty Years, and been nine Years a Citizen of the United States, and who shall not, when elected, be an inhabitant of that State for which he shall be chosen.

* The part included in heavy brackets was repealed by section 2 of Amendment XIV.
** The part included in heavy brackets was repealed by section 1 of Amendment XVII.
*** The part included in heavy brackets was changed by clause 2 of Amendment XVII.
NOTE.—The superior number preceding the paragraphs designates the number of the clause.

⁴ The Vice President of the United States shall be President of the Senate, but shall have no Vote, unless they be equally divided.

⁵ The Senate shall chuse their other Officers, and also a President pro tempore, in the

absence of the Vice President, or when he shall exercise the Office of President of the United States.

⁶ The Senate shall have the sole Power to try all Impeachments. When sitting for that Purpose, they shall be on Oath or Affirmation. When the President of the United States is tried, the Chief Justice shall preside: And no Person shall be convicted without the Concurrence of two thirds of the Members present.

⁷ Judgment in Cases of Impeachment shall not extend further than to removal from Office, and disqualification to hold and enjoy any Office of honor, Trust, or Profit under the United States: but the Party convicted shall nevertheless be liable and subject to Indictment, Trial, Judgment, and Punishment, according to Law.

Section 4. ¹ The Times, Places and Manner of holding Elections for Senators and Representatives, shall be prescribed in each State by the Legislature thereof; but the Congress may at any time by Law make or alter such Regulations, except as to the Places of chusing Senators.

² The Congress shall assembly at least once in every Year, and such Meeting shall [be on the first Monday in December, unless they shall by Law appoint a different Day.*

Section 5. ¹ Each House shall be the Judge of the Elections, Returns, and Qualifications of its own Members, and a Majority of each shall constitute a Quorum to do Business; but a smaller Number may adjourn from day to day, and may be authorized to compel the Attendance of absent Members, in such Manner, and under such Penalties as each House may provide.

² Each House may determine the Rules of its Proceedings, punish its Members for disorderly Behavior, and with the Concurrence of two thirds, expel a Member.

³ Each House shall keep a Journal of its Proceedings, and from time to time publish the same, excepting such Parts as may in their Judgment require Secrecy; and the Yeas and Nays of the Members of either House on any question shall, at the Desire of one fifth of those Present, be entered on the Journal.

⁴ Neither House, during the Session of Congress, shall, without the Consent of the other, adjourn for more than three days, nor to any other Place than that in which the two Houses shall be sitting.

Section 6. ¹ The Senators and Representatives shall receive a Compensation for their Services, to be ascertained by Law, and paid out of the Treasury of the United States. They shall in all Cases, except Treason, Felony and Breach of the Peace, be privileged from Arrest during their Attendance at the Session of their respective Houses, and in going to and returning from the same; and for any Speech or Debate in either House, they shall not be questioned in any other Place.

² No Senator or Representative shall, during the Time for which he was elected, be appointed to any civil Office under the Authority of the United States, which shall have been created, or the Emoluments whereof shall have been encreased during such time; and no Person holding any Office under the United States, shall be a Member of either House during his Continuance in Office.

Section 7. ¹ All Bills for raising Revenue shall originate in the House of Representatives; but the Senate may propose or concur with Amendments as on other Bills.

² Every Bill which shall have passed the House of Representatives and the Senate, shall, before it become a Law, be presented to the President of the United States; if he approve he shall sign it, but if not he shall return it, with his Objections to that House in which it shall have originated, who shall enter the Objections at large on their Journal. and proceed to reconsider it. If after such Reconsideration two thirds of that House shall agree to pass the Bill, it shall be sent, together with the Objections, to the other House, by which it shall likewise be reconsidered, and if approved by two thirds of that House, it shall become a Law. But in all such Cases the Votes of both Houses shall be determined by Yeas and Nays, and the Names of the Persons voting for and against the Bill shall be entered on the Journal of each House respectively. If any Bill shall not be returned by the President within ten Days (Sundays excepted) after it shall have been presented to him, the Same shall be a Law, in like Manner as

if he had signed it, unless the Congress by their Adjournment prevent its Return, in which Case it shall not be a Law.

* The part included in heavy brackets was changed by section 2 of Amendment XX.

[3] Every Order, Resolution, or Vote to which the Concurrence of the Senate and House of Representatives may be necessary (except on a question of Adjournment) shall be presented to the President of the United States; and before the Same shall take Effect, shall be approved by him, or being disapproved by him, shall be repassed by two thirds of the Senate and House of Representatives, according to the Rules and Limitations prescribed in the Case of a Bill.

Section 8. The Congress shall have Power To lay and collect Taxes, Duties, Imposts and Excises, to pay the Debts and provide for the common Defence and general Welfare of the United States; but all Duties, Imposts and Excises shall be uniform throughout the United States;

[2] To borrow money on the credit of the United States;

[3] To regulate Commerce with foreign Nations, and among the several States, and with the Indian Tribes;

[4] To establish an uniform Rule of Naturalization, and uniform Laws on the subject of Bankruptices throughout the United States;

[5] To coin Money, regulate the Value thereof, and of foreign Coin, and fix the Standard of Weights and Measures;

[6] To provide for the Punishment of counterfeiting the Securities and current Coin of the United States;

[7] To Establish Post Offices and post Roads;

[8] To promote the Progress of Science and useful Arts, by securing for limited Times to Authors and Inventors the exclusive Right to their respective Writings and Discoveries;

[9] To constitute Tribunals inferior to the supreme Court;

[10] To define and punish Piracies and Felonies committed on the high Seas, and Offenses against the Law of Nations;

[11] To declare War, grant Letters of Marque and Reprisal, and make Rules concerning Captures on Land and Water;

[12] To raise and support Armies, but no Appropriation of Money to that Use shall be for a longer Term than two years;

[13] To provide and maintain a Navy;

[14] To make Rules for the Government and Regulation of the land and naval Forces;

[15] To provide for calling forth the Militia to execute the Laws of the Union, suppress insurrections and repel Invasions;

[16] To provide for organizing, arming, and disciplining the Militia, and for governing such Part of them as may be employed in the Service of the United States, reserving to the States respectively, the Appointment of the Officers, and the Authority of training the Militia according to the discipline prescribed by Congress;

[17] To exercise exclusive Legislation in all Cases whatsoever, over such District (not exceeding ten Miles square) as may, by Cession of particular States, and the acceptance of Congress, become the Seat of the Government of the United States, and to exercise like Authority over all Places purchased by the Consent of the Legislature of the State in which the Same shall be, for the Erection of Forts, Magazines, Arsenals, dock-Yards, and other needful Buildings;—And

[18] To make all Laws which shall be necessary and proper for carrying into Execution the foregoing Powers, and all other Powers vested by this Constitution in the Government of the United States, or in any Department or Officer thereof.

Section 9. [1] The Migration or Importation of Such Persons as any of the States now existing shall think proper to admit, shall not be prohibited by the Congress prior to the Year one thousand eight hundred and eight, but a tax or duty may be imposed on such Importation, not exceeding ten dollars for each Person.

[2] The privilege of the Writ of Habeas Corpus shall not be suspended, unless when in Cases of Rebellion or Invasion the public Safety may require it.

³ No Bill of Attainder or ex post facto Law shall be passed.

⁴ *No capitation, or other direct, Tax shall be laid, unless in Proportion to the Census or Enumeration herein before directed to be taken.

⁵ No Tax or Duty shall be laid on Articles exported from any State.

⁶ No preference shall be given by any Regulation of Commerce or Revenue to the Ports of one State over those of another: nor shall Vessels bound to, or from, one State be obliged to enter, clear, or pay Duties in another.

⁷ No money shall be drawn from the Treasury, but in Consequence of Appropriations made by Law; and a regular Statement and Account of the Receipts and Expenditures of all public Money shall be published from time to time.

* See also Amendment XVI.

⁸ No title of Nobility shall be granted by the United States: And no Person holding any Office of Profit or Trust under them, shall, without the Consent of the Congress, accept of any present, Emolument, Office, or Title, of any kind whatever, from any King, Prince, or foreign State.

Section 10. ¹ No State shall enter into any Treaty, Alliance, or Confederation; grant Letters of Marque and Reprisal; coin Money; emit Bills of Credit; make any Thing but gold and silver Coin a Tender in Payment of Debts; pass any Bill of Attainder, ex post facto Law, or Law impairing the Obligation of Contracts, or grant any Title of Nobility.

² No State shall, without the Consent of the Congress, lay any Imposts or Duties on Imports or Exports, except what may be absolutely necessary for executing its inspection Laws; and the net Produce of all Duties and Imposts, laid by any State on Imports or Exports, shall be for the Use of the Treasury of the United States; and all such Laws shall be subject to the Revision and Control of the Congress.

³ No State shall, without the Consent of Congress, lay any duty on Tonnage, keep Troops, or Ships of War in time of Peace, enter into any Agreement or Compact with another State, or wlth a foreign Power, or engage in War, unless actually invaded, or in such imminent Danger as will not admit of delay.

Article II

Section 1. ¹ The executive Power shall be vested in a President of the United States of America. He shall hold his Office during the Term of four Years, and together with the Vice President, chosen for the same Term, be elected, as follows:

² Each State shall appoint, in such Manner as the Legislature thereof may direct, a Number of Electors, equal to the whole Number of Senators and Representatives to which the State may be entitled in the Congress: but no Senator or Representative, or Person holding an Office of Trust or Profit under the United States, shall be appointed an Elector.

* [The Electors shall meet in their respective States, and vote by Ballot for two persons of whom one at least shall not be an Inhabitant of the same State with themselves. And they shall make a list of all the Persons voted for, and of the Number of Votes for each; which List they shall sign and certify, and transmit sealed to the Seat of the Government of the United States, directed to the President of the Senate. The President of the Senate shall, in the Presence of the Senate and House of Representatives, open all the Certificates, and the Votes shall then be counted. The Person having the greatest Number of votes shall be the President, if such Number by a Majority of the whole Number of Electors appointed; and if there be more than one who have such Majority, and have an equal Number of Votes, then the House of Representatives shall immediately chuse by Ballot one of them for President; and if no Person have a Majority, then from the five highest on the List the said House shall in like Manner chuse the President. But in chusing the President, the Votes shall be taken by States, the Representation from each State having one Vote; A quorum for this Purpose shall consist of a Member or Members from two thirds of the States, and a Majority of all the States shall be necessary to a Choice. In every Case, after the Choice of the President the Person having the greatest Number of Votes of the Electors shall be the Vice President. But if there should remain two or more who have equal Votes, the Senate shall chuse from them by Ballot the Vice-President.]

³ The Congress may determine the Time of chusing the Electors and the Day on which they shall give their Votes; which Day shall be the same throughout the United States.

⁴ No person except a natural born Citizen, or a Citizen of the United States, at the time of the Adoption of this Constitution, shall be eligible to the Office of President; neither shall any Person be eligible to that Office who shall not have attained to the Age of thirty-five Years, and been fourteen Years a Resident within the United States.

⁵ In case of the removal of the President from Office, or of his Death, Resignation or Inability to discharge the Powers and Duties of the said Office, the same shall devolve on the Vice President, and the Congress may by Law provide for the Case of Removal, Death, Resignation or Inability, both of the President, and Vice President, declaring what Officer shall then act as President, and such Officer shall act accordingly, until the Disability be removed, or a President shall be elected.

* This paragraph has been superseded by Amendment XII.

⁶ The President shall, at stated Times, receive for his Services, a Compensation, which shall neither be encreased nor diminished during the Period for which he shall have been elected, and he shall not receive within that Period any other Emolument from the United States, or any of them.

⁷ Before he enter on the Execution of his Office, he shall take the following Oath or Affirmation:—"I do solemnly swear (or affirm) that I will faithfully execute the Office of President of the United States, and will to the best of my Ability, preserve, protect and defend the Constitution of the United States."

Section 2. ¹ The President shall be Commander in Chief of the Army and Navy of the United States, and the Militia of the several States, when called into the actual Service of the United States; he may require the Opinion, in writing, of the principal Officer in each of the executive Departments, upon any subject relating to the Duties of their respective Offices, and he shall have Power to grant Reprieves and Pardons for Offences against the United States, except in Cases of Impeachment.

²He shall have Power, by and with the Advice and Consent of the Senate, to make Treaties, provided two thirds of the Senators present concur; and he shall nominate, and by and with the Advice and Consent of the Senate, shall appoint Ambassadors, other public Ministers and Consuls, Judges of the supreme Court, and all other Officers of the United States, whose Appointments are not herein otherwise provided for, and which shall be established by Law; but the Congress may by Law vest the Appointment of such inferior Officers, as they think proper, in the President alone, in the Courts of Law, or in the Heads of Departments.

³ The President shall have Power to fill up all Vacancies that may happen during the Recess of the Senate, by granting Commissions which shall expire at the End of their next Session.

Section 3. He shall from time to time give to the Congress Information of the State of the Union, and recommend to their Consideration such Measures as he shall judge necessary and expedient; he may, on extraordinary Occasions, convene both Houses, or either of them, and in Case of Disagreement between them, with Respect to the Time of Adjournment, he may adjourn them to such Time as he shall think proper; he shall receive Ambassadors and other public Ministers; he shall take Care that the Laws be faithfully executed, and shall Commission all the Officers of the United States.

Section 4. The President, Vice President and all civil Officers of the United States, shall be removed from Office on Impeachment for, and Conviction of, Treason, Bribery, or other high Crimes and Misdemeanors.

Article III

Section 1. The judicial Power of the United States, shall be vested in one supreme Court, and in such inferior Courts as the Congress may from time to time ordain and establish. The Judges, both of the supreme and inferior Courts, shall hold their Offices during good Behavior, and shall, at stated Times, receive for their Services a Compensation which shall not be diminished during their Continuance in Office.

Section 2. ¹ The judicial Power shall extend to all Cases, in Law and Equity, arising under this Constitution, the Laws of the United States, and Treaties made, or which shall be made, under their Authority;—to all Cases affecting Ambassadors, other public Ministers and Consuls;—to all Cases of admiralty and maritime Jurisdiction;—to Controversies to which the United States shall be a Party;—to Controversies between two or more States;—between a State and Citizens of another State;*—between Citizens of different States;—between Citizens of the same State claiming Lands under Grants of different States, and between a State, or the Citizens thereof, and foreign States, Citizens or Subjects.

² In all Cases affecting Ambassadors, other public Ministers and Consuls, and those in which a State shall be Party, the supreme Court shall have original Jurisdiction. In all the other Cases before mentioned, the supreme Court shall have appellate Jurisdiction, both as to Law and Fact, with such Exceptions, and under such Regulations as the Congress shall make.

³ The trial of all Crimes except in Cases of Impeachment shall be by Jury; and such Trial shall be held in the State where the said Crimes shall have been committed; but when not committed within any State, the Trial shall be at such Place or Places as the Congress may by Law have directed.

Section 3. ¹ Treason against the United States shall consist only in levying War against them, or, in adhering to their Enemies, giving them Aid and Comfort.

*This clause has been affected by Amendment XI.

No Person shall be convicted of Treason unless on the Testimony of two Witnesses to the same overt Act, or on Confession in open Court.

² The Congress shall have power to declare the Punishment of Treason, but no Attainder of Treason shall work Corruption of Blood, or Forfeiture except during the Life of the Person attainted.

Article IV

Section 1. Full Faith and Credit shall be given in each State to the public Acts, Records, and judicial Proceedings of every other State. And the Congress may by general Laws prescribe the Manner in which such Acts, Records and Proceedings shall be proved, and the Effect thereof.

Section 2. ¹ The Citizens of each State shall be emtitled to all Privileges and Immunities of Citizens in the several States.

² A Person charged in any State with Treason, Felong, or other Crime, who shall flee from Justice, and be found in another State, shall on demand of the executive Authority of the State from which he fled, be delivered up, to be removed to the State having Jurisdiction of the Crime.

³ * [No person held to Service or Labour in one State, under the Laws thereof, escaping into another, shall, in Consequence of any Law or Regulation therein, be discharged from such Service or Labour, but shall be delivered up on Claim of the Party to whom such Service or Labour may be due.]

Section 3. ¹ New States may be admitted by the Congress into this Union; but no new State shall be formed or erected within the Jurisdiction of any other State; not any State be formed by the Junction of two or more States, or parts of States, without the Consent of the Legislatures of the States concerned as well as of the Congress.

² The Congress shall have Power to dispose of and make all needful Rules and Regulations respecting the Territory or other Property belonging to the United States; and nothing in this Constitution shall be so construed as to Prejudice any Claims of the United States, or of any particular State.

Section 4. The United States shall guarantee to every State in this Union a Republican Form of Government, and shall protect each of them against Invasion; and on Application of the Legislature, or of the Executive (when the Legislature cannot be convened) against domestic Violence.

Article V

The Congress, whenever two thirds of both Houses shall deem it necessary, shall propose Amendments to this Constitution, or, on the Application of the Legislatures of two thirds of the several States, shall call a Convention for proposing Amendments, which, in either Case, shall be valid to all Intents and Purposes, as part of this Constitution when ratified by the Legislatures of three fourths of the several States, or by Conventions in three fourths thereof, as the one or the other Mode of Ratification may be proposed by the Congress; Provided that no Amendment which may be made prior to the Year One thousand eight hundred and eight shall in any Manner affect the first and fourth Clauses in the Ninth Section of the first Article; and that no State, without its Consent, shall be deprived of its equal Suffrage in the Senate.

Article VI

[1] All Debts contracted and Engagements entered into, before the Adoption of this Constitution shall be as valid against the United States under this Constitution, as under the Confederation.

[2] This Constitution, and the Laws of the United States which shall be made in Pursuance thereof; and all Treaties made, or which shall be made, under the Authority of the United States, shall be the supreme Law of the Land; and the Judges in every State shall be bound thereby, any Thing in the Constitution or Laws of any State to the Contrary notwithstanding.

[3] The Senators and Representatives before mentioned, and the Members of the several State Legislatures, and all executive and judicial Officers, both of the United States and of the several States, shall be bound by Oath or Affirmation, to support this Constitution; but no religious Test shall ever be required as a Qualification to any Office or public Trust under the United States.

Article VII

The Ratification of the Conventions of nine States, shall be sufficient for the Establishment of this Constitution between the States so ratifying the Same.

DONE in Convention by the Unanimous Consent of the States present by Seventeenth Day of September in the Year of our Lord one thousand seven hundred and Eighty seven and of the Independence of the United States of America the Twelfth. IN WITNESS whereof We have hereto subscribed our Names,

GO WASHINGTON—
Presidt. and deputy from Virginia.

[Signed also by the deputies of twelve States.]

New Hampshire.
JOHN LANGDON, NICHOLAS GILMAN.

Massachusetts.
NATHANIEL GORHAM, RUFUS KING.

Connecticut.
WM. SAML. JOHNSON, ROGER SHERMAN.

New York.
ALEXANDER HAMILTON.

New Jersey.
WIL: LIVINGSTON, WM. PATERSON,
DAVID BREARLEY, JONA: DAYTON.

Pennsylvania.
B. FRANKLIN, THOMAS MIFFLIN,
ROBT MORRIS, GEO. CLYMER,
THOS. FITZSIMONS, JARED INGERSOLL,
JAMES WILSON, GOUV MORRIS.

Delaware.
GEO: READ, GUNNING BEDFORD, jun,
JOHN DICKINSON, RICHARD BASSETT.
JACO: BROOM,

Maryland.
JAMES McHENRY, DAN OF ST THOS. JENIFER,
DANL CARROLL.

JOHN BLAIR—

WM. BLOUNT,
HU WILLIAMSON.

J. RUTLEDGE,
CHARLES PINCKNEY,

WILLIAM FEW,
    Attest:

Virginia.
    JAMES MADISON Jr.
North Carolina.
    RICH'D DOBBS SPAIGHT,

South Carolina.
    CHARLES COTESWORTH PINCKNEY,
    PIERCE BUTLER.
Georgia.
    ABR BALDWIN.
    WILLIAM JACKSON, *Secretary.*

RATIFICATION OF THE CONSTITUTION

The Constitution was adopted by a convention of the States on September 17, 1787, and was subsequently ratified by the several States, on the following dates: Delaware, December 7, 1787; Pennsylvania, December 12, 1787; New Jersey, December 18, 1787; Georgia, January 2, 1788; Connecticut, January 9, 1788; Massachusetts, February 6, 1788; Maryland, April 28, 1788; South Carolina, May 23, 1788; New Hampshire, June 21, 1788; Virginia, June 25, 1788; New York, July 26, 1788; North Carolina, November 21, 1789; Rhode Island, May 29, 1790. It was declared in operation September 13, 1788; by a resolution of the Continental Congress.

ARTICLES IN ADDITION TO, AND AMENDMENT OF, THE CONSTITUTION OF THE UNITED STATES OF AMERICA, PROPOSED BY CONGRESS, AND RATIFIED BY THE LEGISLATURES OF THE SEVERAL STATES, PURSUANT TO THE FIFTH ARTICLE OF THE ORIGINAL CONSTITUTION

Amendment I

Congress shall make no law respecting an establishment of religion, or prohibiting the free exercise thereof; or abridging the freedom of speech, or of the press; or the right of the people peaceably to assemble and to petition the Government for a redress of grievances.

Amendment II

A well regulated Militia, being necessary to the security of a free State, the right of the people to keep and bear Arms, shall not be infringed.

Amendment III

No Soldier shall, in time of peace be quartered in any house, without the consent of the Owner, nor in time of war, but in a manner to be prescribed by law.

Amendment IV

The right of the people to be secure in their persons, houses, papers, and effects, against unreasonable searches and seizures, shall not be violated, and no Warrants shall issue, but upon probable cause, supported by Oath or affirmation and particularly describing the place to be searched, and the persons or things to be seized.

Amendment V

No person shall be held to answer for a capital, or otherwise infamous crime, unless on a presentment or indictment of a Grand Jury, except in cases arising in the land or naval forces, or in the Militia, when in actual service in time of War or public danger; nor shall any person be subject for the same offence to be twice put in jeopardy of life or limb; nor shall be compelled in any criminal case to be a witness against himself, nor be deprived of life, liberty, or property, without due process of law; nor shall private property be taken for public use, without just compensation.

Amendment VI   In all criminal prosecutions, the accused shall enjoy the right to a speedy and public trial, by an impartial jury of the State and district wherein the crime shall have been committed, which district shall have been previously ascertained by law, and to be informed of the nature and cause of the accusation: to be confronted with the witness against him; to have compulsory process for obtaining witnesses in his favor, and to have the Assistance of Counsel for his defence.

Amendment VII   In suits at common law, where the value in controversy shall exceed twenty dollars, the right of trial by jury shall be preserved, and no fact tried by jury, shall be otherwise reexamined in any Court of the United States, than according to the rules of the common law.

Amendment VIII   Excessive bail shall not be required, nor excessive fines imposed, nor cruel and unusual punishments inflicted.

Amendment IX   The enumeration in the Constitution, of certain rights, shall not be construed to deny or disparage others retained by the people.

Amendment X   The powers not delegated to the United States by the Constitution, nor prohibited by it to the States, are reserved to the States respectively, or to the people.
(Ratification of first ten amendments completed December 15, 1791.)

Amendment XI   The Judicial power of the United States shall not be construed to extend to any suit in law or equity, commenced or prosecuted against one of the United States by Citizens of another State, or by Citizens or Subjects of any Foreign State.
(Declared ratified January 8, 1798.)

Amendment XII   The electors shall meet in their respective states and vote by ballot for President and Vice-President, one of whom, at least, shall not be an inhabitant of the same state with themselves; they shall name in their ballots the person voted for as President, and in distinct ballots the person voted for as Vice-President, and they shall make distinct lists of all persons voted for as President, and of all persons voted for as Vice-President, and of the number of votes for each, which lists they shall sign and certify, and transmit sealed to the seat of the government of the United States, directed to the President of the Senate;—The President of the Senate shall, in presence of the Senate and House of Representatives, open all the certificates and the votes shall then be counted;—The person having the greatest number of votes for President, shall be the President, if such number be a majority of the whole number of Electors appointed; and if no person have such majority, then from the persons having the highest numbers not exceeding three on the list of those voted for as President, the House of Representatives shall choose immediately, by ballot, the President. But in choosing the President, the votes shall be taken by states, the representation from each state having one vote; a quorum for this purpose shall consist of a member or members from two thirds of the states, and a majority of all the states shall be necessary to a choice. * [And if the House of Representatives shall not choose a President whenever the right of choice shall devolve upon them, before the fourth day of March next following, then the Vice-President shall act as President, as in the case of the death or other constitutional disability of the President.]—The person having the greatest number of votes as Vice-President, shall be the Vice-President, if such number be a majority of the whole number of Electors appointed, and if no person have a majority, then from the two highest numbers on the list, the Senate shall choose the Vice-President; a quorum for the purpose shall consist of two thirds of the whole number of Senators, and a majority of the whole number shall be necessary to a choice. But no person constitutionally ineligible to the office of President shall be eligible to that of Vice-President of the United States.
(Declared ratified September 25, 1804.)

Amendment XIII

Section 1. Neither slavery nor involuntary servitude, except as a punishment for crime whereof the party shall have been duly convicted, shall exist within the United States, or any place subject to their jurisdiction.

Section 2. Congress shall have power to enforce this article by appropriate legislation
(Declared ratified December 18, 1865.)

Amendment XIV

Section 1. All persons born or naturalized in the United States, and subject to the jurisdiction thereof, are citizens of the United States and of the State wherein they reside. No State shall make or enforce any law which shall abridge the privileges or immunities of citizens of the United States; nor shall any State deprive any person of life, liberty, or property, without due process of law; nor deny to any person within its jurisdiction the equal protection of the laws.

Section 2. Representatives shall be apportioned among the several States according to their respective numbers, counting the whole number of persons in each State, excluding Indians not taxed. But when the right to vote an any election for the choice of electors for President and Vice-President of the United States, Representatives in Congress, the Executive and Judicial officers of a State, or the members of the Legislature thereof, is denied to any of the male inhabitants of such State, being twenty-one years of age, and citizens of the United States, or in any way abridged, except for participation in rebellion, or other crime, the basis of representation therein shall be reduced in the proportion which the number of such male citizens shall bear to the whole number of male citizens twenty-one years of age in such State.

Section 3. No person shall be a Senator or Representative in Congress, or elector of President and Vice-President, or hold any office, civil or military, under the United States, or under any State, who, having previously taken an oath, as a member of Congress, or as an officer of the United States, or as a member of any State legislature, or as an executive or judicial officer of any State, to support the Constitution of the United States, shall have engaged in insurrection or rebellion against the same, or given aid or comfort to the enemies thereof. But Congress may by a vote of two thirds of each House, remove such disability.

Section 4. The validity of the public debt of the United States, authorized by law, including debts incurred for payment of pensions and bounties for services in suppressing insurrection or rebellion, shall not be questioned. But neither the United States nor any State shall assume or pay any debt or obligation incurred in aid of insurrection or rebellion against the United States, or any claim for the loss or emancipation of any slave; but all such debts, obligations and claims shall be held illegal and void.

Section 5. The Congress shall have power to enforce, by appropriate legislation, the provisions of this article.
(Declared ratified July 28, 1868.)

Amendment XV

Section 1. The right of citizens of the United States to vote shall not be denied or abridged by the United States or by any State on account of race, color, or previous condition of servitude.

Section 2. The Congress shall have power to enforce this article by appropriate legislation.
(Declared ratified March 30, 1870.)

Amendment XVI

The Congress shall have power to lay and collect taxes on incomes, from whatever source derived, without apportionment among the several States, and without regard to any census or enumeration.
(Declared ratified February 25, 1913.)

Amendment XVII

The Senate of the United States shall be composed of two Senators from each State, elected by the people thereof, for six years; and each Senator shall have one vote. The electors in each State shall have the qualifications requisite for electors of the most numerous branch of the State legislatures.

When vacancies happen in the representation of any State in the Senate, the executive authority of such State shall issue writs of election to fill such vacancies: *Provided,* That the legislature of any State may empower the executive thereof to make temporary appointments until the people fill the vacancies by election as the legislature may direct.

This amendment shall not be so construed as to affect the election or term of any Senator chosen before it becomes vaild as part of the Constitution.

(Declared ratified May 31, 1913.)

Amendment XVIII

[*Section 1.* After one year from the ratification of this article the manufacture, sale, or transportation of intoxicating liquors within, the importation thereof into, or the exportation thereof from the United States and all territory subject to the jurisdiction thereof for beverage purposes is hereby prohibited.

[*Section 2.* The Congress and the several States shall have concurrent power to enforce this article by appropriate legislation.

[*Section 3.* This article shall be inoperative unless it shall have been ratified as an amendment to the Constitution by the legislatures of the several States, as provided in the Constitution, within seven years from the date of the submission hereof to the States by the Congress.]*

(Declared ratified January 29, 1919.)

*Amendment XVIII was repealed by section 1 of Amendment XXI.

Amendment XIX

The right of citizens of the United States to vote shall not be denied or abridged by the United States or by any State on account of sex.

Congress shall have power to enforce this article by appropriate legislation.

(Declared ratified August 26, 1920.)

Amendment XX

Section 1. The terms of the President and Vice-President shall end at noon on the 20th day of January, and the terms of Senators and Representatives at noon on the 3d day of January, of the years in which such terms would have ended if this article had not been ratified; and the terms of their successors shall then begin.

Section 2. The Congress shall assemble at least once in every year, and such meeting shall begin at noon on the 3d day of January, unless they shall by law appoint a different day.

Section 3. If, at the time for the beginning of the term of the President, the President elect shall have died, the Vice-President elect shall become President. If a President shall not have been chosen before the time fixed for the beginning of his term, or if the President elect shall have failed to qualify, then the Vice-President elect shall act as President until a President shall have qualified; and the Congress may by law provide for the case wherein neither a President elect nor a Vice-President elect shall have qualified, declaring who shall then act as President, or the manner in which one who is to act shall be selected, and such person shall act accordingly until a President or Vice-President shall have qualified.

Section 4. The Congress may by law provide for the case of the death of any of the persons from whom the House of Representatives may choose a President whenever the right of choice shall have devolved upon them and for the case of the death of any of the persons from whom the Senate may choose a Vice-President whenever the right of choice shall have devolved upon them.

Section 5. Sections 1 and 2 shall take effect on the 15th day of October following the ratification of this article.

Section 6. This article shall be inoperative unless it shall have been ratified as an amendment to the Constitution by the legislatures of three-fourths of the several States within seven years from the date of its submission.

(Declared ratified February 6, 1933.)

Amendment XXI

Section 1. The eighteenth article of amendment to the Constitution of the United States is hereby repealed.

Section 2. The transportation or importation into any State, Territory, or possession of the United States for delivery or use therein of intoxicating liquors, in violation of the laws thereof, is hereby prohibited.

Section 3. This article shall be inoperative unless it shall have been ratified as an amendment to the Constitution by conventions in the several States, as provided in the Constitution, within seven years from the date of the submission hereof to the States by the Congress.

(Declared ratified December 5, 1933.)

Amendment XXII

Section 1. No person shall be elected to the office of the President more than twice, and no person who has held the office of President, or acted as President, for more than two years of a term to which some other person was elected President shall be elected to the office of the President more than once. But this article shall not apply to any person holding the office of President when this Article was proposed by the Congress, and shall not prevent any person who may be holding the office of President, or acting as President, during the term within which this Article becomes operative from holding the office of President or acting as President during the remainder of such term.

Section 2. This article shall be inoperative unless it shall have been ratified as an amendment to the Constitution by the legislatures of three-fourths of the several States within seven years from the date of its submission to the States by the Congress.

(Declared ratified March 1, 1951.)

Amendment XXIII

Section 1. The District constituting the seat of Government of the United States shall appoint in such manner as the Congress may direct:

A number of electors of President and Vice President equal to the whole number of Senators and Representatives in Congress to which the District would be entitled if it were a State, but in no event more than the least populous State; they shall be in addition to those appointed by the States, but they shall be considered, for the purposes of the election of President and Vice President, to be electors appointed by a State; and they shall meet in the District and perform such duties as provided by the twelfth article of amendment.

Section 2. The Congress shall have power to enforce this article by appropriate legislation.

(Declared ratified April 3, 1961.)

Amendment XXIV

Section 1. The right of citizens of the United States to vote in any primary or other election for President or Vice President, for electors for President or Vice President, or for Senator or Representative in Congress, shall not be denied or abridged by the United States or any State by reason of failure to pay any poll tax or other tax.

Section 2. The Congress shall have power to enforce this article by appropriate legislation.

(Declared ratified February 4, 1962.)

Amendment XXV

Section 1. In case of the removal of the President from office or of his death or resignation, the Vice President shall become President. .

Section 2. Whenever there is a vacancy in the office of the Vice President, the President shall nominate a Vice President who shall take office upon confirmation by a majority vote of both Houses of Congress.

Section 3. Whenever the President transmits to the President pro tempore of the Senate and the Speaker of the House of Representatives his written declaration that he is unable to discharge the powers and duties of his office, and until he transmits to them a written declaration to the contrary, such powers and duties shall be discharged by the Vice President as Acting President.

Section 4. Whenever the Vice President and a majority of either the principal officers of the executive departments or of such other body as Congress may by law provide, transmit to the President pro tempore of the Senate and the Speaker of the House of Representatives their written declaration that the President is unable to discharge the powers and duties of his office, the Vice President shall immediately assume the powers and the duties of the office as Acting President.

Thereafter, when the President transmits to the President pro tempore of the Senate and Speaker of the House of Representatives his written declaration that no inability exists, he shall resume the powers and duties of his office unless the Vice President and a majority of either the principal officers of the executive department or of such other body as Congress may by law provide, transmit within four days to the President pro tempore of the Senate and the Speaker of the House of Representatives their written declaration that the President is unable to discharge the powers and duties of his office. Thereupon Congress shall decide the issue, assembling within forty-eight hours for that purpose if not in session. If the Congress, within twenty-one days after receipt of the latter written declaration, or, if Congress is not in session, within twenty-one days after Congress is required to assemble, determines by two-thirds vote of both Houses that the President is unable to discharge the powers and duties of his office, the Vice President shall continue to discharge the same as Acting President; otherwise, the President shall resume the powers and duties of his office.

(Declared ratified February 10, 1967)

Amendment XXVI

Section 1. The right of citizens of the United States, who are eighteen years of age or older, to vote shall not be denied or abridged by the United States or by any State on account of age.

Section 2. The Congress shall have power to enforce this article by appropriate legislation.

(Declared ratified July 1, 1971)

Proposed Amendment

Section 1. Equality of rights under the law shall not be denied or abridged by the United States or by any State on account of sex.

Section 2. The Congress shall have the power to enforce, by appropriate legislation, the provisions of this Article.

(Passed Congress March 24, 1972)

GLOSSARY

Affirmative action A policy by which a governmental unit or private group ceases to discriminate against racial, religious, ethnic, or sexual groups and/or actively recruits members of those groups.

Amicus curiae A group not directly involved in a case which submits a brief to the court defending or opposing one of the parties to a suit.

Bill of Rights The first Ten Amendments to the Constitution, specifying most of the basic rights to which a U.S. citizen is entitled.

Caucus A caucus may refer to a meeting of party leaders to nominate party candidates or it may refer to a meeting of members of the legislature of the same party at which party leaders or committee chairs are chosen or at which party policy is formulated.

Civil liberties Constitutional rights of free speech, press, religion, and assembly.

Civil rights The right to be free from arbitrary or discriminatory treatment where public policy is concerned. Historically, the term has had special relevance to black citizens but it is not confined to them.

Closed primary A primary election in which only party members, usually determined by advance registration, may vote for the candidates of that party.

Cloture A petition signed by 60 members of the U.S. Senate calling for the termination of a filibuster.

Coalition A political group composed of diverse political elements which temporarily unite to support a given administration or policy.

Commerce clause "Congress shall have power...to regulate commerce with foreign nations and among the several states...." (Article 1, Sec. 8 of the Constitution).

Direct primary A process enabling members of a political party to directly choose the persons to represent that party for various offices in the general election. (This is contrasted with nomination by party officers or delegates.)

Fair Deal The name given to President Harry S. Truman's domestic policies.

Filibuster An attempt by one or more legislators to either kill or obtain modification of a proposed law by prolonged discussion that prevents the bill from coming to a vote in its current form.

Gerrymander To draw the boundaries of an election district in such a manner as to maximize chances that a given party will elect its candidate. This may involve bizarre boundaries which pull in or exclude areas in which the party is comparatively strong or weak.

Grand jury A group of (usually) 16 to 23 persons who decide if enough evidence of guilt has been offered to them by a prosecutor to warrant bringing a defendant to trial.

Grant-in-aid The granting of funds by a higher level of government to a lower level, usually for certain specific programs.

Great Society The name given to President Lyndon B. Johnson's domestic policies.

Ideology A belief system that explains and justifies a preferred political order, either existing or proposed, and offers a strategy for its attainment.

Incrementalism Changing policy by a series of small steps rather than by more sweeping and comprehensive change.

Incumbent The person currently occupying a political office.

Independent voter A voter who frequently supports candidates of several parties rather than almost invariably voting for members of only one party.

Initiative A petition, signed by a legally specified number of voters, which places a proposed law before the voters for their approval or disapproval.

Interest group A group of persons organized to seek public policies desired by that group or its leaders.

House Committee on Un-American Activities A committee formerly existing in the House of Representatives which inquired into alleged "Un-American" political activities. "Un-American" was never defined.

Left-wing A term describing persons or groups that favor greater governmental control of the economy, usually involving policies believed helpful to lower-income groups. Sometimes used to describe persons with socialist or Communist beliefs.

Legislative liaison agents Executive staff members who seek to obtain legislative support of the executive's policies or nominations.

Limited government A system of government in which the Constitution withholds certain powers from the government, usually in order to protect individual rights.

Literacy test A test to determine if one is sufficiently literate to be able to vote intelligently. Was often used to discriminate against black voters.

Lobbyist A representative of an interest group who seeks to persuade public policy makers to do what his or her interest group wants done.

Merit system A system by which civil servants are appointed and promoted on the basis of their qualifications or demonstrated competence rather than by permitting those decisions to be affected by party affiliation.

Natural Law General laws supposedly applying to persons in all societies, discoverable through the processes of reason.

New Deal The name given to President Franklin D. Roosevelt's domestic policies.

Nonpartisan election An election in which candidates for public office are not identified on the ballot by their party affiliation.

Open primary A primary election in which a voter may vote for the candidates of any party; one need not identify his or her party affiliation in an open primary.

Party regular A voter who almost invariably votes for candidates of one party.

Platform A statement of the principles and policies endorsed by a party seeking popular support at the polls.

Political action committee The organized political arm of an interest group. It may raise money for favored candidates, campaign on their behalf or support favored policies at the legislative, executive or administrative level.

Precinct A small election district of (usually) several hundred registered voters; the voters of this district cast their ballots in a common polling place.

Presidential primary A primary election in which voters either vote for a national convention delegate supporting the party candidate of their choice, or choose unpledged delegates to the national convention.

Progressive tax   A tax which tends to fall more heavily, in proportion to income, on higher income groups.

Recall   A process by which voters can remove an elected official from office prior to the expiration of his or her term. A petition, signed by a legally specified number of voters, must request this election.

Referendum   A process by which voters can approve or disapprove a law already passed by the legislature of a state or local government.

Regressive tax   A tax which tends to fall more heavily, in proportion to income, on lower income groups.

Right-wing   A term describing persons or groups that favor less governmental control of the economy, or that tend to support the status quo. Sometimes used to describe the beliefs of strongly conservative persons.

Seniority principle   The principle which confers a committee chairmanship upon the person who has the longest uninterrupted service on that committee.

Spending clause   National power to *spend* for the general welfare (but *not* to enact whatever laws the Congress may wish to pass to promote the general welfare).

Taxing clause   "Congress shall have the power to lay and collect taxes... to pay the debts and provide for the common defense and general welfare of the United States." (Article 1, Section 8 of the Constitution).

Ticket-splitting   A practice by which voters divide their votes among candidates of several parties.

Trillion dollars   Almost twice as much money as Washington obtains in taxes each year and nearly half of the value of the nation's output of goods and services! More than is expected from royalties from this book.

White primary   A primary election in which only white persons could vote. Was used in the Old South by the Democratic party; persons nominated in this primary were virtually assured of winning the general election.

Writ of habeas corpus   A writ on behalf of someone detained by law enforcement officers, demanding to know for what offense that person is being held.

INDEX

Abortion, 248, 255, 257, 281, 284
Accused, rights of, 40, 247, 255, 281-284
Adams, Sherman, 215
Affirmative action programs, 158, 260, 284, 296
Agnew, Spiro, 147
Albert, Carl, 124, 178
Alien and Sedition Acts (1798), 266
Alinsky, Saul, 156
Alsop, Stewart, 20
American Bar Association, 155, 159
American Constitution, The (Kelly and Harbison), 65
American Farm Bureau Federation, 155
American Federalism (Leach), 62
American Federation of Labor-Congress of Industrial Organizations (AFL-CIO), 136, 155, 158, 161, 165
American Medical Association, 155
American Petroleum Institute, 155
American Political Science Association, 2
American Tobacco Company, 67
Amici curiae beliefs, 251, 257
Anarchy, 52
Anderson, Jack, 93
Anderson, Marian, 89
Angola, 205
Areopagitica (Milton), 269
Arms, right to bear, 280
Articles of Confederation, 31, 33, 62, 194
Assembly, freedom of, 45, 264, 307
Automobile industry, 162

Bachrach, Peter, 158
Bacon, Francis, 24
Bad tendency test, 271
Bail, excessive, 281
Baker, Howard, 167
Baker v. Carr (1962), 255
Bakke case, 284
Baratz, Morton, 158
Barber, James David, 21, 217
Bay of Pigs, 6, 17
Begin, Menachem, 205
Behavioralism, 3-5
Berlin airlift, 91, 202
Bicameralism, 155, 182
Bill of Rights, 38, 46, 51, 248, 255, 264-266, 269-285
Black, Hugo, 260
Blacks, 4, 16
  affirmative action programs, 296
  desegregation, 89, 247, 255, 257
  equal protection clause, 245-246, 284
  riots, 305
  slavery, 245, 252, 254
  voting patterns, 87-89
  voting rights, 36, 46
Block grants, 74, 75
B-1 bomber, 18

Boxer Rebellion, 206
Brandeis, Louis D., 198, 260, 271
Brezhnev, Leonid, 205
Broder, David, 93
Brookings Institution, 169
Brown, John, 304
Brown v. Board of Education of Topeka, Kansas (1954), 247, 256, 259
Bryan, William Jennings, 84, 118
Bryce, James, 105
Brzezinski, Zbigniew, 216
Budget, presidential, 198
Bundy, McGeorge, 214
Bureaucracy, 220-240, 290-295
  controls over, 233-240
  hiring and firing, 223-225
  merit system, 222
  power of, 228-233
  presidency and, 222, 229-233
  red tape, 225-226
Burger, Warren, 247
Burnham, Walter, 128
Busing, 255, 277, 295

Cabinets, 116, 229-230, 231
Calhoun, John, 244
Califano, Joseph, 214, 215
California primary, 145
Cambodia, 205, 207
Campaigns. See Elections
Cannon, Joseph, 178
Capital punishment, 255, 281
Cardozo, Benjamin, 198, 260
Carrswell, Harold, 198
Carson, Rachel, 104
Carter, Jimmy, 52
  B-1 bomber issue, 18
  bureaucracy and, 223, 233
  Congress and, 199
  foreign policy, 203
  1976 election, 16, 18, 93, 116, 120, 145
  1980 election, 141
  personality, 210
  staff, 211, 215
Castro, Fidel, 44
Categorical (program) grants, 73-74
Catholic voters, 85, 87-88, 120
Caucus, 140-141, 142
Central Intelligence Agency (CIA), 97, 198, 203, 210
Checks and balances, 32
Chiang Kai-shek, 205
Church, Frank, 204
Churchill, Sir Winston, 216
Civil Aeronautics Board, 235, 236
Civilian Conservation Corps, 85
Civil liberties. See Assembly, freedom of; Press, freedom of; Religion, freedom of; Speech, freedom of
Civil Rights Act of 1875, 252, 254

Civil Rights Act of 1964, 47
Civil rights movement, 89, 97, 160, 307
Civil service, 2, 124
Civil War, 35, 37, 84–85
Clay, Henry, 244
Clear and present danger test, 270–271
Cleveland, Grover, 113
Clifford, Clark, 214
Cloture, 180, 182
Coalitions, 115–116
Commerce clause of the Constitution, 65, 66–68, 249, 255
Committee chairs, 176–178
Committee for Economic Development, 159, 169
Committee on Political Education (COPE), 136
Committee system, 173–176
Common Cause, 137, 162, 239
Communism, 44, 54, 306
Communist party (American), 93, 97, 246, 254, 256, 268–275
Confederation, 62
Conference committees, 177
Congressional Budget Reform Act (1974), 190
Congressional Government (Wilson), 172
Congressional Research Service, 174
Congress of the United States, 172–191
 campaign financing, 135–138
 change and, 290–293, 297–311
 characteristics of members, 183–189
 cloture, 180
 committee system, 173–176
 Constitution on, 32
 daily routine, 187–189
 filibuster, 180–182
 foreign policy and, 202–208
 incumbents, reelection of, 139, 185–187
 independent regulatory commissions and, 230–236
 interest groups and, 155–166
 leadership, 176–179
 passage of bills, 179–182
 presidency and, 125, 130, 172, 183, 194, 197–203, 205–211
 seniority principle, 176–177
 Supreme Court and, 66–68, 252–257
 tax legislation, 297–299
 voting patterns in, 5–6, 184–187
Conservatism, 95, 98–101, 291, 294–295
Constitution of the United States
 checks and balances, 32
 commerce clause, 65–68, 249, 255
 on congressional powers, 32
 convention of, 30
 elastic clause, 64
 flexibility of, 33
 on national government, 62
 on presidential powers, 32, 194–195
 ratification of,
 separation of powers, 32
 on slavery, 47
 supremacy clause, 64
 on Supreme Court, 32, 244
 text of,
 voting rights, 36, 47–48
Constitutions, 30–40
Consumer Product Safety Commission, 236
Consumer protection, 163
Contract, freedom of, 265
Coolidge, Calvin, 119, 149
Cooperative federalism, 70
Corporations, 136, 295
Corruption, 75
Council of Economic Advisers, 215
Council on Environmental Quality, 215
Council on Foreign Affairs, 169
Counsel, right to, 283
Cox, James, 149
Creative federalism, 70
Crédit Mobilier affair, 165
Crossovers, 130
Cruel and unusual punishment, 281
Cuban missile crisis, 6

Daley, Richard, 122
Dark horse candidates, 142
Davis, John W., 118, 149
Death penalty, 255, 281
Debs, Eugene, 254
de Gaulle, Charles, 205, 216
Democracy, 3, 44–58, 161, 305–306
 defined, 45
 equality and, 46–49
 human rights and, 45–46, 49–54
 majority rule, 54–55
 threats to, 55–57
 types of, 44
Democratic centralism, 54
Democratic national convention (1972), 146
Democratic party. *See also* Elections; Political parties
 beginnings of, 112–113
 voting patterns, 84–89,
Democratic Republicans, 113
Dennis v. U.S. (1951), 272, 274
Desegregation, 89, 247, 255–259
Dewey, Thomas E., 116, 119
Direct-mail solicitations, 135
Direct primaries, 3, 123, 131
Dirksen, Everett, 22
Discrimination, 47
District courts, 260
Dixiecrat party, 119
Dole, Robert, 147
Douglas, Stephen, 17
Douglas, William O., 119, 250, 260
Dred Scott v. Sanford (1857), 245, 252, 254
Dual federalism, 64

Due process of law clause, 40, 246, 248, 282, 283-284, 285
Dulles, John Foster, 88, 215
Durant, Will, 300
Dying, rights of the, 51

Education
　busing, 255, 277, 295
　desegregation, 89, 247, 255-259
　parochial school aid, 277-280
Ehrlichman, John, 231
Eighteenth Amendment, 85
Eighth Amendment, 281
Eisenhower, Dwight D., 21, 85, 86, 113, 116, 139, 147-149, 246
　civil rights and, 89
　personality, 210
　staff, 213, 214-215
Elastic clause of the Constitution, 64
Elections, 134-150. See also Presidential elections
　caucus, 140-142
　direct primaries, 3, 123, 131
　endorsements, 145, 148
　financing, 125, 135-138, 162
　gerrymandering, 140, 162
　issues, 143
　media and, 141, 143-144, 148
　national conventions, 48, 145-146
　opinion polls and, 138-139, 145
　presidential primaries, 140-145
　propaganda and, 149-150
　single member district system, 114
　ticket splitting, 119, 123
　types of, 134
Electoral College, 48, 50, 114-115, 196
Eizenstat, Stuart, 214
Emerson, Ralph Waldo, 101
Empathy, 53
Endorsements, 145, 148
Engel v. Vitale (1962), 255, 278
Entertainment industry, 94
Enumerated powers, 62
Environmental Defense Fund, 164
Environmental Protection Agency, 236, 260
Equal Employment Opportunity Commission, 236
Equality, 4, 45-49, 178
Equal protection of the laws clause, 245-246, 248, 284, 285
Equal Rights Amendment (ERA), 104, 285
Errand running, 173
Ervin, Sam, 249
Establishment, 55
Everson v. Board of Education (1947), 277
Excessive bail, 281
Exclusionary rule, 282
Executive agreements, 203
Executive office, 215

Factions, 35, 112
Fair Deal, 148
Fairness doctrine, 265
Fair trial, right to, 46, 264, 283
Family, socialization and, 84, 86
Federal Bureau of Investigation (FBI), 198, 210
Federal Coal Mine Health and Safety Act, 163
Federal Communications Commission (FCC), 230
Federal Deposit Insurance Corporation (FDIC), 85
Federal Election Committee, 138
Federal Housing Administration (FHA), 86
Federalism, 62-76, 155
Federalist, The (Madison, Hamilton and Jay), 33, 64
Federalist party, 48, 113, 251, 266
Federal Power Commission, 230
Federal Register, 229
Federal Reserve Board, 83, 168, 198, 210
Federal-state relations, 63-76
Federal Trade Commission (FTC), 230, 236
Feminist movement, 178
Fifteenth Amendment, 47,
Fifth Amendment, 46, 65, 143, 264, 281-282, 283
Filibuster, 180-182
First Amendment, 45, 138, 250, 264-266, 269-285, 307
Fischer, John, 19, 21
Ford, Gerald, 116, 141, 147, 149-150, 205
　misstatements of, 143, 145
　Nixon pardon, 82, 149, 200
　staff, 215
Ford Motor Company, 165
Foreign policy, 91, 202-209
Fourteenth Amendment, 36, 47, 246, 255, 264, 284,
Fourth Amendment, 264, 282
Fox, Fannie, 14
Frankfurter, Felix, 260, 283
Freedom, 47
Freedom rides, 307
Freud, Sigmund, 269
Friedman, Milton, 93
Friends of the Earth, 164
Fugitive Slave Laws, 254
Fulbright, William E., 17, 204

Gallup, George, 107, 108
Gandhi, Mahatma, 216
General Accounting Office (GAO), 233
George III, King of England, 32
Gerrymandering, 140, 162
Gibbons v. Ogden (1824), 245
Ginsberg, Eli, 209
Goldwater, Barry, 89, 116, 117, 139, 142, 145, 147, 149

Government of U. of California v. Bakke (1978), 284
Grandfather clause, 47
Grand Old Party (GOP). *See* Republican party
Grants-in-aid programs, 73-74
Great Britain
  Constitution, 30
  political parties in, 121
Great Compromise, 62
Great Depression, 69, 85, 89, 91
Great Society, 148, 304
Greek-Turkish aid plan, 91, 202
Greenfield, Meg, 235

Habeas corpus, writ of, 37, 196
Hagerty, James, 213
Haldeman, H. R., 215
Hamilton, Alexander, 112, 199
Harbison, Winifred A., 65
Harding, Warren, 149
Harlan, John Marshall, 250
Harrington, Michael, 302
Harris, Louis, 107, 108
Harrison, William Henry, 113, 199
Hawthorne effect, 4
Hays, Wayne, 14, 22
Health insurance, 161
Hearing process, 173-175
Highway lobby, 155
Highway Safety Act, 163
Hitler, Adolf, 44, 52, 53, 88, 216
Hofstadter, Richard, 17, 305
Holmes, Oliver Wendell, 245, 260, 271
Home Owners' Loan Corporation, 86
Hoover, Herbert, 149, 201
House of Representatives. *See also* Congress of the United States
  relations with Senate, 182-183
  Rules Committee, 180
  Un-American Activities Committee, 268
  Ways and Means Committee, 190
Huff, Corinne, 14
Hughes, Charles Evans, 198, 249
Human rights, 45-46, 49-54
Humphrey, Hubert, 116, 147

Imminency test, 271
Incrementalism, 300-303
Incumbents, reelection of, 139-140, 141, 185-187
Independent regulatory commissions, 197, 230-236
Independent voters, 101, 119-120, 122
Industrialization, 290
Inflation, 162, 299
Initiative, 3, 44
Intellectual integrity, 94-95
Interest groups, 83, 137, 154-170, 239
  ingredients of power of, 157-162
  lobbying, 164-168
  organized and unorganized, 154-159
  public, 162-165
Interstate commerce, 65-67
Interstate Commerce Commission (ICC), 161, 230, 235, 236
Iowa primary, 145
Iron Law of Oligarchy, 159

Jackson, Andrew, 48, 113, 172, 194
Jackson, Henry, 93
Janis, Irving, 6
Japanese Americans, 37, 254
Jarvis Howard, 104
Jay, John, 202
Jay's Treaty, 82, 202
Jefferson, Thomas, 56-57, 82, 112-113, 244, 273
  Congress and, 172, 199
  executive power, interpretations of, 195
  foreign policy, 205
Jeffersonian Republicans, 251, 266
Jewish lobby, 155, 168
Jewish voters, 88-89, 120
Jim Crow laws, 284
John Birch Society, 44, 248
Johnson, Andrew, 30
Johnson, Lyndon B., 86, 139
  antipoverty programs, 156
  Congress and, 172, 199
  as majority leader, 178
  1964 election, 116
  staff, 215
  as vice-presidential candidate, 147
  Vietnam War, 6, 200, 201, 206, 306
Johnson, Samuel, 310
Jordan, Hamilton, 216
Judicial activism, 257
Judicial restraint, 257
Judicial review, 244, 248, 253-256
Judiciary Act of 1789, 245
Justice, principles of, 53

Kaufman, Herbert, 255
Kelly, Alfred H., 65
Kennedy John F., 17, 20, 88, 148,
  bureaucracy and, 230
  foreign policy, 6, 203, 205
  1960 election, 93, 116, 145, 150
  personality, 210
  press and, 145
  staff, 215
Kennedy, Robert F., 156
Key, V. O., 35
Khrushchev, Nikita, 6, 205
King, Martin Luther, Jr., 150
Kingdon, John W., 6, 186
Kirkpatrick, Jeanne, 129
Kissinger, Henry, 206, 214
Kondracke, Morton, 187
Korean War, 7, 86, 91, 206
Kraft, Joseph, 93

Index

Labor unions, 97, 120, 136, 158, 160, 305, 307
La Follette, Robert M., 118, 154
Laos, 205
Laqueur, Walter, 305
Lasswell, Harold, 5
Leach, Richard, 62, 64
League of Nations, 201
Legislature. *See* Congress of the United States
Lenin, V. I., 216
Leninism, 273
Lerner Max, 251
Liberal democracy, 45
Liberalism, 87, 96–101, 291, 295
Limited government, 55
Lincoln, Abraham, 30, 37, 113, 196, 206, 216, 266
   on blacks, 16
   executive power, interpretations of, 195
   on public opinion, 81
Literacy tests, 36, 47
Lobbying, 164–168
Local committees, 122
Locke, John, 31, 194
Lockwood, Henry, 195
Lodge, Henry Cabot, 147
Long, Huey, 75
Long, Russell, 83
Lycurgus, 35

MacArthur, Douglas, 7, 82
McCarthy, Joseph R., 93, 176, 268, 301
McCormack, John, 124, 178
McCulloch v. Maryland (1819), 63
McGovern, George, 82, 85, 116, 117, 139, 142, 146, 149, 309
McKinley, William, 199, 206
McLellan, David, 170
Madison, James, 32, 244
Magazines, 94, 169
Magna Charta, 30
Majority leader of the Senate, 176, 178, 179
Majority rule, 54–55
Management by Objective (MBO), 234
Mandamus, writ of, 244
Mansfield, Mike, 22, 124, 178
Mao Tse-tung, 44, 205
Marbury, William, 244
Marbury v. Madison (1803), 245
Marcus, Stephen, 301
Marcus Aurelius, 269
Marshall, John, 64, 244
Marshall Plan, 6, 202
Marxism, 269, 273, 302
Media, 13–14, 54, 293
   elections and, 140–145, 149
   politicians and, 12, 13
   president and, 197, 210
   public opinion and, 92–94
Medicaid, 75
Merit system, 124, 222

Metropolitan government, 71
Milbrath, Lester, 135
Military budget, 198
Military draft, 51
Military-industrial lobby, 155
Mill, John Stuart, 269, 272
Miller, William, 147
Mills, Wilbur, 13
Milton, John, 269
Minimum wage, 161, 253
Minority leaders of the House and Senate, 176
Minor parties, 112, 114, 119
Miranda v. Arizona (1966), 247, 255, 282
Missouri Compromise, 252
Modern revolutions, 56
Mondale, Walter, 147
Monroe, James, 202
Monroe Doctrine, 202
Montesquieu, Baron, 32, 194
Morrison, Samuel Eliot, 206
Morrow, Lance, 190
Moyers, Bill, 213
Moynihan, Daniel P., 279
Murphy, Brian, 108
Mussolini, Benito, 44, 55

Nader, Ralph, 104, 137, 162–163
Napoleon I, Emperor, 216
Nasser, Gamel Abdul, 44
National Association for the Advancement of Colored People (NAACP), 160
National committees, 120, 121
National Conference of Mayors, 159
National conventions, 48, 145–147
National Education Association (NEA), 155
National Highway Transportation Safety Board, 236
National interest, 56
National Labor Relations Board (NLRB), 230
National Recovery Act (NRA), 253
National Rifle Association, 155, 161
National Security Council (NSC), 204, 215
National Welfare Rights Organization (NWRO), 159
Nation-centered federalism, 63–64
Nationwide primary, 142
Natural law, 32
Natural rights, 52–54
Neumann, Franz, 56
Neutrality Acts, 202, 205
New Deal, 82–89, 148, 294, 304
New Federalism, 70, 76
New Freedom, 304
New Hampshire primary, 141
Newspapers, 93, 127, 169
New York Times Co. v. United States (1971), 275
Nineteenth Amendment, 48
Ninth Amendment, 51, 281
Nixon, Richard M., 76, 125

Nixon, Richard M. *(continued)*
  bureaucracy and, 230
  executive power, interpretations of, 195
  foreign policy, 202, 206-207
  1960 election, 93, 116, 149
  1968 election, 116
  1972 election, 116
  pardon of, 82, 149, 200
  press and, 145
  public opinion and, 82
  resignation of, 208
  staff, 211, 215
  Supreme Court and, 249, 251
  as vice-presidential candidate, 147
  Vietnam War, 86
  Watergate, 200, 208
North Atlantic Treaty Organization (NATO), 91, 202

Obscenity, 276
Office of Management and Budget (OMB), 198, 215, 233
Office of Personnel Management (OPM), 221
Office of Safety and Health Administration (OSHA), 157, 236, 260
Ohio primary, 145
Oil industry, 162
O'Neill, Tip, 124
One man, one vote decisions, 48, 172, 246, 255, 257
On Liberty (Mill), 269
Opinion polls, 49, 107-108, 138, 145, 186
Oregon primary, 145
Organization of Petroleum Exporting Countries (OPEC), 162

Panama Canal, 195
Panama Canal Treaty (1978), 167, 203, 204
Parochial school aid, 277-280
Patronage, 135, 174, 222
Pearl Harbor, 7, 86
Pendleton Act (1883), 222
Pentagon, 164
Pentagon Papers case, 275
People's Republic of China, 202, 203
Planning, Programming, and Budgeting System (PPBS), 234
Plessy v. Ferguson (1896), 245
Political action committees (PACs), 136
Political elite, 239
Political parties, 35, 112-131
  beginnings of, 48, 112-113
  decentralization and, 120
  decline of, 122-126
  definition of, 112
  functions of, 112, 126-131
  in Great Britain, 121
  loyalty to, 120, 121, 129, 148
  reforms, 129-131
  third parties, 112, 114, 109

two-party system, 114-119
Political revolution, 7-8
Political science
  history of, 2-5
  research, 5-8
Politicians, 12-27
  emergence of, 26-27
  images of, 12-13
  media and, 13-14
  reasons for, 19-22
  stands on issues, 15-18
  successful, 22-26
Politics, defined, 2
Polk, James, 206
Polls, 49, 107-108, 138, 145
Poll tax, 47
Populist parties, 118
Post office, 230
Poverty, 4, 50, 156-157, 295
Powell, Adam Clayton, 15
Powell, Jody, 213
Power, diffusion of, 168-170
Power elite, 54
Precinct organization, 123
President of the United States, 194-217
  appointment powers, 197-198, 209-210, 229
  budget, 198
  bureaucracy and, 222, 229-232
  cabinet, 230
  as chief of state, 195
  as commander in chief, 32, 195, 205-208
  Congress and, 125, 130, 172, 183, 194, 197-202, 205-211
  Constitution on, 32, 194
  election of. *See* Presidential elections
  foreign policy and, 202-205, 209
  interpretation of laws, 197, 228
  media and, 197, 210
  as party leader, 196
  political parties and, 125, 128
  public opinion and, 82
  staff, 211-215
  Supreme Court and, 196
  treaty negotiation, 32
  veto power, 32, 168
Presidential elections
  electoral college, 48, 49, 114, 196
  incumbents in, 141
  national conventions, 48, 145-146
  opinion polls and, 107
  primaries, 140-145
  1896, 84
  1912, 118, 149
  1916, 149
  1920, 149
  1924, 118, 149
  1928, 85, 88, 149
  1932, 85, 149
  1936, 149
  1940, 149

1944, 149
1948, 116, 119, 149
1952, 88, 149
1956, 88, 116, 149
1960, 88, 93, 116, 145, 149
1964, 116, 118, 142, 149
1968, 116
1972, 116, 118, 136, 142, 149
1976, 16, 18, 93, 116, 118, 120, 141, 145, 150
1980, 141
Press, freedom of, 45, 250, 264–269, 275–276
Pressure groups. *See* Interest groups
Primary elections, 129, 140–145
Privacy, right to, 45, 281
Private property, 264
Progressive Movement, 253
Progressive party, 118
Prohibition, 85
Propaganda, 149
Property rights, 31
Proportional representation system 114
Public interest groups, 162–164
Public opinion, 80–108
    importance of, 80–83
    informed voting public, 101–107
    liberal-conservative conflict, 95–101
    media and, 92–94
    personal integrity and, 94–95
    polls, 49, 107–108, 138, 145, 186
    religious and ethnic groups and, 87–92
    socialization and, 83–87

Quorum, 180

Radiation Control Act, 163
Rayburn, Sam, 178
Reagan, Ronald, 118, 145, 150
Reason, 53
Recall, 3
Red Tape (Kaufman), 225
Reed, Thomas P., 178
Referendum, 3, 44, 81
Regulatory commissions, 197, 230–236
Rejai, Mostafa, 7–8
Religion, freedom of, 45, 97, 226, 264, 276–280
Religious groups, socialization and, 86–88
Republican national convention (1976), 145
Republican party, 48. *See also* Elections; Political parties
    beginnings of, 113
    voting patterns, 84–89, 89–90
Revenue sharing, 76
Reverse discrimination, 47
Revolutionary leaders, 7–8
Rockefeller, Nelson, 70
Roe v. Wade (1973), 247, 255
Rogers, William, 214
Romney, George, 145
Roosevelt, Eleanor, 89
Roosevelt, Franklin D., 37, 149, 156, 216, 304

    bureaucracy and, 230
    Congress and, 172, 199
    executive power, interpretations of, 195
    foreign policy, 7, 196, 202, 203, 206
    New Deal programs, 85–89, 113, 294
    personality, 210
    staff, 214
    Supreme Court and, 67, 82, 200, 246, 251
Roosevelt, Theodore, 118, 149
    Congress and, 172
    foreign policy, 202
    personality, 210
    stewardship doctrine, 195
Roosevelt Corollary, 202
Rossiter, Clinton, 195
Rubin, Jerry, 51
Rumsfeld, Donald, 215
Rusk, Dean, 214

Sadat, Anwar, 205
Samuelson, Paul, 93
Schlafly, Phyllis, 104
Schlesinger, Arthur, Jr., 206, 250
School District of Abington Township v. Schempp (1963), 255
School prayers, 43, 256, 257, 278
Schools, socialization and, 86–87
Search and seizure clause, 45, 97, 264, 281
Second Amendment, 280
Secret (Australian) ballot, 48
Self-discipline, 57
Self-incrimination, 46, 264, 282
Senate. *See also* Congress of the United States
    election to, 48, 172
    Finance Committee, 190
    presidential appointments, 210
    relations with House, 182
    treaty ratification, 32, 204
Seniority system, 71, 176
Separation of powers, 32, 155
Seventeenth Amendment, 48, 172
Sexual rights, 50
Shays' Rebellion, 31, 304
Sherman Antitrust Act (1890), 65, 252
Sierra Club, 164
Silent Spring (Carson), 104
Single issue voters, 123
Single member district system, 114
Sit-ins, 307
Sixteenth Amendment, 252, 256
Sixth Amendment, 264, 283
Slavery, 34, 47, 113, 245, 252, 254, 266
Smith Adam, 96, 190, 304
Smith, Al, 85, 88, 149
Smith Act (1940), 272
Social change, 290–311
Social class, voting patterns and, 89–90
Socialism, 114, 266
Socialization, 83–87
Social Security Act (1935), 86

Sorensen, Ted, 214
Southeast Asia Treaty Organization (SEATO), 91
Sowell, Thomas, 296
Sparkman, John, 147
Speaker of the House, 176, 178, 179
Speech, freedom of, 45, 138, 250, 264-275
Spirit of the Laws, The (Montesquieu), 194
Spoils system, 3, 135, 174, 222
Stalin, Joseph, 216
Standard Oil Company, 67
Stare decisis, 250
State-centered federalism, 64
State governments, 63, 245, 264-265
Stevenson, Adlai, I, 20
Stevenson, Adlai, II, 20, 88, 116, 146
Stevenson, Adlai, III, 20
Stewardship doctrine, 195
Stone, Harlan Fiske, 198, 258
Strategic Arms Limitation Talks (SALT), 203
Strict construction, 249
Student unrest, 4, 178, 305
Subcommittees, 175-176, 177, 292
Sukarno, Achmed, 44
Sunset laws, 233
Supremacy clause of the Constitution, 64
Supreme Court of the United States, 168, 210, 244-160
   abortion, 248, 255, 257, 281, 284
   accused, rights of, 247, 255, 256, 282-285
   appointments to, 82, 198, 200, 246
   bad tendency test, 271
   campaign financing, 136-138
   capital punishment, 255
   clear and present danger test, 270-271
   commerce clause, 66, 67, 249, 255
   Congress and, 65-68, 252-257
   Constitution on, 32-33, 244
   counsel, right to, 283
   desegregation, 247, 255, 257
   dual federalism and, 64-68
   due process of law clause, 248, 282, 283-284, 285
   equal protection clause, 245-246, 248, 284, 285
   interstate commerce, 66
   judicial review, 245, 248, 253-256
   obscenity rulings, 276
   one man, one vote decision, 48, 172, 246, 255, 257
   on presidential power, 196
   press, freedom of, 275-276
   privacy, right to, 281
   religion, freedom of, 276-280
   school prayers, 97, 255, 257, 278
   search and seizure, 281
   self-incrimination, 282
   slavery, 245, 252, 254
   speech, freedom of, 270-275
   stare decisis, 250
   taxation, 252, 256
   at work, 257-260

Taft, Charles, 20
Taft, Robert A., Jr., 20
Taft, Robert A., Sr., 20, 22, 124, 178
Taft, William Howard, 20, 118, 149
Taft-Hartley Act (1947), 160
Taney, Roger, 64
Taxation, 47, 71, 136, 158, 252, 256, 291, 294, 297, 307
Taylor, Zachary, 113
Teamsters Union, 155, 161
Technology, 290, 293
Television, 92-93, 123
Tennessee Valley Authority (TVA), 86, 230
Tenth Amendment, 62, 64, 66
Terrorism, 305
Test Ban Treaty (1962), 203
Thieu, Nguyen Van, 207
Third parties, 112, 114, 119
Thirteenth Amendment, 47
Thurmond, Strom, 119
Ticket splitting, 119, 123
Tocqueville, Alexis de, 57
Traditionalism, 2-3, 5
Travel, right to, 45
Treaties, 32, 202-203
Truman, Harry S., 82, 139, 197, 210
   bureaucracy and, 230
   civil rights and, 89
   Congress and, 200
   foreign policy, 7, 86, 88, 202, 206
   1948 election, 116, 119, 149
   as vice-presidential candidate, 147
Two-party system, 113-119

Udall, Morris, 183
Unemployment compensation, 75
Union of Soviet Socialist Republics, Constitution of, 36
Unitary system of government, 62, 71-72
United Mine Workers Union, 162
United States Chamber of Commerce, 155, 166
United States Steel Corporation, 67
United States v. Nixon (1974), 259
Universities, free speech and, 266-269
Unreasonable search and seizure, 45, 97, 264, 281
Unsafe at Any Speed (Nader), 104, 163
Urbanization, 290

Values, 3, 58, 95
Vance, Cyrus, 214
Versailles Treaty, 203, 204
Vice-presidential candidates, 129, 146
Vietnam War, 4, 7, 86, 91, 200-208, 269, 306, 307
Viguerie, Richard, 167
Violence, 304-308
Voting patterns, 84-91, 119-121
   of blacks, 89
   informed public and, 101-107
   of members of Congress, 5-6, 184-187

Voting registration, 103, 149
Voting rights, 36, 45, 46
Voting turnout, 102–103

Wagner Act (1935), 86, 160
Wallace, George, 305
Wallace, Henry A., 119
War on Poverty programs, 156, 295
War Powers Act (1973), 208
Warren, Earl, 246
Washington, George, 20, 82, 172, 199
Watergate, 128, 176, 200, 208
Wealth of Nations, The (Smith), 96, 304
Webster, Daniel, 244
Welfare, 155, 157, 295
Westminster Agreements of 1911, 30
Whig party, 113, 199
Whips, 176, 178
White House staff, 211–216
White primaries, 36, 47

White supremacy, 90, 266
Wholesome Meat Act, 163
Will, George, 93
Wilmerding, Lucius, 195
Wilson, Woodrow, 113, 118, 148, 149, 211, 291, 304
  Congress and, 172, 199, 292
  foreign policy, 203–206
  League of Nations, 201
Winner-take-all system, 49
Wiretapping, 282
Women, rights of, 48, 50
Works Progress Administration (WPA), 85

Yates v. United States (1957), 275
Yazoo land fraud, 165
Yellow-dog contracts, 65, 253

Zero-based budgeting, 233

81 82 83 9 8 7 6 5 4 3 2